who knew?

DOUBLE EDITION

10,001+
Money-Saving Secrets for Solving Everyday Problems

Bruce Lubin & Jeanne Bossolina-Lubin

CASTLE POINT PUBLISHING

Castle Point Publishing
58 Ninth Street
Hoboken, NJ 07030

ISBN: 978-0-9850374-1-3

Please note: While this compilation of hints and tips will solve many of your household problems, total success cannot be guaranteed. The authors have compiled the information contained herein from a variety of sources, and neither the authors, publisher, manufacturer, nor distributor can assume responsibility for the effectiveness of the suggestions. Caution is urged when using any of the solutions, recipes, or tips in this book. At press time, all internet addresses and offers were valid and in working order; however, Castle Point Publishing is not responsible for the content of these sites, and no warranty or representation is made by Castle Point Publishing in regards to them or the outcome of any of the solicitations, solutions, recipes, or tips herein. Castle Point Publishing shall have no liability for damages (whether direct, indirect, consequential or otherwise) arising from the use, attempted use, misuse, or application of any of the solutions, recipes, or tips described in this book.

Printed and bound in the United States of America

10 9 8 7 6 5 4 3 2

Dedication

For Jack, Terrence, and Aidan, as always

Acknowledgments

We couldn't make our books without the generous support of many people, who we'd like to thank here. First, thanks to our families and friends for cheering us on and providing us with millions of tips over the years, long before we started writing down who submitted what. Thank you, too, for putting up with us when we're on a deadline.

We owe great gratitude to Jennifer Boudinot, who is a tremendous partner and friend, and Brian Scevola, who has continued to be an all-around good guy and fight our fights for years now. A big thank you to Joy Mangano, whose vision and enthusiasm inspires us. To Beth, Maureen, Andrea, Joanie, Wendy, Monica, Marianna and everyone else at Ingenious Designs, we owe you a drink! And a nice big bottle of white vinegar. Thanks to all of the designers we have worked with to make Who Knew? books wonderful to read, including Richard Pasquarelli, Christine Heun, Jatin Mehta, and of course, Lynne Yeamans, who proves that old coworkers are the very best kind. We've also been blessed with some great editors over the years, including Heather Rodino, Lindsay Herman, and Rachel Federman. And we have Carol Inskip to thank for all our wonderful indexes! Special thanks to Todd Vanek and Melissa Grover of Bang Printing, who make it possible for us to print all our books in the USA.

We're also grateful for the help we've received from Anthony "Sully" Sullivan and David "Drunkle" Runkle. Arwen Saxon, Pete Donegian, and everyone else at the Billy Mays Memorial Studio, you don't have nicknames yet, but we will come up with some for next time! To Lynn Hamlin, thank you not only for your support, but for your insight and know-how. Mindy McCortney is always amazing, and we are never luckier than when we get to work with her!

Last but not least, thank you to our readers! We couldn't do it without you, and we're humbled by the number of people who have brought our books into their homes! A special thanks to all our readers who have given us their families' time- and money-saving tips, either though the mail, on our Facebook or Twitter pages, or through our website, WhoKnewTips.com. This book is for you!

Contents

who knew?

Bruce Lubin & Jeanne Bossolina Lubin

PART ONE

Who Knew? Heroes

As we searched near and far for the best household tips, we began to notice something: We were constantly running to the kitchen for vinegar, baking soda, salt, lemon, and cooking oil. To this essential tool kit we soon added aluminum foil, and after looking around the house at many of our "repairs," we decided duct tape was an absolute necessity as well. Take a look through this section and you'll be astounded at all you can do with these *Who Knew?* heroes and a little know-how. Soon, your family won't be surprised when you reach for the vinegar at practically every turn.

CHAPTER 1

Vinegar

Label Remover

If you're having trouble peeling off a label or sticker without leaving a gooey mess behind, trying applying white vinegar until it's saturated. It will peel right off!

Vanquish Smells with Vinegar

If you've burnt dinner, welcome to the club. To get rid of the smoky scent in your kitchen, simply boil a cup of vinegar in 2 cups water. In 15 minutes, the smell should be gone.

Power Shower Spray

Save at least one fight in the morning by keeping this daily shower spray within easy reach of all family members. Mix one part vinegar with 10 parts water in an empty spray bottle and you're ready to go. Bonus: You don't have to worry about a toxic cleaner hitting the baby's bath toys.

Who Knew?

The first cookbook ever printed was in 1375. It listed a number of recipes using vinegar, including one in which bread was soaked in a mixture of vinegar and herbs.

Help for Sunburned Skin

You had a great day on the beach, but now your back is burned to a crisp. To help ease the pain of a sunburn, rub vinegar on the affected area with a cotton ball or soft cloth. You may smell a bit like salad dressing, but your skin will immediately feel cooler.

Get Rid of Swimmer's Ear

If your children are prone to swimmer's ear, a bacterial infection of the ear canal, take this precaution when they've been in the pool: Dab a solution of one part vinegar and five parts warm water into each ear three times a day. The vinegar will ward off bacteria and keep your kids' ears pain-free.

Ease Wasp Stings

Stung by a wasp? Apply apple cider vinegar to the area with a cotton ball and the sting will subside.

Make Pots Like New

Remove the stains in clay and plastic flowerpots with vinegar. Just fill the kitchen sink with two-thirds water and one-third vinegar, and soak the pots. In an hour, they'll be good as new! Make sure to wash with soap and water before re-using.

Clean Knives

We used to throw knives in the dishwasher with everything else. Problem was, "gunk" (scientific word for stuck-on food left from chopping onions, raw meat, and tomatoes) would still be on the sides. Luckily, there's a neat trick for cleaning knives without dulling their edges—a cork. Simply dip one in vinegar and use it to rub off the gunk, then wash by hand with a soft cloth. No scrubbing necessary!

Dishwasher Done!

Soap film coating your dishwasher? Run it on an empty cycle using vinegar instead of detergent. It will be sparkling clean, and your next load of dishes will be too.

Get Rid of Greasy Hair

Vinegar is not just for the kitchen; it's also an effective degreaser for oily hair! Simply shampoo your hair as usual, rinse, then pour ¼ cup vinegar over it and rinse again.

Corn Removal

To get rid of corns, soak a Band-Aid in apple cider vinegar, and apply it to the corn for a day or two. You can also try soaking your feet in a shallow pan of warm water with half a cup of vinegar. Either way, finish by rubbing the corn with a clean pumice stone.

> ● **Who Knew? CLASSIC TIP**
>
> Adding 5–10 fluid ounces of white vinegar to the rinse cycle of your washing machine has many benefits, the best of which is the reduction of lint in your clothing. Using vinegar in the wash cycle is also great for dissolving the alkalinity in detergents and getting out stubborn odors from clothes like smoke, gasoline, and bleach.

Vinegar as a Fabric Softener

Never buy fabric softener again! Instead, simply use white vinegar. Use the same proportions as you would for a liquid fabric softener— you'll never notice the difference.

Diapers Love Vinegar

If you use cloth diapers, soak them before you wash them in a mixture of 1 cup white vinegar for every 9 quarts water. It will balance out the pH, neutralizing urine and keeping the diapers from staining. Vinegar is also said to help prevent diaper rash.

Virtually Free Freshener

Vinegar is so perfect for neutralizing odors and cutting back on dust, that we like to keep a little in a small jar near heating vents. Our favorite *Who Knew?* hero will leave your room smelling cleaner than it ever did with air fresheners—just make sure to replace it once a week.

Blanket Fluffer

Before using your woolen or cotton blankets when the weather turns cold, wash them in the gentle cycle with 2½ cups white vinegar. It will leave them fluffy and soft as new.

—*Laura Jean Mucha, Cranford, NJ*

Tar Stain Removal

Tar stains are tough to remove, but vinegar can help. If you've stained cloth with tar, try pouring a few drops of white vinegar on the stain and washing as usual. We've also had luck removing grass, coffee, soda, and fruit stains with vinegar.

Who Knew?

You might think this chapter has an awful lot of uses for vinegar, but in earlier times, there might have been even more. In the Middle Ages, vinegar was thought to cure fever, snake bites, leprosy, and the plague.

Brighten Cloudy Glass

If your glasses are beginning to develop a fine film due to too many trips through the dishwasher, soak them in a bath of warm vinegar for an hour. They'll emerge sparkling clean.

Suede Cleaner

Got a grease spot on suede? Vinegar to the rescue! Simply dip an old toothbrush in white vinegar and gently brush over the grease.

The New Jeans Cure

Every time we get a new pair of jeans, we wash them in white vinegar mixed with water. Why? It will remove their stiffness and make sure they stay color-fast. Just throw them in the wash with 10 fluid ounces of vinegar and your usual amount of soap. Add feel free to add other clothes, too! Vinegar is great for your wash.

Underarm Stains

When dealing with stains left by sweat and deodorant, we always turn to vinegar. Soak underarm areas in vinegar for 10 minutes before washing, and the yellow stain (and the smell) will be gone by the rinse cycle. If this doesn't work, you can also try rubbing a paste of baking soda and vinegar into the stains before washing in the usual way.

White Marks Got You Down?

When you let down hems on clothes such as skirts, dresses, and pants, there is often a white mark where the fabric was turned up. Vinegar can be used to get rid of this pesky stain. First warm up your iron, and then scrub the mark with an old toothbrush dipped in white vinegar that has been diluted with small amount of water. Then press with the iron. The

mark will usually come right out, but if it doesn't repeat the process
until it does. If not, then repeat.

Stuck Gum

To remove gum stuck on fabrics, warm a cup of vinegar in the
microwave. Dip an old toothbrush in the gum and brush the gum until it
comes out. It saved my husband's shorts!

—Paulette Culpepper, Hermitage, TN

Prolong the Life of Your Propane Lantern

If you have a propane lantern, soak the wick in vinegar for several
hours before you use it. This will prolong the life of your wick, helping
you get more for your money.

The Marinade Secret

Vinegar helps tenderize the tough protein fibers in meats, so using it
in marinades and braising liquids helps make your dishes even more
succulent. Simply add some garlic and your favorite spices to balsamic
or wine vinegar and you've got a marvelous marinade!

Diet Dressings

To cut calories, make vinaigrette salad dressings from milder vinegars
like balsamic, champagne, fruit, or rice wine vinegar. They're less
pungent, so you can use a higher ratio of vinegar to oil.

Hard-Boiled Eggs

It's easier to peel hard-boiled eggs if you add a teaspoon of vinegar
and a tablespoon of salt to the water they cook in. The vinegar will also
keep them from cracking.

For a Fluffier Meringue

When making a meringue, add ¼ teaspoon white vinegar for every three egg whites to watch it really fluff up.

Poaching Eggs

If you are poaching eggs in an ordinary saucepan, add a teaspoon of white or cider vinegar to the water in which you are poaching them. The whites will stay better formed, making it easier to cook more than one at a time.

> ### ● Who Knew?
>
> Vinegar can reduce bitterness and balance flavors in a dish. Try experimenting with it in your cooking and see what it can do!

Keep Cheese Fresher!

To keep cheese fresh and moist, wrap it in a cloth dampened in white vinegar and put it in an airtight container.

A Buttermilk Substitute

Next time you need buttermilk in a recipe, don't buy a whole carton that you'll later throw away half-full. Instead, make an easy buttermilk substitute by adding a tablespoon of vinegar to a cup of milk and letting it stand for five minutes to thicken.

Removing Fish Scales

If you're gutsy enough to scale your own fish, make it easier by rubbing it with vinegar five minutes before scaling.

Firmer Gelatin

Add a teaspoon of white vinegar to any gelatin recipe in hot summer months to keep Jell-O salads and desserts firm.

Making Pasta and Rice Less Starchy

Preparing pasta? If you put a few drops of vinegar into the water as it boils, the starch will be reduced, making the pasta less sticky. This also works with rice: For every cup of uncooked rice add a splash of vinegar.

Preserving Sour Cream

To make sour cream last longer, add white vinegar right after you open it (1 teaspoon for a small container and 2 tablespoons for a large container). You won't notice the taste, and the sour cream won't go bad as quickly.

Fluffier Rice

If you've prepared rice and it just won't fluff, add a few drops of vinegar before running through with a fork.

Mold-Free Melons

To keep melons from molding, rub them with a teaspoonful of undiluted vinegar every few days as they begin to ripen.

Get Rid of Weeds

Use white vinegar straight from the bottle to pour on the weeds and grass that come up through the cracks in your sidewalk or patio. After a couple of days, the weeds will die and won't reappear for several months.

Vinegar: Your Iron's Best Friend

When ironing, mix one part white vinegar and one part water in a spray bottle. Use it on your garment to help remove iron-made creases (or make creases where you want them). This vinegar and water solution can also help remove shiny areas on the fabric that can be caused by hot irons. When you're done ironing, spritz the solution on collars and underarm areas to prevent yellow marks. Then sprtiz on the ironing board itself and iron while it's still damp to keep the board fresh. A paste of vinegar and baking soda can also clean the base (sole plate) of your iron.

Keep Away Cats

One of the worst things you can discover in the backyard is that your cat has (once again) used your kids' sandbox as his litter box! Pour vinegar around the sandbox to keep cats away. Reapply about every two months just to be sure.

> ### ● Who Knew? CLASSIC TIP
>
> To get rid of calcium or lime buildup on your shower head, soak it in vinegar overnight. This is easily accomplished by pouring vinegar into a plastic bag, then securing the bag around the shower head with tape or a rubber band.

Increase Soil Acidity

If you live in a hard water area, add 1 cup vinegar to 4 liters water, then use it to water plants that love acidic soil, such as rhododendrons, heather, and azaleas. The vinegar will release iron into the soil for the plants to use.

Neutralize Garden Lime

Rinse your hands liberally with vinegar after working with garden lime to avoid rough and flaky skin.

Keep Flies Away from Your Pool

There's nothing more irritating than having flies and other bugs swarm around you while you're trying to take a dip in the pool. We've had some luck keeping bugs away by applying a liberal amount of vinegar around the perimeter of the pool with a sponge.

Drain Volcano

Most people know the old science fair project of mixing vinegar and baking soda to cause a chemical reaction worthy of a model volcano, but not many know that this powerful combination is also a great drain cleaner. Baking soda and vinegar break down fatty acids from grease, food, and soap buildup into simpler substances that can be more easily flushed down the drain. Here's how to do it: Pour 2 ounces baking soda and 5 fluid ounces vinegar into your drain. Cover with a towel or dishrag while the solution fizzes. Wait 5–10 minutes, then flush the drain with very hot water.

Rust Removal

To remove rust from nuts, bolts, screws, nails, hinges, or any other metal you might have in your toolbox, place them in a container and cover with vinegar. Seal the container, shake it, and let it stand overnight. Dry the objects to prevent corrosion.

Get Paint Off Glass

Accidentally paint the edge of your windowpane while doing some remodeling? Hot vinegar can be used to remove paint from glass.

Just microwave a cup of vinegar in the microwave until hot (about 1–2 minutes), then dip a cloth in it and wipe the offending paint away.

Vinegar for Your Car

If you have to leave your car outside overnight in the winter, mix three parts vinegar to one part water and coat the windows with this solution. This vinegar and water combination will keep windshields ice- and frost-free. A rag soaked in vinegar is also a great way to get rid of lime buildup on windshield wipers and other parts of the car.

Chrome Polish

Need a chrome polish? It's as simple as vinegar. Apply directly on chrome with a rag for a quick, simple shine.

Concrete Stains

Unsightly marks on sidewalks and patios are often caused by tar, gum, and pet urine. These can usually be removed with vinegar, so if you're having trouble removing a stain from concrete, try dousing it with vinegar and letting it sit for a day.

Get Rid of Salt Stains

If your shoes or boots are stained with salt from trudging through winter streets, simply dip a cloth or an old T-shirt into white vinegar and wipe away the stain. It's that easy!

> ### 🌑 Who Knew? CLASSIC TIP
>
> Been out with smoky friends all night? To remove the smoke smell from your clothes, hang them on your shower-curtain rod and fill the bath with warm water. Add a cup of vinegar to the bath water and the smell will be gone from your clothes by the morning.

A Fish's Friend

If your fish tank is marked with hard-to-remove deposits, just rub the tank with a cloth dipped in vinegar, and rinse well. The spots should disappear.

Flower Food

To prolong the life of cut flowers without using commercial plant food, add 2 tablespoons vinegar and 1 teaspoon sugar to the water.

—Kim Brickman

CHAPTER 2

Baking Soda

Dishwashing Delight

If hard water in your home causes spots and stains on items that have been run through the dishwasher, add a spoonful of baking soda to your next load. Your dishes will come out spot-free.

Who Knew?

To be effectively used in cooking, baking soda must be combined with an acid to start a chemical reaction. Some ingredients that are often used to start this reaction are sugar, fruit, honey, and yogurt.

Cleaning Grout

Is there anything more satisfying than nice, clean grout? A simple paste of three parts baking soda and one part water is all you need. Make a new batch each time you plan to attack the space between your tiles.

Too Much Hair Product?

If your hair is starting to feel filmy, blend ¼ teaspoon baking soda into your normal amount of shampoo, then wash as usual. The baking soda will remove the filmy feeling from your hair.

—*Marcia Lubin, Edina, MN*

Great Breath Fast

You don't need expensive mouth washes to get better breath. Simply gargle with a mixture of 1 cup water, ½ teaspoon baking soda, and ½ teaspoon salt. This combo will knock out any germs that are causing your bad breath.

Jewelry Cleaner

Baking soda is safe and effective when it comes to cleaning gold and silver jewelry. For best results, use a paste of baking soda and hydrogen peroxide, and rub gently on your jewelry. It gets rid of dirt, grime, and body oils, and leaves your gold and silver sparkling.

Clean an Icky Brush

To make brushes and combs fresh again, soak them in a mixture of 1 quart hot water and 2 tablespoons baking soda for an hour. Rinse and enjoy your like-new brushes!

Protecting Your Plants from Mildew

Here's an old treatment to prevent plants from suffering from mildew or black spots. Mix together ½ tablespoon baking soda with a drop of vegetable oil and 2 cups soapy water. Spray on both sides of the leaves of plants that are normally affected. Complete this treatment in the evening and never in full sunlight, otherwise the leaves may scorch. While the soap helps to spread the mixture and the vegetable oil causes it to stick, the baking soda makes the surfaces of the leaves alkaline, which will inhibit the fungal spores. The biggest advantage of this is that there will be no adverse environmental impact, thanks to the all-natural ingredients.

Smelly Suitcases

Is your suitcase is a bit musty? The night before packing, pour a cup of baking soda in it, close it and shake. In the morning, vacuum up the baking soda and the smell should be gone.

Who Knew?

Baking soda is inorganic, meaning that it isn't produced from anything that was ever alive. Household odors are mostly composed of organic oils. Baking soda works so well at getting rid of odors because the inorganic powder neutralizes them.

Doormats

Your porch's doormat can be cleaned with a sprinkling of baking soda. Brush vigorously and then sweep away the dirt. The next time it rains, the job will be complete.

Baking Soda for Baby Mamas

Baking soda is a gift to anyone who is feeding an infant. Keep some on hand, and if (and when) your baby spits up, sprinkle baking soda on the spot to neutralize odors and absorb the spill before it sets.

Get Rid of Stains Before They Start

If you're cooking over the stove and grease splatters onto your clothes, think fast. Grab some baking soda from the cupboard and rub it into the spot to absorb as much grease as possible. This will make it harder for the stain to set, and soak up as much grease as possible before it works its way into the fibers of your clothes.

Clean Greens

To wash spinach, Swiss chard, or any other leafy vegetable, fill a large bowl with cold water and add a teaspoon of baking soda. Move the vegetables around in the water, soaking them for three minutes, then rinse. All the dirt will fall to the bottom of the bowl and you'll have clean greens.

Substitute with Soda

If you don't like harsh chemicals, use baking soda instead of scouring powder. Baking soda is slightly abrasive, but still gentle, so it's perfect for getting stains out of countertops, tile, and kitchen appliances.

—*Julie St. John, Brentwood, CA*

Scuff Remover

To remove scuff marks left on your floor by dark-soled shoes, rub some baking soda into the spot with a wet rag. They'll virtually disappear.

Shiny Leaves

Want your houseplant leaves to shine the way they did in the nursery where you bought them? It's easy, even if you don't have time to spray them every day with a light mist. Instead, mix ¼ cup baking soda with ½ gallon cold water and use to clean each leaf with a soft rag. (Fuzzy leaves are better left *au natural*.)

Tobacco Killer

Get rid of stubborn odors and stains from cigarettes by adding a half a cup of baking soda to the wash cycle when doing your laundry.

Cleaning Paint

What's the easiest way to remove crayon, pencil, ink, and furniture scuffs from painted surfaces? Just sprinkle baking soda on a damp sponge, rub clean, and rinse.

Not Even a Mouse

As cute as they are, you don't want a mouse in the house, and certainly not around the kitchen. Shake baking soda around their hiding spots, and they'll stay away. It's safe for pets and kids, and easy to clean up with a broom or vacuum.

Milk Protector

To keep milk from curdling, stir in a pinch of baking soda before you heat it.

Stainless Steel Wonder

To get the cleanest bathroom fixtures you've ever seen, apply a paste of vinegar and baking soda to stainless steel faucets, knobs, and towel bars. Lay old towels or rags on top and wait one hour, then buff off. Rinse the fixtures and then let them dry for sparkling fixtures without a hint of water marks.

Regulating Your Pool's pH

When alkalinity needs to be increased in your swimming pool or hot tub, baking soda can be added to restore a balance if there is too much chlorine.

Cleaning Battery Leaks

If battery acid leaks inside the compartments of your appliances, there's no need to throw them away. Simply take few spoonfuls of baking soda and add water until it's the consistency of toothpaste. Spread it on your battery terminals, let it sit 15 minutes, and wipe clean. The acid should come off easily.

Crystal-Clean Crystal

To clean your cut crystal, mix a teaspoon of baking soda with warm water, then dab it onto the crystal with a soft rag. Rinse with water, then buff with a dry, soft cloth.

Brighten Yellowed Sheets

Make yellow sheets white again by soaking them in a tub with warm water along with a cup of salt and a cup of baking soda. Rinse well and dry.

—*Anna Zaia, Baltimore, MD*

Cleaning Makeup Brushes

If you're having trouble getting your makeup brushes and sponges clean, make a simple cleaning solvent. Combine ½ cup baking soda with 2 tablespoons water and mix together. Then add the resulting paste to one more cup of water and half a cup of fabric cleanser. Dip your brushes and sponges in the final solution, rinse clean, and reshape before allowing to air dry.

● Who Knew? CLASSIC TIP

Prevent flaking and cracking when making cake frosting by adding a pinch of baking soda when mixing it together.

Make Better Coffee

Combine ¼ cup baking soda with 1 quart water and run it through your coffee maker as if you were making a cup of coffee. The baking soda will get rid of any mineral deposits that have built up inside. After your baking-soda cycle, run a pot full of plain water through. Now you're ready to make some of the best-tasting brew to ever come out of your old coffee maker!

Cleaner Plastic

An inexpensive way to clean your plastic storage containers when they start to smell is to wash them with hot water and 2 tablespoons baking soda.

Dispose of Properly

Instead of throwing baking soda away when it's fulfilled its 30-day stint in your fridge, dump it down the garbage disposal with running water. Baking soda will keep your disposal fresh, too!

Restore Shoes

Are your white shoes suffering from scuff marks? Rub a little baking soda into the offending areas and all the marks will practically disappear.

Freshen Your Car

If you don't smoke, there's an even better use for your car's ashtrays. Fill them with baking soda and they'll keep your car fresh without those annoying pine tree–shaped air fresheners. Replace the baking soda every two or three months.

Removing Newsprint from Surfaces

If you've ever left a newspaper on a damp surface, you know that the ink stains that are left behind can be a real pain to get rid of. But with baking soda, it's easy. Make a paste with baking soda and a little water and rub gently until the stain disappears.

Cleaning Blenders and Food Processors

If you haven't had time to do the dishes and dried-on food gets stuck in the blades of your blender or food processor, baking soda can help. Add 1 tablespoon baking soda along with 1 cup warm water to the bowl, put the lid on, and let it blend for 10–15 seconds. Then wash as usual.

Less Yuck

If you have kids, it's happened—you've had to clean up vomit. Use baking soda to make the job a little less gross by sprinkling some on top as soon as possible. It will soak up some of the mess and make the smell easier to deal with when you have to go at it with the paper towels.

Get Gloves on More Easily

Sprinkle a little baking soda into each of your latex kitchen gloves and they'll stick less when you're putting them on and taking them off.

Who Knew?

Baking soda has been a valuable substance for centuries. In fact, the Egyptians used it to keep their mummies fresher—no joke!

Fire Prevention

Because baking soda creates carbon dioxide, it's a useful substance to have around where there are flammable chemicals or grease. Keep a package handy and throw on a fire in case of emergency. The soda will prevent oxygen from feeding the flames.

Perk Up a Room

Guests are arriving and you finally enter the guest room that's been closed off for months, only to find that the mattress smells musty even though it's perfectly dry. To solve this problem, turn the mattress and sprinkle a little baking soda on it before you make up the bed with fresh bedding. You can also sprinkle baking soda into pillow cases to freshen up pillows.

Air Freshener for Carpets

A mixture of equal parts baking soda and cornstarch can be sprinkled on a smelly carpet or rug to freshen it up. Sprinkle it on at night, then vacuum up the powder in the morning and the smell should be gone.

—La'Dasha J., Thomasville, AL

Vacuum Cleaner Treat

Sprinkle some baking soda into the bag of your vacuum cleaner to keep it smelling fresh.

Midas Touch

We tend to think that because gold is valuable it must be hard to clean, but the truth is it's simple. Solicit the kids' help for this one if you'd like. All they need to do is make a paste from ½ cup water and 2 teaspoons baking soda and use a soft rag to rub whatever gold piece you want clean. Then rinse with water.

Who Knew? CLASSIC TIP

You can use baking soda to get rid of oil spots on your driveway. Sprinkle baking soda on the stains, then scrub with a wet brush and hot water. Baking soda breaks apart oil particles, so with a little elbow grease you can have your driveway clean in no time.

CHAPTER 3

Lemon

Worry-Free Carving

To quickly and easily sanitize a cutting board, rub salt into it with a wedge of lemon.

Weightless Cakes

We all know homemade cakes should not double as free weights, but what is the secret to keeping them light? A dash or two of lemon juice added to the butter and sugar mixture. That's it!

> ### ● Who Knew? CLASSIC TIP
>
> Sprinkle lemon juice on guacamole, apple slices, and other foods that brown quickly to keep them from oxidizing, which causes the brown color.

Shower Curtain Saver

If your shower curtain has become more disgusting than you'd like to admit thanks to mildew, first wash it in hot, soapy water. Then rub a wedge of lemon on the stains and leave the curtain out in the sun. By the time it dries the stains will be gone.

Odor Eliminator

To remove the fragrance of bleach (and other cleaning materials) from your hands, pour lemon juice over them and rinse. Bleach is alkaline and lemon is acidic. Together they cancel each other out and balance out the pH of your skin.

Say Goodbye to Mineral Deposits

If mineral deposits have built up in your faucet, cut a lemon into quarters, then shove one quarter up into the faucet until it sticks. Leave for about 10 minutes, then twist the wedge out. Repeat with remaining lemon quarters until the deposits are gone.

> ### ● Who Knew? CLASSIC TIP
>
> To easily extract juice from a lemon, first roll it on the counter under your hand. Heat it in the microwave for 10 seconds, then insert a toothpick. You'll be surprised at how easily the juice dribbles out.

Freshen Your Humidifier

Humidifier smelling musty? Simply add 2 tablespoons lemon juice and it will never smell fresher!

Removing Ink Stains

Ink stains on the carpet? Make a paste of cream of tartar and lemon juice, and dab at the stain. Let it sit for five minutes or so, then clean with a damp cloth.

Solve Your Silverfish Problem

Our boys are pretty tolerant of (read: obsessed with) creepy crawlies, but the delicately named silverfish are too gross even for them. Sliced up lemons are effective in keeping them at bay. Put lemon slices down where they like to appear, and replace with fresh lemons every few days.

Buffing Aluminum and Brass

Lemon is an effective cleaning agent for aluminum and brass. Sprinkle cream of tartar on a wedge of lemon and rub it into the surface. Let sit for 10 minutes, then rinse and buff dry. If you don't have any cream of tartar, you can also try this trick with baking soda.

Fluff Up Your Rice

When cooking rice, add lemon juice to make it fluffier. Simply add 1 teaspoon lemon juice for every quart of water.

—Mary Terlecky, Sandusky, OH

Who Knew? CLASSIC TIP

To get rid of stubborn stains and odors in the microwave, place a bowl of water and lemon slices inside. Heat on high for six minutes. Let stand for a few minutes and then remove. Wipe the inside with a soft cloth and the stains will lift easily.

Refresh Your Lettuce

You've left the lettuce in the crisper for a few days, and now it's too wilted to use for a salad. Perk it right up by submerging it in a bowl of cold water and 1 tablespoon lemon juice. Let sit for 5–10 minutes and it will be as good as fresh.

Cutting Board Stains

Remove stains on cutting boards by pouring lemon juice on the stain and letting it sit for 20 minutes. Then rinse with water.

Easily Clean Graters

Clean soft cheese, garlic, or any other food from your grater by cutting a lemon in half and rubbing the pulpy side against the grater. For extra abrasion, add a little salt.

Soothing a Sore Throat

Relieve your sore throat with a time-tested home remedy. Slice one-third of a lemon off, then take the two-thirds-sized piece and place it on a shish kebab skewer or barbecue fork. Set your gas stove to high and roast the lemon over the open flame until the peel acquires a golden brown color. (This works on electric stoves too, although not quite as well.) Let the lemon cool off for a moment, then squeeze the juice into the smallest cup you have. Add one teaspoon of honey, mix well, and swallow.

Cleaner Glass

Lemon juice makes an excellent glass cleaner, and will even give it an extra shine. Pour it directly onto glass and rub with a soft cloth to dry. Rub newspaper over the area to get rid of any streaks.

Lemon Peels for Kindling

The best thing to use as kindling in your fireplace isn't newspaper (or printed-out emails from your ex). It's lemon peels! Lemon (and orange) peels smell delicious when they burn, and they contain oils that not only make them burn longer, but help ignite the wood around them. Finally, they produce less creosote than paper, which will help keep your chimney clean.

Soothe Stings

If you're stung by a wasp, hornet, or bee, reach for a lemon. Make sure the stinger is gone and quickly rub the area with some lemon juice. It will neutralize the venom.

Ease a Scratchy Throat

Sore throat? Here's another lemon remedy: Gargle with one part lemon juice and one part warm water. Lemon helps fight bacteria and soothes your throat.

Repel Dandruff

To keep your scalp naturally dandruff free, use a little bit of lemon juice. Mix 2 tablespoons lemon juice with 2 cups warm water and pour over your head after you rinse out your conditioner. Let it dry in your hair and it will not only keep dandruff away, it will smell wonderful.

● Who Knew? CLASSIC TIP

Brown spots on your skin are usually caused by dead skin cells. Slough off dead skin and brighten what's underneath by rubbing lemon juice on the spot. Let it dry, then rub vigorously with a washcloth.

Great for Fingernails

Rub a wedge of lemon on your fingernails to whiten the enamel. A perfect activity during downtime while baking!

Go Blonde

If you have brown or dark blonde hair, you can add highlights without chemicals and with hardly any cost. Cut a lemon into quarters or eighths, then cut a slit in the middle, as if you were going to put the wedge on the rim of a glass. Wash your hair as usual, and while it's still wet, place a strand of your hair in the slit, beginning at your scalp and running the wedge down to the tips of your hair. Sit outside in direct sunlight until your hair dries, and you'll have lovely blonde streaks. Repeat in one week to make the streaks even brighter.

Lemon Juice as Toner

There's no need to spend money on facial toners and astringents. Just dab lemon juice on your face with a cotton ball and it will tighten your pores and prevent blemishes. Use it in the morning and the smell will also help wake you up.

A Little Lemon in Your Bath

You've finally found a few secret minutes to have a relaxing bath! But as you're drawing the water you realize you're out of bath salts. It won't be as nice, but to add a bit of scent to your bath, squeeze a lemon into it. Lemon juice is also great for loosening dry skin, so bring a sponge or washcloth with you.

● Who Knew?

Most of our nation's lemons come from California. Why? California gold rushers planted an abundance of lemon trees in 1849 because they valued the fruits as a natural remedy for scurvy.

CHAPTER 4

Salt

Clean Vegetables More Easily

If you're having a hard time trying to get the last pieces of grit off of a vegetable or herb, give it a bath in salt water. It works especially well with leafy greens like spinach.

Easy Egg Clean-up

Salting your eggs may not be good for your health—unless the egg is on the floor. Dumping a pile of salt on top of a cracked egg will make it easier to clean.

Protect Yourself from Grease Splatters

Add salt to the pan when you're cooking greasy foods like bacon, and the grease will be less likely to pop out of the pan and burn your hand.

Who Knew? CLASSIC TIP

To revitalize artificial flowers, forget about using expensive cleaners. Just pour salt into a large paper bag, place the flowers inside petal-side down, and shake vigorously. The dirt will be transferred to the salt.

Frost Fix

If your windows are frosting over, dissolve 1 tablespoon salt in 1 gallon hot water and rub on the panes with a soft cloth. Then wipe away with a dry cloth. This will keep your windows frost-free.

Wicker That Won't Age

To keep wicker from yellowing in the sun, bathe it in salt water with a wet rag when it's new.

Sticky Iron?

Get rid of unwanted residue on the bottom of your iron by sprinkling salt on a piece of printer paper and ironing on a low level with no steam.

Hassle-Free Spill Clean-Up

Oops, that pot in your oven boiled over, and there's a sticky mess on the bottom of your oven! To easily clean any oven spill, sprinkle salt on top immediately after noticing it. After a little while in a hot oven, the spill will turn to ash and it can easily be cleaned.

Chill Drinks Faster

Because salt lowers the freezing point of water, your beverages will cool more quickly if you use salt in your cooler. Simply layer ice with salt, throw in the bottles and cans, and wait for them to chill.

Safety Salt

Water should never, ever be thrown on a grease fire, because it will only spread. If there's a fire caused by grease or oil in your kitchen, throw salt on it until it is extinguished. The salt will absorb the liquid that is causing the flames.

Who Knew?

There are a few stains that salt will actually help set. Never sprinkle salt on red wine, coffee, tea, or cola spills!

Fried Fish's Friend

To keep fish to keep from sticking to your skillet while you're frying it, toss a handful of salt in the pan before the fish.

Keep Milk Fresh

Keep your milk lasting longer by adding a pinch of salt to it after you open it.

For Beet-Stained Hands

If your skin has become stained from beets, sprinkle the affected area with salt, then add a drop of dishwashing liquid and rub.

Lipstick on Your Glass? Use Some Salt

Who knew salt was the best way to remove lipstick from a glass? Rub a little over the stain to remove a pretty imprint on the side of the glass, then wash as usual. Sticking glasses with lipstick on them in the dishwasher hardly ever does the trick, because lipstick is made to resist water. Use this salt pretreatment and you'll get them sparkling.

● Who Knew?

The largest salt flat in the world is the Salar de Uyuni in Bolivia, which has an area of 4,086 square miles. It is so reflective (and the air around it so clean) that it is often used to calibrate satellites that are in orbit over Earth.

Clean Up a Doughy Counter

You've just made a delicious loaf of bread and placed it in the oven, now what do you do about all that dough and flour stuck to the counter? Make your cleaning job easy by first sprinkling salt on the counter. Its abrasive action will help you easily scrub off any sticky spots.

Cleaning Burned Milk

If you've ever scorched milk in a pan, you know it's almost impossible to remove the stain. However, salt can help. Dampen the pan, then sprinkle salt all over the bottom. Wait 10 minutes and scrub away the stain. The odor will be gone, too!

—*Maureen Delepine, Italy*

Perk Up Your Coffee

It's 3 p.m., and with the day you've had, you're headed back for a second (or third) cup of coffee. Unfortunately, once you heat up some cold joe that's been sitting in the pot, it tastes thick and a little bitter. Make your coffee taste like it's just been brewed by adding a pinch of salt and a dollop of fresh water to your cup. Heat it up in the microwave and you're ready to power through the rest of your workday.

Make Colors Last

Brighten rugs that have faded by rubbing them down with a rag that has been soaked in salt water (then wrung out). You can also submerge throw rugs and drapes in a solution of salt water, then wash as usual.

Yellowed Counter?

If the enamel on your counter or tub has turned yellow, add a handful of salt to turpentine and rub onto the enamel, then wash as usual. Make sure to test on a small area of the counter to ensure it doesn't harm it.

Drip-Free Candles

To keep candles from dripping, soak them in a strong salt-water solution after purchasing. To make sure your salt water is as strong as possible, heat up some water and add salt until it won't dissolve anymore—then you'll know the water is completely saturated. Leave your candles in this solution for two hours, then remove and dry.

Make Sponges Like New

Whether it's your kitchen sponge or the head of your mop, porous cleaning materials can be revived with a little salt. Fill a bucket with a mixture of ¼ cup salt and 1 quart warm water. Then soak your mops and sponges for 8–10 hours and their grunge will be gone.

Loosening Soot

If you throw some salt in your fireplace every now and then, soot will be easier to clean from your chimney. It will also make your fire burn a cool yellow color!

Put Out a Fire

You're ready to go to bed, but the fire you started a few hours ago is still awake, glowing with its last few embers. Instead of making a mess with water, throw some salt over anything that's still burning. It will snuff out the flame and you'll end up with less soot than if you let it smolder.

Freshen Shoes

Get rid of nasty shoe odors by sprinkling salt in them and leaving overnight. The salt will absorb moisture and odors.

Drain Renewal

Pour a half a cup of salt down the drain of your kitchen sink with warm running water. The salt will freshen your drain and keep it from getting bogged down with grease.

Removing Cooking Odors from Hands

A quick way to remove the smell of garlic or onion from your hands is to rub them with a bit of table salt. It will absorb the oil and smell in a matter of seconds.

Make a Broom Last Longer

There are all kinds of new products available to get your floor clean, but sometimes a simple straw broom is your best bet. Soak your straw broom's bristles in a bucket of warm salt water for a half an hour and then let dry. It will keep your broom lasting longer.

—*Crystal Garito*

Make a Room Smell Wonderful

Who hasn't had a beautiful bouquet of flowers that they wish they could make last longer? Give your flower petals a second life by layering them with non-iodized salt in a small jar—this works best with flowers that have pulpy petals and woody stems, like roses, lavender, and honeysuckle. The salt will bring out their natural scent and help freshen your entire room. Keep a lid on the jar when you're not around to make the scent last even longer.

Dandruff Problem?

If you're afflicted with dandruff, try this homegrown fix. Rub 2 tablespoons of salt into your scalp before shampooing and watch those flakes become a thing of the past.

Fix Puffy Eyes

Soak cotton pads in a solution of ½ teaspoon salt and 1 cup hot water, then apply them to your eyes and relax. Your eyes will be less puffy in 15 minutes or less.

Who Knew? CLASSIC TIP

If you're having trouble sleeping, try this salty tip: At bedtime, drink a glass of water, then let a pinch of salt dissolve on your tongue, making sure it doesn't touch the roof of your mouth. Studies have shown that the combination of salt and water can induce a deep sleep.

Poison Ivy?

To help relieve the itching of a rash caused by poison ivy, soak the affected area in a strong salt bath. Make sure the water is warm to fully get the itch out.

Repel Pantyhose Runs

If your nylons seem prone to getting runs, try soaking them in salty water before you wash and wear them. Use a half a cup of salt for each quart of water, and let them soak for 30 minutes. Then launder as usual.

Displaying Fake Flowers

Make a holding place for your fake flowers using salt. Fill your vase with salt and add just enough cold water to get the salt wet, but not submerge it. Then stick the stems of your artificial flowers inside. The salt and water mixture will turn hard, keeping your flowers exactly where you want them. When you're ready to take the flowers out, fill the vase with warm water until the salt starts to dissolve.

Make Copper and Brass Shine

To clean and polish brass and copper, make a paste of one part salt, one part flour, and one part vinegar. Rub this paste into the item using a soft cloth, then rinse with warm water and buff with a dry cloth for a glistening shine.

CHAPTER 5

Vegetable and Olive Oil

Duct Tape Residue

If you've been using the last chapter of this section (Duct Tape) a lot, you may need this tip: To get rid of duct tape residue, simply rub with oil. Let it sit for 5–10 minutes, then wipe up. The residue should now be much easier to scrape off with the rough side of a kitchen sponge and some warm water.

Untangling Necklaces

For annoying tangles in thin chains, place on a glass surface. Add a drop of oil and use a pin to tease out the knots. Then rinse in warm water.

> ### ● Who Knew?
>
> Olive oil does not get better with age—it's best to use as close to its production date as possible. Store in a dark place that isn't too airy to preserve it as long as possible.

Better Than Hand Soap Alone

To remove oil-based paint from your hands, simply rub them with a drop of oil, then wash off with soap and water.

Quick Candle Clean-Up

Rub a bit of oil on candlesticks before inserting candles and they'll be easy to remove. Any dripped wax will also peel off with ease.

Olive Oil and Eggs

If your recipe requires eggs but you don't want the calories of egg yolk, use the egg white mixed with a teaspoon of olive oil instead. This gives a better consistency than using the whites on their own, which can make the mixture too light, plus you'll reap extra health benefits.

—*Cheryl Dunn, New York, NY*

The Trick for Sticky Pasta

If your pasta came out too sticky, let it cool, then sauté it with enough olive oil to lightly coat each noodle. Make sure to stir or toss while reheating.

Silence Squeaky Hinges

Who needs WD-40 when you have vegetable oil? Simply rub oil on squeaky hinges with a cloth, letting the oil run down the sides of each hinge.

Who Knew?

Vegetable oil has a higher smoking point than olive oil, which means that it's better for cooking foods on high heat, like pan-seared fish and fried chicken.

Unstick a Zipper

Zipper won't budge? Try adding a tiny bit of vegetable or olive oil to the stuck teeth with a Q-tip, being careful not to get any on the fabric. This will lubricate your zipper and allow it to move more easily.

Wood Cleaner

Out of Pine Sol? Use vegetable or olive oil to dust your wooden furniture.

Keep Bugs Away from a Birds' Bath

Just a few drops of canola or vegetable oil will keep mosquitoes from laying eggs in the water in your birdbath and won't hurt the intended residents.

For the (Humming)birds

Are ants overrunning your hummingbird feeder? Rub a bit of olive oil on the tip of the feeding tube, and they'll stay away. The ants can't get through the oil, but hummingbirds can.

Say Goodbye to Moles

Use olive oil in the yard to keep moles away: just soak an old rag and stuff it into a mole hole. They hate the smell and will stay away.

Greasing the Racks

After you've cleaned your oven racks, coat the sides with a bit of vegetable oil. They'll slide in and out of the oven with ease.

—*Claire Beevers, Essex, UK*

Unstick Stuck Glasses

You reach to get a glass out of a stack of glasses, only to realize they're stuck together. Reach into the cabinet again to get some vegetable oil, then pour a bit down the side of the glass to unstick them without the risk of breaking the glass.

Scratch Eraser

For tiny scratches in your wooden table or floor, rub vegetable or canola oil into the surface. The oil will darken the area and help it blend in.

Quick, Cheap Makeup Remover

A wonderful, inexpensive way to remove eye makeup is to dab a little olive oil under your eyes and rinse off with a washcloth. You can also use hair conditioner!

Who Knew?

In ancient Greece, women used olive oil to make eye shadow by mixing it with charcoal.

Cuticle Cure

Using a Q-tip, dab a bit of oil on your cuticles to keep your nail bed moisturized. You'll be less likely to get hangnails!

Soften Rough Feet

For the softest feet you've ever experienced, try this before-bed routine: Rub down your feet with vegetable oil, then put on some old socks. When you wake up, the oil will be gone and your feet will be supersoft.

Is This How Popeye Shaves?

Shaving cream feels great, no doubt, but did you know it's actually not the most efficient way to get a good shave? Next time, try shaving with olive oil instead—you'll get a closer, smoother shave.

Paint Be Gone

If your kids love to paint like our sons do, they'll inevitably get some paint in their hair—or in the dog's! Don't fret, though—acrylic paint is easily removed from hair by using a cotton ball soaked in olive oil.

Fur-tastic Olive Oil

Add up to ¼ teaspoon olive oil to your cat's moist food to stave off hairballs and make his coat extra shiny.

Help with a Splinter

Got a splinter you can't get out? Try soaking the area in vegetable oil for several minutes. It should soften your skin enough to allow you to ease the splinter out.

CHAPTER 6

Aluminum Foil

Fix Your Flooring

If your vinyl flooring is coming up, put it back where it belongs! Lay a sheet of foil on top (shiny side down), then run a hot iron over it several times until you feel the glue on the bottom of the tile remelting. Place something heavy, like a stack of books, on top and leave it overnight to set.

Broken Toy?

If you have an electronic toy whose batteries are loose due to a missing spring, don't throw it away or pay to get it fixed. Simply ball up a small amount of aluminum foil and put it in the spring's place. The aluminum will conduct electricity in lieu of the spring.

Protection While Painting

Before you begin that big painting project, cover doorknobs, drawer pulls, and any other small object you're worried about catching spills with aluminum foil. The foil easily molds to any shape and comes off when you're done.

> ● **Who Knew? CLASSIC TIP**
>
> Covering your ironing board with foil before you iron your clothes will get them wrinkle-free twice as fast, saving you time and energy!

Silverware Saver

To keep your silver from becoming tarnished, store it on top of a piece of aluminum foil. You can also wrap clean silverware in plastic wrap, then in foil, for tarnish-free long-term storage.

Polish Your Silver

You can also polish silver with aluminum foil, but not in the way you think. Line a pan with aluminum foil, add a tablespoon of salt, and fill with cold water. Then add your silverware to the mix and let it sit for a few minutes before removing and rinsing. The aluminum acts as a catalyst for ion exchange, a process that will make the tarnish transfer from your silver to the salt bath.

Make Your Grill Super Hot

To get your grill even hotter (making sure the bar marks on your steak are extra impressive), cover it with a large sheet of foil for 10 minutes before cooking. This will keep the heat from escaping.

Pie Crust Saver

Keep your pie crusts from getting too brown by covering the edges of your pie in strips of aluminum foil.

Cool Pan Handles

The handles on pots and pans can get very hot, hence the invention of potholders. If you have hollow handles, however, you can place some aluminum foil inside to keep them cool. It seems counterintuitive, but the foil blocks heat from traveling up from the burner. Don't tell anyone how you did it. Use your bare hands. Impress your friends!

Easy Oven Clean-Up

Cooking something messy in the oven? Cover the rack below the one you are using with aluminum foil. It will make it easy to wipe up any drips, and is safer than lining the bottom of the oven.

Fuzzy TV Signal?

If the picture on your television isn't crystal clear, it may be caused by interference. Place a sheet of aluminum foil between any electronics (like your DVD player, cable box, or TV) that are stacked on top of each other and those wavy lines will be history.

Soften Brown Sugar

If you find that everything in your brown sugar box is one giant lump, place it in a ball of foil and bake in a 350° oven for five minutes. It will be back to its old self in no time.

Perk Up Houseplants

If your houseplants aren't getting enough sun, maximize the amount of light they *are* getting by placing them on top of a table covered in foil (shiny side up). The foil will reflect the light, and your plants will thank you.

Keep Bugs Away

Protect your soft drinks from bees and other bugs when you're enjoying a beverage outside. Cover the top of the cup or can with foil, then poke a straw through. Now you can sip in peace!

Deter Hair Dye

When dyeing clients' hair, I use this tip when they want to catch up on *Cosmopolitan* but can't read without their glasses! Just cover the arms of the glasses in foil and you'll make sure none of the strong hair dye gets on them.

—*Shelia H., Carlisle, PA*

A Giant Vessel

When you started preparing the recipe, you didn't realize its contents would double in size! If you run out of space in your bowl and you're in a pinch, simply line your entire kitchen sink with foil and throw your ingredients in there. Then serve in smaller containers.

Who Knew? CLASSIC TIP

When you're done grilling, place a large piece of aluminum foil over the entire top of your grill, then put the top back on and let it sit for 10–15 minutes. The caked-on mess from the burgers and hot dogs will turn to ash.

Keep Away Wetness

Whether you're on a big camping trip or your kids are just sleeping in the backyard for fun, place a long sheet of aluminum foil underneath sleeping bags to keep moisture from sinking into the fabric.

Deter Pests in Your Garden

If you've ever bitten into a shred of foil that was stuck to a piece of candy, you know how unpleasant the sensation is. Rodents hate the feeling of foil between their teeth, too, so placing strips of foil in your garden mulch will help deter rodents and some bugs. If rodents are eating the bark of your tree, you can also wrap the trunk in foil.

Funnels of Foil

If you have aluminum foil in your kitchen, you don't need a funnel. Simply fold a sheet of foil in half width-wise and roll into a funnel shape. You can make a funnel of any size and to fit any hole!

Fireplace Quick Clean

Cleaning out a fireplace is easy when you line the bottom with aluminum foil. Just wait for the ashes to cool, fold up the foil, and lay a fresh layer out.

Makeshift Platter

If you're looking for a platter for deviled eggs, brownies, or other picnic items, simply cover a piece of corrugated cardboard with aluminum foil (dull side up), then throw it away when you're finished!

Mattress Protector

If you need to accident-proof your child's mattress and you don't have a waterproof mattress cover, just lay overlapping sheets of foil on top of your mattress, then cover with a couple of old towels and the rest of your sheets. Now onto the harder task: Coming up with a potty-training strategy!

Fresher Paint

Keep paint in half-used cans from developing a film on top. Before you close the can for storage, place the lid of the can on top of aluminum foil and trace around it. Cut out the circle, then drop it gently into the can so it covers the paint. When you open the container later, just take out the foil and you won't have any messy dried paint bits to worry about.

Toasty Toes

This trick is an old family favorite. Wrap rocks in foil and place them in your campfire. When it's time for bed, place them at the bottom of your sleeping bag and they'll be comfortingly warm.

—*Greg Schoenfeld, Dawson, MN*

Replace Steel Wool

You have a pot that's in need of a good scrubbing, but you're out of steel wool. Simply reach for the aluminum foil! Roll it into a ball and use it (with some dishwashing liquid) to scrub off caked-on grease. This is also a great way to reuse foil before you recycle it.

Brighten a Backyard

You're hosting a backyard barbecue that's turned into an evening affair. Unfortunately, your outdoor accent lights aren't bright enough, but you don't want to have to turn on the glaring light by your door. Instead, fold pieces of aluminum foil in half (shiny side out) and wrap like a bowl around the bottom of the light, then attach with a few pieces of electrical tape. The foil will reflect the light in a nice, shimmering pattern.

● Who Knew? CLASSIC TIP

Brrr, it's cold in here! Wrap a very large piece of corrugated cardboard in aluminum foil (shiny side out), and place it behind your free-standing radiator. The foil will reflect the heat, and you won't have to keep telling your landlord to turn up the boiler.

Fisherman's Friend

If you're caught without a lure and have a fishing trip ahead, use aluminum foil instead. Cover your hook with foil, then rip it away in small sections so that it will dance in the water. Fish will be attracted to the movement and reflected light.

Arty Aluminum

Art project? Make paint-mixing easy by using a piece of cardboard covered in aluminum foil as your artist's palette. Kids will especially love it if you cut the cardboard in the shape of a palette first.

Clean an Iron

If you've been ironing too many clothes with starch and your iron is starting to get sticky, run it over a piece of aluminum foil to clean it.

Who Knew?

Have you ever wondered why aluminum foil has one shiny side and one dull side? The shininess is produced during the foil's final press at the factory. However, foil is so thin that it's virtually impossible to create a press that can press something that thin. Therefore, two sheets are pressed at the same time. The sides of the foil that are on the inside (touching each other) end up dull.

Leaking Gutter?

If your steel gutter is leaking, aluminum foil can help. First patch the hole with roofing cement, then cover the cement with foil and another layer of cement. For an even heavier-duty fix, add an additional cement-and-foil layer. This combination will plug the hole better than cement alone.

CHAPTER 7

Duct Tape

Quick Fix for Long Pants

You've bought a great pair of jeans, but they're too long and you don't have time to hem them before you need to wear them. Simply fold them up and tape with duct tape. The hem will last the whole night—and maybe even through a couple of washings. This is also a great tip if you're not sure exactly where you want to hem your pants. Have a "trial run" using the duct tape, and they're all ready to sew.

Out of Rope?

Duct tape is so sturdy, you can use it as a rope by twisting it around itself. Use as a backup for clotheslines, leashes, tying twine, or anything else you would normally use rope for.

Winterize Your Door

If you have a sliding glass door that's rarely used during the winter, seal the top, bottom, and sides with duct tape to keep cold air from coming in.

—Belinda Duchin, Portland, ME

Mend a Shingle

If one of your roof's shingles has fallen off, you can make a temporary replacement using duct tape. Cut a ¼-inch thick piece of plywood to match the same size as the missing shingle. Then wrap it in duct tape (you will need several strips) and wedge it in place.

Camper's Aid

Always, always pack duct tape when you're going camping. It's a must-have to repair rips or holes in tents and air mattresses, and can be used to string up food so it's out of bears' reach.

Reinforce Folders

For a pocket folder you know is going to take a beating—like the one we keep near our tool kit that holds instructions—reinforce it on the sides and pockets with duct tape. It will last forever!

●⸱Who Knew?

Duck Products, a manufacturer of duct tape, sponsors an annual competition that offers a college scholarship to the person who creates the most stylish prom dress made from duct tape.

Picnic Pleaser

When going on a picnic, bring a roll of duct tape. Use the tape to tape the sides of the tablecloth to the picnic table, and you won't have to worry about it blowing away.

Reinforce Hockey Sticks

Make your hockey sticks last longer by covering the bottom with a layer of duct tape and replacing it when it gets nicked and worn.

Make Hanging Holes

If tubes of glue, caulk, and other home-repair necessities are cluttering up your work bench, hang them from the wall with nails. Create holes that the tubes can hang from by wrapping a piece of duct tape from front to back on the bottom (non-dispensing end) of the tube. Leave an extra ½-inch flap of tape at the end that doesn't touch the tube and just folds onto itself. Then poke a hole through this part and you'll have a handy hanging hole. Wrap another piece of tape around the tube the other way to reinforce the tape you've already applied.

Secret Key

Duct tape a spare key to the undercarriage of your car or in a wheel well and you'll never get locked out again. Make sure to do it in a location other than near the drivers' side door, where thieves may check.

Who Knew? CLASSIC TIP

Duct tape may be the best aid for a last-minute Halloween costume. Make a robot or the Tin Man using a brown paper bag or box as a mask. Cover it, as well as a shirt and an old pair of jeans, with duct tape, then send your kid out for some much-deserved candy.

Goodbye Flies

Each summer we travel to our cabin, and when we arrive there are always droves of flying insects inside. We tape five to ten pieces of duct tape to themselves (making a ring with the sticky side out), then hang them from the rafters near the overhead lights. The bugs become stuck, we throw out the tape, and our problem is solved!

—*Frank R., Michigan City, IN*

Keep Kids' Hands Warm

If your child refuses to wear gloves or mittens, don't give him the opportunity to take them off once he goes outside to play. Duct tape the cuffs of the gloves to the cuffs of his coat!

Perfect for Boots

Make your winter boots a little warmer—and make sure they're completely waterproof—by lining the bottom of the insides with duct tape. The tape will create a waterproof seal, and the shiny silver will reflect your body heat back onto your feet.

Vacuum Fix

If your vacuum hose has developed a crack and is leaking air, simply cover the crack with duct tape and keep on cleaning.

Leaky Shower Arms

If you have a shower that has a detachable shower head, use duct tape to repair any holes when the connecting arm inevitably begins to leak.

Customize Tools

If the screwdriver, hammer, or other tool that you're using is hard to grip, wrap duct tape around the handle until it more easily fits your hand.

Who Knew?

Even given its name, duct tape is not actually safe to use on heating ducts. This is because the adhesive can be ineffective at high heat.

Vacuum Bag Fix-Up

If your disposable vacuum cleaner bag is full and you don't have replacement on hand, it's duct tape to the rescue! Remove the bag and cut a slit straight down the middle. Empty it into the garbage, then pinch the sides together at the slit and fold over. Tape the fold with a liberal amount of duct tape. The bag will hold a little less, but you'll be ready to vacuum again without having to run to the store.

Splinter Removal

If you get a splinter, a little duct tape does the trick to get it out. Cut off a piece and gently press it to the affected area.

Big Hat (or Small Head)?

Make your ball cap tighter by cutting a piece of duct tape lengthwise and wrapping a few layers around the sweat band.

Pool Liners

When pool liners tear, it can be very costly to repair them. But duct tape can do the job. Simply cover the tear, and keep and eye on it to make sure it doesn't start to peel off. Believe it or not, a single piece of duct tape can usually last underwater for an entire summer.

A Hiking Must-Have!

Before you start out on your hiking trip, tape your pant legs to your boots with duct tape. This will ensure you'll get no bites from ticks, flies, and mosquitoes.

Protect Your Grill

Make sure squirrels, mice, and other critters don't chew through the rubber pipeline that connects your propane tank to your grill—reinforce the entire thing with duct tape. This is a good idea for anything else in your yard made out of rubber, as this is a favorite chew toy of rodents!

Keep Wood From Splitting

When cutting plywood, first reinforce where you plan on cutting with a strip of duct tape. The tape will keep the wood from splitting as you saw, and then you can peel the tape right off.

Trash Can Tip

If your curbside trash can has a crack, the easiest way to repair it is to just slap some duct tape over it on both sides. Duct tape can withstand the rigors of the outdoors, and it's not like you're worried about your can looking nice, anyway.

Who Knew?

The television show *MythBusters* may have discovered some of the most fun uses for duct tape. In their duct tape–centric episode, they lifted a car with it, constructed a boat out of it, and created a cannon made entirely out of the beloved tape.

Goodbye, Hose Thieves!

Our hose hookup is on the side of our house, and unfortunately, we had our hose stolen twice! We were forced to keep rolling it up and putting it in our garage until a neighbor mentioned why she thought her hose had been spared—it was full of holes that had been repaired by duct tape. We slapped some duct tape on our hole-free hose, and it hasn't been stolen since.

—*Janice K. Smith, AZ*

Quick Seal

If the seal around the window in your car is leaking air and making an annoying sound as you drive, patch it up with duct tape until you have the time (and money) to take it to the shop.

Make Your Slippers Even Better

To make your slippers waterproof and therefore safe to wear on a quick trip outdoors, simply cover the bottoms with—you guessed it—overlapping layers of duct tape.

Basket Mending

If you have a plastic laundry basket that has cracked or has a handle partially torn off, cover the rip with duct tape on both sides. It may not be pretty, but it works just as well as a new basket.

Cleaning Velcro

It's hard to get bits of lint and hair out of Velcro...unless you have some duct tape. Firmly press it into each side of the Velcro several times to easily clean it.

Let's Twist Again!

If you're having trouble getting a dead light bulb out of its socket due to arthritis or a particularly tricky bulb (we always have trouble with those enormous floodlight bulbs with the long, flat fronts), use some duct tape to help you. Pull off a strip of tape that is about two feet long, then fold about six inches of the middle portion back on itself, sticky side to sticky side. You'll now have a six-inch "tab" of duct tape with two sticky ends. Tape these ends to either side of the bulb, then twist the tab to get some leverage. Replace the bulb and thank duct tape for another job well done!

A Better Way to Take-In Pants

If you have a child who is super-skinny (despite his grandmother's best efforts to fatten him up), you've probably taken in your fair share of sweatpants using a safety pin. However, using duct tape will allow you to take in the pants without worrying about the pin being uncomfortable. Simply fold the elastic band of the pants onto itself, then tape the fold with duct tape.

Protect an Injury Quickly

If you receive a cut or gash while hiking in the woods, working at a jobsite, or somewhere else where medical care isn't readily available, duct tape can help. Use a bit of tape to cover cuts and hold your skin together if they're deep. This isn't a permanent solution, of course, but the tape will keep germs out while you go to get help.

Duct Tape for Warts

It's long been stated as fact—then disputed—that duct tape can help cure warts. It may seem strange, but medical studies have concluded that when patients cover their warts with duct tape every day for a month, 85 percent of them will see a reduction in the wart. That's compared to only a 60 percent reduction in patients who used cryotherapy (having the wart frozen off by a dermatologist). It's hard to believe, but many people swear by the treatment! Our opinion? Especially if you don't have health insurance, it's worth a shot!

Who Knew?

Enough duct tape is sold each year to make a duct tape rope that extends all the way to the moon.

PART TWO

More Time- and Money-Saving Tips

Want to know the easiest way to carry drinks at a party? The best recipe for a homemade foot bath? How to keep your energy costs down? What to do when you spill paint on the rug? Our Household Help section will tell you all this and more, but it's not just about knowing that corn syrup will remove grass stains or that an old toothbrush holder makes a great vase. It's about making your day easier and (hopefully) stress-free by giving you simple solutions to simple problems. So the next time you oversalt the soup, bees overrun your party, or your bills never seem to get paid on time, don't fret.

CHAPTER 1

Cleaning Wonders

Cleaner Windows

Do you feel like you can never get a window completely clean? Here's an easy tip that will help you to tell which side of the pane those godforsaken streaks are on. Simply wash your windows from top to bottom on the inside, then switch to washing side-to-side on the outside.

● Who Knew? CLASSIC TIP

Do you have streaks and lint on your windows after washing them? Stop cleaning them with paper towels—try newspaper. It's cheap, easy, and green!

Homemade All-Purpose Cleaner

A good all-purpose cleaner is essential to any well-run home. Keep this one on hand at all times (but out of reach of the kiddos). Start with ¼ gallon water and mix in ½ cup rubbing alcohol, a squirt of dishwashing liquid, and ¼ tablespoon ammonia (non-sudsy). Fill a spray bottle and you're ready to go.

Rings Around the Table

If you've got kids, you probably have watermarks on your finished wood table. Since they may never listen to your pleas to use a coaster, use a little petroleum jelly to remove the white stains. Just rub the area with the jelly and let sit for several hours (or even overnight). Then rub again with a soft cloth and the stain should disappear.

How to Easily Clean a Dirty Radiator

Dreading cleaning your radiator? Here's a simple way to get the job done. Hang a damp cloth or damp newspapers on the wall behind it. Then use your hair dryer to blow the dust off it. The dust will stick to the wet surface behind it, and then you can simply throw it away.

Polish Marble

Polish marble surfaces by first pulverizing a piece of chalk using a mortar and pestle or a hammer. Sprinkle the chalk dust on the marble, then rub in with a soft, damp cloth. Buff with a clean cloth for a brilliant shine.

Restore Robust Rugs

To get the color back in your carpet or rug, take a small bucket and pour 2 cups white vinegar, 2 gallons hot water, and 2 teaspoons ammonia into it. Mix well, dip a washcloth into it, and scrub away on the carpet. Soak up any excess with a dry towel.

—*Carla Renaudo*

Cast Iron Cookware Cleaner

To remove charred food from your cast iron cookware, boil a mixture of salt and vinegar in it and let simmer for 10–20 minutes. Rinse your pan thoroughly and then re-season it with vegetable oil before storing it.

Sparkling Can Opener

When even your can opener is super clean, you know you have mastered the art of home maintenance. Putting it in the dishwasher can lead to rust so just churn a folded paper towel through it after each use to remove the residue, then quickly wash and rinse.

Clean Fiberglass

This is, unfortunately, an adults-only chore. Using plastic gloves in a well-ventilated room, mix together 1 cup vinegar, ½ cup baking soda, ½ cup clear ammonia, and 1 gallon warm water. Designate a sponge just for this purpose (or use a rag) and make sure not to let the solution touch your skin as you rub it onto any fiberglass that needs cleaning.

 Who Knew? CLASSIC TIP

Keep tarnish off your silver in storage by keeping a couple pieces of chalk wrapped in cheesecloth with them. The chalk absorbs moisture, keeping tarnish away.

Fireplace Finisher

If you've been burning a lot of fires this winter, get your brick fireplace nice and clean in the spring with a simple household solution. Take 3 cups vinegar, 3 cups ammonia, and 3 cups borax, mix the ingredients thoroughly, and scrub the bricks clean. This will work for any bricks inside or outside your home.

Paint Spills

If you've spilled paint on your carpet, stop cursing and head to the kitchen. Mix together 1 tablespoon vinegar, 1 tablespoon dishwashing liquid, and 1 quart warm water. Douse the area with this mixture and try rubbing it away. If that doesn't work, you may be out of luck. Wait for the paint to dry and snip off the area that has paint on it—your carpet's "haircut" will be less noticeable than a giant paint stain.

Paint on Windows

Were you a little sloppy when painting around your windows? To easily remove paint from glass, dab the area with nail polish remover, then wash off after 2–3 minutes.

Restore Shine to a Plant's Leaves

Easily dust your houseplant by rubbing the inside of a banana peel on each leaf. Not only will it remove dust, it will also leave the leaves even shinier than before.

Quick Carpet Cleanser

If you've got guests coming over and need a last-minute way to clean your dirty carpet, simply mix a cup of ammonia with a quart of water. Use a mop to rub this solution onto the carpet, and it'll help remove the grime. You might want to test this method beforehand on an unseen area of carpet—such as underneath a chair—and make sure to never use it on wool carpets.

The Black Bag Treatment

Make your oven racks easier to clean by coating them with cleanser, placing them in a black plastic trash bag, and setting them outside in the sun. After a few hours, they'll be ready to spray off with a hose.

—*Trish Mackay, Newark, DE*

Garbage Disposal

Cleaning your garbage disposal is as easy as throwing a few ice cubes down your drain. Run the disposal until you no longer hear grinding, and your job is done! The cold cubes will congeal any grease in the drain, allowing your disposal to break it up. Add a peel from any citrus fruit to give it a fresh scent!

Dust is mostly composed of biological matter, the largest percentage of which are mold spores. To keep mold from forming, clean your home regularly and keep dampness from setting in.

One Great Beverage Deserves Another

Coffee stains can be frustrating, but did you know you can get them out of your carpet by pouring beer on them? That's right—just pour a couple of sips onto the stain and it should vanish. Dab up the extra beer with a paper towel, and if the coffee stain doesn't go away completely, repeat the task a couple more times. This works for tea stains, too.

Venetian Blinds

The easiest way to clean blinds is to wrap a kitchen spatula in an old cloth and secure it with a rubber band, then dip it in rubbing alcohol or your favorite cleaner, close the blinds, and go to it!

Pledge Allegiance to Your Sink

You already know Pledge has many household uses, but did you know that one of the best ones is keeping your sink clean? If you've got a stainless steel sink, wipe wood cleaner over it after you wash it out. If you do this at least once a month, the cleaner will keep your sink shiny by preventing water and food stains from taking hold.

Greasy Wallpaper

To eliminate grease on wallpaper without chemical cleaning products, first cover the area with a brown paper bag or craft paper. Apply a warm iron and the paper will absorb the grease.

Untarnished Silver

Here's an easy household solution we use to polish up our old heirloom silver. Combine 1 quart whole milk with 4 tablespoons lemon juice, and let your silver items soak in the solution overnight. The next day, just rinse it off with water and dry it.

A Great Future for Your Plastics

There aren't many cleaners made especially for plastics, but it's easy to make your own. Simply take a quart of water and mix it with three tablespoons of either lemon juice or white vinegar. Mix it together and put it in a spray bottle, and you've got some plastic cleaner.

Clean Grease Like Lightning

If you have kids, you're going to end up with a grease stain on your carpet sooner or later, guaranteed. The big thing to remember is to not touch the stain at all—don't sop it up, wipe it, or anything else. Instead, pour a large amount of cornstarch on top of the spot and gently stir it with your finger. Let it sit for a day, and make sure not to walk on it. The next day, use your vacuum cleaner's hose attachment (the plastic one, not the one with bristles) to suck away the cornstarch. The stain should have mostly disappeared, but if not, keep repeating this tip until it's completely disappeared. You can then use the brush attachment to clear away the last remnants of cornstarch.

Clean, Then Clean Your Dust Mop

The most efficient way to clean a dust mop without making a mess is to put a large paper bag over the head of the mop, secure it with a rubber band, and shake vigorously. The dust on the mop will fall into the bag, and then you can throw it away.

—Ceclia Oczkowski, Patterson, CA

Your Shower Likes Wine, Too

Rid shower doors of stains and lime scale by wiping them over with a bit of white wine—the cheapest you can find, of course.

Erase Vacuuming Mistakes

You can prevent marks on baseboards and walls when you vacuum by covering the edges of the vacuum head with masking tape. That way, you won't leave behind dark smudges from the metal when you inevitably bump the wall.

Cleaning a Crystal Chandelier

Our kids are getting better about pitching in with housework, but this is one chore we tend not to delegate to them. (We also don't tell anyone how easy it is!) First, make sure the light switch is off. Next, lay a blanket underneath the chandelier in case any pieces fall. Now mix ½ cup rubbing alcohol with 1½ cups water in a jar. The crystals clean themselves—all you have to do is bring the jar up to each one and dip it in, then let it air dry. You can use a little bit of the solution on a clean cotton rag to wipe areas that can't be dipped.

Another Way to Eradicate Crayon Marks

To remove crayon marks from wood, rub mayonnaise over the area and leave on for 10 minutes, then easily wipe off.

> ### ● Who Knew?
>
> If the hole in one of the burners of your gas-powered stove is clogged, never use a toothpick to clean it out, as toothpicks can easily break instead. Instead, use a straight pin or a pipe cleaner.

The Best Way to Deodorize Your Freezer

Add a shallow bowl of freshly ground coffee, uncovered, to your freezer. Leave for a few days and any funky freezer odors will disappear.

Getting Rid of an Iron Disaster

If you've ever had scorched, melted polyester or vinyl on your iron, you know what a mess it can be. Wait for your iron to cool, then rub the melted muck with a rag that has been dipped in nail polish remover. Scrape off the mess with a wooden spoon (or anything else made from wood—metal can scratch). Wipe with water before ironing again.

It's Not Easy Being Green

We admit we kind of like the look of that green coating (patina) over copper, and it was popular as a pigment in oil paintings in the Middle Ages. But the deposit signals damage and should be removed from jewelry, antiques, coins, nameplates, and the like. Using a soft cloth but lots of elbow grease, rub a mix of equal parts baking soda and deodorized kerosene into the affected item. If it's a utensil that can take the abrasion, use fine steel wool and/or a toothbrush to get in between tiny pieces.

Ceramic Tile

The easiest way to clean ceramic tile is with rubbing alcohol. Just pour it straight on, and mop until it dries.

 Who Knew? CLASSIC TIP

For a great glass cleaner, fill a 3-cup spray bottle with ½ teaspoon liquid dish detergent, 3 tablespoons white vinegar, and 2 cups water. For very dirty glass, use more detergent.

Get Rid of Food Odors

To remove odors from dishes, bottles, or plastic containers for good, add a teaspoon of mustard to hot water and let the item soak in it for five minutes. The mustard will get rid of the smell, and you can wash as usual.

Scrub, Baby, Scrub!

You love steel wool for its abrasive cleaning power, but hate the rust stains it sometimes leaves. One idea is to keep your steel wool pads in an ordinary soap or sponge dish, but an even better idea is to use the tray part of a terra-cotta plant pot. These are made to soak up water—so put them to work!

Wax Splatters

Nothing is more disheartening than discovering hot wax has just dripped on your sofa. But there may be a way to fix it. Place a brown paper bag on top of the wax, then iron the bag with an iron set on medium heat. The wax should transfer to the bag, and you can peel it right up.

Preventing Fingerprints

You just bought the coffee table of your dreams, but when it was sitting in the store you didn't realize it would attract fingerprints like bees to honey. To get rid of a persistent fingerprint problem, rub down the tabletop with cornstarch. The surface will absorb the cornstarch and it will repel prints.

Cornmeal Cure

Cornmeal absorbs grease stains on light-colored fabric or upholstery. Just pour enough on to cover the soiled area and let sit for 15–30 minutes, then vacuum. The stain will be gone!

Cleaning Leather

The best advice for clean leather furniture is to keep your children and pets away! But there are a few ways to clean it if it becomes dirty. Treated leather can be rubbed down with a damp cloth, and an occasional date with warm soapy water won't harm it. If you get a spot on your leather furniture, try removing it by rubbing it with artists' gum—a super-powerful eraser that can be found at art supply stores. If you accidentally get a liquid that badly stains on your leather, blot up as much as you can, then apply hydrogen peroxide with a cotton ball to wipe it up.

When to Clean Your Bathroom

The best time to clean your bathroom is right after you've taken a shower. The steam loosens dirt and grime and makes it easier to get that perfect shine.

Safe Septic Tank Cleaner

When buying your first new home, you probably thought about the backyard parties and a basement rec room. Cleaning the septic tank? Not so much. Still, the time will come when it needs to be done. Add 2 teaspoons baker's yeast and 2 cups brown sugar to 4 cups warm water. Flush the mix down the toilet and let sit overnight.

Refrigerator Drawers

If you never feel like contending with a filthy vegetable drawer again, line it for easy cleaning. Newspaper will keep veggies from getting too moist, while bubble wrap will make sure your food stays bruise-free. Either will make for an easy clean-up job: just remove and replace!

Glass Dishes

To remove baked-on stains from a glass casserole dish, fill it with warm water and add two tablets of Alka-Seltzer or denture cleaner. Leave for an hour and the stains will be gone.

—Sandy Martis, Sandpoint, ID

Stuck-On Food

If the bottom of your pot or pan is a burnt-on mess, stick it in the freezer for an hour or two. The stuck-on food will freeze and be easier to remove.

Stained China

Impossible-to-remove stains on your china? There may be hope yet. Apply a bit of nail polish remover to the spots with a soft cloth, then wash as usual. The spots should quickly fade.

Get Rid of Greasy Fingerprints

Believe or not, a good way to get greasy fingerprints off walls or wallpaper is to rub the area with a slice of white bread.

Cleaning Hard-to-Reach Places

Unless your arms are six feet long, dusting behind radiators or under appliances can be a real drag. Try making a dusting tool by slipping a heavy-duty sock on a yardstick and securing it with a rubber band. Spray it lightly with dusting spray (we like water and a little bit of fabric softener) and you're ready to finally grab all that dust you've been avoiding.

● Who Knew? CLASSIC TIP

Removing candle wax from your wood floor is easy: First soften the wax with a blow dryer, then wipe with towel soaked in vinegar and water.

Microwave Window

To clean the smudged, greasy, food-flecked window of your microwave, use ashes from your fireplace. Rub them on the window with a wet rag, then rinse clean.

Removing Red Wine

What's the easiest way to remove red wine spills from your carpet? Try applying a bit of shaving cream (after checking that the carpet is colorfast) and letting it sit for a minute. Then wipe away. Shaving cream will also work on grease stains.

Easy Clean for a Dishwasher

To get rid of mineral deposits and iron stains in your dishwasher, run it through an empty wash cycle using powdered lemonade mix instead of detergent. The citric acid in the mix will eliminate your problem.

Cleaning a Melted Plastic Mess

It's happened to us tons of times, and it's probably happened to you, too—a bag of bread is in the wrong place at the wrong time while you're making breakfast, and you end up with melted plastic all over the toaster. To remove melted plastic from metal, glass, or other plastic, first make sure the surface is cool (that is, unplug the toaster!). Then rub the affected area with nail polish remover until the plastic scrapes off. Wipe down the surface with a damp sponge, let it dry, and you're back in business.

Forgotten, But Not Gone, Grime

It's time to do what you've been dreading: Clean the caked-on grime that's been accumulating on top of your refrigerator. But don't worry, the job's easier than you think. Simply mix 1 tablespoon ammonia with 1 cup hot water. Apply a generous amount to the top of your fridge with a sponge or rag and let set for 5 minutes. Then wipe away with ease.

Burning Hair Dryer Smell?

If it's beginning to smell like fire every time you blow dry your hair, your dryer's motor may be clogged with hair and lint. Use an old toothbrush to brush clean the back of the dryer, where it sucks in air. Now you can dry your hair without someone poking their head in the bathroom to make sure everything's okay!

For Caked-On Filth in Your Bathroom

If your porcelain sink or tub has rings that refuse to be removed, it's time to call in the big guns: oven cleaner. Oven cleaner can eat through a plastic shower curtain and bleach colored porcelain fixtures or tile, but if your sink and tub are white, this is the cleaner for you. Simply spray oven cleaner on the affected areas, wait about an hour, and rinse off. It's that easy!

Best Gum Remover

The best way to get gum out of carpet, clothes, or hair is with a chemical called methyl salicyclate. Luckily, you don't have to make any methyl salicyclate yourself. Just look for it in an analgesic heat rub like Bengay. Put it on the gum and then apply heat in the form of your hairdryer set on low. Then press a plastic sandwich bag on the gum and pull it away easily. Make sure to wash the area after you've removed the gum.

Caked-On Food, Go Away!

If you're cleaning your oven, make the job a bit easier with this solvent. Blend a quarter cup of ammonia with a box of baking soda to make a soft paste. Apply this paste to the stained, cooked-on spots inside your oven and let sit overnight. Rinse it well with regular water the next day, and your oven will look good as new.

● Who Knew?

In a survey of British residents, people rated cleaning the oven as their most-hated chore.

Ceiling Clean

It seems cruel that, after spending so much of your time cleaning your home, dust still manages to get places you never thought to clean— like your ceiling. To vanquish this last bit of dirt, use a clean, dry paint roller with a long arm to quickly dust above your head.

Lampshade Lifter

Dust your lampshades using a fabric softener sheet and their static-fighting properties will keep the shades cleaner for longer.

Shiny Countertops

For a scratch-free cleaner that will make your countertops sparkle, apply club soda with a moist sponge.

Dirty Kitchen Sponges

To quickly kill the dangerous bacteria that makes its home in your kitchen sponge, simply wring them out, then microwave on high for 30–60 seconds.

Coffee-Stained Carpet

Your best bet for removing coffee stains from carpeting is to rub a beaten egg yolk into the spot, leave for five minutes, then rinse with warm water. This will also work for coffee stains on clothing!

Keeping Trash Bins Clean

When cleaning kitchens and bathrooms, sprinkle a little scouring powder like Comet (or better yet, a generic brand) at the bottom of trash cans. The powder will soak up any liquids if there is a leak in your bag, repel mildew, and keep your bin smelling fresh.

Get Rid of That Ring

If your shaving cream can is leaving rusty rings on the side of your tub or sink, perform this trick right after you purchase a new container: Coat the rim around the bottom of the can with clear nail polish, then let it dry. The nail polish will keep out water and prevent rust.

Remove Old Stickers and Labels

To remove the gummy remains of a label or sticker on glass or a mirror, cover it in mayonnaise and let it sit for 5–10 minutes, then gently scrape off with a putty knife.

Another Use for Alka-Seltzer

Effervescent tablets aren't just good for curing hangovers—dissolve a tablet in warm water at the base of a vase to remove stains and leave it shiny-new.

Easy Ashtray Emptying

To make ashes slide right out of your ashtray without leaving a mess behind, first clean it and then coat it with a fine layer of furniture polish.

Your Electric Dustpan

Forget the feather duster—the easiest way to get loose dust off your knick-knacks and anywhere else in your home is to blow it away with a hair dryer.

Get Ahead of Grime

Instead of spraying your shower down every time you use it, try this solution for keeping your shower mildew- and grime-free. Apply a thin layer of car wax to a completely clean shower, then buff with a dry cloth. Your cleaning job will be much easier, and you'll only have to reapply the wax once a year. You can also perform this trick in your refrigerator to keep food stains at bay.

Rusty Sink

As long as you're very careful, you can use lighter fluid to buff out rust stains on your sink! Just make sure to thoroughly wash your hands and the sink afterward.

Who Knew?

Even if your carpet doesn't look dirty, you should still vacuum it regularly. Dust mites, which are invisible to the naked eye, love rugs and carpeting! Nearly 100,000 dust mites can live in one square yard of carpet. Ick!

Easy Toilet Bowl Cleaner

For a cheap and easy way to clean your toilet, use mouthwash. Just pour 1 capful into the bowl, leave for 10–15 minutes, and wipe clean with your toilet brush.

Shower Door Scum

Easily erase soap scum from shower doors by rubbing them with a fabric softener sheet.

Mildew-Fighting Booze

For an unusual mold and mildew fighter, try vodka! It works especially well on the caulking around your tub. Just spray on, leave for 10 minutes, and wipe clean.

Keep the Lid Up

This may go against years of training your boys, but in rarely used bathrooms the lid on the toilet should always be kept up. Keeping the lid up allows air to circulate in the bowl, which will prevent mold and mildew from forming. Also make sure to leave toilet lids up when you go on vacation!

—Jennifer Pilcher, Olathe, KS

Toothpaste Trick

Most optometrists will try to sell you an expensive cleaner when you buy your glasses. Instead of buying theirs, simply use a tiny dab of white toothpaste (not a gel) on both sides of the lenses to polish them and keep them from fogging up.

Impromptu Glasses Cleaner

The next time you're digging through your pockets looking for a cloth you can clean your glasses with, try a dollar bill. Press hard and it will do the job of a glasses cloth in a pinch.

Quick Drain Fix

Not only is drain cleaner expensive, it can weaken your pipes. Instead of using Drano to unclog a slow-moving drain, use a gel dishwasher detergent like Cascade. Pour the detergent into the drain and chase it with boiling water.

Cleaning Golf Clubs

By now you've probably realized that we have a substitution for just about every household cleaner. But what about when your prized golf clubs get dirty? Resist the urge to spend money on fancy cleaners. Instead, soak your clubs for one minute (no longer) in a bucket of water that you've dissolved one scoop of laundry detergent in. The detergent has the exact same ingredients as those expensive club cleaners.

Another Reason to Love Coca-Cola

When you buy a rust remover, what you're really paying for is phosphoric acid. However, phosphoric acid can also be found in something you probably have around the house—cola. Dip screws or anything else that needs de-rusting into cola and leave for several minutes. Then scrub away the black substance that remains and repeat if necessary.

Fireplace Cleaning Secret

Before cleaning the ashes from your fireplace, sprinkle some damp coffee grounds over them. They'll weigh the ashes down and keep dust to a minimum.

Easy Sponge Disinfection

Another way to make your kitchen sponges and brushes last longer is to wash them once a week in the utensil compartment of your dishwasher with a load of dishes.

Clean Ceiling Fans

To easily clean a ceiling fan, spray glass cleaner or a mixture of half vinegar and half water on the inside of a pillowcase. Put the pillow case over one arm of the fan, then pull the pillowcase off while applying gentle pressure toward the floor. The pillowcase will wipe the top of the blade clean.

Beautiful Brass

To clean brass, apply white, non-gel toothpaste on a soft cloth, and then rub firmly on the brass. Use a fresh cloth to wipe clean.

Good Fix for a Bad Sink

Your stainless steel sink has seen better days, but it might not be beyond repair yet. For a sink that's been scratched, stained, and treated with every harsh chemical in the book, it might be time for a facelift. Use chrome polish to buff it back to life.

Mirror Makeover

For a unique cleaner for the mirrors around your home, use aerosol air freshener. It will bring your mirrors to a glossy shine and will have people wondering where that flowery scent is coming from.

Spilled Hair Dye?

To remove hair dye from wooden furniture and cabinets, wipe with a cotton ball dipped in fresh hydrogen peroxide. This method is tried and true by hair salons.

—*Jennifer Pilcher, Olathe, KS*

Clean with a Coffee Filter

We always prefer to clean our windows with something reusable, like an old rag. But if you like to go the disposable route, try coffee filters instead of paper towels. They won't leave behind any lint or paper pieces.

Stained Containers?

If you have plastic containers that have been stained by tomato sauce or curry, the solution isn't ten rounds in the dishwasher or simply throwing them away. Instead, place the containers in direct sunlight for a day. The sun will bleach out the stain naturally and your plastic will be as good as new.

A Fix for a Pull-Cord Problem

There always seems to be one thing around your house you just haven't figured out how to clean easily. At our house, that thing used to be the pull cords on our Venetian blinds. They were grimy from years of use by greasy hands, but taking down the blinds always seemed like too much work. Finally, we found this solution: Get a step ladder or something else that you can rest a jar on top of that is the same height as the top of the blinds (where the pull cord begins). Then fill the jar with cold water and add a tablespoon of bleach, soak the cord for two to three hours, and rinse. Just make sure to pull your blinds up first, so the maximum amount of cord possible is exposed.

CHAPTER 2

Around the House

Mark Your Tape's End

Nothing's more irritating than trying to find the end of a roll of packaging tape. So after you tear off a piece, stick a toothpick to the tape at the end of the roll. It will make it easy to find and easy to lift.

Make Scouring Pads Last Twice as Long

When we use scouring pads, a lot of the surface tends to get wasted, so we cut them in half before using them. That way the box lasts twice as long—and it'll help sharpen your scissors, too.

For a Great-Smelling Home

To freshen your whole house fast when it's too cold to open the windows, place a couple of drops of vanilla extract on your furnace's filter. Your house's heating system will do the rest of the work for you.

Plants Like It Warm

When watering houseplants, always use lukewarm water. Cold water may chill their roots.

Easy Roach Repellent

To get rid of roaches, chop up cucumber skins and bay leaves, mix together, and spread around the areas that have been invaded. The hideous creatures will steer clear, meaning you don't have to do the dirty work of throwing the dead ones out as you do with traditional traps (one of our least-favorite chores).

A Solution for Mice

If you've got problems with mice getting into places they're not supposed to, fill in any openings or gaps with steel wool. This will kill the mice by causing internal bleeding after they eat it. If you'd rather not kill them, just put some caulk into the crevice, too, which will keep them out altogether.

—*Tayshaun Boyd, Chanute, KS*

 Who Knew? CLASSIC TIP

Here's a trick that could save you hundreds: If your cell phone gets wet, first take the battery out and dry it with a paper towel. Then bury the phone and the battery in a bowl of uncooked rice for 24 hours. The rice will draw the rest of the water out of the phone, and hopefully it will be back in business again.

Picking Up After a Glass Accident

You've just shattered a vase or glass, and there are shards of glass everywhere. Don't panic. Put on some shoes, keep kids and pets away from the area, and then head for your newspaper bin. Wet several sheets of newsprint (usually an entire section will do) and use them to wipe up the mess. First pick up any big pieces, then wipe the newspaper on the floor. The small pieces will stick to the wet paper, making sure you get every last piece.

Light Candles Without Burning Your Fingers

To light hard-to-reach wicks at the bottom of jar candles, use an uncooked strand of spaghetti. Light the end of it, then use it like a fireplace match.

Eternal Flame

If you have a favorite candle you may wince each time you go to light it, knowing it will eventually be gone. Yet letting it sit unused on the shelf seems like bad feng shui. As a compromise, try this: Let your favorite candle be a candleholder. When there's a big enough hole worn down the middle, put another, smaller candle inside and light that one. Votive candles work well for this and can be easily replaced when they burn down.

Green Thumb Water Test

No matter how long you've been gardening, it's still hard to tell exactly how much water each plant needs. Our son loves performing this test to see when a plant has had enough to drink. (It's just like sticking a fork in a pan of brownies to see if they're done.) Poke a pencil into the dirt and pull it back out. Clean means it's time to water. Soil on the pencil means the plant is okay for now.

Plants Like Beer, Too

If you host a big party at your house, don't throw away all the beer from those half-empty bottles. Instead, pour it into a bucket, let it sit for a day or two until the beer gets flat, then pour it on your indoor or outdoor plants. The nutrients from the beer will give the plants an extra boost. Wait a minute, wasn't this in *Little Shop of Horrors*?

Neat Way to Dry Gloves

You've just come in from outside, and your snowy gloves have quickly turned into sopping wet ones. To dry them out in time for your next excursion into the winter air, pull them over the bottom of a jar, then place the jar upside down on top of a radiator or heating vent. The warm air will fill the jar and dry out your gloves in no time.

Get Rid of Telltale Creaks

Back when our kids were still tiny, this trick was a lifesaver. There's nothing worse than finally getting a grouchy baby to sleep and tip-toeing out of the room only to have the wooden floor in the hallway creak like the second coming. Shake talcum powder over the cracks and rub in with an old rag, and you can escape in silence!

Fun Fern Facts

If you have a fern that's seen better days, water it with lukewarm salt water and that'll help it recover. If your fern is plagued by worms, that problem is easily solved, too. Just stick half a dozen unlit matches into the soil, coated end facing down. The sulfur content in the matches will keep the worms away.

Select Your Pot Carefully

Although fancy pots may look pretty, the best kind of container to grow plants in is an unglazed clay pot. It's porous, which allows the soil to breathe, and the hole at the bottom makes it difficult to over-water. Be wary of both plastic pots and decorative glazed clay pots.

Tea Plants

If you have any doubt that tea really is a panacea, here's one more amazing use for it: nurturing your plants and keeping them moist. Place a lining of tea bags along the bottom of the plant container, then pot and water as usual.

No More Gnats

If you suspect that one of your plants has a gnat problem, here's how to find out for sure. Slice off one-third of an uncooked potato and place it face down (peel side up) on top of the soil. Leave it for a week to 10 days, and if the potato is still clean, there are no gnats to worry about. If gnats are present, however, there will be larvae on the underside of the potato slice. To rescue your plant, kill the gnats with vodka. (Yes, vodka.) Mix one part vodka to three parts water, pour it into a spray bottle, and spray away. Do this for a week and the pests will be long gone.

Who Knew? CLASSIC TIP

If you have a scratch in your wood floor or furniture, cut a pecan in half and rub the meat of the nut over the scratch. The dark color of the nut will blend right in.

A Must for Musty Areas

If a closet, garage, or rarely visited corner of your home is starting to get musty, use this trick to get rid of excess moisture. Fill a coffee can halfway with charcoal briquettes, then punch some holes in the lid and put it back on the can. Place one or two of these cans in the area and the mustiness will be a thing of the past.

Get Rid of Roaches

To repel roaches, make a "tea" with catnip by submerging the leaves in hot water and straining them. Then spray the solution in your kitchen, bathroom, and other areas where roaches like to stray. Repeat every time you mop or vacuum to permanently keep cockroaches away.

—Anna Boudinot, Los Angeles, CA

Easy Wasp Killer

If some wasps have found their way into your home, don't panic. Fill a wide-mouthed jar with 1 cup sugar and 1½ cups water. The wasps will be attracted to the sugar, and drown in the water trying to get to it.

Best Bait for Mice

If you've seen a lot of Disney movies, you probably think mice live for cheese. But when you're baiting a mousetrap, a better bet is peanut butter. Since it's sticky, you can be sure the mouse won't grab it and run, and some people say they love its sweet scent even more than your best piece of cheddar.

Tread on Traction

Those nonslip bath strips aren't just good for providing traction in the tub. They can provide traction for anything that slips you up, whether it's the stairs to your attic or a tiled floor, and are available at any hardware store.

Find a Lost Contact Lens

Nothing's worse than crawling around the floor trying to find a lost contact. If you've been looking, one-eyed, for too long, try this trick. Get an old nylon stocking and secure it over the end of your vacuum hose using a rubber band. Then run your vacuum where you think you lost the contact. The lens will stick to the stocking.

Waterproof with Wax

To waterproof something you've written with marker on your child's school supplies or on a package you're sending, rub over the writing with a white candle. The wax will repel water, but you'll still be able to see through it.

Fruit flies are always a pain, because they usually hover around fruit baskets and other areas where you don't want to spray poisonous bug spray. Instead, spray a little rubbing alcohol on them. They'll fall to the floor and you can scoop them up and throw them away.

Repair a Braided Rug

If your braided rug is coming undone, it's not a goner yet. Try repairing it by using a hot glue gun. Just lay down some newspaper, then carefully apply a small amount of glue in between the braids. Press them back together again and hold for a few seconds for the glue to dry.

Fix Stuck Plugs

If an electric plug on an appliance fits too snugly and is difficult to pull out, rub its prongs with a soft lead pencil and it will move in and out more easily.

Potpourri Substitute

Instead of spending money on costly potpourri, give your house a delightful aroma much more inexpensively. Heat your oven, toss some ground cinnamon on a sheet of foil, and leave the oven door slightly ajar. The cinnamon will unleash its delicious aroma as it warms up, giving your home a delightful scent.

—Evelyn Quigley

The Only Way to Dry Wood

If a piece of your wood furniture or a wooden windowsill have gotten wet, resist the urge to dry it out with a space heater or hair dryer. Too much heat will make wood crack and warp. Instead, keep the area at room temperature and aim a fan at it.

Free-Flowing Electronics

Use a pencil eraser to wipe off the metal contacts on rechargeable items such as your cordless phone and drill and they'll get a better charge. You can also use this trick for your cell phone, iPod, or between batteries and their contacts in electronics.

Boost Your Alarm Clock's Power

If "brrrring!!" isn't enough to wake you up anymore, maybe it's time to make your alarm even louder. Place it on a cookie tin lid, metal tray, or ceramic tile. The material will amplify the sound, creating a "BRRRRING!!" you can't ignore.

Plant Revival

Give dying indoor plants a second chance with this odd little treatment. Let three empty eggshells sit overnight in a couple of cups of water. (Multiply the amounts as needed.) Then use the eggshell water the next day when it's time to water the plants.

Debug a Plant

To get rid of bugs that are harming your houseplant, place the entire plant (pot and all) in a clear, plastic dry-cleaning bag. Throw several mothballs in with it, and tie a knot at the top. The sun will still get through, but the bugs will die after a week in seclusion with the mothballs.

Hit the Right Switch

The switch for our garbage disposal is right next to the one for an overhead light, and I used to always flick the disposal switch when I just wanted more light in the room. It's bad for the disposal to run without any water running, not to mention the fact it would always startle me half to death! To get rid of this problem I finally found a very simple solution. I put a dot of red nail polish on the disposal switch. No more accidental grinding!

—*June Panella, Phoenix, AZ*

Repel Frost on Windows

To keep your windows or sliding glass door from frosting over on the coldest days of winter, wash them with a mixture of 1 quart warm water and ½ cup rubbing alcohol. Now you'll be able to see clearly, even if it's too cold to actually venture outside.

Protect Your Table

An easy way to protect your dining room table is to purchase table pads that go underneath your table cloth. But since they usually have to be custom-made, they can cost a bundle. For a large, rectangular table, use a twin-size mattress pad instead. It's not as nice, but it will do the job.

So Long, Static

You know, of course, that dryer sheets remove static cling from your laundry—but did you know they remove it from just about everything else, too? Just wipe down your computer screen, television—or even your hair!—with a sheet of Bounce, and the static cling will disappear.

This Solution's a Corker

Avoid slamming kitchen cabinets by putting homemade silencers on them. Just save the cork from your next bottle of wine, slice it into skinny pieces, and glue them onto each inside corner of your cabinet. Problem solved!

Cheapo Paper "Shredder"

Worried about identity theft, but can't afford a proper paper shredder? Use your washing machine instead! Put the papers in a stocking, tie the end, and throw them in for a wash. By the time the cycle is over, the ink will be bleeding, the papers a shredded mess, and your secrets safe from anyone picking through the trash.

A Better Way to Hide Things

Instead of leaving your valuables where burglars can find them, hide them out in the open. For instance, wash out an old mayonnaise jar and paint the inside of it white. Let the paint dry and then place your money, jewelry, and other items inside. Store it in the back of your fridge and it'll still be there even if you're burglarized.

Stamp Removal Stamp of Approval

We don't recommend snooping, but if you need to unseal a letter, or get an unused stamp off an envelope, simply leave it in the freezer overnight. The next morning, the glue will be undone and you should be able to use a pair of tweezers to complete the job. Another way to get a stamp off an envelope is to leave it in a cup of water for a few hours. It'll float right off; then just let it dry and use paste to stick it onto the new envelope.

Makeup to the Rescue

To fix tiny furniture scratches, use an eyeliner in a matching color to fill in the hole.

—*Margie Parker, Tampa, FL*

A Shocking Solution

If you can't escape static electricity on your carpet, here's an easy fix. Mix 3 cups water with ½ cup liquid fabric softener, put it in a spray bottle, and apply to your carpet. Not only will the static electricity disappear, but the mixture will serve as a carpet deodorizer too.

Minty Magic Insect Repellent

Here's a great way to use the gum you regularly confiscate from unruly offspring—leave the mint-flavored variety in the pantry to keep away insects. A few slices (even wrapped) can do wonders.

Bees Begone

Swatting at bees is unnecessary (and never leads to anything good). Just turn out the light and open a window. The light from outside will attract them even more than your nice, juicy arm.

Silence a Squeaky Door

If your door won't stop squeaking and you're sick of constantly reapplying WD-40, try this trick. Take the door off its hinges, then rub them all over with a candle. The wax will stick and prevent the parts of the hinges from rubbing against each other, which causes that annoying sound.

Avoid Musty Books

If you're placing some old books in storage and don't want them to acquire a musty smell, here's the solution for you. Just place a new sheet of fabric softener inside the pages, and that old copy of *To Kill a Mockingbird* will stay nice and fresh until you need it again. If you fail to follow this tip or if you have books that are *already* musty, just place them in a paper grocery bag with an open box of baking soda. Fold over the bag, staple it shut, and let it sit for a week or two. Your books should smell considerably better when you take them out.

Freshen That Air

Here's an easy way to make your own eco-friendly air freshener with ingredients you have around the house. Mix 2 cups warm water with 2 tablespoons baking soda and ½ teaspoon orange or vanilla extract. If you prefer, you can use an essential oil for the scent: lemon, jasmine, rose, and lavender all smell wonderful. If you leave out the extract or oil, it's safe to spray around pets, kids, and most furniture (although you might want to spot-check first).

Quiet a Loud Washer

Does it sound like there's an earthquake in your laundry room every time you run the washer? If your washing machine's vibrations are driving you nuts, try placing a scrap of carpet underneath. The carpet should keep the machine from dancing around. For safety reasons, just make sure the carpet you choose is flame-resistant.

Stuck Photos

If your photographs are stuck to each other or to a glass frame, the solution is steam. Use a steamer, a steam iron set on its highest setting, or a pan of boiling water to get steam as close as you can between the photo and whatever it's stuck to (being careful not to burn yourself). As the photo gets warmer and wetter, it should become easy to peel away. Lay out to dry, then flatten with a fat book if it has curled.

How to Store Stamp Pads

Here's one for your home office: Always store stamp pads upside down. This will ensure that they don't dry out in between uses.

Easy Fix for Some Broken Umbrellas

Before you throw away an umbrella, see if you can fix it by sewing the fabric back onto the metal arm—easily accomplished with a simple sewing kit!

Another Way to Bring Back Old Books

Make your old, musty book smell like new with this simple trick. Sprinkle a half an inch of cat litter in the bottom of a container that has a lid, then seal the book inside for 12–24 hours. It will come out smelling like a book again.

—*Nina Harbert, Mt. Vernon, WA*

Keeping Utensils Safe

If your plastic lids, baby spoons, and other small items in the dishwasher keep falling through the rack, place them inside a zippered mesh bag that is usually used for washing delicates in the washing machine.

Never Buy Flypaper Again

To get rid of crickets or other critters, place packaging tape sticky-side up along the wall in your basement or wherever else you find them. This inexpensive flypaper will snag the insects so you can stomp them out and throw them away.

Carpet Cleaning Work-Around

Finally getting around to shampooing your carpet? You don't necessarily have to remove all your furniture from the room. Slip plastic bags over the feet of tables and chairs and secure them with rubber bands. You can clean underneath, then move the furniture a bit and wash where its legs were. The plastic will keep the furniture from getting wet.

Stuck Drawer?

If you've been fussing with a drawer that won't open, it's probably expanded due to humidity. Dry it out with a hair dryer, or place a work lamp with a 60-watt bulb inside and leave for 30 minutes. Once you can get the drawer out, rub its runners or anywhere else it seems to be sticking with a bar of soap or a candle. This should grease it up enough to get it moving again.

See It Quickly

It's often hard not to misplace your household scissors, cell phone, and remote control...and the list goes on! Find lost items more quickly by slapping on a piece of reflective tape. The shimmering surface will pop out at you, even from between couch cushions.

● Who Knew?

According to the American Time Use Survey, 52 percent of women and 20 percent of men do housework every day.

Broken Shoelace?

If you or your child's shoelace breaks, use a ribbon as a replacement. It often looks better than the original!

—*Francie J. Shor*

Halve Your Paper Towels

Many paper towels now offer rolls with "half sheets"—that is, the perforated lines are closer together. We were shocked at how much longer our paper towel roll lasted when we bought one of these brands! And if your favorite brand doesn't offer half sheets, you can simply tear them in half yourself, of course!

Avoid Falls

If you've ever accidentally skipped the last step of your basement stairs and fallen on your face, you'll take us up on this tip immediately. Paint the last step a bright white. Even if your basement is pitch black and your arms are full, you still won't miss it.

Houseplant Favorite

Forget expensive food for your houseplants. Just feed them flat club soda periodically and they should thrive. The minerals in club soda are beneficial to plants.

Replacing a Cracked Bulb

If a shattered light bulb needs replacing, don't try unscrewing it with your bare hands, since there are almost always shards of glass left behind. Instead, make sure the lamp is unplugged, then put on some dishwashing gloves and use a wadded-up piece of newspaper. If there is a substantial amount of the bulb left, you can also use a wedge of apple. Place the apple on top and force it down onto the shards until it sticks, then turn.

Roach Resolution

If you've tried every other solution and those pesky roaches still want to call your house home, it's time to make roach balls. Here's how: Combine 2 cups borax, ½ cup sugar, ½ cup chopped onion, 2 tablespoons cornstarch, and 2 tablespoons water in a bowl, then roll into small balls. Place three balls into an unsealed sandwich bag and place the bags wherever your roach problem exists. Remember, though, that the roach balls are poisonous; be sure to place them where kids and pets can't reach them.

CHAPTER 3

The Great Outdoors

Covered in sand after a day at the beach? Sprinkle baby powder on yourself to easily brush the sand off. This is also a great tip for when your kids have spent the afternoon in a sandbox.

Preparing a Garden

If you've never had a vegetable garden, now is the time to start! Here's how: In the fall, decide where you'd like your garden to be and mow away the grass. Then cover the area with several layers of newspaper. Add as much mulch and leaves as you can to the top (aim for five inches), then get the entire area wet with a hose. By the time spring rolls around, the area will be grass-free and primed for planting.

Gardening After Heavy Rain?

If it's too muddy for even your beater sneakers out in your garden, keep them clean by sticking plastic bags over them. Secure them with rubber bands and you're ready to go to work.

Starting Seedlings

Don't buy cardboard "seed starters" from your garden store. Instead, use a cardboard egg carton, or toilet paper and paper towel tubes. The tubes will need to be cut in halves or fourths, then placed on a tray, while the egg carton can be used as is. Put a little soil in each, place in a warm, moist area (it doesn't even need to get any light), and wait for your seeds to sprout with some regular watering.

Early Bird Gets the Water

Early morning is the best time to water your lawn or garden because you'll minimize evaporation. The absolute worst time to do it is during the bright sun of the afternoon.

A Must-Have for Growing Carrots

The best thing you can give your carrot seeds is also what keeps you going during the day—coffee! Mix carrot seeds with coffee grounds before you plant them. Having some extra bulk to plant will ensure they don't end up all lumped together, and the coffee will provide your growing plants with much-needed nutrients.

Food for Your Geraniums

Who knew geraniums love potatoes? They contain all the nutrients a growing geranium plant needs, and can also make it easier for you to transplant these beautiful flowers. Simply carve out a hole in a raw potato using the end of a vegetable peeler and insert the stem of a geranium, and then plant the entire thing in its new pot or in your garden.

Healthy Pepper Patch

This advice definitely sounds like an urban legend, but it's such an easy way to grow fantastic sweet peppers that you have to try it. A matchbook buried with each pepper plant will transmit sulfur, a great fertilizer for them. To give these nutrient-seeking plants the magnesium they also need, add 2 tablespoons Epsom salts to ½ gallon water and soak the plants with the mixture when you see the first blossoms of the year.

Daily News Keeps Weeds Away

The most inventive idea to keep weeds away we've heard of is this: Wet newspapers and layer them around the plants (then cover with dirt and mulch so your yard doesn't look like a trash heap).

Critter-Free Garden

Try this easy, natural recipe to keep cats and squirrels away from your property. First mix ⅓ cup flour, 2 tablespoons cayenne pepper, and 2 tablespoons powdered mustard. Then use the mixture to sprinkle around the perimeter of your yard. Or, mix it with 4 cups water and 4 cups vinegar to make a spray.

Keep Pests Out of Your Trash

To keep raccoons and other critters out of your garbage, regularly spray the side of your cans with a mixture of one part ammonia and one part water.

—Holly L., Wenham, MA

● Who Knew?

Half of all Americans only get outside to enjoy outdoor recreational activities once every other week.

Get Mosquitoes to Scram

It's a little-known fact that mosquitoes hate basil and tansy. Keep those plants in your yard and around your porch. If you're not familiar with it, tansy is a pretty yellow perennial, which has been harvested for its medicinal properties for several thousand years. In colonial times it was used to preserve meat and keep insects away. It's a low-maintenance flower, except for the odor, which irritates some people almost as much as the bugs.

From the Kitchen to the Garden (and Maybe Back Again)

Cut down on the trash your family generates and help your garden at the same time with these easy composting ideas.

- ✦ Mix dried banana peels in with the soil next time you plant something new; you'll give it the potassium and phosphorous it needs to grow beautifully.

- ✦ Coffee grinds can go straight into the garden as fertilizer to provide nitrogen to roses, azaleas, rhododendrons, sunflowers, and many other plants and trees.

- ✦ Finally, transfer fireplace ashes to your flowers in the spring. Keep wood ashes away, however, from potatoes, blueberries, rhododendrons, azaleas, and any plants that like acid. And be careful handling the ash: Use gloves and protection for your eyes and make sure you spread it out to prevent clumping and leaching.

Snow Shoveling Made Easy

Here's a tip that you northerners will appreciate. Before going out to shovel snow, coat the blade of your snow shovel with cooking spray. That way the snow and ice will slide right off the shovel instead of sticking to it. This works on both plastic and metal shovels.

An Alternative to Rock Salt

Icy sidewalk? Throw cat litter down instead of rock salt. It won't harm your grass, stain your clothes, or hurt the environment, but it will provide plenty of traction for safe walking and driving.

Make Your Birdbath Shine

If your birdbath is dirty, it could be spreading germs to birds who alight there. To safely and easily clean it, drain all the water, then spread newspapers that have been soaked in bleach on top. After 30 minutes, any algae should be history. Rinse the birdbath, then add some colorful marbles to attract neighborhood birds.

Brown Lawn?

If your grass turns brown after mowing, either you've cut it too short or the lawn mower's blades are dull. Dull blades tear up the grass instead of clipping it cleanly. It may be time for a new mower.

Bees, Spiders, Mosquitoes—Oh My!

Use this (almost) all-natural insect spray to make your yard and garden a little less all-natural. Chop 1 small onion and 1 head of garlic. Mix together with 4 cups water, 4 teaspoons cayenne pepper, and 1 tablespoon liquid dish soap. Spray around your deck and in places where your children play rather than on the children themselves. This mixture will last a week or so if stored in a jar with a tight-fitting lid and kept in a dark, cool place.

Cleaning Wicker

If your white wicker deck furniture has turned a grimy brown, you have some work to do. But take heart, it isn't hard! First, vacuum up the free-standing dirt on the seat and arms. Then cover the whole piece with a mixture of 1 gallon warm water and 3 tablespoons ammonia. Scrub it with a brush to get between the fibers, then let it sit in a shady area to dry.

Silence Squeaky Lawn Furniture

If your wicker seems to scream every time you sit in it, it's become too dry. Take off any cushions and spray the wicker with a hose. The water will give it enough moisture to silence the squeaks.

Vanquishing Anthills

Ants hate oranges, so blend orange peels with water and pour the concoction wherever the little guys are bothering you. Some people also swear by hot chili peppers. Use whichever smell you prefer to have permeating your living space!

Get a Leg Up on Centipedes

Borax works for repelling centipedes and millipedes. Sprinkle around areas where you've spotted them making a run for it. (It also works for the less offensive cricket.) Unfortunately, borax is not pet- or kid-safe, so sprinkle wisely.

Rusty Concrete

If you have rust stains on your concrete, pour on a little cola and let it sit. By the next time it rains, the stains will be gone.

—*Jess Holman, Syracuse, NY*

Coil Your Cord

Do you have a long extension cord you use with your electric mower, weed-whacker, or power washer? Keep it from getting tangled and running all over your garden's plants with a big bucket. Drill a hole in the bottom of the bucket and run the end of the cord through it. Then coil the rest of the cord inside. The cord will easily pull out and easily coil back up when you're finished.

Mosquito Secret

Mosquitoes are attracted to dark blue clothing. (It's true!) If you usually have trouble with mosquito bites, trying wearing light clothes when you're outdoors.

Remove Ticks with Ease

Oh no, you've got a tick! If you're having trouble prying the little bugger off, apply a large glob of petroleum jelly to the area. Wait about 20 minutes, and you should be able to wipe him off with ease.

Who Knew?

While 68 percent of children aged 6–12 participate in outdoor activities such as camping, picnics, sporting events, hiking, and fishing, only 26 percent of adults over the age of 65 do.

Eco-Friendly Way to Water the Lawn

Unless you live in a desert (where technically, you should not have a lawn), you don't need a lot of water to keep the grass green and healthy. One inch a week is all you need. To find out how long you need to run the sprinkler, mark a jar with a piece of masking tape or permanent marker at one inch and place it on your lawn. Start the sprinkler and see how long it takes before the water reaches the mark. Next time, skip the jar and just set the timer.

Never Clean a Lawnmower Again

Before mowing your lawn, spray the blades of your lawnmower with nonstick cooking spray. They'll keep cut grass from sticking to its insides.

How to Kill Spider Mites

Do you have trees that are infested with spider mites? You can make a mixture to get rid of them using ingredients already in your kitchen. Take a pound of flour, five gallons of water, and a cup of buttermilk, mix it all together in a large bucket, and put it in a plastic spray bottle. Use it on your trees once a week, and that should keep the mite population under control.

A Spray a Day Keeps Pests Away

One way to keep unwanted pests out of your garden is to infuse it with a garlicky odor that will be unpleasant for insects. Take a ¼ cup garlic and mix it with 2 cups water in a blender, strain it with an old nylon stocking, and scrape the paste into a jar. Add 2 teaspoons mineral oil and several squirts of liquid dish detergent. Carefully replace the lid on the jar and shake well. Transfer the solution to a spray bottle and use it on your garden in the early morning hours.

Snail Solution

Did you know that snails and slugs like beer almost as much as people do? If you're tired of these pests invading your garden, leave a flat, shallow container—such as a pie tin—in your garden and fill it with a can of beer. Let it sit there for a couple of days, and you'll probably find it full of drowned slugs.

So Long, Squirrels

If squirrels are making a nuisance of themselves around your home, keep them away with a homemade pepper spray. Take a cup of your favorite hot sauce, add a spoonful of cayenne pepper and a capful of Murphy's Oil Soap, and mix together. Spray the mixture in whatever areas you want the squirrels to steer clear of.

—Megan Rye, Washington, DC

Green Gardens

Make your garden work for you by filling it with plants that repel pests, add fertilizer to the soil, and more. Here are some super-powered flora to get you going.

+ Plant savory and chamomile throughout your garden; they'll attract the "good" kinds of insects that will help pollinate your plants.

+ Plant mint and nasturtiums, which will repel white flies and aphids.

+ French marigolds are practical because they have a strong odor that helps bewilder insects in search of their preferred eating plant.

- ✦ Garlic planted everywhere will help keep away beetles and aphids.

- ✦ If you plant basil, it will add to the flavor of whatever other plants grow near it.

- ✦ Fertilize your garden for free by planting clover, which will help repair the soil while also providing a nice green carpeting.

Aphid Awareness

Are aphids invading your garden? Here's another easy, organic way to keep them out. Chop up an onion, place it in a cup of water, and puree it until it's liquid. Pour the concoction into a plastic spray bottle and use it to mist the plants aphids are attracted to. For best results, try it at dawn before the sun starts blazing.

Keep Your Plants Covered

If you have smaller outdoor plants, you don't necessarily need to bring them inside to keep them protected from frost. Simply cover them at night with small plastic garbage bags (the kind that have pull handles), and tie the handles snugly around the pots. Don't forget to remove the bags in the morning, though, so the plants can soak up the sun.

You Say Tomato, I Say Grow Faster!

If the end of growing season is nigh and you'd like your tomatoes to ripen on the vine more quickly, there are a few things you can try. Remove damaged, dead, or diseased leaves, and cut off all new flowers. Keep a daily eye on the tomatoes and pick them as soon as they're ripe, so the plant can devote its effort to developing new fruit.

Harvest the tomatoes when they're red, but still firm. Believe it or not, watering the plant less will ripen the tomatoes more quickly!

The Many Benefits of Epsom Salts

Did you know Epsom salts are one of the best natural lawn fertilizers around? They're composed of magnesium and sulfur, both of which are highly beneficial to grass. Magnesium kick-starts seed germination, and is also a player in manufacturing chlorophyll, the substance that plants manufacture from sunlight in order to feed themselves. Sulfur, meanwhile, also helps with chlorophyll, while also enhancing the effects of other fertilizer ingredients such as nitrogen, phosphorus, and potassium. It also deters certain pests such as ground worms. With all these benefits, it's no wonder that savvy lawn care specialists have been using Epsom salts for years. You can either sprinkle them on your lawn using a spreader, or make a liquid solution out of them by adding some water and putting it in a spray bottle.

The Egg and the Rose

Did you know that eggshells help rose bushes grow? The nutrients contained in the shells are a great benefit, especially if you crush up the eggshells and deposit them under the surface of the soil, near the bush's roots. The same applies to water that you've used to boil eggs in—when you're finished cooking, just dump the nutrient-enriched water on your rosebush.

Reviving Plants

This may sound like a cure from the Middle Ages, but garlic does a fine job of reviving diseased plants. Grate two cloves into four cups water and use as much as you need to quench the thirst of your struggling plant. Given the myriad health benefits garlic offers to humans, it's not surprising it can help the immobile organisms that share your home (and we don't mean your spouse and kids).

Keep Good Neighbors (Protect Your Fence Posts)

When it comes to chores around the house and yard, we're not the handiest family on the block, so we like those one-time projects that last a lifetime. It's true the ingredients for this fence post protector sound like they're meant for a witches' brew, but it really does work like magic! Mix together pulverized charcoal and boiled linseed oil to get a paint-like consistency, then simply paint onto the bottom of each post.

● Who Knew? CLASSIC TIP

Your garden hose will last twice as long if you store it coiled, rather than folding it, which can lead to crimps and cracks.

Get Rid of Plant Fungus

If your garden is infected with fungus, mix one piece of ground-up aspirin with a quart of water and use it to water your plants once a week. (Be careful, as too much aspirin can damage your plants.)

Keep Bees Away

For an easy way to keep away bees, put a sheet of fabric softener in your pocket. The yellow pests will buzz right by you!

—*Miahua Huang, Dale City, VA*

Deer Repellant

If deer are getting to your flower garden, throw a few mothballs on the ground. Deer hate the smell of mothballs. (Who doesn't?)

Reclaiming Your Yard from Raccoons

Have the raccoons grown rather bold around your backyard and trash cans? Try this equivalent of a phony "Beware of Dog" sign by distributing dog hair around your property. You can also try planting cucumbers, which both skunks and raccoons avoid like the plague.

Check for Compost Collection

You've just weeded your entire yard, put new edging along your flower beds, and trimmed your bushes. Now what do you do with all that garbage? Check with your town to see if they collect yard waste to turn into compost. Many municipalities will even come pick it up for you.

For Easy-to-Raise Plants

At PlantNative.org, you can find lists of flowers, shrubs, trees, vines, and grasses that are native to your area. This means they'll not only be less expensive to buy, but they'll also hold up well in your garden.

Woodpecker Problem?

If woodpeckers in the garden bother you, try hanging a metal pie plate to the tree where the pests reside. The reflection off the plate will scare the birds away.

Keeping Neighborhood Cats Away

If your neighbors' cats are causing havoc in your yard, don't even try to go talk to their owners—once the cats are let out there is really nothing they can do to keep them fenced in. Instead, sprinkle the edge of your yard with orange peels and coffee grounds. Cats don't like the smell, and they'll eventually create great compost for your lawn.

> ### ● Who Knew? CLASSIC TIP
>
> To get rid of ants for good, sprinkle cornmeal near ant hills. They'll eat it, but they can't digest it, which will cause them to die out. Wait a couple of weeks and see if your ant problem improves.

Feeling a Bit Rusty?

Don't just toss your garden tools in a bin or bucket when you're done with them; they'll eventually rust. To prevent this, keep them in a bucket of sand instead, and just submerge the metal parts in the sand whenever the tools are not in use. (Better yet, add some mineral oil to the sand.) Make sure the sand is stored in a dry place where rainwater can't get into it, though. If you decide you don't want to store your tools in sand, then a good thing to do is toss a handful of tea leaves in whatever container you keep them in. For whatever reason, the leaves will help keep the metal nice, new, and rust-free.

Protect Roses from the Japanese Beetle Invasion

Keep your rosebush the pride of your garden by getting rid of those icky Japanese beetles. Pour a bowl of self-rising flour and go outside, sprinkling it over the whole bush like it's some kind of magic potion (which, in this case, it is).

Tough Love for Trees

Treating your fruit trees like they're bad will yield a good crop. A newspaper rolled up works well to smack the trunks and get the sap moving more efficiently through the branches, which, in turn, helps the tree produce more fruit. Think of it like a massage to increase blood flow. And be prepared for strange looks from passers-by.

Tree Sculpting

Pruning will be less of a chore if you keep your eye on the goal of a strong and healthy tree. If it's more of a motivator, though, remember you don't want to get sued if a weak branch falls on a neighbor. On pruning day follow a simple plan: First get rid of any branches that are clearly dead, dying, or infested. Then home in on the ones that are too long, criss-crossing each other, or growing weak. Step back and admire your work.

Protect a New Lawn

If a scarecrow doesn't work to keep birds from feasting on your grass seeds, try this modern-day equivalent before you resort to netting. Place stakes at the four corners of the area you want to protect. Now cut two pieces of string, long enough to reach diagonally in an X across the lawn. Every foot or two along the strings you'll want to tie one-inch strips of aluminum foil. The breeze will keep the aluminum pieces flapping about and scare off would-be invaders.

Ramp Up Your Mowing Game

Save yourself the boring task of poking holes in your soil to aerate it. Instead, multitask the easy way by wearing spiked golf shoes or soccer cleats to aerate while you mow your lawn.

A Second Life for Seafood Shells

You may not have time to build a compost bin (or the stomach for a bucket full of worms), but you can easily crush shells from last night's seafood dinner and scatter them over your lawn. The calcium helps the grass grow.

● Who Knew? CLASSIC TIP

Never pay to have your gutters cleaned again! To easily keep falling leaves from clogging them up, place a Slinky (yes, the child's toy) in your gutters. Stretch it out, then fasten the ends to your gutters with binder clips. The coil will allow water to get through, but keep leaves out.

Inventive Weed Killer

If you had a hammer, you wouldn't have so many weeds. Kneel down, turn the hammer backward, and bang it onto the soil to catch the weed between the claw. Now just pull. Yes it *is* okay to hammer when you're in a bad mood. As long as you can check something off your to-do list while you are at it.

Get Rid of Poison Ivy

When it comes to poison ivy, an ounce of prevention really is worth a pound of cure. So if you've got a patch of this pernicious vine on your property, kill it. Mix ½ gallon soapy water with a 1½ pounds salt, spray the plant, and run in the other direction.

Plant Doctor

A broken stem doesn't have to mean the end of a flower. If you catch it in time, you can save the limb by making a little splint out of a toothpick and tape. It looks a little funny, but your kids will get a kick out of it and it makes a great lesson in resilience.

Ripen Tomatoes

There's a frost predicted for tonight, and you have several unripened tomatoes on the vine. Don't risk them getting bitten by frost. Instead, pick them now and bring them inside. Place them inside a paper bag or wrap them in newspaper, then place them in an airtight container and put them in a dark area like a cabinet or closet. Check back in a few days and they'll be just-off-the-vine ripe.

Make Your Own Bonemeal

As you may know, bonemeal is an excellent source of nutrients for your plants. But instead of spending $8–$10 on a bag at your local gardening store, make your own! Bonemeal is just bones, after all. Save bones from chicken, turkey, steaks, and stews, then dry them out by roasting them in a 425° oven for a half an hour or microwaving them on high for 1–6 minutes (depending on how many bones you have). Then place them in a plastic or paper bag and grind them up by hitting them with a hammer, then rolling them with a rolling pin. The resulting powder is a life-producing treat for your plants, and you didn't spend a cent.

Wise Way to Wash Your Hands

Sometimes running your hands under the hose isn't enough to clean off all the dirt and grime that comes with gardening. Meanwhile, even stepping into the house with those filthy hands usually means something's going to get smudged. Fix this problem by keeping a bit of soap near your outdoor spigot. Tie it up in the leg of an old pair of pantyhose or a mesh bag and hang it nearby.

Repel with Peels

Another ingenious way to keep mosquitoes from biting you? Rub any exposed skin with orange or lemon peels. Mosquitoes hate the smell and will find someone else to attack. Ants also don't like to smell of lemon and orange peels, so grind them in your blender with some water, then spread in areas you find ants to keep them away.

Looking for Worms?

If you're getting ready for a big fishing trip by looking for bait in your backyard, begin by soaking an entire newspaper with water, then spreading it out in one hunk in your garden or on your lawn. Lift it up in the early morning, and loads of worms will be underneath. To keep your worms alive until it's time to use them, store them in a can with soil and coffee grounds.

Gone Fishing

If you use a hollow plastic tub jig on your fishing line, slip a small piece of Alka-Seltzer or denture cleaner inside before tossing it into the water. It will release a string of bubbles that will attract fish.

Sweet Fish Bait

Did you know that fish have a sweet tooth? It's true! To make some scrumptious bait, mix 2 cups flour, 2 cups cornmeal, and 2 tablespoons molasses into a thick dough. Roll it into balls and boil in water for 20 minutes. Place the balls directly in an ice water bath after removing them from the boiling water, and now you're ready to catch some fish.

An Easy Way to Identify Your Campsite

When going camping, mark your campsite by tying brightly colored helium balloons to a few trees nearby. Your tents will be easy to find even from far away.

—*John T., Murfreesboro, TN*

Who Knew?

Almost 12 million Americans go camping each year.

Can't Start a Fire

Rain on a camping trip is enough of a bummer; it doesn't have to ruin your campfire as well. Melt paraffin (available from the supermarket) in a coffee can inside a pot of water on the stove. Remove the can and begin to mix in sawdust until you have about three parts sawdust to two parts paraffin. Pour into paper cups and let cool. Then all you need to do is pop them out of the cups and store them in a Ziploc bag. They'll light up easily when the time comes. Now all you need is a spark.

Another No-Fail Fire Starter

Before your camping trip, smear petroleum jelly on some cotton balls and keep them in a Ziploc bag. Even if you find yourself camping in the middle of a rainstorm, these bits of kindling will definitely get your fire roaring.

CHAPTER 4

Celebration Time! Tips for Holidays and Entertaining

Great Decorating Tip for Any Holiday

Fresh flowers and greenery make beautiful holiday decorations, but where do you put them? All you need are some empty wine or other bottles (like beer or juice bottles), old newspaper, and spray paint. Place the bottles outside on the newspaper, spray paint them gold, silver, or the holiday color of your choice, and let them dry. Voilà!— unique vases that will have your guests guessing as to where you purchased them.

Stock Up a Year Ahead of Time

We always hit up stores after each holiday to check out what kind of deals we can get on decorations or gifts for the following year. Also keep in mind that many stores start discounting holiday items a week before the holiday—so if you're willing to wait until the last minute, you can save big.

Holiday Flowers

Flora-lovers don't need fancy arrangements to celebrate every holiday with style. Start your own tradition of dyeing white carnations whatever color is fitting for the occasion. You can use various shades of red and pink for Valentine's Day, green for St. Patrick's Day, a combination of red, white, and blue for July Fourth, orange and black for Halloween, and so on. It's also fun to do favorite colors for birthdays. All you need to do is add a bit of food coloring to your flowers' vase with some warm water. Half the fun watching the flower take on the new color as it sucks up the water, so make sure the kids don't miss out.

"Oh Yeah, Those Other Holiday" Trees

Whoever had the idea for the first Christmas tree must have retired young. Why not spread the wealth and decorate an indoor tree you already have for other holidays? Our kids love to hang eggshell ornaments and tie pastel ribbons on the dracena in our kitchen at Easter. And when they were younger, we used to arrange their stuffed bunnies, ducks, and lambs on a blanket spread out on the floor underneath the tree. For Valentine's Day, a simple afternoon project of making and hanging paper hearts cut out of last year's Valentines (hole-punch the top and tie a ribbon) can become a family tradition.

 Who Knew? CLASSIC TIP

If you've just removed your candlesticks from the cupboard for a party and they're covered in wax, try this handy trick: Just stick them in the freezer for a couple of hours. The wax will harden and chip right off.

The Gift of Memory Lane

For the couple who has everything, why not show them how much they've already had? A tour of places they used to live (or went to school or worked) is a personal and moving way to celebrate a special day. For an anniversary, find out where they met, where they had their first date, and where they got married. You can start out narrating, but be prepared for the recipients to take over. They'll likely enjoy telling stories as much as anything else you can give them.

—*Marge Lenkel, Laguna Beach, CA*

Think of Your Guests During the Super Bowl

Having a Super Bowl party? Consider having two TVs—one of which is reserved for the hardcore fans only. A lot of people will come to the party just looking to socialize (and maybe watch the halftime show), so let them watch away from the football freaks, who will want to be able to catch every moment of pig-skinned glory.

Free Valentines

It's Valentine's Day and you haven't gotten a card! Instead of buying a valentine for your sweetie, trying making your own with magazine clippings or colored paper. If you're not the creative type, visit DLTK-Holidays.com/valentines/cards.htm, which has links to various websites that offer free valentines that you can print and send.

Early Morning Valentine

Instead of worrying all day about how to make the perfect romantic dinner for your valentine, try breakfast in bed and get a whole day's worth of credit for it. A flower, a chocolate, and a heart-shaped placemat are all you need to make eggs, toast, and a fruit bowl look especially festive.

Easy Easter Egg Dye

Never, ever pay for egg dye! Simply mix ½ cup boiling water with ½ teaspoon white vinegar, and add food coloring until you get a hue you like. For a striped egg even the Easter Bunny would be proud of, wrap tape around the egg before dipping. Once the egg dries, remove the tape, tape over the colored parts, and dip again in a different color. You can also use stickers in the shapes of hearts, stars, and letters.

Egg Dyeing for Toddlers

You might think only older kids can dye Easter eggs, but we started our boys off when they were still in diapers. Give your little helpers a plastic container filled with food coloring, water, and a little vinegar.

Let them drop the hard-boiled egg in, help them seal it closed, and tell them to "Shake, shake, shake." Pure magic.

O Say Can You...Be Careful With Those Sparklers?

It's Fourth of July and time to bust out the legal explosives. Kids love to hold sparklers, but make sure their hands are safe by sticking the sparkler in Play-Doh inside its container, which is the perfect size for the kids to wrap their patriotic hands around.

Add Halloween Atmosphere

Adding stretchy cobwebs to the door jambs and corners of your home is a great way to add Halloween flair to the entire house. Instead of buying the ones packaged as spider webs, though, simply go to a craft store and buy a bag of fiberfill. It's the exact same stuff, and a 16-ounce bag of fiberfill is less than half the cost. You can usually find bags of plastic spider rings for super-cheap at party supply stores or superstores—add them to the webs and on tables around your house for more atmosphere, and encourage your guests to take them home!

Looking for a Last-Minute Costume?

For ideas on how to make costumes out of clothes and materials you may have around the house (no sewing!) head over to CostumeIdeaZone.com. This is the perfect site for your pre-teens who want to dress up, but want to do it themselves and don't want a big fuss made over the whole thing.

Creepy Halloween Drinks

Getting dry ice to put at the bottom of the punch bowl is a bit difficult, so to make your punch seem haunted quickly and easily, freeze grapes to use as ice cubes. Once they're frozen, peel off the skin and they'll look like creepy eyeballs.

An Inexpensive Thanksgiving

If you're trying to save this Thanksgiving, don't be afraid to make it a potluck! Most guests love to bring a dish that shows of their culinary skills, and those who don't can bring the wine!

Fun Thanksgiving Activity

Give hyper kids something to do *and* decorate your table at the same time this Thanksgiving by sending them out into the yard to find the last remaining yellow, red, and orange leaves. Make sure they're not visibly dirty, then arrange them along the middle of the table in lieu of a runner. We love this activity because it's good for kids of any age, and the older ones can help the younger ones.

Hot Potatoes

Skip the last-minute panic on major holidays and mash the potatoes first thing in the morning. Transfer them to a slow cooker while you move onto the stuffing and string beans. Two hours before you're ready to serve the meal, turn on the slow cooker. You won't have to give the potatoes another thought until the guests are seated and it's time to serve the meal.

—*Sue Pratt, Jasper, GA*

Smells Like the Holidays

This little gem of a recipe will give your home an instant cozy and home-for-the-holidays feel. Mix whole cloves, crushed cinnamon sticks, bay leaves, juniper berries, orange peels, nutmeg, and allspice. (You can store the mixture in a jar until you are ready to use it.) To get the smell to disseminate, boil water in a saucepan and pour in some of your homemade potpourri. Simmer gently and your house is guaranteed to start smelling like Christmas.

Deck the Halls—and the Wreath

If you're getting tired of that old drab-looking Christmas wreath, don't get rid of it—just spruce it up a little. Use a glue gun to attach some pinecones from your yard onto it, or buy some cheap doo-dads at your local crafts store and do the same. You'll get a brand-new wreath for a fraction of the cost.

Do It With Ribbon

Used wisely, a little holiday ribbon can go a long way. Wrap it around just about anything—a vase, throw pillow, lamp shade, curtain, pillar candle, and the list goes on—to create a festive atmosphere at little or no cost.

Be the Color Police

If you want your home to look super-Christmassy, scan your living room for brightly colored objects that aren't red or green, and move them to invisible or inconspicuous locations for the season. Without the other colors to distract people's eyes, your red and green Christmas decorations will stand out even more.

Outdoor Christmas Decorations

When pruning your trees and bushes in the spring or summer, make sure to save some branches for later use. Then spray paint them red, white, silver, or gold and you have an instant Christmas decoration! Place them in planters of flowers that are dead for the winter, and add lights or ornaments for extra flair.

Long-Lasting Wreaths

We love the look of a pine wreaths and garlands, but hate it when needles get all over the floor. To keep the needles from falling, spritz your holiday greenery with hair spray right after you purchase it. The hair spray will keep the needles moist and where they belong.

Sappy Hands

The scent of evergreens is pure magic, but you could do without the sticky sap left on your hands after collecting branches for a wreath or making one. Bring out the Hellmann's (or whatever mayonnaise you have on hand). Rub a small spoonful on your hands like lotion and the sap will wash right off.

It's a Wrap! Tips for Wrapping Holiday and Other Presents

Keep gift-wrapping fun and inexpensive by coming up with different materials to decorate your presents. Here are some of our favorite ideas.

◆ Use pages from the past year's calendar (photo-side up, obviously) to wrap smaller gifts—two taped together are great for books or DVD sets.

◆ Copied sheet music makes for unique and festive wrapping paper. At your local library it should be easy to enough to find books of whatever music suits your friend (classical, show tunes, rock music, etc.). Make a copy on colored paper if you can, and be sure the title of the piece shows when you fold it over the gift.

◆ Instead of doling out cash for fancy bows to decorate gifts, use your actual dollars to *make* the bows. Fold a dollar bill (or more, if you're a high roller) accordion-style and affix with a ribbon over a wrapped gift. As a variation, give a nod to Chinese New Year by putting two dollars inside a traditional red envelope and taping it to the top of a gift for good luck.

◆ Do you have collections of paper napkins that are "too pretty to use"? Then use them in a way that takes advantage of their design—as wrapping paper for little gifts or candy bars.

◆ Have your kids draw on some taped-together printer paper and use it to wrap gifts that are "from them."

◆ Quickest buzz kill when wrapping presents: trying to reuse tired out, wrinkled tissue paper and hoping the recipient won't take it personally. Turns out you can iron used tissue paper on low to get it to look "like new!" Amazing.

✦ After everyone's done opening their presents, don't forget to save bigger sheets of paper, bows, and pretty cards (to use for next year's gift tags). We keep our stash in one of those giant popcorn tins with a Christmas design from years ago!

Make Your Own Cards

Show your friends you care and save money by making your own cards to send for birthdays or other occasions. Look through old magazines for funny photos (or shots of your friend's celebrity crush) to use for the front. Or for something more complicated, visit Card-Making-World.com for ideas and free backgrounds and embellishments to download.

● Who Knew?

Approximately 1.2 billion birthday cards are purchased every year. Time to buy stock in Hallmark!

Shipping Secret

When packing up those holiday presents, make sure nothing rattles in the box and the lid closes firmly (without being easily depressed into the box). This will ensure your presents arrive safely, even if heavier boxes are stacked on top (plus, the post office won't insure your package if it sounds like it contains loose items!). To help fill out the space in a big box, use Ziploc bags. Seal them all the way, then open them up just enough to fit a straw through. Blow through the straw to inflate them, then reseal—a homemade air pillow!

A White, Salty Christmas

You can easily dust your Christmas wreath with "snow" by using salt. Go outside in the backyard with a large paper grocery bag and half a cup of salt. Pour the salt in the bag, place the wreath inside, and fold the bag closed. Then shake gently for 20 seconds and your wreath will look as good as new.

Save Energy This Christmas

Did you know that one strand of traditional Christmas lights running five hours a day for 30 days can add up to $10 to your electricity bill? This Christmas, make sure you use LED lights, which will only run you 12¢ for the same amount of time. LED lights also last much longer!

Free Tree Stand

Instead of buying a stand for your Christmas tree, simply fill a bucket with sand. You can still water it, and you won't have to deal with the hassle of readjusting the stand so the tree isn't crooked.

Watering Your Christmas Tree

If you have trouble getting a watering can to reach underneath the lowest bows of your Christmas tree, throw several ice cubes into the base each day to easily keep it watered.

—Fran Kaiser, Shalimar, FL

Easy Christmas Decorating

Put those unused holiday ornaments to good use by using them for an inexpensive centerpiece. Simply pick your favorites and put them in a clear punch bowl, and add tinsel or pine sprigs around the base. It works great with those solid-colored orbs we always seem to have so many of!

Frost Your Windows

If you want your windows to look like they've been touched with frost this holiday season, just mix 1 tablespoon Epsom salts with 1 cup beer, then brush onto the window with a small paintbrush. When you're ready to remove the frost, just wash it off with ammonia and water.

Film Canister Ornaments

It's easy to turn film canisters into little Christmas treasure boxes. Any scraps from the arts and crafts table (glitter, sequins, bits of wrapping paper, mini buttons) can be applied with a hot glue gun to decorate the outside. Fill with little candies or toys from the five and dime store. Miniatures have a certain holiday magic and kids never seem to grow tired of them. To make into hanging ornaments, simply knot a ribbon into a loop and glue to the top.

—*Rachel Federman*

Walnut Treats

For a holiday treat, carve the nuts out of split walnut shells and place fortunes or little prizes inside. Glue back together and decorate with sparkle paint. When the shells are dry, collect them in a basket for a unique centerpiece and a fun activity one dark night of the advent. Pass around the table after dinner and let family members take turns reaching for a walnut and cracking it open to find out what's hidden inside.

Make Your Own Poppers

These are a favorite Christmas tradition in our house. We cut paper towel tubes into three pieces and then load them up with candy, little toys, and tissue paper crowns. Then we use wrapping paper to cover the tubes completely, leaving extra paper on each end that we tie up with ribbon. Everyone gets a popper with his or her place setting for Christmas dinner. Our kids love to show guests how to yank from the sides, so that the poppers actually pop!

Handmade Gift Soaps

Soaps never seem to lose their appeal as holiday gifts. They're useful and don't add clutter to people's houses (something we're always trying to avoid in ours). You can make your own by grating white, unscented soap it into a bowl with warm water. For color, add a few drops of food coloring. Next, add a drop or two of an essential oil (lavender or rose are lovely), then knead like pizza dough and make into little balls. As an alternative, use candy molds for fun shapes. Leave them to dry on wax paper for a day or so.

Frugal Christmas?

If opening presents is going to take drastically less time than usual this year, fill the gap by starting some new Christmas traditions. Make a popcorn string for the tree, cut out sugar cookies with different-colored sugars for decoration, or try this game to make gift-opening take longer (it's a favorite at our gatherings): Find as many holiday present rejects as you have people playing—all those candles with scents you can't stand, weird gifts from office gift exchanges, or your silliest finds from the dollar bin at Target. Wrap each one and have each guest pick a gift. Go around the room clockwise, starting with the youngest person. Before opening their gift, guests can decide to trade with someone else (even if that person's gift has been unwrapped). After one round of gift opening, have one more round of trades, with players deciding if they want to keep their current gift or switch with someone else. You'll be surprised which gifts people actually like, and "you'll have a laugh" at the expense of the person left with the worst one.

Coasters: More than Just Drink Holders!

Keep an eye out during the year for cool drink coasters that are served at bars. These cardboard circles and squares are great for gift tags and ornaments. Simply punch a hole through the top, insert a ribbon, and hang!

Easy Ornament Storage

The best container we've found for storing Christmas ornaments is an empty case of wine or liquor (no comment on how we came across this!). Keep the cardboard dividers inside, and you have a handy place to ball up your ornaments with newspaper and keep them safe until next year. These boxes are also great for storing rolled-up artwork and posters.

How to Keep a Poinsettia Blooming

Poinsettia plants are gifts that keep on giving, if *you* give *them* a little extra care. After the last of the Christmas decorations are packed away, bring your poinsettia plants down to the basement (or elsewhere) where it's cool and dark. Then keep them like prisoners, giving them very little water, until they're almost dried out but not quite. Toward the end of April, bring the plants back out, trim them down about halfway, and give them lots of water and sun. You'll be amazed at how well they re-bloom. When nights are warm enough for just a sweater, we sometimes plant them outside in a sunny spot to enjoy from the deck all summer long. Then bring them back inside in the fall, where they still get full sun and lots of water. Just remember that poinsettias can be toxic to pets.

The 365 Days of Christmas

Eventually, you do have to give in and take down the Christmas tree, but before it goes out the door, pull off a few handfuls of needles that you can keep as simple potpourri. Little cloth bags are readily available in craft stores, or you can make your own out of old nylons. Just cut a scrap into a square, place the needles inside, bundle up, and tie with a ribbon. There's no reason not to enjoy that woodland scent all year long.

Clean and Easy Tree Removal

The holidays have been over for weeks, but you've been dreading the removal of your Christmas tree, which has been shedding pine needles pretty much ever since you bought it. To get a dead tree out of your house without too much mess behind you, find the biggest, strongest garbage bag you can. Open it up so you can see the bottom, then place on the floor next to your tree. Once you free the tree from its stand, place the trunk squarely in the middle of the bag, then work your way around the tree, pulling the bag up as far as you can over its branches. (This is often easiest as a two-person job, with one person holding the tree and one person moving the bag.) Even if you can't get the bag all the way over your tree, you can still hold the bag in place while you carry the tree out to the curb. By the time you get there, there will be a huge pile of needles at the bottom of the bag that never made it onto your carpet.

Auld Lang Time

Here's an original idea for a cheap New Year's Eve decoration: Gather all the devices you use to tell time—stopwatches, alarm clocks, calendars, pocket planners, even the little hourglasses from board games—and place them on a tray next to the champagne bowl. Tell all your guests to set their alarms for midnight and do the same with the items you've collected.

Who Knew? CLASSIC TIP

Wondering how much food to make for your big soiree? Wonder no longer. At a cocktail party (no dinner served), 10–12 bite-sized portions per person is a good bet. If you're also serving a meal, figure on 4–5 bites per guest. For dip, figure 2 tablespoons per person (plus veggies or crackers for dipping), and for cheese, get 4 ounces for each person.

Housewarm with Houseplants

Clippings from a houseplant make great (and free!) housewarming presents. Cut your plant at the "knuckle" (or joint) section of the stem, then place in a cup of water until it grows roots. To present it, wrap the bottom in a wet paper towel and place in a plastic bag, tying it up with ribbon. Or plant in an old mug!

A Party Is About the People...

...Not how much money you spent on it. Before you throw a huge bash, write out your priorities in terms of what you think is most important to spend your money on (for example, the least on decorations and the most on food). Then figure out how much you're willing to spend on the highest item on your list, and work your way down. Friends always ask, "Can I bring anything?" and you shouldn't be afraid of asking your good friends to bring a dessert or appetizer. And don't forget—potlucks and picnics are cheap and always popular.

Party Photo Pleaser

When taking photos at night, sometimes the flash from your camera can leave an ugly glare on people's faces (making sure they'll never let you post the pics online!). Get rid of glare by taping a tiny piece of white coffee filter over the flash. The scene will still light up, but won't be as harsh.

Card Table Trick

This simple trick offers peace of mind when several folding tables are placed together to form a bigger table. Use cleaned-out coffee cans as holders for adjoining legs from different tables and rest assured that your grandmother's hand-blown glass punch bowl is safe.

Cork Control

Uh oh, you were uncorking a bottle of wine, and didn't do a very good job. You're not above drinking wine that has a little cork floating in it, but you definitely don't want to serve it to guests! Simply hold a coffee filter over a carafe and pour. It will filter out the cork pieces and your reputation will be saved...for now.

● Who Knew? CLASSIC TIP

Here's a great way to display dip on your table. Cut off the top of a bell pepper, then hollow it out and spoon your dip inside. You can also use a sturdy bread like pumpernickel as a hollowed-out dip container. Put spinach dip inside, then cut the bread you removed into large cubes and use for dipping.

Be Creative With Ice

If you're serving punch at a party, pour some of it into ice cube trays and freeze. This way, you can keep the punch nice and cold without diluting it. This also works well with wine, iced tea, or any number of other beverages. If you want to get really exotic, mint leaves are a great thing to make ice cubes out of—just fill the ice tray with water like normal and then stuff the leaves so that they rest below the surface.

Keep the TV Going

During parties, our giant TV suddenly becomes a dead spot in the room (when normally it's the center of attention!). Pop a movie into the DVD player and let it run on mute. Play a scary movie if it's a Halloween party, or a Christmas classic if it's a holiday party. Or play movies from your teenage years or favorites amongst your group of friends. And if it's your birthday, of course, it's your pick! Once you've picked your theme, pile the rest of your DVDs that fit it on top of the player and change the movie throughout the night.

Easily Label Drinks

Keep a handle on whose drink is whose by pressing window decals onto the sides of glassware. This is a perfect trick for a party that takes place around a holiday, when you can use festive decals that are easy to find at party stores.

Ice Bucket Solution

It's nice to keep an ice bucket next to your drinks on the table, but once the ice melts you're left with a few cubes soaking in a puddle of water. To fix this problem, place a colander on the top of your ice bucket and fill *it* with the ice. Water will drip through the bottom, and the ice will be easier to grab with some tongs.

—*Cynthia Ferris*

No-Spill Party Drinks

We love anything that gives us more time to talk to our company and cuts down on hosting duties during a party. One simple way to hand out drinks—use muffin trays instead of flat trays. You can easily carry two dozen glasses without breaking a sweat and even younger family members will be able to help.

The Secret to Day-Ahead Salad

It's so much easier to prepare food a day ahead for a dinner party—but what to do about the salad? Making the salad before guests arrive usually leads to a soggy mess, but here's a tip to allow you to make most of the salad without it going soft. Gather lettuce and any of the following ingredients: broccoli, cabbage, carrots, cauliflower, celery, cucumbers, onions, peppers, and radishes. Chop them up and place them in a large bowl. Then completely cover all your ingredients with water and keep the bowl in the refrigerator until you need it. Then add tomatoes, croutons, and any other toppings and enjoy a crisp, delicious salad.

Who Knew? CLASSIC TIP

Nothing gets the summertime party going faster than firing up the backyard grill. Just make sure you keep all that smoked and grilled meat coming—it's unforgivable to run out of fuel before the last kebab is bobbed. Even without a gas gauge, there is a way to figure out how much fuel you have left. Here's what to do a day or two *before* the flip-flopped masses are set to arrive. Boil water, then pour it down the side of the tank. Place your hand on the side: The cool part has propane inside, the warm part is empty.

Great Grilling

To get the most out of that grilled flavor everyone loves so much, add a few sprigs of your favorite herbs, such as rosemary, thyme, and savory, directly to the top of the charcoal as you grill. It will infuse whatever you're cooking with mouthwatering flavor.

Butter Corn With Ease

If you're serving bread with your barbecue, use a slice to easily butter your corn. Spread a generous amount of butter onto the bread, then gently wrap it around your corn. Twist the cob until the butter has gotten into every crack, then enjoy perfectly buttered corn and bread with melted butter.

A Makeshift Fish Cage

If you have two small wire racks, you can easily cook a fish (and impress your friends) on your outdoor grill. First, find toaster-oven or cooling racks and some fireproof wire. Oil the racks, then put the fish between them and tie the racks together. Grill the fish on one side, then flip your newly constructed basket with large tongs or a spatula. This makeshift cage will keep delicate fish from breaking apart.

Save Some Beer for the Bugs

The next time you're having a party in your garden, place a few cans of open beer around the perimeter of your yard—insects will be more attracted to the beer than to your guests.

BBQ Squeeze

A Sunday afternoon barbecue is one of our favorite summer traditions. The not-so-great part? Clean-up. One way to make it easier is to eliminate the entire barbecue sauce brushing routine, which is arguably just a way for guys to flex their muscles as they prepare for a big fire. Instead, use one of those disposable sport water bottles with the squirt top to store the sauce and squeeze while cooking as needed. Keep in the fridge when not in use.

Having a Picnic?

Include some sprigs of fresh mint in your picnic basket when eating al fresco. Bees and wasps don't like mint, so add some to your plate to keep it stinger-free.

The Secret Storage Secret for Coolers

Before stashing away your cooler for the winter, stuff it with a few balls of newspaper. The newspaper will absorb any lingering odors, so it won't be a mildewy nightmare when you open it back up in the spring.

You Can Catch More Wasps With Honey Than Vinegar

If you can't beat 'em, join 'em (kind of). At your next picnic party give stinging party crashers a treat of their own—a sugar-covered grapefruit. They'll go for the fruit and stay away from your guests.

Party Like It's Wednesday Night

If your children's birthday parties are putting a hurt on your budget, there's a simple solution—have the party during the week instead of on a weekend. Sure, everyone wants a weekend party, and that's why restaurants and other popular birthday locales charge a lot more for Saturday and Sunday events. They'll be only too happy to accommodate your request for a weekday party, and it might even be easier for you, too—just offer to pick up your child's playmates from school that afternoon and have them picked up from the party later. Your child will have just as much fun as they would at a weekend party, maybe even more, since it's a rare weekday treat. A great, but rarely utilized, location for a summer party is your local minor league baseball park. Tickets are cheap, kids will love interacting with the mascot, and there's no need to stay the whole game—five innings or so should suffice. The team might even offer you discounted group tickets and flash your child's name on the scoreboard.

The Perfect Candle Holder for Kids' Cakes

Life Savers are an excellent accent for your child's birthday cake. Not only do kids enjoy sucking on them, but they are perfect for holding candles! Use the regular size (not the jumbo kind that come individually wrapped in bags), put them on top of the cake, and then insert the candle in the middle. The candy will hold the candle straighter and is easily disposed of if wax drips on it.

Make Ice Cream Shapes for a Perfect Dessert Plate

Here's a fun and unique way to serve ice cream next to cake. Buy a pint-size container of your favorite ice cream, then slice right through it (cardboard and all) with a serrated knife, making ice cream "rounds" that are about 1-inch thick. Peel off the remaining cardboard, then use cookie cutters to make various shapes. Store them in your freezer in between pieces of parchment paper until you're ready to serve. And if you don't use the entire pint of ice cream, the top will still sit flush against your "short stack" to keep it fresh for later.

Tablecloth Substitution

Your daughter's party is about to start, and you just realized you don't have a plastic tablecloth on which to serve the cake. Don't worry, your dining room table isn't ruined yet. Just use the mat from your Twister game. It's covered with colorful dots, and food wipes right off.

Pass the Present

Here's a cheap and easy game for a kids' party that's become a favorite of our kids. Before the party, gather up enough party favors for each child who will be playing, then add a "special" party favor for just one child. Put the favors in a box and wrap it with an old scrap of wrapping paper. Then wrap it 6–12 more times (depending on how many guests you're expecting). When you're ready to play. Sit the children in a circle and start up some music. While the music plays, the children pass the present around to their right. When the music stops, the kid holding the present gets to unwrap a layer of wrapping paper. The game continues until the last child unwraps the present, and discovers the special prize for herself and the ones for everyone else.

All's Fair in Love and Piñatas

When it comes to piñatas, the spoils go to the bullies, but not if you separate the candies and prizes into Ziploc bags for each guest before stuffing them inside the papier-mâché animal. The kids will still get a rush of excitement when the piñata drops, but the game won't dissolve into an "Are we having fun yet?" moment when they start fighting over Tootsie Rolls and Milky Ways.

CHAPTER 5

Tricks for Getting Organized

Scrunchies Saved

Stop hunting around the house every time you need a hair band! Get a toilet paper tube and wrap the bands around it. Keep it in your bathroom or on your dresser and you'll never be without a ponytail holder again.

—*Jackie Bavel, Manahawkin, NJ*

Extra Storage for a Three-Ring Binder

If your kids are like ours, they have all kinds of problems keeping their school supplies organized. You can help remedy this by taking a heavy-duty Ziploc freezer bag, punching holes so that it fits in their three-ring school binder, and filling it with pencils, erasers, and other easily misplaced items.

Shoe Box Dividers

Keep bureau drawers under control by using shoe boxes to separate underwear, socks, tights, and whatever else gets stuffed in there when company comes.

Sewing Board

If you use a sewing machine often, mount a small bulletin board on the wall next to it. Then fill it with pushpins or straight pins. That way when you've got your hands full, you can use the pins to hang extra thread, buttons, bobbins, and other miscellany on the board until you need it.

Cut Your Clothing Clutter

Are you afraid you'll be buried in a fabric avalanche every time you open your closet? It's time to take control of your wardrobe. Going through your clothes and figuring out what you have and what you don't need has a lot of money-saving benefits. First of all, you can take unwanted clothes to a resale shop and either make some money or exchange them for new clothes. Second, you'll have a better handle on what clothes you need for the season, cutting down on duplicates and making impulse buying less likely. If you tend to buy a lot of items that are similar to each other, try organizing your closet by color, so when you pause by that black polo shirt at the store you'll remember just how many black short-sleeve shirts you already own.

Organize Those Bunches of Cords

Don't throw away empty toilet paper rolls! Use them to store the millions of cords running behind your entertainment center. Not only will the rolls keep the cords untangled, but if you also write which appliances the cord belongs to on the roll, you just might be the most organized person in your neighborhood.

Who Knew? CLASSIC TIP

Use an old egg carton to sort small items like nails, screws, and nuts. It can even be used for earrings!

Keep Track of Computer Logins

In these modern times, everyone is registered for more websites than they can count, making it next to impossible to remember all of one's usernames and passwords. Instead of forgetting these all the time, just create a computer document listing all your logins and passwords, and place it on your desktop. Whenever you sign up for a new site, it'll take about 10 seconds to add the new login to the document.

God's Gift to Organization

Clear plastic storage bins may be the greatest thing we have going for us. If you feel like your house is constantly cluttered, go to your nearest organizational store, superstore, or even a dollar store and stock up immediately. But before you go, take a look around your house to find empty areas for some covert storage. Buy long, flat bins for under the couch and you can store board games, video games, and DVDs. Buy tall, stackable ones for keeping items in a closet. And buy whatever fits best under your bed to maximize this perfect space for storing off-season clothes. Make sure to keep some where it's easy to reach—we have one that's simply for all the *stuff* we find in our living room that needs to be put back elsewhere in the house.

Old Cassette Cases Are Good for Something!

Looking for a container to store iPod earbud headphones where they won't get tangled? Coil the cord and then place them inside an old cassette case. Your headphones will be safe, and your friends can admire the *Flashdance* soundtrack decoration on the outside. So retro!

Meds on the Go

For the perfect container for keeping medicine with you in your purse or pocket, try a contact lens case. Since it comes with two handy sections, it's easy to store different pills in different compartments and label them, if necessary.

Remote Remedy

If you're always searching for the remote control, pick one designated place for it and try to always return it to that spot when you're done watching television. You can always keep it on the same end table, or attach self-adhesive Velcro to it and to your TV and affix it there. If you have two (or three, or four, or five) remotes, keep them together in a small basket by your favorite chair.

Organize Your Yarn

Doing some knitting? Keep yarn from getting tangled, especially if you're working with two strands at a time, by running the ends of the rolls through straws. If you pull the yarn through straws as you knit, they'll straighten out each strand.

—*Missy Miller, Loveland, CO*

How to Hide Your Hiding Spaces

Here's a quick and ingenious way to make a cover for under your sink or a small table that will hide anything underneath it. Take an old pillowcase or two and cut through the seams on the top, bottom, and unopened side. Then run a ribbon or piece of elastic through the hemmed portion on the end where you formerly would have stuffed a pillow. Wrap the ribbon around the tabletop or the base of the sink—you may need to string more than one pillowcase on to get full coverage. Tack or tape the string to the wall or the back of the table, then stuff all your power cords, cleaning supplies, or anything else you want out-of-sight underneath!

Pantyhose Problems?

Is pantyhose overrunning your sock drawer? Place each pair in its own resealable sandwich bag. Write any pertinent information (like the size, or whether or not it's control top) on the outside. If they're still taking up too much space, place them in a plastic storage bin under your dresser or somewhere else out of the way.

Bag It!

One of our favorite organizational tools is a hanging shoe organizer. These canvas contraptions are made to allow you to store your shoes on the back of a door, but their individualized compartments make them perfect for storing anything. Keep one in the bathroom for bobby pins, make-up, and lotion; one in your kitchen for spices; and one in the TV room for rarely used remotes and video game controllers. We keep one in each of our children's rooms, so that when we yell, "Clean up your room!" they have a handy place to stow toy cars, action figures, and the 20 million other little things that find their way onto their floors.

Solve Linen Closet Madness

Easily keep your cloth napkins and other matching linens together when you store them by using binder clips to keep like kinds together. You'll never have to dig through the closet looking for a lost place setting again.

Who Knew?

In a survey of 400 adults, 384 of them said they could save time every day by becoming more organized. What are some tweaks you could make to make your day run more smoothly?

Declutter Your Desk

If your desk seems cluttered, make sure you're taking advantage of the space above it. Install a shelf or two for books and folders, and make sure to attach some hooks on their undersides. Hang small baskets on the hooks and now you have a hiding place for paperclips, pens, glue stick, tape, and the hundred other things that are taking up room in your office space.

Get Rid of Menu Mayhem

If you live in an urban area, you probably get a take-out menu stuck under your door every day. To get rid of the clutter caused by having menus stacked up in a drawer, on a table, or practically all over your house, pick a storage method and stick to it. We use a sturdy, waterproof pocket folder for our menus, but you can also use a magazine holder, an inbox, or an old box with the flaps cut off. If you have a three-hole punch handy, you can even store them in a three-ring binder. Whatever you decide, go through your menus first and get rid of any duplicates. Also throw away any menus that serve similar food to a restaurant you order from regularly—once you find your favorite Chinese joint in the area, you're unlikely to try the mediocre one from the next neighborhood over. Make sure to tell your family where your menus now reside, and next time someone says, "Time for takeout," dinner really will be a breeze.

The Key to Keys

You'll never fumble with the wrong key again if you color-code them with a dot of nail polish. Just apply a thick coat of a different shade to the top of each key.

Finding the Card You Need: Priceless

A Rolodex is so old-school, but not if you use it in a new way. How many gift cards or store credits expire before you use them? What about those self-multiplying rewards cards? They slide all over the place in your wallet, and are always out of sight when you make a purchase. Organize them into a Rolodex so you'll never leave home without the right one again.

Clothespin Your Way to Organization

Glue one side of a sturdy clothespin to the inside of cabinet doors, the front of your washing machine, and elsewhere around your home. Hanging clothespins are great for holding plastic shopping bags, and plastic shopping bags are great for holding trash, clean rags, cleaning supplies, and more.

—Katie N., Philadelphia, PA

Getting a Handle on Pan Lids

Forget buying one more specialty-organizing device and instead use the time to actually organize. A dish rack or V-rack (meant for roasting) both make great containers for sorting pan lids in the cabinet. Act now and do away with banging and rummaging for good. Simply reach for the lid you need!

What Uses Can You Think of for a Giant Magnet?

Magnetic strips made to hold knives in your kitchen are useful in many other ways as well. Use them to hold keys, nail clippers and other bathroom must-haves, office supplies—even family photos with a magnet.

Jewelry Organizing Secret

This organizational tip is also a great bedroom decoration. Buy a bulletin board and lots of sturdy push-pins, then use them to hang your bracelets, necklaces, rings, and hook earrings. With all your jewelry on display, you'll be able to more quickly decide what you want to wear, and it won't be a tangled mess. You'll also get a chance to look at beautiful pieces that may not make it into your regular rotation.

—*Devorah Klein, Sliver Spring, MD*

How to Hide a PIN

Here's a question we often get asked: "Where's a safe place to keep PINs for bank cards and the like?" The answer isn't so much *where* as *how*: Hide them inside a fake phone number. For example, if your PIN is 1234 (and hopefully, it isn't!), scribble 347-1234 on the inside of your day planner or somewhere else accessible. Would-be thieves won't know it's the number they're looking for.

Make Bed-Making Easier

Want to know the quickest way to a perfectly made bed every time? Stitch a small *x* in the center of your flat sheet and blankets, then line them up with the center of the headboard. Presto!

—*Stefanie Pole*

Pillowcase It

Our closets are kind of a mess, but we manage never to misplace part of a sheet set. That's because after washing and folding them, we put them right inside one of the pillowcases, which is a convenient way to make sure everything stays in one place.

Quick Serve

If your kids are like ours, they tend to grab whatever snacks are most easily accessible in the fridge. We've solved that problem and encouraged healthier eating by keeping a sandwich basket right in front, containing all the ingredients necessary for a quick meal—deli meats, cheese, condiments, and so on.

Medicine Cabinet Organization

If you have a metal medicine cabinet, mount a magnet inside it, and you'll be able to place nail clippers, tweezers, safety pins, or other handy items at your fingertips. And if your cabinet is made of metal, just glue the magnet inside.

Bountiful Bathroom Storage

Those three-tiered baskets that you usually find holding fruit in the kitchen are also perfect for bathrooms. Store brushes, hair gel, band-aids, or whatever else is taking up space in your medicine cabinet. If hung out of reach of your kids, it's also a great place to store shaving supplies.

Great Tip if You've Ever Said, "Where's My Ring?!"

Screw a small hook into the wall near your kitchen sink. It will make a handy place to store your rings while you're doing the dishes.

—*Tawnya Crawford*

Make Your Own Closet

You're in desperate need of more closet space, but you can't afford a fancy armoire. Here's what to do: Find two old doors at a yard sale or scrap yard. Paint or decorate them how you please, then hinge them together. Place the doors in the corner of the room at a 90-degree angle to each other so that you make a "box." Use one as the door of your new closet, and the other to hang shelves and attach a bar to. Suspend a clothes line between them for additional hanging. It may not be fancy, but we bet your friends will be impressed!

Who Knew?

January is National Get Organized Month. Celebrate by organizing your entire house! Or at least clean out that junk closet.

CHAPTER 6

Make Cooking
A Breeze

Mom's Omelet Secret

The best omelet you will ever eat has mustard in it. Just add ¼ teaspoon fancy mustard for each egg, and mix in when scrambling. The mustard will add a hint of mysteriously delicious flavor to the eggs, as well as making them the perfect consistency.

—*Aggie Bossolina, Jupiter, FL*

Chop Up Your Veggies

When cooking, avoid crunchy vegetables by slicing them up a bit smaller. If you chop your veggies into tinier pieces, they'll cook more evenly throughout. As an added bonus, they'll finish cooking more quickly, too.

Wilted Lettuce No More

When we grew up, making a salad with wilted lettuce was a sin on par with serving moldy bread. Do your best to dry the leaves after you wash them. Once you put them in the salad bowl, you can keep off excess water by piling them on top of an upside down plate that's on the bottom of the bowl. Moisture will still collect along the bottom, but the lettuce will remain a safe distance away.

Quickly Ripen Tomatoes

To bring already-picked tomatoes from green to red, place them in a closed paper bag with an apple.

Double Frosting

This simple little trick saves money and calories. You may not have time to make your own frosting, but you can blend store-bought frosting with a hand mixer to double the volume.

Spoon Slipping Solution

At our house, all of our wooden mixing spoons have a rubber band wrapped tightly around the top of the handle. Why? Because they keep the spoons from falling into whatever you're stirring. Wrap some rubber bands around your spoons and you can safely rest the spoon on the side of the bowl without it slipping.

Cleaning Utensils as You Go

This cooking tip operates on the same principle as a kindergarten paint session. Just keep a jar with warm soapy water on your counter and place whatever knife or other utensil you're working with in it when you're done with that part of the recipe. When you need it again, you don't have to stop what you're doing to wash it. A quick rinse will do. Then again, one of us (not naming names) saves time by just reusing dirty utensils for the rest of the night.

Get Rid of Fish Odor Before It Starts

When frying up fish in a pan, add a dollop of peanut butter. It won't affect the taste of the fish, but it will affect the odor—peanut butter contains a chemical that absorbs that stinky fish odor, so your whole house doesn't have to.

—Marlena Kahn, Steubenville, OH

Cup a' Joe with a Twist

Flavored coffee is such a treat, but most families can barely manage to keep enough of the regular stuff stockpiled. Luckily, it's easy to add your own flavors with ingredients you have on hand. Orange peel, vanilla extract, cinnamon, allspice, or ground-up roasted nuts can all be added to coffee grinds before you brew. To make six cups of coffee, you just need ¼ teaspoon of whatever flavor you choose. Experiment to get the proportions exactly right.

Fix a Salt Shaker

You love your antique rooster-shaped salt shaker, but every time you shake it over something way too much salt empties out. Easily fix this problem by painting over a few of the holes with clear nail polish.

Sweetest Corn

To make the sweetest, freshest tasting corn you've ever had, add ¼ cup powdered milk to the pot while you're boiling it.

Award-Winning Pies

You'll impress even Martha Stewart with this one. After you've crimped the crust, but before you place your work of art in the oven, go around the edge again, this time carefully lifting the crust up ever-so-slightly from the dish so it won't stick while baking. When you go to serve pieces "just like Grandma made" they'll come out in one clean swoop rather than insides slopped on the plate followed by hacked up pieces of the crust.

Strawberry Days

Hate the waste of lopping off strawberry stems with a knife but like to serve the delicious summer treats ready-to-eat? Try this: After washing, push the stems out from the bottom up using a plastic straw.

Getting Your Cake to Come Clean

Your beautiful cake is perfect except for one thing—you can't get it out of the pan! Lay out a sheet of wax paper and gently turn the whole thing over. Next, put a dishtowel over the pan and iron it with a hot steam iron. After a few minutes the pan should be ready for lift-off.

Keeping Pasta Warm

Here's a trick that will keep freshly cooked pasta warmer longer. Place a large mixing bowl underneath your colander as you drain the pasta. The hot water will fill the bowl and heat it up. Once the bowl is warm, dump out the water and put the pasta in the bowl instead. Then cover the bowl and take your time finishing the rest of your meal.

Husking Corn

The easiest way to husk corn is to cut off both ends, then roll the corn on your counter for a moment. The husk will then peel right off!

—*Sona Gajiwala, Chicago, IL*

Bag Your Fruit

If you have some unripe fruit that you'd like to ripen faster, simply place it in a plastic garbage bag. The gases released by the fruit will remain trapped in the bag, causing it to ripen more quickly. Make sure not to seal the bag airtight, though—a little bit of ventilation is necessary.

A Different Kind of Soup Stone

Have you ever had to throw out a batch of soup because you accidentally oversalted it? Not anymore! Potatoes contain starch, which absorbs salt, so all you need to do is peel a raw potato or two and toss it in the soup. Let the pot simmer for about 15 minutes before removing the potato, and your soup will be almost good as new.

Stuck Marshmallows?

It's time for s'mores, but when you take the marshmallows out of the cupboard, they're all stuck together! Separate them by adding a bit of cornstarch to the bag, then shaking vigorously. The cornstarch will absorb the moisture that is keeping them stuck together and break them apart.

Protecting Your Cookbooks

A well-worn cookbook is a good sign, but company shouldn't be able to guess your favorite recipes just by inspecting the splatters. So here is yet another use for one of the million plastic bags taking over your pantry: Use one to cover the binding and pages surrounding the recipe you are using. You can then lay a sheet of plastic wrap over the page you are on.

Who Knew?

Sugary or tomato-based BBQ sauces should be added only at the end of the grilling process, because both will burn easily.

Make Leftover Onion Last Longer

You've chopped up half an onion and you'd like to save the rest for later. Make sure the onion lasts longer in your fridge by rubbing the cut end with butter, then wrapping in plastic wrap.

Quick Fix for Curdling

If you've added too much citrus to dairy and caused it to curdle, add an ice cube to the mix and you'll be back in business in no time. The cold will actually reverse the curdling process.

—*Charles Strohm, Calgary, AB*

Pitting Cherries

For a quick and easy way to pit cherries, use a pastry bag tip. Just set the tip on a cutting board with the jagged edge pointed up, then firmly press the cherry down on top of it. Be careful not to cut your fingers!

Make Your Pans Last Longer

When cooking on a gas stove, the flame should extend no farther than two-thirds up the pan. (If it does, opt for a bigger pan.) Never leave an empty pan on a hot stove for more than a couple of minutes, and keep an eye out for shiny rainbow-colored marks on the pan. These are signs that you've been cooking at too high a heat.

Remove Rust from Your Knife

If your knife is rusty, it's time to chop some onions. Believe or not, onions will remove rust from metal objects. Plunge the knife into the biggest onion you can find, let it sit for a few seconds, then pull it out. Repeat this process until the rust has dissolved, then wash as usual and dry.

Stop Stove Disasters

Keep pots of pasta or rice from boiling over by adding a tablespoon of butter to the water when you add the pasta or rice.

Freshen Your Hands

Reach for the mouthwash when you're cooking with garlic, onions, fish or anything else that can leave a scent on your hands. Just pour a few tablespoons into your palms, rub your hands together, and the smell will disappear.

Grapes Are Easy

After rinsing newly purchased grapes, leave them in the colander for refrigerator storage. Grapes are actually helped by lots of cool air, and the holes in the colander will allow the air to more freely circulate around them.

—*Teddy Levy, Casper, WY*

Who Knew? CLASSIC TIP

If you know to put toothpicks in a cake before covering it with plastic wrap for travel, you're halfway there. The only problem is that sometimes the toothpicks poke right through the wrap and defeat the purpose. The solution? Miniature marshmallows, of course. Our six-year-old loves to carefully place one marshmallow on the top of each toothpick (and then pop the rest in his mouth). Much better results than when we let him apply the actual frosting.

Separating Eggs

Even if you don't have an egg separator, it's easy to separate an egg's yolk from its white. Place the smallest funnel you have over a container, then gently crack the egg into it. The white will slide into the container, while the yolk will stay behind.

Fix a Cookbook Problem Before It Starts

Oops! You just spilled on your favorite cookbook. Don't despair. Simply blot the page with a paper towel and then insert a piece of waxed paper on the page before closing the book. The pages won't stick together.

Makin' Bacon?

Always rinse bacon under cold water before frying—it will reduce the amount the bacon shrinks when you cook it.

Smooth Grating

Problem: You want to break your addiction to buying pre-grated cheese in bags, but cleaning up the cheese grater is always a pain. Solution? Put the grater in the freezer or run it under cold water for several minutes before grating, and the cheese won't stick. You can also try spraying it with cooking spray before each use.

Goodbye to Dry Burgers

The secret to juicy burgers is simple. Just let them sit, covered, at room temperature for an hour before you cook them. This is safe to do as long as it isn't too hot (over 80°) where they will be resting.

Decrystalizing Honey

There's nothing more sweetly delicious than real honey, but we find it often gets thick and full of crystals after a little while in the cabinet. To get it back to its former consistency, simply place the open container in the microwave, then heat on high for 10 seconds and stir. Continue microwaving in 10-second increments and stir until it's back to its lovely, spreadable self.

Nice Ice Cubes

Yes, even ice cubes can be perfected. Do yours look like they've melted and refrozen a hundred times? Make them beautiful and clear by using water that you've boiled, cooled, then poured into the tray.

For That Last Bit of Ketchup

The last bits of tomato sauce, ketchup, salsa, or chutney left in their bottles and jars are great to use in marinades. Simply add some vinegar and oil to the bottle and shake. The liquid will pour out easily. Now add a little onion, garlic, and spices, and you have a marinade!

—*Lupe Velasquez*

Beating Egg Whites

When you're going to beat egg whites for a recipe, let the eggs sit at room temperature for 30 minutes before using them. The egg whites will then beat to a greater volume.

Who Put the Apples in the Cookie Jar?

Chewy, homemade cookies are one of the great pleasures in life. So it's hard not to get disappointed when cookies dry out and turn crispy in the jar. It turns out a few apple slices thrown in will keep them as chewy as the day they were made (or brought out of the box). If your cookies have already hardened, soften them back up by brushing them with a little bit of milk and heating them in a 225° oven for five minutes.

Storing Fresh Herbs

Fresh parsley and cilantro are crisp, flavorful additions to any dish, but they always go bad so quickly. Both will last for at least a couple of weeks if you store them in a jar. Just clip the stems of the herbs, and place them in a jar with water in it, stems down. Cover loosely with a plastic bag and refrigerate.

Mess-Free Mashing

The quickest way to "chop" nuts is to place them in a sealed plastic bag, then roll over them with a rolling pin. This is also a clean, easy way to break up graham crackers or vanilla wafers to make a pie crust.

Cork Your Soda

Lost the cap to your soda bottle? Use a wine cork instead! They're usually the perfect size.

—Maria Delakis, Shaker Heights, OH

Picking Up Persistent Ice Cubes

If you're trying to retrieve a stubborn ice cube from the ice cube tray, here's a surefire trick. Run your finger under running water for a second, then press it to the center of the cube. The ice will stick to your finger long enough for you to transfer it into your glass.

Who Knew? CLASSIC TIP

When you finish a stick of butter, don't throw the paper wrapper away. Instead, fold in half and store in a plastic bag. Next time you need to prepare a buttered bowl or pan, use the buttered paper—it's easy and neat!

Bungled Beaters

If your hand mixer isn't what it used to be thanks to jiggling beaters, hardened food in its sockets may be to blame. Take out the beaters and clean out the sockets with a toothpick or bobby pin.

Give Your Potatoes an Apple

To keep your potatoes from producing buds before you use them, store them in a bin with an apple. The apple will slow down sprouts before they start.

Extra Cooling Rack

Keep your cool during holiday baking days. When you're covered with flour, have no idea where the kitchen table used to be, and just pulled the fifth blistering hot tray of gingerbread men out of the oven, simply flip over cardboard egg trays (you'll need two, spaced a little bit apart) and set the baking pan on top.

It's Burger Time

When freezing burgers or chops, always separate with sheets of parchment paper before storing in freezer bags. The paper makes it easy to remove the meat when it's time to cook.

Slicing Chicken

Cutting chicken into bite-sized pieces for dishes like pastas and stir-frys is easier when it's half frozen. Place fresh chicken in the freezer for two hours before you start dinner for easy cutting. Or, place frozen chicken in the microwave and cook on the defrost setting for about five minutes, turning halfway through.

Secret to Easily Peeling Garlic

To get garlic cloves to separate from their skins, break apart each individual clove from the head and heat on high in the microwave for 5–10 seconds. This tiny bit of cooking should make them easily slip out of their skins.

—*Jennifer Nelson, Philo, CA*

For Carrots That Keep

Always store your carrots with the tops removed. The green parts will pull moisture from the carrots while they're in the bin.

Jar Problem?

It might be handy to have a man around the house, but you won't need one with these jar-opening tips. If you have a jar you can't open, first try putting on some latex dishwashing gloves. If it still won't budge, wrap a few rubber bands around the lid for extra grip. If that doesn't work, run some hot water and hold the lid underneath it, turning the jar so the water hits all the edges of the lid. Then tap the edges several times with a butter knife, dry the lid, and try opening it with the gloves again. As a final attempt, smack the bottom of the jar squarely with the flat of your palm, then immediately try the lid again. This will send an air bubble to the top of the jar to hopefully help your cause.

Perfect Rice, Reheated

Ordering in Chinese always left us with leftover rice, but it never tasted quite right when we reheated it. I finally perfected (OK, stumbled upon) the perfect microwaving method. Place the rice in its original container or in a microwave-safe bowl. Cover it, then microwave for one minute on medium (50 percent) heat. Stir, then re-cover and heat for another minute on high. Let sit for one minute more and you'll have perfect rice.

—*Brian Shelby, Brooklyn, NY*

Shower Caps in the Kitchen

Plastic wrap is perfect for covering bowls of rising dough, but if you leave the room for too long the dough will push the wrap right off, leaving it susceptible to germs in the open air. Solve this problem by switching out the plastic wrap for a plastic shower cap—the elastic will fit perfectly over your bowl, and the plastic will stretch enough to allow for expansion.

Overdone Spaghetti?

If you forgot your simmering pot on the stove and your noodles are limp and mushy, try this trick. First run them under the coldest water possible—this will stop the cooking process immediately, and make the starch inside them contract. If you're making a dish with tomato sauce, heat them back up directly in the sauce, as the acid will help them hold up even better.

For Pancakes That Are as Light as Air

Substitute club soda for water when making pancakes, and they'll be fluffier than clouds.

Breaded Cutlets: Hold the Crumbs

Breaded cutlets are less appealing when the breadcrumbs have all dropped off in the oven. One extra step is all you need. After coating with crumbs, let the cutlets dry on a baking rack for 10 minutes, *then* cook.

Use a Potato to Erase Food Stains

This is a great tip that was taught to me by my grandmother after a grueling day of Thanksgiving cooking: To remove food stains on your hands, rub them on a peeled, raw potato. They'll come off like magic!

—Megan O'Brien, Lovelock, NV

If you grind the average pepper mill 10 times, you'll have ¼ teaspoon pepper. Figure out how many grinds your pepper mill takes to make a teaspoon and you won't have to measure every time a recipe calls for black pepper.

Born Again Chips

It's 2 a.m.—do you know where your chips are? Yes, but unfortunately, they've been there way too long. Microwaving, which turns bread to mush, has the opposite effect on chips. Just give them a whirl for a minute on a glass plate. Be careful when you bring them out; they may need to cool down a bit before you can eat them.

Say Goodbye to Stuck Dumplings

To prevent delicate dumplings from sticking to your steamer while cooking, first line the steamer basket with lettuce leaves. Sticky dumplings will be a thing of the past.

Designing With Chocolate the Easy Way

Adding a chocolate design to cakes, brownies, and other confections gives them a sophisticated touch sure to be appreciated by your friends. To easily use chocolate for decorating, place old candy, unwrapped, in a plastic sandwich bag. Microwave for 30 seconds at a time, turning until melted. Then snip off the corner and use like a pastry bag to write words and create embellishments.

Perfect Cake Slicing

Keep crumbling to a minimum when slicing a cake by dipping your knife in cold water between every slice.

Leave the Seeds

When using only part of a red, green, or yellow pepper, cut it from the bottom or the sides, leaving the seeds attached, and it will remain moist for longer. You can put the rest in a resealable plastic bag and use it 3–4 days later.

Cleaner Basting Brushes

There's nothing like a gooey, smelly basting brush to ruin your mood. Put a stop to it today! After your usual washing routine with hot water and soap, dry it off a bit by shaking. Here's the cool part, which might remind you of your eighth-grade science class. Pour coarse salt into a cup and place the brush inside. Any remaining wetness will be absorbed by the salt, leaving the bristles as clean as can be.

Truss With Floss

You might know that "trussing" means tying the wings and legs of a bird down for more-even cooking. But do you know the best string to use for trussing? Dental floss! Not only does it come in a small container, it's usually easy to get for free at your dentist's office. It's also very strong, and won't burn in high heat.

Storing Milk and Eggs

It turns out the refrigerator door isn't the best place to store your milk and eggs. Because the temperature fluctuates more there, your dairy products may not stay as cold as they need to to stay fresh for a long period of time. Instead, place them on a shelf inside.

Quick Baked Potatoes

Halve the oven time for baked potatoes by placing each medium-sized potato in a muffin tin on its end. Turn over after 10 minutes, and they'll be ready in a half-hour or less.

The Many Uses of a Pizza Cutter

Pizza cutters can be used for a lot more than just pizza. Use your pizza cutter to quickly slice tortillas, sandwiches, pancakes, omelets, brownies, and even stale bread to make croutons.

Hot Sugar!

You're making cookies, but forgot to soften the butter beforehand. Instead of the trial-and-error involved in attempting to soften (but not melt) butter in the microwave, zap the sugar instead. Mixing butter with warm sugar will soften it in a second.

—Lindsay Herman

All the Kings Horses Could Not Peel This Egg

We could have saved years of our lives if we had known this trick earlier, not to mention many a cranky morning. When your eggs are boiled, put them inside a container filled with cold water and close the lid. Give a good shake until the eggs crack. That little pesky skin will separate from the white and stay out of your way when you try to peel the egg.

Extra Foam, Please!

A frothy, foamy cappuccino at home can really cheer up the family on a long, rainy afternoon (decaf for the younger crowd). But you don't need to buy an espresso machine or spend hours holding the milk up to one of those little steamers. Instead, once the milk is heated, simply beat it with a handheld mixer. You'll know it's ready when those white, luminous peaks are nicely holding themselves up. Pour into a mug, spoon the foam, and add cinnamon or chocolate powder. Voilà.

Fish Fix

If you're cooking fish but it comes out too dry, brush it with a mixture of equal parts melted butter and lemon juice and some dried or fresh herbs. The butter will help make it moister, while the lemon juice will help it hold together and cause your diners to salivate—perhaps making them less likely to notice your cooking error.

Stuck Cookies

Are your cookies stuck to the cookie sheet? Remove them easily by working some dental floss in between each cookie and the sheet.

Shabby Chic Trivets

Hardware and home improvement stores have lots of ceramic tiles that can be adapted as mix 'n' match trivets. Choose from a variety of designs and colors to add unique accents to your table setting. It's easy enough to affix felt corners (peel and stick) underneath.

Banana-Peeling Secret

When peeling bananas, peel from the bottom up. This will eliminate the banana "strings" you get when peeling from the top down.

Reheating Pizza

The best way to heat up leftover pizza is in the toaster oven, but if you don't have a toaster oven you don't need to endure the soggy crust that results from microwaving a leftover slice. Just place the piece in a covered skillet and heat over medium-low heat until warm.

Bar Cookie Perfection

Want to know the secret to perfectly cut bar cookies? As soon as you remove your sweet creation from the oven, make a ¼-inch incision with a knife and outline your bars. Then once they've cooled, cut all the way. This will ensure that the edges of your cookies are as smooth as can be.

Another Way to Unstick Stuck Cakes

The bad news is that your cake is stuck to the bottom of the pan. But the good news is that it's easy to get out intact—you just need to heat the bottom back up. This is easily accomplished by submerging the bottom of the pan in hot water. Once the pan heats back up, use a knife to easily dislodge your still-perfect cake.

Lower-Calorie Sweetener

In spiced recipes like muffins and biscuits, try reducing the amount of sugar in your recipes by half and doubling the cinnamon. Not only will the cinnamon taste help retain sweetness with the least calories possible, it has also been shown to help control blood sugar levels.

Who Knew?

Spices and dried herbs keep their flavor better if stored in a cupboard away from heat, light, and moisture, all of which impair flavor, change color, and shorten life. Herbs and ground spices will generally retain their best flavor for a year. Whole spices last one year.

Butter Your Veggies

When you scrape out the last of the margarine from the tub, don't throw the container away just yet. Throw some vegetables into the tub, microwave it for a few seconds, and voilà!—instant yummy veggies.

Intoxicating Tenderizer

Do you tend to buy those tougher, bargain-priced meats at your local supermarket? If so, you can tenderize them without spending extra money on powdered tenderizer. Just let your meat soak in a can's worth of beer for at least an hour, and that should do the job.

Turkey Trouble

When you're stuffing that Thanksgiving turkey with dressing, you may have trouble with the stuffing sticking inside the bird after cooking. To prevent this, wrap the stuffing in cheesecloth before cooking. When the turkey is done, pull out the cheesecloth and the stuffing will slide right out.

Pancakes: Heinz's 58th Variety

If you're the family pancake chef, make your job a lot easier by thoroughly rinsing out a squeezable ketchup or salad dressing bottle. Pour the batter in and squeeze, and you'll have neater, rounder, and more precise pancakes. You can even store the leftover amount in the fridge for next time.

Cut Your Cake and Eat It Too

If you've got a delicate cake that falls apart and sticks to the knife when you cut it, use dental floss—yes, dental floss—to cut it instead. Hold the floss tight and give it a slight sawing motion as you move it down to cut through the cake. This trick also works for blocks of soft cheese.

Don't Let Apples Go to Waste

If you have a bunch of apples that are going to go bad soon, here's how you can use them up quickly: Cut them into wedges or smaller chunks, dump them in a saucepan, and sauté them in butter over medium heat. When that's finished, sprinkle a half sugar/half cinnamon mixture on top, and you've got a yummy treat that the kids will love. You can even use them as the start of a homemade apple pie!

Butter Softener

Whenever I need soft butter and all I have is hard, refrigerated sticks, I simply shave off the needed amount with a vegetable peeler. In a matter of seconds, the butter shavings will be soft.

—*Grace Carrick, Arlington, VA*

Who Knew? CLASSIC TIP

Bread gone stale? Simply wet your fingers and flick some water on each surface. Then wrap in foil and heat in an 250° oven for 10 minutes.

Measuring Hint

When measuring sticky foods like peanut butter or cream cheese, first rinse the inside of the measuring cup with hot water. The food you're measuring will slide out easily into your bowl.

Getting Cutting Boards to Stay Put

Cutting boards that slip around on the counter are an obvious no-no, yet it's amazing how often we turn cutting a watermelon into an extreme sport in our house. We finally figured out that all that extra shelf liner in the pantry *did* in fact come in handy one day. We simply cut it to the right size to use as a placemat for the board and it never slipped again.

Corn's Up

According to the unwritten laws of *The Guy's Guide to Life and Cooking*, everything edible can be grilled, but even our little guys had to concede that grilled mac 'n' cheese just wasn't working. Grilled corn, on the other hand, really is good. The trick is to shuck it down to the last layer of the husk and cut off the furry edges with scissors. Pop those babies on the grill and watch for the moment when the husk starts to show the outline of the kernels and the top edges begin to peel down. The ears are ready.

Hand Me That Cob

Yes, there's a utensil specifically designed for pulling corn out of boiling water (tongs). But if you can't find them and the corn is just right, a potato masher does the trick quite nicely with a tiny bit of balance. And our 11-year-old says airlifting the cobs this way is great practice for the crane machine filled with toys at the arcade!

Perfect, Easy Deviled Eggs

Here's a method for making deviled eggs that's so simple you'll want to make them for every picnic you go to. After hard-boiling eggs, slice them open and place their yolks in a resealable plastic bag. After mashing them up through the bag, add the mayonnaise and the rest of the ingredients. Mash some more to blend, then cut off the corner of the bag and use like a pastry bag to easily dispense the mixture into egg halves.

Say No to Flour

Hate that white floured look your cakes end up with after you flour the edges of your cake pan before baking? Make it a thing of the past by reserving a small amount of cake mix, then using it instead of flour to flour your pans.

Bake Me a Cake

Remember the rest of the line from this nursery rhyme? "As fast as you can." Those pre-made mixes from a box are so easy, but you can recreate the effect *and* maintain bragging rights to a homemade dessert. Measure things out a few days before you plan to bake. Store the mixes in Ziploc bags (for dry) and plastic containers (for wet), making sure wet stuff gets into the refrigerator. Eggs should be added the day of. We find this trick especially great for holiday bake-offs when we like to give tins of various cookies to neighbors and friends.

The Right Pan at the Right Time

You shouldn't need a ruler in the kitchen. Yet when a recipe gives you cooking times for five different pan sizes, you wish you knew the actual measurements of your baking pans. And now you will. All you have to do is use nail polish to mark the dimensions on the bottom of each pan. Then put that ruler back in the home office where it belongs.

CHAPTER 7

Dogs, Cats, and Other Pets

Due Doggie Diligence

When you're choosing what kind of pet to buy, make sure to research the different breeds before selecting one—even Wikipedia is a big help. For instance, did you know that dalmatians are among the most high-strung dogs, while beagles will often scamper away because they're always following their noses? It's always best to select a pet that's been raised by a friend or a reputable shelter; avoid puppy mills, which tend to mass-produce poorly adjusted pets. Remember, too, that while purebred animals are supposedly status symbols, they're also much less hardy and more prone to diseases than mutts.

Who Knew? CLASSIC TIP

Never have to throw away an ant-infested bowl of pet food again. Simply sprinkle some ground cinnamon around the bowl, and the ants will stay away.

How to Handle Pet Hair

If you don't have the heart to banish your pet from the couch, here's a solution for removing all that hair from your sofa. Just put on some rubber kitchen gloves or surgical latex gloves and then wipe the hair into a pile with your hand. Discard it and then repeat the process. After you've gotten most of the hair, take a sheet of fabric softener from the laundry room and use it to pick up the rest—the hair will be naturally attracted to it. When that's done, use a vacuum cleaner to add the finishing touch.

Help Pet Food Stay Put

If your pet's food dish always ends up three feet from where it started by the time he's done eating, make it skid-proof. With a glue gun, make a thin strip of glue around the bottom rim. The hardened glue will make it much harder for the bowl to slide across the floor.

Untangle Fur

Pet owners know that matted hair can make brushing your animal a frustrating experience for you—and a painful one for them. To prevent this, rub your pet with baby powder prior to brushing. It'll be easier to remove the tangles, for which both you and your pet will be grateful.

Save on Your Pet's Care

We all love our pets and will go to any length to make sure they are happy and healthy, but this shouldn't mean taking out a second mortgage to pay vet bills. Look at your local shelter to see what services they provide. Many will spay/neuter and administer vaccinations and annual shots for less than half the price of your friendly neighborhood vet.

Mutt Munchies

If your dog is teething, you can create a cheap chew toy by soaking an old washcloth in water, twisting it into a fun shape, and leaving it in the freezer. Give it to your pup fully frozen, and when it thaws out, simply repeat the process. Be careful doing this with tiny dogs, though, as they can get too cold if they chew on frozen toys too often.

Ease Painful Pads

If your poor pet's pads are cracked or dry, the solution is simple. Gently rub a little petroleum jelly into her pads while she's sleeping. It will moisturize the area and is completely safe if your pet decides she wants to lick it off later.

Butter Up Pills

If you have trouble getting your cat to swallow pills, try rubbing them in butter first. It will make them taste better to your cat, and they'll slide right down his throat.

Rein in Pet Hair

Cleaning out your own brush is bad enough, but cleaning out the one that belongs to your furry companion can be a half a day's work. Instead of getting angry next time you snag your pantyhose, give them a second life. Cut strips of hose and lay them over your pet's clean metal brush, poking the pins of the brush through. The next time your cat or dog locks like he just stepped out of a salon after a heavy brushing, all you'll have to do is remove the scraps of material, throw them out, and replace with new strips.

● Who Knew?

If you have both cats and dogs, you may be tempted to feed your cat dog food. Don't do it! Besides being highly insulted if he happens to see the can, your cat needs certain nutrients that are found only in food made specifically for cats.

Routine Is Key

If you've ever had your pet wake you up precisely five minutes before your alarm goes off so she can be fed, you know that animals are creatures of routine. Changes in behavior could be a sign that something is wrong with your pet. Just to be sure, you should take her to the vet if you notice changes in appetite, thirst, frequency of urination, energy level, hiding behavior, or anything else that seems strange to you. Your pet will thank you!

For Smelly Cats and Dogs

Sometimes, your pet is just plain stinky. If you're beginning to notice pet odor when you open your front door, it's time to take action. Add a bit of brewer's yeast (1 teaspoon for cats and small dogs and 1 tablespoon for bigger dogs) to your pet's food and your pet will secrete less of those unpleasant odors.

Get Rid of Fleas

You can remove pesky fleas from your pet's coat without having to pay for expensive flea collars or medications. Simply bathe your pet in salt water, and the fleas will stay way. You can also try steeping rosemary in warm water and using that as bathwater. Better yet, use a combination of the two.

Treat Your 'Keet

If you have a parakeet or other bird, make sure you have perches in various diameters. Birds' talons don't get a proper workout unless they have different things to grasp. Use tree branches or store-bought perches, especially those with a rough feeling, to keep your bird exercised and happy.

Beware Poisonous Plants

If your pet likes chewing on plants, beware: Some common house and garden plants are poisonous to animals. They include rhododendron, daffodils, crocus, lilies, poinsettia, holy, mistletoe, lantana, laburnum, taro, yew, cyclamen, foxglove, hyacinth, hydrangea, rhubarb, narcissus, and the pits of many fruits like apricots, plums, and peaches. If you see your pet eat any of these, take him to the vet immediately!

To a Cat, Anything (and Everything) Is a Toy

Cats love toys, and they aren't picky about where they come from! Don't spend money on expensive cat toys. Instead, use a balled up piece of paper, a cork, a jingle bell, or anything else they can bat around the house. To make the toy extra enticing, throw it in a tissue box that has the plastic part removed. Cats will love sticking their paws inside to try to fish out the toy.

Secret to Shiny Fur

To make your short-haired cat's fur extra-shiny, rub it down with a piece of silk, velvet, or chamois cloth.

Build a Doggie Path

If your dog tends to track mud into the house, you can confine that mess to one area by creating a walkway for him to use before entering. The best bet is filling a path with gravel, which helps keep mud off the pooch's paws and keeps the house cleaner.

> ### Who Knew? CLASSIC TIP
>
> When getting a "treat" for being good, most dogs are just excited about a special snack, not that it's in the shape of a bone. Instead of paying extra for dog treats, keep a separate container of dog food where you normally keep the treats, then give your dog a small handful when he's done something reward-worthy.

Scent of a Pet Owner

If you're going to be unable to pay attention to your pet for a while—such as when she's in a carrier on a long trip—put an old, worn T-shirt (the best are ones you've recently exercised in) inside the pet carrier with her. Your scent will help ease your pet's worries.

Pet Mess

If you're training a new pet, here's the best way to get accidental wet spots out of the carpet. First soak up as much of the pet mess as possible with paper towels. Then combine 2 cups warm water, $\frac{2}{3}$ cup vinegar, and 2 teaspoons dishwashing detergent. Mix everything together, then blot the stain carefully with the solution, making sure not to apply excess liquid. Rinse it off with tap water and dry it with paper towels. When the carpet is completely dry—usually the next day—kill off the lingering smell by sprinkling a heavy dose of baking soda on the spot and letting it sit for one hour before vacuuming up.

Stave Off Shedding

Even regular brushing can't get every last stray hair off your pet, but a dryer sheet can. Run a dryer sheet over your pet's coat and static will cause any loose hairs to be picked up.

Fat Cat?

If you have trouble getting your cat to play with toys for exercise, make him or her work a little for food! First you'll need a cylindrical container—a yogurt container (with the yogurt and foil removed) that has a top for granola or candy works well. Cut a hole in one or both ends and re-enforce with masking or duct tape, to make sure there are no sharp edges in the plastic. Then put some dry food inside and put it in front of your cat. Cats love the noise the food makes when rattling around inside, and will continue to bat at the toy to get the food to come out.

Provide Ice Cubes During Transit

You're taking your pet on the plane, but you're worried about her getting water while you travel. Instead of filling a water dish with water, which can splash out during transit, put a few ice cubes in the dish. Once your pet's cage is settled in cargo, the ice cubes will melt, giving her some much-needed refreshment.

—Art Gallagher, Burnside, CT

A Bath for Your Goldfish

Before you clean out your goldfish's bowl, first prepare a salt-water bath for him. Even though goldfish are freshwater fish, salt will help your fish absorb much-needed electrolytes and kill any parasites on his fins. To get the salt water ready, run tap water into a bowl and let it sit for a day to allow the chlorine to evaporate (you should do this when filling his freshwater bowl, too). Add a teaspoon of non-iodized salt and mix until it dissolves. Then let Goldy go for a swim in the salt water for approximately 15 minutes.

When the Cat's Away Your Plants Will Be Happier

Here are two ways to keep feline visitors away from your indoor garden. Make a protective circle of crushed-up pine cones around the stems of your plants and mist the leaves with a combination of water and a few teaspoons of vinegar.

Prevent Sunburn

Did you know that light-colored animals can get sunburn, too? Guard against this by dabbing a bit of SPF 15 sunscreen on your pet's nose and the tips of his ears.

Eliminating Cat Smell

If the smell from your in-heat housecat's spray has more than nine lives, try mixing one cup hydrogen peroxide with ½ tablespoon baking soda and two squirts liquid dish soap. Pour into a spray bottle and use wherever Fluffy has left her trademark. (Be sure to spot-check as you run the risk of bleaching certain materials.)

Easy Dog Toy

Dog toys are expensive and can be made from harmful materials. In the colonial era, kids made their own dolls from rags. A canine version will make Fido just as happy as any designer plush toy. All you need to do is braid together three old dishtowels. Before you start, cut two strips off the side of two of them. Then use these to tie the tops and bottoms of the braid together.

Traveling With a Pet?

To make pets calmer while traveling with them in a car, add a few drops of Bach's Rescue Remedy to their water. Its all-natural ingredients will help pets stay calm just as well as it helps humans do.

Get Rid of Ear Mites

A great household remedy for ear mites is to rub a cotton ball soaked in 1 teaspoon baking soda that has been dissolved in 1 cup warm water. Of course, if you see a pet scratching his ears, you should always take him to the vet first, just to be sure.

Time for a Bath

You've finally trained your dog how to be good while getting a bath in the tub, but his tiny hairs always slip through your drain's catcher and clog up your pipes. To keep this from happening, stuff some steel wool into the opening (but not too far down). It will catch every hair from even the furriest of creatures. When you're done bathing, make sure to fish the steel wool out immediately.

Fido Being Finicky?

If you've bought a new brand of food and your dog doesn't want to eat it, put a piece of beef jerky in the bag and reseal it. By the next day, the smell will have worn off on the food, making it seem much more appetizing.

Birds Get Lonely, Too!

It may seem silly, but not to your bird—put a mirror in his cage to make sure he doesn't get lonely. The bird will see the reflection of himself and think it's another bird to keep him company. Of course, the other solution is simply buying your bird a real feathered friend!

● Who Knew? CLASSIC TIP

Is your dog leaving brown spots on your lawn where he decides to pee? Put a few drops of vinegar into his water bowl every time you refill it and brown spots will be a thing of the past.

Does Your Cat Have a Weak Stomach?

If you have a cat who frequently vomits, you should (of course) take her to the vet. Unfortunately, your vet might tell you that some cats just throw up a lot. (Why do we love them so much again?) If your cat frequently vomits, it could be because she's eating too fast. Try leaving dry food out all day, to let her eat at her own pace. But if she becomes overweight, this might not be an option. Another trick to try is pulverizing some mint with some fresh catnip and seeing if she'll eat it—mint is good for calming stomachs.

Removing Ticks

You and your dog just enjoyed a fun romp through the forest, but now the poor guy has ticks in his fur! To more easily remove them, first wet a Q-tip with rubbing alcohol. Dab it on the tick, and he'll loosen his grip. You should then be able to pull the tick straight off your dog.

Bad Breath Bomb

If your cat or dog has horrible breath, try adding some fresh chopped parsley to his food.

Easiest Way to Clean a Fish Tank

Having fish is fun, but not when you have to periodically replace the water. Make your job easy with the help of some old pantyhose and a wet/dry shop vac. Place two or three layers of pantyhose over the nozzle of the hose and secure it with a rubber band. Remove your fish to a safe location, then stick the hose in the tank and start sucking. The dirty water will find its way into the vacuum, but the rocks won't make it through the nylon.

Ant Problem Solved

Petroleum jelly will keep ants out of a pet food dish. Simply rub a small amount on the rim around the bottom of bowl.

Get Rid of Litter Box Odor

If your cat's litter box smells like, well, a litter box, rinse it out and add a half-inch of white vinegar in the box. Let it stand for half an hour, then swish it around, rinse, and dry the box.

Keep Small Animals Calm

If you have a rabbit, guinea pig, hamster, or other small pet who lives in a cage, try refilling his water dish by sticking a turkey baster through the bars. It will allow you to give him something fresh to drink without scaring him by opening the door and moving things around.

Easier Than a Bath

Washing a pet can sure be a hassle—especially if it's a cat. Save yourself the trouble (and several scratches) by using cornstarch instead. Sprinkle cornstarch on your pet's coat, then work it into his hair. It will soak up grease and odors, and even fluff up his fur.

How to Discipline a Cat

Unfortunately, cats rarely respond when you tell them "no." So to make sure they have a reason to not repeat bad behavior, spray them in the face with water from a spray bottle when you catch them being bad. If this doesn't work, try spraying them with air from a compressed air can (usually used to clean electronics and computer keyboards). Cats hate the feeling of air on their faces.

⬤ Who Knew?

It seems like a silly habit of guilty "dog parents," but it's true: Leaving the TV or radio on low in the room next to your pup will keep him calm while you're away.

Scaredy Cats

All cats will run and hide if they hear a loud noise, but some cats seem particularly flighty. If your overly anxious cat runs when she hears regularly occurring noises like shut doors, loud steps, or even sound effects from the TV, here's how to help. Begin by tapping a wooden spoon very gently against or pot or pan while he is eating. Make sure the sound is loud enough that he notices, but not so loud that he gets scared. After you've done this for a couple of days, you can begin slowly increasing how loudly you tap. Once your quiet tap is a loud bang and your cat is still calm, change the surface you're tapping to wood, or try to incorporate a sound that has easily spooked him in the past—just make sure to begin quietly and work your way up again. Finally, begin introducing these sounds into your cat's daily life. Eventually he won't even notice that clap of thunder from outside.

Get Groomed for Less

The busiest days at the pet groomer's are Friday, Saturday, Sunday, and Monday. Find a groomer who offers discounts on Tuesdays through Thursdays, or ask your groomer if she will offer you a discount for coming midweek.

Come Boy, Come!

If your dog simply won't come when called, it might be time to start from scratch. Once a dog has decided that a word doesn't mean anything to him, it's much harder to make him understand that "come" means "come to me," not "do whatever you want." Pick a different word like "here" or "move," and begin your dog's training over again by standing several feet away, saying your new word, and offering scraps of food when he obeys. Your friends at the dog park might think it's weird when you shout, "Draw nigh, Rover!" but it's way better than having him run the other way.

Pacify a Chewing Puppy

If your new puppy isn't adorable enough to make up for all those chair and table legs he's been chewing, head to your local vitamin or health food store and ask for some clove oil. Oil of cloves smells great to us but terrible to dogs. Wipe it on the legs of anything wooden and he'll stay away.

Pleasant-Smelling Litter

Don't spend extra money on scented cat litter. To keep cat litter fresh-smelling, simply mix a bit of baby powder into clean litter.

—Peter and Sarah Bailey, Fitchburg, MA

Lazy Lizards

If you have a lizard, you know how much they like to relax! But did you know that one of their favorite resting places is a hammock? Make one yourself by stringing up an old piece of cloth between two items in your lizard's cage, and you'll soon seem him taking a nap in style.

Lost Your Snake?

If you have a pet snake who's gotten away, help yourself find him with a little aluminum foil. Place the foil around the room and in potential hiding places. When your snake is done lying low, you'll be able to hear him slithering across the foil.

CHAPTER 8

Sanity-Saving Kid Tips

Numb the "Ick" of Taking Medicine

Nothing's worse than having to give a sick child medicine he can't stand the taste of. To make things a little easier, have him suck on a popsicle for a few minutes before taking the medicine. The popsicle will not only act as an incentive, it will numb his taste buds a bit, making the medicine easier to swallow.

Good Backpack Fix

If your child tears his backpack, there's no need to buy a new one. Just thread some floss onto a needle with a large eye, and use that to sew up the hole. It's sturdier than regular thread and will hold up well.

Don't Drop the Cup

If your children, like our youngest, have graduated past the sippy cup stage but still have problems getting a grip on "grown up" glasses, try putting five or six small rubber bands around the glass. That'll help them hold on, which means fewer spills for you to clean up.

● Who Knew? CLASSIC TIP

To keep melting ice cream from leaking out of the bottom of an ice cream cone, just drop a couple of mini marshmallows at the bottom before topping with ice cream. The marshmallows will act as a delicious plug.

Journey of 1,000 Untied Shoes

We carry emergency ChapStick around with us for the boys, but for their shoes, not their lips. A little rubbed on the laces around the knot keeps them in place, and means we get from the car to the rink (or football field, or school) in about half the time it would otherwise take.

Cheap Child-Proofing

Use a shower curtain ring to keep a toddler out of your cabinets. Just run the ring through two handles that are close by and latch.

—*Randy Rodriguez, Waxahachie, TX*

Rolling in Dough

Don't spend money on store-bought Play-Doh; make your own at home instead with the following ingredients: 2 cups flour, 2 cups water, 1 cup salt, 2 tablespoons vegetable oil, 1 tablespoon cream of tartar, and the food coloring of your choice. Combine the ingredients in a large saucepan and stir continuously over medium heat until a solid ball forms. Remove it from the heat, knead it until all the lumps are out, and you should end up with a finished product nearly identical to the real thing. Make sure to store it in a completely airtight container; you might even want to dab a few drops of water on the underside of the container lid before sealing it.

Bath Entertainment

For more fun at bath time, take all those little plastic toys your kids have gotten from vending machines and goody bags, and place one or two in each hole of a muffin tin. Then fill the tin with water and freeze. When it's time for a bath, pop one out and throw it in the tub. Your toddler will love watching it melt in their hands and then having a toy to play with.

Frozen Juice Box

When packing a sack lunch for your child, place a juice box in the freezer the night before and place it in the lunch bag while still frozen the next morning. It'll help keep the lunch cool, and as an extra bonus, the juice will be nice and cold when your child finally gets around to drinking it at lunchtime.

—Adriana S., Youngstown, OH

Make Your Kid Stand Out

If you know you're going to a crowded place, make sure to dress your children in bright colors so you can easily spot them. To make them stick out even more, buy each kid a cheap helium balloon and tie it around their wrist. Kids love balloons, and so will you when you realize you can see them from a mile away at the mall.

Who Knew?

Your teen or preteen may be more stressed than you think. According to an American Psychological Society survey, only 2–5 percent of parents said their child was highly stressed, while 14 percent of preteens and 28 percent of teens said they were.

Toy Parachutes

Make an old action figure fun again by creating a mini parachute. First, cut out a square from a plastic sandwich bag. Poke a hole in each corner, then thread a foot-long piece of dental floss through the hole, tying a knot at the end so the floss can't be pulled back through. Once you've threaded a piece of floss through each hole, tie their other ends around the arms or—dare we say it—the neck of the figurine. Now you're ready to launch.

Get the Dents Out of a Ping-Pong Ball

The sound of ping-pong balls being paddled all over the basement is worth every minute of keeping your kids busy! Unfortunately, they finally emerge from downstairs with tons of dented balls. To get the balls round again, fill a jar to the brim with warm water, then place the balls inside and close the lid so that they're submerged. In 20 minutes or less, the water's pressure will make them pop back into place.

Instant Indexing

Our kids, like many, are incorrigible procrastinators when it comes to schoolwork. When they need index cards at a moment's notice, however, a late-night trip to the store is unnecessary. Simply take an ordinary paper plate and measure out a 3-by-5-inch or 4-by-6-inch rectangle. Cut it out and use the first card as a stencil for the rest.

—Nathaniel M.

Interesting Art Project

Get creative with watercolors and candles—but perhaps not in the way you think. Give your child a white tapered candle and have her "draw" a picture on a piece of paper. She won't be able to see the drawing, of course, until she adds a little watercolor to the paper—and the picture will come to life. This is an especially good activity for two kids. Let them write "secret messages" to each other, then exchange the papers, apply some watercolors, and see what happens.

Teacher Appreciation

It can be a struggle to find the right gifts for teachers, and yet it's not hard when you think along the lines of something that will enhance their classrooms. Here are some ideas: books, magazine subscriptions, educational games, posters of material they teach (the solar system or animal kingdom, for example), art supplies, easy-to-care-for plants, and gift certificates to bookstores. Many teachers use their own money for classroom supplies, so this kind of gift will be especially gratifying.

Make Your Swing Set Safer

You've just bought your kids a new swing set, and you're peering out the window just waiting for one of them to fall off. Fear no more! Place carpet remnants or free carpet samples from a local store underneath the swings for extra padding. They'll kill the grass underneath, but your kids would have done that anyway.

● Who Knew? CLASSIC TIP

Here's a great recipe for homemade bubble solution: 1 tablespoon glycerin, 2 tablespoons powdered laundry detergent, and 1 cup warm water (add a couple of drops of food coloring for colored bubbles). Use a wire hanger to make your own bubble blowing device, or stick a straw into the mixture and blow into it to create tiny bubbles that will float onto the surface and dissipate.

Make Ripping off Band-Aids Painless

Before removing a bandage from your child's skin, douse the area with baby oil. The baby oil will soak into the bandage and make it easy to remove without hurting her.

Eat Those Veggies!

If your child never wants to eat his vegetables at dinnertime, try putting out a plate of raw veggies like carrots, celery, and broccoli right before dinner. Since he'll be hungry (and probably pestering you in the kitchen), it will be more likely that he'll succumb to this healthy snack.

—*Terry Gallo, Breeding, KY*

Swap Out Your Toys

When you notice your kids getting bored with a toy (and they always do), don't buy them a new one. Instead, stash the disfavored toys away in a bag or box. Once you have several toys, swap with a friend for toys her kids have gotten sick of. Not only will you save money, you'll save on the clutter of continually purchasing new playthings for your kids.

Do It Yourself

Organized activities for your kids are great, but the expense of enrolling them can take a toll. Instead of paying for a pricey arts and crafts class, for example, simply search online for the necessary information and hold the "class" yourself. Instead of paying for swimming lessons, just take your kids to a relative's pool or a public pool. Spending on beginner-level instruction is often a waste, but if your child shows an aptitude for a certain activity or sport, *then* you can spend that money on more advanced instruction. If you have to cut down on activities or sports they're already involved in, ask your children if there are any they don't really like. You might find they're just playing soccer, for instance, because their friends are on the team.

Make Your Own Baby Toy

Here's a free, soft toy for your wee one: an old sock! Stuff it with old pantyhose, fiber fill, or even more old socks, then sew it shut to make a soft ball. Sure, it might not look as impressive as the $10 ones you'd buy at a toy store, but your baby won't know the difference!

Getting Rid of Lice Naturally

Nothing strikes fear in the hearts of parents like the words "lice outbreak." The harsh chemicals that are used to fight lice are almost as bad as the lice themselves. Luckily, there is a cheap, natural alternative, and it's as close as your refrigerator. Massage a liberal amount of mayonnaise into your child's scalp, then cover with a shower cap or towel and let it sit as long as possible (overnight is best—but with complaining kids you might have to settle for letting it sit through two movies and a round of video games). Then shampoo as usual, using a fine-toothed comb to snag any remaining lice bodies. To make sure you killed any eggs, repeat this procedure in one week.

Video Game Strategy

If your kids love video games, try to buy games that can be played over and over (such as puzzle games) rather than ones that aren't fun once you "win" them—you'll go a lot longer before you start hearing requests to buy a new game! When you finally do cave, make sure to buy used games whenever possible.

Homemade Glitter

If your kids need glitter in an emergency (and who hasn't had a glitter emergency?), you can make your own at home. Just take a cup of salt, add 10–15 drops of your favorite food coloring, and mix it thoroughly. Microwave on high for 2–3 minutes, then spread it out on a sheet of nonstick foil or wax paper to dry. If you don't use it all right away, make sure to store it in an airtight container.

Rainy-Day Shaker

Short of shaking vitamin bottles, this might be the easiest instrument a human can make. Put dry beans between two paper plates, then tape the plates together. Decorate with markers, crayons, sequins, or anything else you have on hand. Your kids will love creating rhythms with their new toys.

Make Your Own Ceramics

When they were younger, our kids always loved making ceramic objects out of clay. You don't need to sign them up for an art class, either: the clay is easy to make at home. Thoroughly mix the following ingredients in a bowl: 4 cups flour, 1½ cups salt, ¾ cup white glue, 1½ teaspoons lemon juice, and 1½ cups water. When you've got it all mixed together, you should end up with a pliable clay that can be either sculpted into different shapes or sliced with cookie cutters. When your kids are done molding the clay, let their creations sit overnight, allowing them to harden and air-dry. Then they can apply paint and/or glaze.

Exercise Weights as a Balancing Act

If your stroller has become unbalanced thanks to the hundreds of shopping bags you have hanging from the handles, use arm and ankle weights that are used for exercise to more evenly distribute the weight. Attach the weights (which come with Velcro) to the bars of the stroller right above its front wheels. Now when your child jumps out, you won't end up with your bags all over the sidewalk.

—*Donna Inklovich, Calumet City, IL*

Make Slides More Fun

If your kids have tired of that expensive playground set you bought them, make the slide even more fun by giving them each a large piece of wax paper. If they sit on the paper as they're going down the slide, they'll move much faster, and they'll never call it boring again (or at least not for a few weeks).

Homemade Swords

Here's a quick, homemade toy that will keep your kids busy for hours, if not days: Take a large piece of corrugated cardboard and cut it in the shape of a sword (use two pieces and tape them together, if necessary). Wrap the handle with electrical tape and the "blade" with duct tape. Your kids can practice their fencing skills against each other, and since they're playing with cardboard you won't have to worry about them getting hurt.

Take Off Temp Tats

There's nothing kids love more than temporary tattoos—until they decide they hate them. To easily remove a temp tat before it rubs off itself, dab some cold cream on the area, then wipe it off with a washcloth.

Getting Pen Marks Off Skin

Our kids drive us crazy by writing notes and drawing all over their hands (thankfully not answers for tests, as far as we know). The fastest way to get them ready for company: Green or black tea bags. You use the actual wet bag itself to dab at the stains, once you're done brewing a cup with it.

Who Knew? CLASSIC TIP

If you've got kids who never seem to know when enough is enough, add water to your hand soap. Your hands will get just as clean, but the soap will last longer! You can also find foaming soap dispensers at a lot of stores, which are also good for keeping the amount of soap you use to the minimum you need.

Cheap Fun That Lasts for Hours

If your young child likes building toys but you don't want to pay for expensive blocks, buy plastic cups in several different colors and use those instead. They're extremely cheap and just as fun to knock down!

Making Puppets

For a fun craft project, have your children make paper lunch bags into puppets. All you have to do is turn the bag upside down, then draw a face on what would be the bottom of the bag. Draw the mouth so that it's half on the bottom, half on the bag itself—that way, when someone puts their hand inside, they can open and close "the mouth." Give your kids extras from your sewing box such as trim, fabric scraps, and buttons to embellish the puppets.

Temper Tantrums Solved

When I'm taking trips with my children, I always bring along a bottle of bubbles. If (and when) a tantrum hits, I take out the bubbles and start blowing. This distracts them enough so that they calm down and I can actually speak to them! By handling over the wand and letting them help, I not only reward them for stopping the screaming, but it allows them to take deep breaths and become even more relaxed.

—Mary Bowers, Salt Lake City, UT

Perfect Bottle Holder

We're a little embarrassed to admit this, but when our boys were young we had the perfect holder for extra bottles for the babysitter: an old six-pack container. If you don't think it's funny to have "Heineken" written on the side, cover with contact paper, wrapping paper, or stickers. Your baby won't know the difference, and you'll make sure to leave with as many bottles as you came with.

Goodbye to Popsicle Drips

Keep messy melting popsicles from getting all over your kids' hands (and the floor) by poking the stick-end of the popsicle through a coffee filter before you hand it over. The filter will act like a bowl, catching any drips.

Popcorn, Without the Dishes

If you're serving popcorn to the kids but don't want to wash a bunch of bowls afterward, consider using coffee filters as disposable bowls.

Kids' Shoelaces Coming Untied?

If your children's shoelaces (or your own) often come untied, you may be tying them wrong. Bows that we tie with shoelaces work by using a square knot—and you may remember the adage "right over left, left over right, that's what makes a square knot nice and tight." Unfortunately, most of us do what's easiest for our hands—and that's tying both the beginning knot and the bow "right over left." If you look down at the shoes and the loops from the bows are pointing toward you rather than laying flat across the shoes from left to right, then you aren't tying a square knot properly! To fix this, simply reverse the way that you tie the beginning knot for your bow. In other words, if you normally cross the right shoelace over the left at the beginning, switch so that you're crossing left over right. It might take your hands a while to get used to it, but your bows will stay so well you won't even need to double-knot them.

Who Knew?

In a survey by the Early Childhood Investment Corporation, parents cited simply being with their children as the best part about parenting, and discipline as the worst part of parenting.

It's Camp Time

The best time to sign your kids up for camp is right after camp has ended. Many camps allow you to pay in advance for the next summer and save 5–10 percent. Ask at your camp as you're picking your kids up this year!

CHAPTER 9

Automotive Advice

Make the Most of That Expensive Gas!

With gas prices as high as they are, it's worth it to try to use the least amount of gas possible when driving. Here are some tips to get the most out of your mileage.

+ Keep your tires inflated. It's much harder for your engine to get your car to move when your tires are even a little flat. Invest in a gauge, and make sure to keep them as inflated as possible without over-inflating.

+ Go manual. If you're buying a new car and can't afford a hybrid, consider going with a stick-shift rather than automatic. Manually changing gears saves energy because your car is only using as much energy as it needs to—it's never in a higher gear when it shouldn't be. Being able to coast down hills also saves you tons.

+ Stay under the speed limit. Your car will begin to lose fuel efficiency once it gets over 60 mph. One of the easiest ways to save money on gas is to always go the speed limit—and it's safer, too.

+ Change your oil regularly. As oil ages, it gets thicker and harder to push through the engine, causing more energy to be used. By changing your oil regularly you'll make sure you get the best fuel economy possible.

+ Remove excess weight. Take anything heavy out of your trunk or back seat that doesn't need to be there (kids don't count). An extra 100 pounds in your car can decrease your miles per gallon by 2 percent.

- ✦ Pick the best route. Stopping and starting and going up hills will cause you to use more gas. Consider taking a route that will allow you to make fewer adjustments as you are driving, even if it takes a little longer.

- ✦ Roll up your windows on the highway. Having the wind streaming through your hair might be fun, but it increases drag on the car and makes it take more energy to run. In this case, it's actually usually cheaper to run the AC.

- ✦ Group your errands. Obviously, if you're driving less distance by not traveling from home each time you'll save on gas, but the Department of Energy also reports that several short trips beginning from a cold start use almost twice as much energy as a single trip of the same length. Keep your engine warm and your car won't have to work as hard.

● Who Knew? CLASSIC TIP

If your windshield wipers are smearing your windshield while they work, wipe the blades with rubbing alcohol.

Educate Yourself Before You Buy

After gas, one of the biggest costs associated with having a car is from the interest you pay on the loan. Before you go buy a car, get a loan in place first—the financing the car dealership will offer most likely won't have a rate that is as good. Know your credit rating, and check with your employer's credit union or look online for deals on car loans. A good place to begin is a page that lets you compare rates and find out information on car loans. One site we like is BankRate.com. Click on "Auto" from the homepage.

Easily Remove Window Frost

Instead of scraping away frost from your car's windows and windshield, spray them with rubbing alcohol when you go out to start up your car. By the time you come back to drive, the frost will easily wipe away.

Keep Car Doors from Freezing

It's hard enough having to dig out your driveway and scrape off your car after a snowstorm. Save yourself the trouble of worrying about car doors freezing closed by spraying WD-40 in the lining. Once in the beginning of the winter should do it.

Condition Your Car

After washing your car, give it a second round just like you would your head—use hair conditioner! You might think we're crazy, but applying conditioner, leaving for five minutes, and then rinsing it off will give your car a just-waxed shine. As an added bonus, it will more effectively repel water!

For Supple Leather

If you car has leather seats, regularly apply a thin layer of baby oil to the leather and let it dry. This will prevent your seats from drying out and cracking.

Put the Brakes On

If an advertised price for fixing your brakes seems too good to be true, it is. Garages can't make a profit on $100 brake jobs, so rest assured that these places are either doing shoddy work, or are counting on sticking you with hidden extra costs. Whenever you get your brakes done, make sure to ask beforehand for an estimate of the final total cost, including all labor fees and other extra charges.

Get the Whole Part

Sometimes unethical mechanics will use cheap or knockoff parts—they're a lot more prevalent than you might think—and try to pass them off as the real thing. Whenever you're having parts replaced, make sure to insist on a brand-name part and ask to see the box it came in as proof.

Transmission A-OK

If you're not an automotive expert, you should be aware that small metal shavings in a transmission pan are a perfectly normal sign of usage. If a garage shows you a pan like this and uses it to pressure you into a new transmission, walk away. They're likely not being honest with you.

—*J.D. Morse*

● Who Knew?

Only 5 percent of cars actually run better on premium gas as opposed to regular. Make sure to check your owner's manual to see what it recommends.

Don't Blow Off a Chipped Windshield

Never, ever ignore a chip in your windshield—get it fixed right away. A chip will often eventually grow into a crack, which will raise your costs from about $100 for a chip repair to $1,000 or more for a full windshield replacement. There are even companies that will repair the chip right there in your driveway; just do a Google search for something like "mobile windshield repair" near your home.

Turn a Visor Into an Organizer

Turn your car's visor into a handy place to store paper and other flat items by using rubber bands. Wrap several rubber bands snugly around the visor, then slip papers, CDs, or anything else under the rubber bands.

Covered in Tar?

You took a trip over some recently tarred roads, and now your bumper is covered in black spots. Get rid of tar with an unexpected item from your fridge—mayonnaise. Wipe on, wait five minutes, then easily wipe off both the mayo and the tar.

Take Two Aspirin for Yourself, Then Two for Your Car

If your car battery has died and you don't have jumper cables, don't get a headache just yet. First, try dropping a couple of aspirin tablets into the battery. The acid in the aspirin can provide it with just enough charge to get you to the nearest service station.

Free Floor Mats

If your car's floor mats need to be replaced, consider going to a carpet store and finding some samples to use instead. You'll always be able to find samples that are gray or another color to match your car, and they're free!

If your car gets stuck in an icy patch and your wheels aren't getting any traction, help free it by using your car's floor mats. Take them out and place under the tires, then drive to a safe place, retrieve the mats, and be on your way.

Time to Remove Those Parking Stickers

If your windshield is covered with parking permits and inspection stickers from years gone by, you'll love this tip. Pour nail polish remover over the decals until they're soaked. Then scrape with a razor blade and they'll come off cleanly in seconds.

Get Rid of Grease Stains

If your driveway or garage floor has become an easy place to do some Rorschach testing thanks to the grease, oil, and transmission fluid stains all over the place, take heart—clean concrete is only 10 minutes away. Spray any stained areas with oven cleaner, then let sit for 10 minutes. Rinse off with a hose and the stains will disappear.

Wait Till Monday

A mechanic friend (who shall remain nameless!) once confessed to us that he does his worst work on Fridays, because he tends to rush the job to get ready for the weekend. If it can wait, take your car in on Monday, when it will get the time it deserves.

Organize Your Pickup

Sick of things rattling around your truck bed? Divide it into several compartments for storage by using spring-loaded shower curtain rods. Brace the rods against the sides of your truck bed and each other. They'll keep larger items from shifting during flight.

Put 'Em to Work!

Want to know how to never have to pay for a car wash again? Make the kids do it! All you need is a bucket, a few squirts of car-washing detergent, and some sponges. Then put the kids in their swimsuits and get out the hose. Kids will love the water and suds, your car will get clean, and they'll be tired by bedtime!

Clean a Spot With Cat Litter

If your car has leaked oil in your garage, easily clean it up by applying some cat litter to the area (preferably the non-scoopable kind). Its super-absorbing properties will make the stain disappear in a day.

Make Your Battery Last Longer

Epsom salts can extend the life of your car battery. Just dissolve an ounce of Epsom salts in 1½ cups warm, distilled water and fill each battery cell.

Patch Up Your Upholstery

Oh no, your kids tore a hole in your car's seat. (Okay, so it wasn't the kids, it was you.) Instead of getting an expensive upholstery replacement, use an iron-on patch instead. Hold the patch in place with a few straight pins while you iron. If you don't have a long enough extension cord to bring the iron into your car, set the iron on one setting higher than the directions on the patch recommend. When it heats up, unplug it and quickly bring it out to the car.

Remove the Rack

We bought a mini-van that has a luggage rack, but we find that we almost never use it unless we're on a long vacation. If that applies to you, too, then you should remove the rack until you actually need it. Driving with the rack on top increases wind drag and helps kill your gas mileage. Removing it can be a real money-saver.

—*Francesca R., Portland, OR*

Find the Cheapest Gas

If you're on the road and know you're going to need gas soon, have the person in your passenger seat send a text message to gas@fuelgo.com. Just type your zip code as the body of the message, and they'll text you back with the lowest fuel prices in your area.

Who Knew?

All told, Americans drive over 245 billion miles per month.

It's Clean-Up Time

After working on your car, easily clean grease and oil off your hands by rubbing a bit of baby oil between them, then washing as usual with soap and water.

Tip for Car Buyers

If you're in the market for a new car, make sure you test drive it at night. Driving in the dark will give you an opportunity to make sure its lights work, and will draw your attention inward toward its dash, making sure you take in all of its interior features and whether or not you like them.

Buy a Program Car

Program cars are cars that are driven by people who work at a car dealership, and are sold after they reach 100,000 miles. Since it's often car mechanics themselves who drive these cars, they're always kept in good shape. Ask your local dealerships if they're selling their program cars and you can save big.

Keep Your Battery Clean

To prevent your car's battery from corroding, wipe down the battery posts with petroleum jelly once every couple of months.

Is It Time to Change Your Car's Air Filter?

A clean air filter can improve your car's mileage by up to 10 percent, so make sure yours is replaced regularly. Your car's filter should be changed at least every 8,000 miles, but if you live in a sandy or highly polluted area, you should change it more often. A good rule of thumb is to simply have it changed when you get your oil changed.

Know What's Under Warranty

Did you know that by law, emissions controls for your vehicle have an eight-year/80,000-mile warranty? When purchasing new parts for your car, check with the manufacturer to make sure you can't get them for free first.

Muffle a Motorcycle

If your motorcycle is too loud (yes, there is such a thing), stick a number-3 grade steel wool pad into the muffler.

—*Jason Selway, Blacksburg, WV*

Get Your Old Parts Back

When visiting a mechanic to have a part replaced, always ask for the worn/damaged part back. This way, you'll be sure it was actually replaced and that you're not getting a bum deal.

Don't Wait Until Empty

You should always fill up your gas tank before it dips below a quarter of a tank. Always having a little bit of fuel will ensure your car's fuel injection system stays healthy.

Removing Bumper Stickers

We hate to break it to you, but John Kerry and John McCain lost their elections. Get those old bumper stickers off and bring your car up to date. Rub cold cream on the stickers and wait 10 minutes. Then say goodbye to your former favorite candidate and peel the bumper stickers right off.

When Accidents Happen

Been involved in an accident? The best thing to do is to leave the vehicles where they are and call the police. Whether anyone is ticketed or not, your insurance company will usually require you to complete a police report, which will help them decide which party is to blame. But if the damage is minor and you either don't have time to call the police or have to move your car out of traffic, you should document what happened. Use your cell phone's camera to take as many pictures possible of the accident, so you can prove what happened later.

Impromptu Shovel

Stuck in the mud or sand with no way to dig yourself out? A shovel may be closer than you think. Just detach your hubcap and use it instead.

Cleaning Off Break Dust

To remove break dust—that fine, black powder—from your car's tires, spray on a bit of cooking spray or vegetable oil, then wipe right off.

The Perfect Parking Spot

If you have as much stuff stacked up in your garage as we do, you'll love this tip for making sure you don't run into it when you pull in. First, drill a hole through the middle of a tennis ball, then run a long piece of clothesline through it and knot the end so it won't pull through. Safely and successfully park your car in its ideal garage location, then tie the other end of the clothesline to the rafters of your garage so that the ball is hitting your windshield. Next time you pull in, you'll know when to stop without having to slowly inch your way in.

—Bill B., Davenport, IA

Stop Ice Before It Starts

To keep your car's door locks safe from ice during the cold winter months, place a refrigerator magnet over the lock. You can even take an old magnet (that 2008 calendar from a local realtor, perhaps) and cut it into pieces that fit perfectly.

It Pays to Restart Your Engine

If you are waiting for longer than 30 seconds in your car, turn off the engine. You use more fuel idling after 30 seconds than you use to restart your car.

Who Knew?

Half of respondents in a 2009 *Consumer Reports* survey said that they need a new car, but are putting off buying one. Most cited financial trouble as the reason.

Is Your Child Safe?

Nothing is more important than the safety of your child, so make sure your car seat has been installed properly. If you've read the directions a hundred times and are still unsure, head over to your local police station. Most police officers are trained on how to properly install a car seat, and will be happy to check yours to make sure you've done the job correctly.

CHAPTER 10

Don't Sweat it! Home Repair

Do It Yourself

Before you call a repairman, try basic household fix-its yourself by getting a general manual, looking for information online, or simply following the instructions that come with replacement parts like doorknobs and faucets. You'll be surprised how many of these repairs are easy enough for you to do yourself.

Wooden Dent Removal

As long as the wood hasn't broken apart underneath, you may be able to fix dents in wooden floors or furniture. Here's how: Run a rag under warm water and wring it out, then place it on top of the dent. Apply an iron set on medium heat to the rag until the rag dries out. Repeat this process until your dent is gone.

Easy Way to Smooth Caulk

Caulking can be tricky business—it's hard to get perfect lines, but if you try smoothing them down with your finger, it sticks, creating an even uglier sight. When you need to smooth down caulk, try using an ice cube instead. The cold will help set the line, and it won't stick to the ice.

● Who Knew? CLASSIC TIP

When painting steps, paint every other one as you work your way down. When those are dry, go back and paint the rest. This way, you'll still be able to use the stairs while your paint is drying (as long as your careful!).

Silence Squeaky Faucets

If the handles of your sink shriek when you turn them, try this simple fix. Unscrew the handles and rub petroleum jelly on all the threads. The jelly will keep them lubricated and (hopefully) squeak-free.

Clean Up a Spill With a Straw

You're trying to make a repair in a drawer or somewhere else with a tight corner, and you keep dripping glue that's nearly impossible to wipe up. Solve your problem by folding a drinking straw in half. The v shape is perfect for getting into tiny corners and crevices.

Untangle Twine

If you're working with a ball of twine that keeps getting tangled, find two baskets and overturn one to make a cage. Place the ball inside and run the end of the string through the cage. The ball will be caught inside while the string unspools freely.

Unhelpful Holes?

If a hole in your wall (or whatever else you're working on) is too stripped to hold a screw, dab some glue on a tiny piece of steel wool (which can be cut with scissors) and stuff it into the hole. Once the glue dries, you can screw in your screw without a problem.

—Jian Liu, Charlotte, NC

Patch It Up

To make a simple putty for quick patches, combine a tablespoon of salt with a tablespoon of powdered starch. Mix them together with just enough water to make a paste. Apply while still wet.

Rid of Rust

If you're trying to keep something rust-proof, here's a solution you can make. Combine two cups petroleum jelly and half a cup of lanolin in a microwave-safe bowl and heat the mixture until it melts together. Stir frequently, and make sure to apply to the rust-prone item while the mixture is still warm. Remember, don't wipe it off; allow the paste to dry on the item.

Pipe Down, Pipes

If your water pipes are banging and pounding, you may be able to get rid of the noise without paying for a plumber to visit. First, turn off your main water valve, which is usually located near the water meter. Turn on all your water faucets, set them to cold, and let them drain until dry. Then close them again. Turn your main valve back on, then turn each faucet back on as well. After making spitting and coughing noises for a few moments, they should now flow freely with no noise coming from the pipes.

Beware the Caulk

When caulking the edges of your bathtub, keep in mind that the caulking will often expand and crack the first time you fill the tub with hot water. To combat this, fill the tub with water *first*, then caulk away.

Who Knew? CLASSIC TIP

Sanding wood and want to know if it's completely smooth? Slip an old nylon stocking over your hand and run it over the wood. If there's a rough spot, the nylon will snag.

Sandpaper Your Ladder

Most stepladders are perfectly safe, of course, but if you want to amp up the non-skid surface of the rungs, there's an easy way to do it. Just paint the steps of the ladder and, before it dries, sprinkle fine-grained sand on top. The sand will stick to the ladder and create a sandpaper-like surface.

Crack Goes the Ceiling

If you have a crack in your ceiling but you can't quite afford to re-plaster yet, you can fake it with some readily available household supplies. Take one part white glue and one part baking soda, mix them together thoroughly, and then dab the paste onto the crack using your fingers, a Q-tip, or similar object. If your ceiling isn't white, you can try mixing different food colorings into the paste until you get exactly the right shade.

Fill a Hole in Your Vinyl Floor

If there's a small hole in your vinyl floor, here's how to patch it up without anyone noticing the spot. Find a tile that is the same color, or better yet, one that you've saved for a replacement. Make some vinyl shavings from the tile using a cheese grater, then mix them with a small amount of clear nail polish. Dab the nail polish into the hole and let dry. Voilà! Your floor is like new again.

Painting?

Even if you clean your paintbrush thoroughly, the bristles are likely to be stiff after they dry. Keep them soft and flexible with ordinary hair conditioner. Just add a tablespoon of conditioner to a pint of warm water, and after cleaning the brush, dip it in the solution for a few minutes.

Paint Tray Problem Solved

The easiest way to clean a paint tray after you're done rolling on paint in a room is to never get it dirty in the first place! Instead of using plastic wrap or foil, put the paint tray in a plastic bag and pour the paint on top. Once you're done, simply turn the bag inside out and throw away.

Keep Drips Away

Maybe we're just messy painters, but when we paint a room that rim around the paint can is never a big enough trough to catch the paint that has slopped over the edge—eventually it fills up and runs down the can. To solve this problem, we make several holes in the bottom of the rim with a small nail and hammer. Now the paint drips back into the can rather than running down the side.

A Different Way to Get Rid of Excess Paint

Another way to make painting neater is to wrap a wide rubber band around your open paint can from top to bottom. The rubber band will run right over the opening to the can, and you can use it to wipe the excess paint from your brush instead of the edge of the can. Then when you're done painting, wrap the band around the paint can the other way, at the exact level that the paint is at inside. That way, you won't have to open the can to see how much paint is left.

Paint Odor Remover

To get rid of that overwhelming paint odor after you've redone a room, place a bowl or two of ammonia, vinegar, or onion slices in the room. They will absorb the smell of the paint.

Finding Imperfections

Filling and sanding every hole in the wall before you paint can be enough of a pain, but sometimes it's hard to find every crack, hole, and imperfection. Make your job easier by turning off the lights in a room, then slowly running a flashlight over the entire surface of the wall. The light will cast different shadows in these areas, making them easier to see than in the daylight.

Warm Your Paint

Did you know that enamel paint spreads more smoothly when it's warm? To get it up to a higher temperature, place it in a warm bath before you use it.

Brush-Shopping Secret

We'll usually tell you to go for the cheapest option, but when it comes to paint brushes, quality matters. To make sure you're buying a high-quality brush, look at the tips of the bristles. If they have a lot of split ends, they'll spread paint more evenly.

Who Knew? CLASSIC TIP

The fastest way we've found to clean a paintbrush is in a solution of ½ cup liquid fabric softener and 1 gallon of warm water. Stick the brush in a bucket of this solution, then swirl it vigorously for 20 seconds.

Wall Hole Solution

Before spackling small holes in your wall caused by nails, first cut a Q-tip in half and insert in the hole, stick end first. Then spackle as you normally would. This will completely fill the hole and make sure you won't have to go back for a second pass.

Make Your Door Stop Sticking

Your bedroom door has expanded, and realigning the hinges didn't work. Instead of taking the entire door down to sand the bottom, try this trick instead. Place enough newspaper under the door until it can just barely close on top of them. Then tape a piece of coarse sandpaper on top of the newspaper, and open and close the door until it glides over the floor without a noise.

Stud Finder Substitution

Looking for a stud and don't have a stud finder? Use an electric razor instead. Most razors will change slightly in tone when going over a stud in the wall.

Prevent Leaks With Floss

Instead of using expensive Teflon tape to preventing leaking between pipes and other parts that screw together, just use dental floss. Wrap the floss around the item's threads and you'll have a tight connection.

Screwy Screws

If you're having trouble with your screws falling off your screwdriver as you're trying to get them into the wall, first poke the screw through a piece of plastic wrap. Hold on to the wrap while you're screwing, then pull it away when you're finished.

Removing Old Wallpaper

Putting up new wallpaper? Here's a great trick to quickly and easily get rid of the old stuff. First, score the paper with a utility knife by cutting slashes through several parts of the paper. Then, dab on a mixture of half water and half liquid fabric softener. Leave on for 10–15 minutes, then watch your old wallpaper peel right off.

—*Lora Boudinot, Woodridge, IL*

Make Hanging Wallpaper Easier

Take your wallpaper out of its roll a few days before you hang it and re-roll it the opposite way. This will make it less curly and easier to hang.

A Better Fix for Wallpaper

If your wallpaper needs a fix-up in a small area, don't use scissors to cut off the replacement pieces. Instead, tear if off with your hands. The ragged edges of the new piece will blend in better than a straight edge.

A Home for Your Soldering Iron

If you regularly use a soldering iron, place several pieces of steel wool in an old coffee can. When you're done soldering, you can easily place the iron tip-down in the can to make sure you don't burn your work area.

Who Knew?

American homeowners spent an estimated $109.7 billion on home improvements in 2009.

Moving Large Items

Moving a large appliance or piece of furniture? Make your job easier by first placing carpet scraps (carpet-side down) under each corner—or do the same with flattened, waxy milk cartons. Either way, the piece of furniture will slide easily along your floor. If you're moving something in the kitchen (like a refrigerator), try squirting liquid dish detergent all over the floor. Watch your step, because it will be very slippery! So slippery, in fact, that your large appliance will just glide to the other side of the room.

How to Remove Superglue

Superglue's claim to fame is that it sticks to everything—and is impossible to get off. But if you accidentally get some on your work project or, heaven forbid, your fingers, there is one substance that can get your out of your "bind." Soak the corner of a soft cloth or paper towel in nail polish remover, then hold it on the area until the glue dissolves. Be aware, however, that nail polish remover will eat away at varnish and other finishes.

Impromptu Sawhorse

Need a sawhorse? Don't worry, it isn't time to cash in on that favor from a handy neighbor just yet. Instead, turn a sturdy ladder on its side. It works almost as well.

Replacement Cap

If you lose the tiny cap to your glue or caulk tube, stick a screw in there instead! We actually prefer long screws to caps, because they'll clean out the narrow area in the tube and make sure the glue or caulk doesn't harden between uses.

Repair a Scratched Floor

If you've scratched your floor while doing some home repairs, it's time to ask your kid for help. No, really! Go to his box of a million different-colored crayons, and pick the one that most closely matches the color of your floor. Cut off half the crayon and place it in an old take-out container (or something else you won't mind getting crayon all over). Melt the crayon in the microwave, then spread the hot wax into the crack. Wax your floor and it will look like new.

Fix a Squeaky Floor

If that squeak in your floor is about to drive you mad, you may be able to easily repair it yourself. Most squeaks are caused not by the floor boards themselves, but by the support beams that hold up your floor, called joists. If a joist gets too dry, it will shrink, causing the boards under your floor to rub against them rather than being held flush. To fix a squeak, first find the joist closest to it using a stud finder or a nail. Joists are usually located 16 inches apart and run lengthwise from the front to the back of your house. Once you find the joist, drill a number 8 wood screw through the floor into it. This should fix your problem.

A Handy Holder for Tape

If you use tape a lot near your work bench, make searching for rolls a thing of the past. Attach a toilet paper holder or a wall-mounted paper towel holder to the wall, and you have an easy holder for tape rolls.

Hold Screws More Tightly

If you're using a flat-head screwdriver and are having trouble keeping the screw on the end, try rubbing each side of the screwdriver with a piece of chalk. The chalk will increase the friction and give you a tighter hold.

—*Jim Dwyer, Gettysburg, SD*

Rein in Remodeling

If you're planning a big remodel of your home but don't want to spend a bundle, try to keep toilets and other major plumbing appliances like kitchen sinks where they are. These types of improvements can cost around $1,000 apiece, and could be a major portion of your renovation budget.

Add Marbles for Easy Painting

Before stirring paint, place a few old marbles in the can. They'll stir the paint so well you should just be able to give it a good shake to remix the paint before its next use. To make shaking and storing even easier, first empty the paint into a plastic jug with a funnel.

CHAPTER 11

Decorating Done Easily

Two Thumbs Up: Movie Poster Decorations

For fun wall decorations for kids' rooms or a family room, frame movie posters from your family's favorite movies. Try asking at video stores or movie theaters to see if you can have their posters when they are done with them. Often, they'll just give them to you for free. If you're looking for an older movie, you can also find them inexpensively on the internet. Just type in the name of the movie and the word "poster" into Google or another search engine. Another inexpensive decoration option is buying old magazines and hanging vintage ads and photo spreads in frames.

Glossy, Decorative Leaves

For an easy decorating project, gloss colorful autumn leaves. The whole family can collect them together and spread them out on newspaper inside. To gloss, combine equal parts milk and water and paint over the leaves or brush over with a clean rag. When the leaves are dry, use them to adorn indoor plants, fill a vase with them for an eye-catching centerpiece, spread them out on the mantle, or place them underneath candles to catch the drips.

Bargains for a Buck

Your local dollar store can be a boon for home decorating, even if you're not using the items for the purpose they were intended. A cheap, small plate can become a candle holder, while a teacup or bowl can be used as a pot for indoor plants.

—*Carol Ann Laplante, Omak, WA*

Suitable for Framing

Instead of spending tons of money on impressive, expensive frames, give your photos a personal touch. Buy the cheap frames at the store and repaint them yourself. Not only will they look almost as good as the expensive kind, but you can customize them to perfectly match your home decor.

Matching Not Necessary

You've probably noticed this at the restaurants you frequent, but it's becoming more and more acceptable nowadays—even hip—to eat your meals on vintage, mismatched chairs. Instead of spending a fortune on a dining-room set, go for the mismatched look and hunt for your chairs at thrift shops and used furniture stores.

Don't Discard Dingy Dressers

If your furniture is weathered or out of style, that's not necessarily a reason to replace it. There are plenty of ways to spruce up old dressers, chairs, and tables. Everybody loves quilts, so why not drape one over that old chair that needs reupholstering? You can also try using colorful fabrics on the fronts of nightstand and dresser drawers. Just get some scrap cloth from your last project or from a fabric store, and attach it to the dresser drawers with a staple gun. To have even more fun with it, we like to paint part of the piece and color-coordinate it with the cloth we're using.

A Beautiful Vanity Accent

To turn an old picture frame into a lovely tray for your vanity, take out the glass and pry off the arm that allows it to sit on a shelf. Reinforce what is now the bottom of the tray with a piece of cardboard and a nice fabric of your choosing.

Who Needs Frames?

To make a fun display for your favorite photos, hang twine in a corner and place clothespins on it like a clothesline. Then clip on photos, artwork, or your children's drawings to show off.

Bring Back a Treasured Vase

Just because there's a crack in your grandmother's old vase doesn't mean you can't use it for fresh flowers anymore. Just line it with one of those clear plastic bags you get in the produce section of your grocery store, and your problem is solved. It makes for simple cleaning as well! Just dump the water out, then throw away the bag with the dead flowers in it.

A Place for Firewood

Instead of buying an expensive container to hold firewood and kindling next to your fireplace, use a ceramic flower pot instead. They're cheap and easy to find in tons of different designs.

—*Lamar Wallace, Shiprock, NV*

Table It

If you have a room whose decor seems disorganized or mishmashed, place a dark brown or black piece of furniture, like a table, in the center. The darker item will attract the eye and focus people's attention.

Don't Rip Up That Carpet Just Yet

If you're thinking of getting new carpet put in, consider getting your old one professionally cleaned first. You'll be shocked at what a difference it makes, and it might change your mind about replacing the carpet. If there are still stains that even a professional cleaning won't remove, a strategically placed rug or chair can hide them.

Handled With Style

If your cabinets are getting old and worn, you can make them look nearly new just by replacing the knobs and handles. A good variety should be available inexpensively at your local hardware store. They'll make your kitchen or bathroom look brand new!

Read All About It

For something new and interesting to decorate your coffee table, why not coffee-table books? Choose a few of the most interesting ones from your collection (including this one, of course) and leave them out for visitors to peruse. If you really want to go the extra mile, you can also select a couple of random, heavy doodads to use as bookends.

Color Coordinate

You can easily create an attractive tabletop display by color-coordinating. Gather whatever objects you have that are the same color, and they'll catch the eye more easily. If you have more than one space to fill, create different displays using different colors for each.

Mirror, Mirror on the Wall

Do you have an old, dusty picture hanging in a place of prominence on your wall? Has it finally worn out its welcome? If so, replacing it with a large mirror can help brighten and reinvigorate your room.

Ditch the Drapes

Here's the thing about drapes: They're expensive and unnecessary. High-quality shower curtains are much cheaper and can serve the same purpose. Nobody will be able to tell the difference!

Raise the Rod

Who knew your windows will appear larger—and will let a little more light into the room—if you just raise the curtain rod a few inches? You'll be surprised how much of a difference this makes.

Make Your Own Clock

An easy way to add custom knickknacks to your home is to buy clock mechanisms from your hardware store. These do-it-yourself clocks are just the hands and the motor, so you can add them to household items and turn them into clocks. Add them to tins, plates, photos with

a cardboard backing, or just about anything else in your home. All it
takes is a little creativity!

Fun Addition to a Child's Room

Here's a great decorating idea for a child's room: Make a magnetic
chalkboard out of the wall! This can be easily accomplished by
purchasing a can of magnetic paint and a can of chalkboard paint, both
of which should be available at your local hardware store and will run
you about $15–$25 apiece. Mark off the area that you're going to paint
with masking tape, and remember that it can be any shape or size.
Then paint several layers of the magnetic paint, waiting for each layer
to dry before adding another layer on top of it. Finally, paint on a layer
of the chalkboard paint and let it sit for 2–3 days. With the help of some
magnets, you'll be able to hang your child's artwork on the wall, and
she'll be able to doodle to her heart's delight.

Who Knew?

According to *Nursing Standard* magazine, clowns are the
worst possible choice you can make for decorating your
child's room. They surveyed 250 pediatric patients and
found that every single one of them hated being in a ward
with clowns painted on the wall.

Repurpose Old Furniture

If your country kitchen is running out of room, consider a dresser. Even
though you're used to bureaus being only for bedrooms, it can be a
valuable addition to a kitchen for storing napkins, utensils, and more.
Repaint the dresser in colors to match your kitchen and you'll have
guests asking where you got your newest piece of kitchen furniture.

Jazzing Up Outdoor Plants

Sure you can stick with plain flowerpots for your outdoor foliage, but here are some ideas for days when you're feeling more inspired: Pretty watering cans, an old mailbox, a leather boot, crockery from a second-hand shop, a broken teakettle, or a dresser drawer. You'll need holes in the bottom (cut or drill as appropriate) of whatever items you choose, and you might want to add little stones as well.

How to Light Up a Room

If you have the interior decorating bug, but don't have much to spend on home accents, here's an easy way to add ambience: Use Christmas lights. They're great over a doorway, winding up a large houseplant, along a counter, or out on your patio, and you'll be surprised how many compliments you'll get for this simple technique. They're especially great to implement in January, when all the holiday decorations are half off!

Get Flowers to Bloom

If you've tried cutting their stems at an angle and changing their water but the flowers in your vase just won't bloom, try a hair dryer. Put a diffuser on it and set it to low, then point it at your bouquet and slowly sweep it back and forth for five minutes. The warmth simulates the sun, which may get your shy flowers to open up.

A Better Way to Hang a Poster

Kids love to put up posters on their walls, but kids being kids, of course, those posters will often sag or fall off completely when the thumbtack holes get torn. To prevent this, just place a strip of tape—electrical, packing, or strapping tape will work—on each corner of the back of the poster *before* tacking it to the wall. The tape will be unseen once the poster is hung, but it will reinforce the tack holes and the poster will stay on the wall considerably longer.

Fix a Tilted Frame

If you have a picture frame that won't stop tilting, simply stick a bit of something sticky behind one of the corners. Two options are "sticky tack," which can be found at office supply stores, and mounting putty, which can be purchased in hardware stores.

—Tamara Joseph, Saginaw, MI

Dust Ruffle Alternative

A dust ruffle is one item that can safely be consigned to the "things you really don't need" category—unless you're trying to hide everything you've stored under the bed. Make your own with a sheet or tablecloth. Only the sides of the bed that show need to have something hanging down over them. A more streamlined option is simply to cover the box spring with a fitted sheet.

Furniture Floor Samples

Let's be honest. If you have kids or pets, your furniture is going to be banged up. So why not get deep savings on furniture that already has a few dings on it? Almost all furniture stores sell floor samples of their merchandise. Ask a sales representative if the store is willing to sell the floor samples; often, stores have sales specifically for floor samples and the salesperson can tell you when that happens. Otherwise, they may only be willing to sell the floor sample if it's the last piece left. Ask if you can leave your phone number for when the rest run out, and don't be afraid to bargain on the price!

Jar Displays

Have some beautiful clear jars, but don't know what to do with them? Try putting photos inside! Add marbles, rocks, colored sand, or other decoration at the bottom, then bend the photo ever-so-slightly so it fits the curve of the jar.

● Who Knew?

When asked what kind of decorating style they prefer in a survey, 27 percent of respondents said "country style."

It Beats Buying Limited-Edition Prints

If you've got lots of bare wall space that you need to fill, there's a way to fill it cheaply and attractively. Buy a pile of cheap frames at the store, and then head to your nearest used bookstore to find a discounted art or photography book on a subject that interests you. When you find an image you like, use a box opener or X-Acto knife to cut the image out of the book cleanly. (Instead of a book, you can also use your favorite wall calendar from a year gone by.) If all the images you use come from the same book, the pages will all be the same size, which will enable you to arrange the frames in a cohesive way on the wall.

Cool Tips for Cut Flowers

Who doesn't love a bouquet of flowers displayed in a vase? Unfortunately, it's not always easy to keep your display looking fresh and beautiful. You probably know that you should keep your flowers' water fresh and regularly cut their stems, but here are more ideas to keep your flowers lasting longer and your bouquet at its best.

✦ To keep your cut flowers smelling fresh, make sure you remove any of the stem leaves that will be underwater in your vase. If left underwater, leaves rot quickly.

✦ If you've perfectly arranged a vase of flowers that's filled to the brim, water it without disturbing your design by filling a turkey baster with water, then slipping it between the stems.

✦ A drop or two of bleach can keep fresh flowers "alive" longer. This always struck us as odd, until we stopped to think that you use bleach to kill bacteria, viruses, and germs in general. Why not flower germs? You can also add aspirin and a little sugar.

✦ To prevent flowers from wilting, gently spray the undersides of petals and leaves with a little bit of hairspray. It really works!

✦ If you're cutting flowers from your garden, do it first thing in the morning. Flowers have more moisture then and will last longer if cut early in the day.

✦ Ever have the problem of a beautiful bouquet spreading out too much in the vase? It ends up looking rather sad and scrawny, but here's a simple fix: Use a hair elastic to hold stems together.

✦ If the opening of your vase is too large, make a grid by crisscrossing clear tape over the top. Then stick stems into the individual holes created by the tape.

- ✦ Your flowers may be indifferent to the inebriating effects of vodka, but you should feed it to them all the same. Pour a small shot of the cheapest vodka you can find into the vase, and your bouquet will stay fresh longer.

- ✦ To easily transport cut flowers, slip a balloon over the faucet and fill it with some water, then pull the opening over the stems of your flowers and secure with a rubber band. It's an unmessy way to let them have a drink in transit.

Internet Art

Hanging any image you'd like on your wall is as easy as a color printer and some internet-searching know-how. To find images that won't be too small or fuzzy when you print them out, go to Images.Google.com and click on "Advanced Image Search." Enter a the subject of your desired picture (for example, "moon") in the box labeled "Related to any of the words" and select "Large" next to "Image size." Even "large" images won't be poster-sized, but they'll still have enough pixels per inch to make sure it's not blurry when you print it out.

Another Tip for Hanging Frames

When a picture refuses to hang straight, wrap clear adhesive tape around the center of the wire to prevent it from slipping sideways.

● Who Knew? CLASSIC TIP

Store your candles in the freezer. Once you light them, they'll go hours before they start dripping.

Decorate With Fruit

Fill a large, glass bowl with citrus fruit for a bright centerpiece that's especially good for the dining room table. Use whatever is on sale— lemons, limes, oranges, or a mixture.

Spice Up a Bathroom

Want to add a little style to your bathroom? Replace old, boring shower curtain rings with pretty ribbon that matches your curtain. Just run it through the grommets and tie a bow on top of the rod.

Kitchen Decorating Idea

A fun and vintage-looking decoration for a kitchen is framed seed packets. Dig through whatever is available at your gardening store, then carefully slit the top to let the seeds loose. Center the empty pack on a matte or solid-color background, then glue with rubber cement or white glue. Frame, then hang on the wall for the perfectly themed picture.

Hang Pictures Easily

To get rid of the guesswork that comes with putting a nail in the wall to hang a picture, try this easy trick. Place a dab of toothpaste on the back of the frame on the hook or string (whatever will touch the nail). Then hold the frame up to the wall, position it carefully, and press it against the wall. The toothpaste will leave a mark that you can hammer a nail through, then wipe away.

Dress Up a Bedroom

If you love the look of lace, add some to your bedroom or guest room with this inexpensive trick. Buy a rectangular lace tablecloth that is 70-by-90 inches, and you can place it directly on top of your existing comforter. You'll have friends asking how you could afford to dress up your bed with lace!

Sliding Solution

If you're finding it hard to keep a floor rug in one place, buy some self-adhesive Velcro strips. Attach to the floor and to the corners of the rug and your skidding problems will be over for good! This also works great for keeping cushions on chairs.

—Robert Lepovetsky, Camp Hill, PA

Make Your Room Look Bigger (and Brighter!)

To make a ceiling look higher, all you need to do is change the lighting. Floor lamps that have the shade below the light bulb—like halogens—reflect the light onto the ceiling, which will make it look farther away.

Postcard Pizzazz

For beautiful art at cheap prices, try the gift shop of an art museum. They sell a wide variety of prints from their collection (and sometimes famous works as well) available in several different styles. Our favorite gift shop buy, however, is art postcards. Buy some cheap, black plastic frames, pop your postcards inside, and you have a lovely mini art display for your wall.

Liven Up an Already-Bright Room

For a sunny room that gets a lot of light, try this neat decorating trick: Fill clear bottles with water and add food coloring, then place on the windowsill. The sun will filter through them, casting brightly colored shades and shapes reminiscent of stained glass around the room.

Color Matching

If you're shopping for accessories to match a color on a bed spread, couch, or piece of art, taking a photo often doesn't cut it. Especially if you print it out on your home printer, the variance in color from the photograph to the actual article can be dramatic. Instead, go to a paint store and pick up paint swatches that you think are close in shade. Then go home and find the closest match. Mark that color, then bring the swatch to the store instead.

Striping Solution

Looking to add some character to a room by painting stripes on the wall? Make it easy by first adding "stripes" to your paint roller. Run masking tape around it in several places to mat down the roller. When you paint, the masking tape won't touch the wall, leaving clearly defined stripes behind.

See Your Carpet for What It Is

When shopping for carpet, make sure you do more than just leave your swatches on the floor. When you've narrowed your decision down to a few different shades, take them outside and get them a little dirty! You may surprised how well dirt is hidden—or revealed—on each sample.

Make Your Flowers Taller

Got some nice flowers whose stems are too short for the vase you want to put them in? Take a clear plastic straw and cut a segment off, then slide it over the bottom of the flower stem. Your floral display will now stand tall!

CHAPTER 12

Jeanne's Best Beauty Secrets

The Truth About Moisturizers

If you're looking for a way to cut back on cosmetics, the first place to start is with your moisturizer. Whether it's night cream, day cream, anti-aging lotion, or anti-wrinkle solution, it's all pretty much the same. Pick a moisturizer with an SPF of at least 15—other than that, go with a less expensive brand with a fragrance you like. Your wallet will know the difference, but your face never will.

Save on Shower Necessities

Transfer your shampoo, conditioner, and body wash into pump bottles. Your products will not only be easier to dispense, but you'll make sure not to use too much. One pump is all you should need!

—*Alexis Raizen-Rubenstein*

 Who Knew?

The average American woman spends more than $1,000 per year on beauty products. Read this chapter carefully to see how you can save!

Make Your Bath Luxurious

Don't spend a bundle on bath salts. Instead, make your own by combining two cups Epsom salts and two drops essential oil. Essential oils can be found online and in vitamin shops, health food stores, and in some drugstores. Find your favorite scent, then add it to Epsom salts for a relaxing bath.

Trick for Puffy Eyes

Fix a puffy under-eye area by rubbing egg whites on it. As the egg whites dry, you'll feel the skin get tighter. Leave on for a few minutes after it dries, then rinse off with cool water. You can also try applying a few slices of cucumber or potato to your eyes and leaving on for 15 minutes.

Brighten Skin Naturally

Rubbing a slice of pineapple or papaya onto your skin will help remove dead skin cells. Leave for five minutes, then rinse off with water. Alternatively, use olive oil mixed with salt for an abrasive action.

Callus Be Gone!

Get rid of ugly, unwanted calluses by dabbing them with chest rub, then covering them with bandages and leaving overnight. Repeat this procedure several days in a row and your calluses will disappear in no time. Believe or not, chest rub is also good for curing toenail fungus!

Surprising Use for a Coffee Bean

To freshen your breath, try sucking on a coffee bean. It's much cheaper than a breath mint, and tastes great to us coffee addicts!

Tiny Purse? Tiny Powder!

You're headed out for a night on the town with that fantastic new clutch you found, but once you shove your cell phone, wallet, and keys in there you barely have room for your lipstick. So what do you do with the powder compact you were counting on for touch-ups? Simply take some of those pieces of pressed powder that inevitably break off of the mass and keep them in a tissue. When it's time to refresh, rub the tissue across your face.

Make Perfume Last Longer

Before putting on a splash of your favorite scent, rub a pit of petroleum jelly on your skin. It will keep your fragrance from fading.

Fast Dry for Nail Polish

You have just enough time to touch-up your nails before you leave—but not enough time to dry them. Make your nail polish dry more quickly by spraying your final coat with cooking spray. The oil will help them dry faster, and moisturize your cuticles, too!

Who Knew?

When shopping for perfume, hair spray, nail polish, and other cosmetics, keep an eye out for phthalates on the ingredient list. Phthalates can be absorbed through the skin and have been found to damage the liver and reproductive system. They have been outlawed in Europe, but they're still legal in the US, so make sure you check the label before you buy.

Don't Dare to Neglect Hair Care

If you want to strengthen your hair, make sure to brush or comb it thoroughly each night. This will increase circulation in your scalp, loosen dry skin, and help moisturize your hair with your body's natural oils.

Keep Dandruff Away

Aspirin may help reduce dandruff if you crush a couple of tablets and add them to your normal shampoo. Just make sure to let the shampoo sit on your hair for 1–2 minutes before washing out.

Hand-Brewed Shampoo

It may surprise you to discover that beer has practical uses other than guzzling, but it's true. One of the best ones is enlivening flat hair. Mix three tablespoons of your favorite brew with half a cup of warm water, and after shampooing, rub the beer solution into your hair. Let it sit awhile before rinsing it off, and your hair will get that lively bounce back.

Blondes (Usually) Have More Fun

Ever heard the one about blonde hair turning green in a swimming pool? We've seen it happen. Thankfully, there is a solution: our 40th president's favorite "vegetable." Coat your hair with tomato ketchup and let it sit for a half an hour or so before you rinse it off. Then follow with your regular hair washing and conditioning routine. Remember to use up those packets stockpiled from fast-food places!

Summer Scalp

Hot summer sunshine can increase sweat production and make your scalp look and feel much greasier. To counteract this problem, try more frequent washings with a small amount of shampoo, and use a much lighter conditioner than you use in the winter.

Helping Oatmeal Help You

Have you ever noticed that oatmeal is often a main ingredient of bath products? Well guess what—you have that very same oatmeal in your kitchen! Unfortunately, it's not as easy as just throwing some into a hot bath. First, grind the oatmeal down in a blender or coffee grinder to expose its inner skin-soothing qualities. Then place it in a piece of cheesecloth with a few drops of your favorite scented oil. While you're running your bath, hold it under the faucet, or tie it with a bit of string. You'll have a luxurious oatmeal bath, and even a little sachet you can use as a washcloth to help you exfoliate your skin.

Foot Bath Formula

If you need a good soak in a foot bath, here's a soothing recipe to use. Pour a gallon of water into whatever container you use for foot soaking, and then add 1 cup lemon juice, 1 tablespoon olive oil, and ¼ cup milk. Mix thoroughly, stick your feet in, and relax!

 Who Knew? CLASSIC TIP

Instead of buying expensive shaving creams or foams, try shaving with hair conditioner. (Buy the cheapest kind.) The conditioner will soften the hair and provide a layer of protection between your blade and your skin. You'll even find your shave is closer.

Brighten Your Nails

If your fingernails have become stained by wearing dark nail polish, here's a quick fix: Plop a denture-cleaning tablet into a glass of water and soak your nails for a couple of minutes. The stain will come right off.

Moisturize Your Cuticles

To keep the cuticles of your nails super soft, pour mayonnaise into a small bowl and keep your fingers submerged in it for five minutes. Keep the bowl covered in the fridge and take it out three or four times a week to repeat this admittedly strange beauty routine.

Freshen Feet

Stinky feet? Keep them fresh by sprinkling a bit of cornstarch into your shoes once or twice a week. The cornstarch will absorb moisture and odors, making you unafraid to slip off those uncomfortable dress shoes under your desk.

Too Much Perfume?

Oops! You accidentally put on way too much perfume, and you're afraid the restaurant you're going to will smell like someone just let off a flower-scented bomb! To make your perfume less strong but still a little fragrant, dab a bit of rubbing alcohol wherever you applied the scent with a cotton ball. Your friends will thank you!

Natural Acne Fighter

Sprouting pimples like they're going out of style? Try this neat trick to clear up your face. Cut a raw potato in half and rub the flat end over your face. Leave the juice on for 20 minutes before rinsing off. The starch in the potato will help dry out your oily skin.

Wrinkle Cure and Face Massage in One

When you're feeling too lazy to hit the gym, work out your face instead! Doing facial exercises can help keep your skin looking fresh and young. Begin with this exercise for tired eyes: Simply look up and down with your eyes closed. Then move on to massaging your temples, which not only feels nice, but also helps relieve headache tension and can help prevent wrinkles. Pulling your skin from the eyebrows outward is also a good wrinkle-preventer. Exercise your cheeks by rubbing them in circles, chewing gum, and blowing on an instrument or into a straw.

Who Knew?

Sophia Loren once said, "Beauty is how you feel inside, and it reflects in your eyes. It is not something physical." If one of the most beautiful women in the world thinks so, it must be true!

The Best Place to Store Soap

If you've just purchased a new bar of soap, take it out of its box or wrapper and place it in your linen closet. Being exposed to the air will make the soap harden slightly, which will help it last longer. Meanwhile, it will freshen your closet while it's waiting to be used in the shower.

Make Your Own Liquid Soap

Shower gel can get expensive, so make your own from the cheapest bar soap you can find. Grate two bars of soap of your choice with a cheese grater and add to 2½ cups warm water. Add a soothing oil of your choice (baby or almond oil work well), as well as rose water or an essential oil like eucalyptus or marjoram. Refill an empty soap dispenser and shake. (You may need to shake each time you use it.)

—Emma Louise Haydu

Who Needs a Soap Dish?

Instead of letting your soap sit in standing water on your soap dish, put it in a mesh bag (like the kind you would get a bunch of onions in) and tie it to your faucet or an in-shower towel rod. The water will run right through.

How to Clean Your Iron

If your curling or straightening iron is getting a little gross from caked-on hair product and other dirt, head to the kitchen and reach for some oven cleaner. Spray it on, then let it sit for an hour and wipe off. Then wipe the iron with a damp cloth and make sure to let it dry before you use it again.

A Pool No-No

Never wear silver jewelry in pools, because chlorine can cause pitting, small indentations in the surface. It's not a particularly good idea to wear gold jewelry in chlorinated water either, so make sure to leave your valuables at home before heading to the pool.

Fix Broken Jewelry

If a stone has popped out of a piece of your jewelry and you were lucky enough to save it, you can easily put it back in place with a tiny dab of clear nail polish.

To whiten your teeth naturally (and cheaply), mash 4–5 strawberries with ½ teaspoon baking soda. Brush onto your teeth with a toothbrush and let sit for 10–15 minutes. Then rinse out and brush your teeth as usual, making sure no strawberry seeds got caught between your teeth. Repeat this process every night and you'll start to see results in 3–4 weeks.

Treatment for Tired Feet

To rejuvenate tired feet, treat them to this home spa treatment. Massage some butter into your soles, then wrap your feet in warm, moist towels and let sit for 10 minutes. When you unwrap them they may smell a little like popcorn, but they'll be soft and feel great.

Natural Toner

Toner is a final layer of beauty product to use after cleaning your skin. It will help you get a fresh look, reduce puffiness, and tighten your pores. To make your own all-natural version, combine a quarter of a cucumber (no need to peel) with 1½ tablespoons witch hazel and 1 tablespoon water (distilled if you have it) in a blender. Add a little lemon juice and blend until smooth (which should only take a minute). Push through a mesh tea strainer and throw out the solids. Store the toner in the fridge, and when you're ready to use it, dab on your face with a cotton pad or ball. It can be used daily and should last a few weeks. Enjoy! Once you try it you'll never go back to the store-bought kind.

Get Rid of Dead Skin

Another way to slough off dead skin easily is by applying mayonnaise over any dry, rough patches. Let sit for 10 minutes, then wipe away with a washcloth that has been dampened with warm water.

Sylists in Progress

Get your haircut on the cheap by students who are studying to be beauticians. You may risk a less-than-professional 'do, but it's probably better than having a friend do it. Student haircuts are also great for kids, whose simple cuts are usually hard to screw up. To find a beauty school near you that offers cuts and styles at low prices, go to BeautySchoolDirectory.com.

Trim on the Cheap

If you're used to getting an expensive haircut, it's hard to switch to a bargain salon such as Supercuts. But what you can do to save yourself hundreds of dollars a year is to get a hairstyle that doesn't need a lot of upkeep. When you need a trim in between cuts, go to an inexpensive salon. While hair stylists at the bargain salons sometimes can't give you the fancy cut you want, they can usually handle a simple trim, following the path of your normal stylist. If you just need your bangs cut, ask at your usual salon if they offer free bang trims in between cuts.

Your Hair Won't Know the Difference!

For a cheap alternative to hair gel, try a light hand lotion instead. If you have a short cut, it works great to weigh down curls and frizzies, and costs less than half the price of hair gel. Hand lotion is also great as a hair product because you can find it in so many scents—you'll probably find one you like even more than your normal hair-care product!

Too Much Hairspray?

If you've gotten hairspray on your eyeglasses, just wipe them down with rubbing alcohol and you'll be seeing clearly again.

Cheap Make-Up Remover

For an inexpensive way to remove mascara, eye liner, and shadow, try baby shampoo. It contains many of the same ingredients as eye-make-up remover, and works just as well. Dispense a small amount on a tissue or cotton ball, rub over closed eyes, and rinse with water.

Strong Foundations

Some of the most expensive kinds of make-up are foundation and powder. Make them last longer by buying a shade darker than your natural shade, then mixing it with moisturizer (for foundation) or baby powder (for powder) until it matches your normal color. You'll have more than twice as much, and you'll never be able to tell the difference!

Who Knew?

Many forms of make-up are sensitive to the sun due to their preservatives. Make sure to keep your make-up away from the window to ensure it lasts as long as possible.

Watch Your Wardrobe

The biggest thing people do wrong when trying to hide their weight is to buy loose-fitting clothes. The truth is, baggy clothes will just make you look bigger. Instead, find an outfit that accentuates the positives—whether that's your hourglass hips, great legs, or beautiful neckline.

Getting clothes that are tailored, but not tight, will not only draw attention where you want it to, but will let people know that you're still confident about your appearance—which is way sexier than losing a few pounds around your waist.

Play Up Your Best Features

The whole point of jewelry is to enhance your beauty. So if you're self-conscious about your neckline, by all means steer clear of a dramatic choker. Try bracelets and elegant headbands instead. If those daily crunches are starting to pay off, wear a flashy belt or a bright scarf wrapped around just above the hips to draw attention to your slimming waistline.

Keep Static Away from Stockings

If you've ever had your skirt or slip stick to your pantyhose due to static electricity, you'll love this tip. Just spritz a little hair spray on your nylons and they'll not only be free of static, they'll be less likely to run.

—*Francie J. Shor*

Quick Bracelet Fastening

Having trouble getting that bracelet on? Make fastening easy by attaching the bracelet to your arm with a bit of tape. Then clasp, pull the tape off, and go!

Make Shoes Shine

After polishing your shoes, spray them with a bit of hairspray. People will wonder how you got them so shiny!

The Trick for New Shoes

Cobblers will stretch out your new shoes for you, but there's no need to pay their price. Do it yourself by wearing your new shoes around the house and out to run errands for a few days, and wear two pairs of thick socks with them. The extra padding will stretch out the shoes until there is plenty of room for your feet, and will also make your feet less likely to get blisters when you're ready to wear your new shoes out on the town.

—*Betsy Beier, Viroqua, WI*

Two-Minute Slimdown

You don't need to purchase a shaper and certainly not a corset to make yourself look five pounds slimmer. Try leotards, tight-fitting tank tops, leggings, and spandex running pants. The trick is to layer them underneath your nice outfit so you don't get the "Are-those-pajamas-you're-wearing?" look. You'll feel firmed up and pulled-together, at least until you catch sight of your hair.

Who Knew?

Never paint your nails on a wooden table. Even one drop of nail polish is hard to remove, and nail polish remover will strip the varnish. Paint your nails over newspaper and you'll make sure to avoid an expensive repair bill!

Get Rid of Static

If brushing your hair makes it practically stand on end, run your brush under cold water before running it through your hair.

Fight Dandruff With Thyme

If your scalp is getting flaky, try treating it with a mixture of 2 tablespoons dried thyme and 1 cup water. Let the water boil, then add the thyme and wait 5 minutes. Remove from the heat and let cool, then strain out the thyme and pour the water on your hair and scalp after you've washed and rinsed it. To let it work, don't rinse it out for 12 hours—but don't worry, your hair will dry fine (and smell delicious)!

Another Way to Combat Chlorine Coloring

If you're a fair-haired person and an avid swimmer, you've probably noticed that the chlorine in pools can wreak havoc on the color of your hair—often turning it green! If you want your old hair color back, just dissolve a half-dozen aspirin in a bowl of warm water and rub it into your hair. Let it sit for 20 minutes and then wash it out with tap water, and your hair will be good as new. Alternatively, you can rub cider vinegar into your hair *before* jumping in the water, which helps prevent color change.

Help Dry Hair

Suffering from dry hair? Here's a surefire way to make your hair moist again. Mash a banana and mix with a teaspoon of almond or olive oil. Rub the mixture into your hair and scalp, and let sit for 20 minutes. Rinse off and shampoo and condition as usual. You'll be surprised at the results!

Face Masks for Every Skin Type

Face masks aren't only good for your face, they're also a relaxing treat. Make girls' night even more interesting by making your own! With these homemade face mask recipes, you'll get the same results as store-bought masks, and they're easy too!

✦ Simple avocado: Just mash up a ripe avocado (the fruit shouldn't be tough, and it give a little when touched). Apply to your face and let it dry for 15–20 minutes. Add some cucumbers to your eyes for extra relaxation! Rinse with warm water.

✦ Go bananas: Bananas are great for oily skin. Mash one banana with a teaspoon of honey and a couple of drops of lemon juice. Apply to your face and let sit for 15 minutes before washing with a cool washcloth.

✦ The solution for dry skin: Mix one egg yolk with a teaspoon of honey and a teaspoon of olive oil. Leave on your face for as long as possible, then wash off. The vitamin A in the egg yolk is great for your skin!

✦ Exfoliant: Mix ¼ cup brown sugar with 1½ tablespoons whole or 2 percent milk. Rub into your face, then leave on for 10 minutes. The brown sugar will exfoliate while the milk will moisturize. Tastes pretty good, too!

✦ Clay: You won't believe it till you try it, but clay cat litter is actually the exact same clay that's found in some of the most expensive face masks on the market. Find some cat litter labeled "100 percent all-natural clay" and mix it with water until it gets to the consistency you want. Adding a couple drops of scented oil will also help make it seem less like you're applying cat litter to your face. Wash the mask off after it hardens.

✦ Skin soother: This face mask is perfect for sunburned or irritated skin. Combine ¼ cup full-fat yogurt with 2 tablespoons oatmeal. Mix vigorously for one minute, then apply to your face. Leave on for at least 10 minutes, then wash off with warm water.

Getting Your Eyebrows Waxed?

The next time you get your eyebrows waxed, bring a container of eye drops with you. Applying the solution to your brows after your wax will greatly reduce the redness that comes with it.

For That Last Bit of Mascara

You've just spent more time than you'd like to admit perfecting your make-up when you realize you're out of the finishing touch—your mascara! Don't despair. You can still get a little bit more out of the tube. Tightly close the cap and run the mascara under hot water for 15 seconds. The water will heat up the mascara on the sides of the tube, allowing it to flow more freely. Unscrew the cap and stick the brush back in a few times and you'll have enough mascara for one more night on the town.

CHAPTER 13

Simple Solutions for Better Health

Exercise the Easy Way

Oftentimes, surveying the latest home exercise equipment or worrying about which gym to join are just excuses to put off actually getting in shape. Start getting in shape *today* by using your stairs (if you have them) and cans of food as hand weights. You can march in place anywhere, do squats while waiting for the pasta to cook, and rotate your arms while talking on the phone with a headset. If you do have some equipment, but want access to more, try circuit training with a neighbor—you have a bike and treadmill, she has a weight machine and rower. Trade every other day. Even without any machines you can create your own little circuit, setting up stations to do sit-ups, push-ups, jumping jacks, and even a few yoga poses if you're feeling adventurous.

Original Hiccup Cure

When "Boo!", drinking upside down, and holding your breath don't work, try this to get rid of your hiccups. Insert a Q-tip into your mouth and gently dab the back of the throat under the soft palate. You're trying to hit the uvula, which requires good aim, a diagram, or both! If this doesn't work, try putting sugar under the tongue and letting it dissolve, or swallowing a tablespoon of lemon juice.

Instant Hand Sanitizer

To avoid spending money on expensive hand sanitizers, make your own at home with these ingredients: 2 cups aloe vera gel, 2 teaspoons rubbing alcohol, 4 teaspoons vegetable glycerin, and 15 drops eucalyptus oil. Mix the ingredients well and you should be able to use it the same way you'd use the commercially made version.

Foot Bath for Health

If you find that you're susceptible to athlete's foot, here's a trick that will keep that nasty fungus at bay. Once or twice a week, soak your feet in a hot bath with two cloves of crushed garlic mixed in. The garlic will kill athlete's foot before it starts, and you won't be afraid to walk around in sandals. To treat a case of athlete's food that has already begun, try soaking your toes in mouthwash. It may sting a little, but the nasty fungus will be gone in just a few days.

Binder Clips to Build Strength

If you suffer from arthritis, try this trick to make it easier to open jars and perform other daily tasks. Take a medium-sized binder clip and push back the wings with your thumb and index finger. Hold for 5–10 seconds, then move on to each finger of each hand. Do this a few times a day and it should help your grip.

Back Pain? Check Your Wallet

If you're a man who suffers from back pain, your wallet may be to blame. Sitting on a bulky wallet can cause your spine to become misaligned and your muscles to compensate. Try carrying your wallet in a front pocket (where it's also safe from pickpockets) or make sure it's as thin as possible.

Homemade Heating Pad

Don't spend your money on an aromatherapy pillow! Instead, add uncooked, long-grain rice to a sock and tie it shut. Whenever you need a little heat after a long day, stick it in the microwave on high for 1–2 minutes and you'll have soothing warmth. To add a little scent to the pillow, add a few drops of your favorite essential oil to the rice.

Keeping Finger Bandages Dry

You put a Band-Aid on your finger to cover up a scratch, but you still have to go through your day full of hand-washing, child-bathing, and dishes-doing. To keep the bandage dry while you work, cover it with a non-inflated balloon—any color will do!

The Fish That Don't Kill You Will Make You Stronger

Eating some fish will seriously jeopardize your health because of the mercury content, but eating others will help you live to 100. Which are which? These types are safe and have lots of omega-3s for a healthier heart: anchovies, Chinook salmon, farmed salmon, herring, Atlantic mackerel, sablefish, striped bass, Pacific oysters, sardines, albacore tuna, and freshwater trout. Swim clear of these five, which you should only have once or twice a month, or not at all if you're pregnant or under five years old: king mackerel, swordfish, marlin, tuna steak, and shark tilefish.

Get Your Ducts in a Row

If you find yourself getting headaches or sinus trouble more often than you used to, it might be that your home's ducts simply need a good cleaning. Whenever air conditioning or heating is on, tiny particles that have accumulated inside the ducts blow out too, including mold, mouse droppings, and plain old dust. If you have sensitive allergies, a professional duct cleaning may be just what the doctor ordered.

Help for Stings

Believe it or not, meat tenderizer works wonders on all sorts of stings—bee, wasp, even jellyfish. That's because it contains papain, which helps break down the proteins in venom. Make a paste with the tenderizer by adding a few drops of water at a time, then rub on the affected area.

After-Sun Soother

Lots of people swear by aloe lotion, but green tea is a cheaper option and just as effective for treating sunburns. Use a washcloth soaked in tea that has been cooled in the refrigerator as a compress on your tender skin. (Some people say topically applied green tea may even protect against skin cancer.) This is also a great way to ease a sunburned scalp. After washing and rinsing your hair as usual, pour the cooled tea over your scalp. Your poor skin will thank you!

A Different Kind of Ice Pack

If you're a vodka drinker, you're well aware that it doesn't solidify in the freezer. For this reason, it's also a great tool for making your own homemade gel ice pack to use on aches or injuries. Just pour two cups of water, one-third cup of Smirnoff, and a few drops of green or yellow food coloring (so everyone will know not to eat the contents) into a heavy-duty Ziploc freezer bag. Put it in the freezer for a while, and you've got an instant ice pack. If you don't keep vodka around, you can simulate the same effect with liquid dishwasher detergent. (If you do use detergent, though, make absolutely certain to label the bag so nobody ingests it.)

Desk Discomfort

If you find sitting at your desk is causing lower back pain, try slightly elevating your feet. And old phone book is perfect for the job.

Three Cheers for Turmeric

Making tumeric—a Southeast Asian relative of the ginger root—part of your diet can pay off in many different ways. It reduces cholesterol, and lab tests have indicated that it may also inhibit tumors. It's also a natural antibacterial agent and helps detoxify the liver. You can mix the powder into drinks or baked goods, or even sprinkle it on ice cream!

Bug Bite?

A great way to treat mosquito bites is with a dab of ammonia, which stops them from itching. In fact, ammonia is the main ingredient in many of the itch-relief products currently on the market. You can also try a dab of rubbing alcohol.

Get Rid of Chiggers

There may be nothing more disgusting in this world than chiggers. After picking them up in the forest, chiggers will lay eggs in the folds of your skin, causing a poison ivy–like rash. If you think you've been exposed to chiggers, take a hot bath. The heat will cause the larvae to die, making your pain (and disgust!) short-lived.

Rub Away the Bloat

Feeling bloated? It could just be trapped gas. Encourage it to move by gently stroking from your right hip up toward your ribs, then across the bottom of your rib cage and down toward your left hip. Repeat several times.

Cure for Canker Sores

Hydrogen peroxide may help reduce and relieve canker sores. Simply mix one part peroxide with one part water, then dab on any affected areas several times a day or swish around in your mouth for as long as possible.

Sun-Lovers Take Note!

Don't wait until you are out in the sun to apply a protective lotion to your skin. Sunscreen needs time to work, so smooth it on about 20 minutes before you go outside, and don't be stingy with it—use liberal amounts and reapply after doing any swimming.

Drink Up to Stop Stiffness

If you find you're often stiff after exercising, you probably just need more water. Dehydration is a major cause of post-exercise muscle soreness. Drinking water regularly while you work out should keep water levels high enough to combat pain.

Lose Weight Without Lifting a Pound

Hot, spicy foods can help the body burn up calories. Using spices like cayenne pepper and chili powder elevates the body temperature, which makes the heart beat faster and requires more energy.

Slightly Less Sugar

You can reduce your children's calorie and sugar intake by diluting their apple and orange juice with a bit of water. When you open a new bottle, empty a quarter of the juice into a pitcher, then fill the original juice bottle back to the brim with water. It'll still taste delicious, but the kids will get less of a sugar rush, and the juice will last longer to boot.

—*Rosemary Deibler, Harrodsburg, KY*

Sanitize a Cut

You just got a nasty cut on your hand, but don't have anything to clean it out with before you put the bandage on. Luckily, there's something in your medicine cabinet that you may not have thought of—mouthwash. The alcohol-based formula for mouthwash was originally used as an antiseptic during surgeries, so it will definitely work for your cut, too.

> ### Who Knew?
>
> If you're over 50, taking 400 IU of vitamin D every day will reduce your risk of osteoarthritis in your knees.

Pepper Yourself for Pain

Cayenne pepper contains a substance called capaicin, which stimulates the brain to secrete endorphins, which are peptides that help block pain signals and reduce chronic pain, such as that from arthritis and a bad back. If you suffer from pain, try sprinkling a little cayenne pepper into your food.

Keep the Doctor Away

If you need medical treatment but can't afford a doctor, consider a walk-in clinic. Walk-in retail clinics can be found in many drug and even department stores. You'll see a nurse or nurse practitioner and may get everything you need, with the convenience of the pharmacy on-site. Besides the quick service and low cost, you'll appreciate the extended evening and weekend hours. Remember that these clinics are meant for minor illnesses and injuries such as colds and flus, sprained muscles, pinkeye, burns, and ear infections. If your situation goes beyond the scope of the clinic, you'll be advised to see a doctor.

—*Samantha Chumley*

Drink Tea for Better Bones

The caffeine in coffee is thought to deplete calcium levels, contributing to osteoporosis, but the same isn't true for tea, which actually has the opposite effect. Drinking tea can reduce fracture risk by 10–20 percent, probably because of its estrogen-building isoflavonoid chemicals.

Cold Cure

Stuffy nose? Don't spend money on decongestant—head to your fridge instead. Cut the "root" end of two scallions and carefully insert the white ends into your nose (being cautious not to shove them too high!). You may look silly, but your nose will start to clear in a couple of minutes.

Reflexology: Health in Your Hands

Take your health into your own hands (literally) with reflexology, which is the practice of applying pressure to the feet and hands to help ease pain and prevent disease. For instance, if you experience eye strain, you can pinch the webbing between your fingers or toes to help alleviate it. For colds, press about halfway down the side of your thumb. It may sound crazy, but it's been practiced in Asia for years, and China has recently been recruiting reflexologists to cut down on health care costs. For learn more, visit your local library or Reflexology-Research.com/whatis.htm.

Sore Throat?

To cure a sore throat in a day or two, mix equal parts vinegar and honey and take one tablespoonful every two hours.

—Ruth Leibenguth

Root Out Nausea

Ginger root, taken as a powder or in tea, works directly in the gastrointestinal tract by interfering with the feedback mechanisms that send sickness messages to the brain. Take some when you're feeling nauseated to help alleviate your symptoms.

Headache Pain

Many headaches are caused by dehydration. Before you reach for the pain reliever, try drinking two or three glasses of water or an energy drink like Gatorade. You may find you're back to normal in no time.

Toothpaste Hero

A white, pasty toothpaste (not a gel) like original Colgate should be a part of everyone's medicine cabinet—and not just for clean teeth. This kind of toothpaste can be used to clear up pimples and even as a salve for burns. Simply dab a small amount onto affected areas and leave overnight.

Who Knew? CLASSIC TIP

Having trouble sleeping? Before you turn to the prescription medication, try valerian root. Used in sleep remedies for generations, valerian is a natural sleeping aide.

Soothing Back Pain

If you have chronic back pain—especially associated with arthritis—or other sore muscles, try adding yellow mustard to a hot bath. Add a few tablespoons for mild pain, and up to a whole 8-ounce bottle if the pain is severe. The bathwater may look strange, but your aching back will thank you.

Watery Eyes?

If your eyes are itchy, try this quick fix to cut down on your misery: Rub a small amount of baby shampoo on your eyelids. It should reduce your symptoms dramatically.

Steam Away a Cold

Steam is a wonderful household remedy for colds, especially with some aromatherapy oils mixed in. Try pouring hot water into a bowl and breathing in as you lean over it. Stick your tongue out as you do it—this will open the throat and allow more steam through, which prevents membranes from drying out. Add aromatherapy oils to the water that are especially known to alleviate the symptoms of congestion, such as black pepper, eucalyptus, hyssop, pine, and sweet thyme.

Alleviate Neck Tension

Been leaning over your work too long? Try this to help a hurting neck. Inhale and raise your shoulders up to your ears, pulling them as high as they will go. Then let go with an "ahhh" and drop them slowly back down. Repeat several times to release muscle tension.

Get Rid of Toenail Fungus

If you have yellow toenails, you may have a fungus problem. Get rid of this unsightly affliction by soaking your toes in mouthwash for 10–15 minutes each evening.

Are Your Eyes Causing Headaches?

Less-than-perfect eyesight can trigger headaches because the muscles around the eyes squeeze in order to focus. If your headaches come on after reading or working at a computer, make sure you give your eyes a rest every 15 minutes by focusing on a distant object for at least a minute. You may also want to get your eyes examined to see if you need glasses.

Hangover Cure

Party too hard last night? Just spread a little honey on your favorite crackers. The honey provides your body with the essential sodium, potassium, and fructose it needs after a raucous night out!

Hard Cheese for Healthy Teeth

Serve hard cheese like romano and aged cheddar as an after-dinner snack. They'll help scrub your teeth of acids found in other foods, and the calcium inside helps make teeth stronger.

Pummel Pollen

If you have a pollen allergy, try to keep these sneeze-inducing allergens out of your home. Take a shower immediately after doing any yard work to get rid of pollens you may have carried in on your hair and skin, and throw your clothes in the laundry basket. Animals can carry in pollen, too. After taking your dog for a walk or letting your cat out, wipe them down with a wet rag or baby wipe.

Olives for Healthy Joints

People who eat the most olive oil and cooked vegetables are about 75 percent less likely to develop rheumatoid arthritis than those who eat the fewest servings. So use olive oil in your cooking, and consider buying some gourmet olive oil that you can mix with pasta and eat as-is.

Get Rid of Headaches

An old-fashioned and effective way to treat headaches is to cut a lime in half and rub it on your forehead. In a few minutes, the throbbing should subside.

Who Knew?

It's official—children have known it for years, but scientists now admit that eating ice cream can actually make you feel better. Eating a spoonful of ice cream lights up the same pleasure center in the brain as winning money!

When Bees Strike

When you're stung by a bee, carefully grasp the stinger and pull it out as fast as you can. The less venom that enters your body, the smaller and less painful the resulting welt will be. Ice the area immediately to reduce the swelling. If it still hurts, try cutting an onion in half and applying the fleshy side to the sting. It should help ease the pain.

High Blood Pressure?

If you have high blood pressure, and particularly if you take cholesterol-lowering drugs, make sure your diet is high in Co-enzyme Q10 (CoQ10). It can help lower blood pressure and protect against heart disease, breast cancer, and gum disease. Good sources include organic meat and eggs, rice bran, wheat germ, peanuts, spinach, broccoli, mackerel, and sardines.

Satisfy a Sweet Tooth

Trying to lose weight but keep craving something sweet? Keep a bunch of grapes in your fridge and grab a handful when the hunger hits. Grapes release sugar quickly, so they are great for satisfying your sweet tooth. If you don't feel like the grapes are hitting the spot, wait 10 minutes and see how you feel before reaching for the candy!

Nuts for a Healthy Heart

Nuts are rich in unsaturated fats and vitamin E, which have been linked to a reduced risk of heart disease. Nut-eaters are a third less likely to suffer heart disease than others, so get some trail mix and get to munching!

Headache Help

If you tend to get headaches in the late mornings, late afternoons, or after a long nap, they might be due to low blood sugar, also known as hypoglycemia. These headaches can be helped by eating foods that release sugar slowly, such as bananas, whole grains, and oats.

Natural Remedies for Motion Sickness

If you get nauseated every time you ride in a car, boat, or train, take some lemon wedges with you. Suck on them as you ride to relieve nausea. You can also try sucking on a piece of ginger or drinking ginger tea.

Sore Throat?

Aspirin does more than just relieve headaches! If you have a sore throat, dissolve two non-coated tablets in a glass of water and gargle. Just make sure to note that this only works with aspirin—don't try it with other pain relievers like ibuprofen.

CHAPTER 14

Stain-Fighting Miracles and Other Laundry Wisdom

Save with Steam

Save time and money by steaming your clothes at home rather than taking them to a dry cleaner. Choose a steamer with 1,200 to 1,500 watts of de-wrinkling power—anything above that may cause a short circuit, and anything under that may not be effective. Hang suits, shirts, and skirts on a shower rod and steam several items at once. You may find it doesn't take too much longer than dropping them off at the dry cleaner's!

A Detergent Secret from a Professional

We'll never forget a friendly repairman who, while fixing our washing machine, told us, "You know, you only need half of the detergent that they tell you you need." If you do as much laundry as we do, this tip will save you money right away. If you miss the smell of lots of detergent, add an extra half of a dryer sheet to the dryer. You can also use half the amount of dish detergent in your dishwasher!

Not Your Mother's Mothballs

Mothballs have that telltale old attic smell and even worse, they contain a carcinogen. Use a pretty-smelling natural potpourri made of rosemary, mint, thyme, ginseng, and cloves for the same effect. You want about eight times as many cloves as the other ingredients, since they are what actually keeps the moths away. You can also add lemon peel and tansy. Store in little sachets, which you can buy in a craft store, or tie up in old rags. If you have moths on an item of clothing, put it in your freezer for two days and then clean as usual.

Keep Clothes Color-Fast

The secret ingredient to keeping your clothes from bleeding in the washing machine may surprise you—it's pepper! Throw a teaspoon of ground pepper into the washing machine with your dirty clothes and they'll be less likely to bleed and more likely to keep their bright colors longer.

For Wrinkle-Free Sheets

Though we like wrinkle-free linens as much as the next person, we simply don't have the time to iron bed sheets like our mothers used to. Still, there are a few things you can do to stop wrinkles before they start. Believe it or not, drying your sheets in the dryer can actually increase and set wrinkles. Instead, fold the sheet into quarters or eighths, snapping it and smoothing it out after each fold. Then place the last fold over a clothesline. The fabric is so light, it will easily dry, with only a few wrinkles still intact.

> ### ● Who Knew? CLASSIC TIP
>
> Trying to get an ink stain out? Try spraying ultra-stiffening hairspray on the spot, then laundering as usual. Hairspray will usually remove the stain.

Restore Worn Velvet

If your velvet dress, shawl, shirt, or—dare we say it—pants are getting a shiny mark from too much wear, you may be able to remove it. Try lightly spraying the area with water, then rubbing it against the grain with an old toothbrush.

Say Goodbye to Ring Around the Collar

If your dress shirts are getting stained around the collar, wipe the back of your neck with an alcohol-based astringent before you get dressed in the morning. The alcohol will prevent your sweat from leaving a stain.

Suntan Oil Spill

You had a great time at the beach, but you accidentally got suntan lotion all over your wrap. To remove this stubborn stain, cover with liquid dish detergent and rub in. Then turn your kitchen sink on at full blast and run under cold water.

Paint Stains

Got paint on your clothes? Unfortunately, it's often impossible to remove. Before you give up completely, however, try saturating the stain in a solution of one part ammonia and one part turpentine, then washing as usual.

Give Buttons Some Wiggle Room

When sewing on buttons, place a toothpick between the button and the garment. This will ensure you're not sewing it too close to the fabric.

—*Joyce Barone, Hoboken, NJ*

Help Sweaters Stay in Shape

Be careful when drying sweaters! Common laundry advice, but it usually stops there. You can't throw them in the dryer. You can't let them hang and fall out of shape. So what *are* you supposed to do? Once pantyhose have lost their shape, run the legs through the arms of your sweater so the waist is up at the sweater's neck. Use a hanger with clips to grab the ends of the pantyhose (the feet) and hang.

Hiding Marks on White Canvas Shoes

Uh oh, your new white canvas shoes just got a big, black scuff on them. The best way to get them looking like new again is to dab a bit of liquid white-out on the stain. You won't be able to tell the difference when looking down from above.

> ## ● Who Knew? CLASSIC TIP
>
> Nothing stinks on your clothes like gasoline! To remove the odor, place the offending clothes in a bucket of cold water, and add a can of cola and a cup of baking soda. Soak overnight, then line dry outside if possible. If there is still any odor left, just wash as usual and it should be gone.

For Dye-Bleeding Blunders

If you open the washer and everything's vaguely the same color as your new red shirt, don't despair. Skip the dryer and soak any garments that have been accidentally dyed in the wash in a bucket of rubbing alcohol, then rinse. Repeat the process until your clothes are their original color, then wash as usual.

What to Do with Grass Stains

Try a little corn syrup to remove stubborn grass stains from clothing, instead of those expensive pre-soaks. Just rub the syrup into the stain and launder as normal.

Easy Way to Thread a Needle

To quickly thread a needle, spray the end of the thread with a bit of hair spray. It will stiffen the thread and make it much easier to get through the eye, leaving you ready to darn all those socks.

Make Mending Easier

If you're mending a hole on a sleeve or pant leg, it's easy to miss a stitch when the fabric gets all balled up. Make your job easier by rolling up a magazine and placing it inside. It will partially unroll as far as the sleeve or leg will let it, creating just enough tension to hold the fabric in place.

Who Knew?

When given a list of household appliances in a survey, people rated their washing machine as the number one appliance they can't live without. Following the washing machine were their microwave, dishwasher, DVR, and coffee maker.

Neat Pleats

Bobby pins keep the shape of pleats so you won't ruin them with the iron (and we know you iron every Sunday night at least).

Never Throw Away a Needle

If your needle has grown dull, sharpen it up again by running its tip back and forth on an emery board several times.

—Patricia S., West Plains, MO

Stitching Sheer Wear

It's fun to work with sheer materials for curtains and lingerie, but they can be very unwieldy when you're using a sewing machine. If you first sew them to paper (which you'll rip off as soon as you're done), they will stay smooth. Make sure to use needles made for lightweight fabric and fine thread.

Keep Your Clothes Lasting Longer

Once you've found the outfit of your dreams, make sure it lasts! Here are some tips to prolong the life your favorite clothes.

+ Many of your clothes can be worn several times before you wash them, especially sweaters. Most items get more wear and tear from being in the washing machine than they do on your bodies!

+ Turn knitted clothes and T-shirts with designs on them inside-out when washing and drying.

+ Synthetic fabrics wear faster, while naturals like linen and wool will last longer.

+ When pre-treating a stain, try to wash the item within an hour after applying the stain remover.

+ When ironing clothes, especially dark ones, iron them from the inside. Make sure to use distilled water if you use a steaming iron to prevent stains.

+ Line dry your clothes. Not only is air-drying less harsh, you'll love the real smell of sun-dried linens. If you don't have a clothesline, use hangers to hang shirts and pants on tree limbs! Just make sure not to put brights in the sun, as they made fade.

Quick Fix for Heavy Drapes

To give heavy drapes or bedding a fast fluff-up, run them on the delicate setting of your dryer with a damp towel.

Who Knew?

It's important never to rub a fresh stain with a bar of soap. Many stains can set further when treated with soap.

Scorch Mark?

If you have a scorch mark on fabric, your quest to remove it begins in the kitchen. Cut the end off of an onion and grate about a fourth of it into a bowl using a cheese grater. Rub the stain with the grated onion, blotting it with as much of the onion juice as you can. Let it sit for 8–10 minutes, and if necessary, reapply the onion juice. Once the stain is gone, launder as usual.

Suede Stains

The emery board that you normally use on your nails can remove small stains from suede. Gently rub the file across the stain a few times to remove the mess.

Take Them for Another Spin

If you find your clothes are still dripping wet when you take them out of the washing machine, put them back in and set the cycle to spin. The extra spin time will wring them out even further, and use less energy than extra time in the dryer will.

Prevent Underarm Stains

Here's a great tip if you get those pesky yellow stains on the armpits of white shirts. Coat the would-be stained area on the inside of the shirt with a spray adhesive (available at your local craft store). The adhesive will seal the fibers, so that sweat and your deodorant can't get inside— or stain the cloth. You can also try sprinkling on a little baby powder before you iron the spot.

> **● Who Knew? CLASSIC TIP**
>
> To make your jeans last longer, iron patches on the inside as soon as you purchase them. Place the patches where the jeans usually wear out quickly, such as at the knees or the inner thighs.

Iron Woman

A great way to defend the purchase of a straightening iron for your hair is to point out the contribution it will make to the household: ironing those hard-to-reach places between buttons on a blouse or dress shirt!

Need to Iron a Straw Hat?

Rescue a straw hat by placing a damp cloth between the straw and a warm iron. Rest the brim underside up on the ironing board and press, rotating the hat. For flat tops, place cardboard inside and pack with crumpled newspaper before pressing.

Keeping Lace Lovely

Nervous about ironing lace items? Don't be. Before ironing, simply dip the lace in sugar water, and your item should emerge from ironing unscathed.

Remove Scuff Marks from Shoes

Just about any scuff mark can be removed with the help of some nail polish remover. Wet a rag with some, then rub on the scuff mark lightly but quickly. You may need to give your shoes the once-over with a damp cloth afterwards.

Grease Be Gone

Liquid dish detergent is made especially to get out grease—which is why it is perfect for removing grease stains from your clothes. Pretreat grease-stained clothes with a bit of dishwashing liquid, then launder as usual.

Revive Water-Resistant Items

Do you have a jacket, backpack, or tent that used to be water-resistant, but has lost its effectiveness over time? Set your hair dryer to its highest setting and blow air evenly over it. The warmth will reactivate the coating on the cloth that makes it repel water.

A Coat of Coffee Does the Trick

If your black cotton items are starting to look more like they're dark blue, wash a load of only black items. But first, brew a strong pot of black coffee, then add it to the rinse cycle.

Hand-Washing Tip

When you're hand-washing cashmere and wool, add a drop of baby oil to the water during your last rinse. The oil will make the fabric more pliable, so you can more easily move it back into its original shape for drying.

—Cece Barrington, Shelby, NB

Fix Frustrating Trousers

Keep the waistband of your slacks from curling up by ironing a strip of rug binding onto it. Problem solved!

Who Knew? CLASSIC TIP

To make your clothes dry more quickly, throw a dry towel in with each load.

Tea Stains

Tea and lemon are best friends—even in the laundry room. Rub a tea stain with equal parts lemon juice and water. Just make sure the mixture only gets on the stain, using a Q-tip or eyedropper if necessary.

Blood Stains

Here's a unique way to remove blood stains, in case you've tried everything else and it's failed. Mix unseasoned meat tenderizer with a bit of water to form a thick paste, then apply it to the stain. Let sit for a half an hour, then rinse and launder as usual.

Brighten Your Whites

Add ½ cup lemon juice to the wash cycle of your washing machine to brighten your white clothes. They'll also smell wonderful!

Bird Got Your Leather?

If you were enjoying a nice day outside until a bird pooped on your leather jacket, don't go get your BB gun. Instead, rub a bit of petroleum jelly into the spot and let set for five minutes. It should rub right off.

How to Wash Lace

Even if you hand-wash it, lace can get easily tangled and torn when cleaning. To prevent this from happening, safety-pin the lace to a sheet or smaller cloth. Wash gently as usual, then unpin when dry.

Smelly Shoes?

Place a fabric softener sheet in your shoes overnight to get rid of any foul odors. This also works for hampers, gym bags, or anything else that needs a little freshening.

Even Smellier Shoes!

Here's another great tip for preventing smelly shoes. Take a couple of old socks without holes and fill them with scented cat litter. Then place them in the shoes when you're not wearing them. They'll suck up any moisture, and odor along with it.

Don't Give Up, Get Creative

If you can't get a coffee or tea stain out of a white tablecloth, there is one last solution. Soak the tablecloth in a bucket of strong coffee or tea (depending on the type of stain) for two hours. You won't get the stain out, but you will dye your linen a lovely earth tone!

Shiny Pearls for Life

Pearl buttons, whether they're real or fake, can benefit from a coating of clear nail polish.

Storing Leather and Suede

When storing leather and suede garments, don't cover them in plastic. These materials need a little breathing space, or they'll quickly dry out.

Spotty Situation

It never fails that the second our family is all dressed up in their Sunday Finest (which is definitely not every Sunday), a leaky pen materializes out of nowhere. Luckily this powerful fix is made from ingredients we always have on hand. Mix white vinegar, lemon juice, milk, and borax in a bowl (go heavier on the vinegar and milk, easy on the other two). Lay one paper towel over the stain and one underneath. Use a clean sponge to apply the solution to the stain gently (you don't want to rub it into the fabric). Rinse with cold water and repeat as necessary.

Gummy Mess

If you've gotten gum on your clothes, try rubbing them with egg whites using an old toothbrush. If that doesn't work, you can also try placing a piece of wax paper on the affected area, then ironing the wax paper. The gum should transfer from the cloth to the paper—problem solved!

Winterize Your Shoes

To protect your shoes from getting damaged and stained by too much rock salt in the winter months, coat them with hair conditioner and let it soak in. The conditioner will repel the salt, and help keep leather shoes supple.

Who Knew? CLASSIC TIP

Dab a small drop of clear nail polish on the front of a button to keep the threads in place and never lose a button again.

Mismatching Socks

When your kids' socks finally need to be thrown away (or turned into rags) because of holes, rips, or stains, make sure to keep their mates. Since you probably bought them in a pack, it's only a matter of time before another one just like it bites the dust. And if you end up with mismatching socks, your kids can still wear them around the house or to bed.

—*Debra R. Young*

How to Fix a Shrunken Sweater

If you've accidentally shrunk a sweater in the dryer, there may still be hope. Let it sit in a bucket of water with a generous amount of hair conditioner mixed in. The chemicals in the conditioner can untangle the fibers in your sweater, making them expand back to their original condition. If that doesn't work, it's time to cut up the sweater and make some new mittens!

Storing Sweaters

When putting away your sweaters for the spring and summer months, wrap them in newspaper and tape the sides. The newspaper will keep away both moths and moisture.

How to Save a Stretched-Out Sweater

Somehow, our boys always manage to stretch out the cuffs of their sweaters. If you have a sweater-stretching problem, too, use this quick fix to get them back into shape. Spritz the area with warm water, and then turn your hair dryer on it. The heat will cause the wool or cotton to shrink back into place.

Stuck Shoelaces?

If you can't get the knot out of your shoelaces, here's a simple trick to make the job easier. Just sprinkle your laces with talcum or baby powder. The powder will provide extra friction that will make them easy to untie in seconds.

CHAPTER 15

Don't Throw it Away: Second Lives for Ordinary Items

Plastic Hanger Covers

We hate throwing out *anything* at our house. Even plastic from the dry cleaners is turned into trash bags by tying a knot by the hanger hole. They're great for showing off pretty wastebaskets because they're clear!

Mouse Pads Without Mice

Extra mouse pads can do a lot more than take up space in a desk drawer. Put the ones that don't have a plastic coating to use in the kitchen as hot plates so you can keep the fancy trivets clean for company. Repurposed pads can also be used as shelf liners, mini placemats for kids, or kneepads for gardening and playing with sidewalk chalk.

Squeeze Bottles Still Have Air!

Save plastic squeeze bottles, but not to store things in. Wash them out and let them dry, and they make the perfect substitute for bottles of compressed air, which are used to clean out computer keyboards, electronics, and other tiny crevices. This works especially well with squeeze bottles with small spouts, such as lemon juice dispensers.

Oven Mitts for Your Car

When it's time to retire your oven mitts because they're covered in stains and burn marks, don't throw them away. Save them for use with your car. Oven mitts are great to use when handling hot engine parts or even as a washing mitt.

Coffee Can Lids

Instead of throwing away the lids to coffee cans, use them as a washable, greener alternative to parchment paper. Place them between slabs of burgers in the freezer or use them to set things on in the microwave while you're heating them up.

—*Caren C., Red Bank, SC*

Yarn Container

Yarn can get out of control very quickly (especially if you have cats), so keep each ball of yarn in a dispenser made from an appropriately sized soda bottle (cleaned out, of course). Cut a hole in the bottom big enough to slip the yarn through, then place your skein inside and string it out through the bottle opening.

Checkbook Covers Turned Organizers

When you receive new checks in the mail, don't throw away the plastic cover that often comes with them. Instead, use it as an organizational tool to store receipts, itineraries, or other papers that find their way into your purse or wallet.

What to Do with Wet Umbrellas

Need a cover to store your wet umbrella in while you're on the go? Look no further than the end of your driveway. The plastic bags newspapers come in are waterproof, and are the perfect size.

Shower Curtain Liner

When it's finally time to replace your shower curtain liner, keep the old one and use it for a drop cloth while painting or doing art projects.

Binder Clips

If you're one of those people who prance around town without a purse or giant bag, then we envy you, because we're sure we look like we're moving to another country most days. If you can pull off a fanny pack, more power to you. Otherwise, get that free and easy look (and feel) by pinching a couple of binder clips from the supply closet at work. Use them to fasten your keys and dollar bills to your pockets, belt or waistband. Look Ma—no hands!

Quick Fix for a Loose Button

After rifling through your clothes for a half an hour, you've finally decided on the perfect outfit to wear—but a button is loose! If you're about to lose a button and you're already halfway out the door, use a twisty tie instead. Just remove the paper covering, then twist it through the holes in the button and fasten on the other side of the cloth. Just make sure to replace with real thread later!

Makeshift Vase

When you're serving breakfast in bed, don't despair if you can't find a vase for that elegant touch of fresh flowers. Grab a toothbrush holder, which gives a mod look and holds the flowers up quite nicely.

Recycled Inbox

Cereal boxes make great stacking trays for your home office. Carefully cut off the top and back of the box, and you have an inbox waiting to happen. If you don't like the Total, Wheaties, and Chex look, spray the boxes with silver spray paint and let dry before using.

—David Dean, Fairbanks, AK

Repurpose an Old Candle

You've lost the wick of an old candle, and you were never really crazy about the scent anyway. Turn your old candle into a pincushion by simply sticking pins in the top or the sides. The wax will even help them slide more easily into cloth.

Venetian Blinds

Before you toss out that set of old Venetian blinds, cut out a dozen of the blinds to use as straight edges. They're great for home projects, because if you get any paint, varnish, or other material on them, you can just throw them away. We especially like them in lieu of using tape to make sure paint stops at the ceiling, because it's easier than trying to tape a straight line. As for the rest of the blinds, take the ladder-shaped strings that hold them together and give them to your kids. You'll quickly find that action figures and small dolls always have a use for ladders.

Garden Hose

Old hose finally kick the bucket? Before you throw it away, cut two portions that are each about a foot long, then cut a slit in them. They'll make perfect covers for the blades of ice skates.

DIY Comforter Cover

Even the sewing-challenged can manage to make a cover for their comforter using two sheets sewn together. Mix and match patterns if you'd like. Ours has a flannel sheet on one side, which makes it extra cozy. Don't forget to leave one side open (with a few buttons intact) so you can remove the cover for washing.

An Ingenious Way to Cover Up Ugly Toilet Bolts

If the caps to the bolts at the base of your toilet have cracked or gone missing, you've probably discovered that they're hard to replace. A perfectly suitable replacement are the protective caps used on some stick deodorants that need to be removed before you can apply the deodorant for the first time. So go buy a few new sticks of deodorant, and make sure to take a look at the cap color before you buy!

Winter Time-Saver

If you park your car outside during winter, you can save yourself scraping and wiping time each morning by wrapping your side mirrors and windshield wipers in old plastic bags.

Breath Mint Containers

The containers to Tic Tacs and other breath mints are perfect for storing tiny items like pins, needles, buttons, beads, and nails. Plus, they'll still smell minty fresh when you open them!

Keep that Carton

Don't discard that partitioned wine or liquor carton! Instead, cut the top off and keep it in the garage for storage of sporting goods, fishing poles, and other sundries.

Bottles for Boots

One-liter and other-sized plastic bottles are perfect for propping up leather boots. Just clean the bottles and place one in each of your knee-high boots, and you won't have to worry about them getting wrinkles from folding over.

Match Point Jar Opener

You've seen those nifty, colorful jar openers in cool houseware shops, but you might not realize you've got a bunch of tools that are just as effective lying around your garage or basement. Using an X-Acto knife, slice open an old tennis ball and you've got two handy openers——point, set, match. Now pass the olives.

Pantyhose and Other Nylons

If your tights, knee highs, or other nylon items have holes that can't be solved with the old clear nail polish trick, use them as extra stuffing in sagging throw pillows.

Who Knew? CLASSIC TIP

It's hard to get more than a few wearings out of a pair of pantyhose, but luckily there are lots of uses for them once they get runs. Save them to use as dust rags, or use them to buff your shoes. We find they polish even better than a normal cloth.

Turn Extra-Large Tees into Extra-Stylish Tees

If you're like us, you have a million XL T-shirts that you've gotten from various organizations and events. Unfortunately, all of them make you look like a formless blob. Fix them into something you would actually wear by getting a little creative. To make a scoop-necked shirt that's perfect to wear over bathing suits or tank tops, cut off the piece of fabric that runs along the neck hole with a pair of scissors. Try the shirt on, and cut a little at a time until it fits your style and shape. To make a fitted tank top from your XL shirt, cut off the sleeves, then slice up the sides of the shirt and stitch them back together more tightly to fit your form. For instructions on how to perform these T-shirt surgeries and many more (most of which don't even require a sewing machine), check out the book *Generation T* by Megan Nicolay. (And make sure to get it for free at the library!)

Dryer Sheets

After you pull your clothes out of the dryer, save the fabric softener sheet! Tape it to your heat or air conditioning vent and it will freshen the whole room.

—*Marge Backes*

A New Use for Dustpans

Instead of throwing away an old dustpan (even a cracked one), wash it thoroughly and throw it in with your kid's sandbox toys. It makes a great scoop.

Wipes Dispenser Turned Organizational Tool

An old plastic cylindrical dispenser for baby wipes or disinfectant wipes is perfect for holding your child's chunky markers. (Cut to size if necessary.)

Homemade Exercise Weights

If you have teenage boys, odds are they'll sign up for a sport at some point that requires them to do minor strength conditioning at home. If you can't afford a set of weights, just take some empty plastic milk jugs and fill them with dry pinto beans. The result won't be perfect, but it'll be good enough to fake it.

Save Your Bottles

If you're looking for a cheap and practical toy for kids, thoroughly wash old ketchup, salad dressing, and shampoo bottles and let the kids use them to play in the swimming pool or bathtub. They're also a good way to wash shampoo out of hair at bathtime.

Make Your Own Watering Can

Don't spend money on a watering can unless it's for decorating purposes—it's much more practical to make your own. Simply wash out an old 1-gallon milk jug, then poke or drill very small holes below the spout on the side opposite the handle. Fill it with water, screw the top back on, and you have a homemade device to water your plants!

Perfect Storage Containers

Instead of throwing away the boxes that powdered laundry detergent comes in, we keep them to store household items. We have one in the garage for tools, one for my wife's sewing supplies, and we give them to the kids for toys. They're perfect because they're easy to carry and lined with waterproof wax. Just make sure to rinse them out first!

—*Eggbert Joliet, Toronto, ON*

Homemade Bath Pillow

To make your own bath pillow, reuse a household item no one seems to be able to get rid of: packing peanuts! Pour packing peanuts into a large, resealable freezer bag, then let out some of the air and seal. Place in the bath as a soft resting place for your head.

White-Out

There's still a use for old-fashioned liquid paper, so if you've still got it, don't throw it away. Use it as touch-up paint for white appliances, like your refrigerator. If your fridge has a ding but it's not white, try buying a small amount of touch-up paint from a car detailer.

Tops to Condiment Bottles

When you've used all the ketchup in a plastic squeeze bottle, throw the cap in the dishwasher and wash until the caked-on ketchup is gone. Keep it, along with other tops to condiment bottles, handy in the kitchen. When your current bottle gets all mucked-up, simply switch it out with a clean top and throw the dirty one in the dishwasher.

● Who Knew?

Each day the population of the United States throws away enough trash to fill 63,000 garbage trucks.

Garlic and Onion Skins

Yes, there's even a second use for the skins of garlic and onions. Save them for the next barbecue and toss them into the fire just before grilling meats or vegetables. The flavor is terrific.

The Perfect Tie Holder

Don't throw away the little z-shaped hooks that come with dress socks—use them as tie holders! Slip them onto a hanger and they are perfect for hanging the tie that accompanies that particular suit. Who knew?

Butter Box

If the butter you buy comes in a flat box of four, don't throw away the container when you're done. These square boxes are perfect for stowing sandwiches! Now I can just put my lunchtime sandwich in my purse and head to work without worrying about it getting smushed.

—Sarah Parkarvarkar

Fun with Old Crayons

If your child has lots of little crayon pieces left over, turn them into a fun craft project by removing the paper and melting the pieces together in an old muffin tin. Your child will love the new, enormous crayon with unpredictable colors!

Clean That Jar

After your jar candles burn out, they can be cleaned out and reused for any number of things—including other candles. One way to clean a candle jar is by setting your oven to 200°, melting the leftover wax, and then pouring it out. An even better way, though, is to put it in the freezer for an hour and then pry out the frozen block of wax. It should fall right out.

Shower Caps

Shower caps that you receive for free in hotel rooms are perfect for wrapping your shoes before you pack them in your suitcase. The plastic cap will keep the rest of the items in your suitcase from becoming dirty.

Use Easter Eggs All Year Round

Instead of packing away those plastic Easter eggs for once-a-year use (or tossing them out altogether), you can keep using them throughout the year. For instance, instead of putting snacks in Ziploc bags in your child's sack lunch, put the snacks inside the eggs. They can be filled with M&Ms, Skittles, Cheerios, Goldfish crackers, and a variety of other things.

—Hadley Moore, Hartford, CT

Shower Curtain Rings

Got new curtain rings (or took our advice to change them out with ribbon)? Use the old ones to organize your coat closet. Hammer a nail into the wall, then hang a couple of curtain rings on it. They can be used to grasp items like gloves and hats, or you can run a scarf through one.

Dryer Lint

Instead of throwing away lint you've cleaned out of your dryer's screen, use it as kindling for your fireplace. It lights quickly and can be stuffed places paper can't.

Old Toothbrushes

There are many uses for an old toothbrush—the biggest being to clean crevices and other tiny spaces like the molding between bathroom tiles. Our favorite second life for an old toothbrush, however, has to be in the kitchen. Use an old toothbrush to quickly and easily remove the silks from a fresh ear of corn.

● Who Knew? CLASSIC TIP

Forget about expensive plant food! Just save the water when you boil potatoes or pasta, let it cool, and use it to water your plants. They'll love the starchy water.

Six-Pack Containers

Six-packs are a must-have at a barbecue—and not just for the beer. Turn an old six-pack container into a holder and carrier for condiments like ketchup, mustard, and relish. You can even stick napkins and plastic utensils inside. To make it extra strong (and waterproof), wrap in duct tape!

Egg Cartons

Cardboard egg cartons are great to use when starting fires (in your fireplace or outside in a pit, of course). Fill them with bits of wood and pieces of paper that would be too small to use on their own, like receipts. You can also fill an egg carton with charcoal and use it to start your barbecue grill.

Produce Bags

The plastic bags you put your produce in at the grocery store are perfect for makeshift gloves. Slip your hands inside and fasten around your wrists with rubber bands.

Cardboard Boxes

Place the side of a large cardboard box near your door during snow storms so family members can pile their filthy, slushy boots and winter gear on top while keeping your home clean.

Velcro

Before you throw away something that has Velcro on it, first cut out the part of the article that has the "hooked" side of the Velcro. It's perfect for getting the little pills off of sweaters, scarves, and other clothing items.

Camera Saver

When packing, a plastic container for bar soap is usually the perfect size for stowing your digital point-and-shoot camera inside.

Eggshells

Even eggshells have a great use before you throw them away: getting rid of rings on hard-to-clean places in vases. Fill the vase mostly full with warm water, then add a drop of dishwashing liquid and the egg shells. They'll act as an abrasive to scrub off the stains.

Versatile Speakers

If you're getting rid of a computer, make sure to keep the speakers if they are detachable. Plug them into a portable CD player or mp3 player, and you have an inexpensive stereo for your kitchen, bathroom, or workspace!

—Christopher James

Tissue Box

An empty tissue box is great for holding plastic shopping bags that are waiting for their chance at a second life. As you place each bag in the box, make sure its handles are poking up through the hole. Then thread each new bag through the previous bag's handles. That way, when you pull a bag out of the box, the next one will pop right up.

Mittens

Mittens that you no longer use make great glasses cases! You can also use them during their "off-season" to hold sunglasses in the summer.

Who Knew?

According to recent studies, between 2 and 5 percent of what we throw away each day is potentially reusable.

Coffee Cans

Coffee cans are the perfect container for more than just coffee. You can also use them to bake dough! Use like you would a loaf pan, making sure to grease them first, and only fill halfway if you're making a bread with yeast in it.

Candle Tubes

Looking for a container to store long, tapered candles in? Now you have one: The tube that Pringles potato crisps come in. It even has a lid!

Bottles for Candles

Here's another great use for used, clear 2-liter bottles. Cut off the tops and bottoms, then place the middle portions over candles that you're using outside. The plastic will act as a shield to keep wind away and the fire lit.

Fish Tank Water

Even old water from your aquarium can be used again. Use it to water your houseplants—they'll love the extra "fertilizer" the fish provided.

Repurposed Paintbrush

Before you throw away that old paintbrush, use it as a cleaning brush. Cut the bristles very short and use in hard-to-reach places like the corner of the tub.

A Comb for Your Broom

Use an old wide-toothed comb to get the lint and hair out of the midst of your broom's bristles. And always store brooms upside down to make sure the bristles stay straight.

Packing Peanuts Turned Beauty Product

Here's another use for those packing peanuts that you never seem to be able to get rid of. Save eight of them and use the next time you're painting your toenails. Insert one between each pair of toes to separate them and more easily give yourself a pedicure.

Unwanted Perfume

Someone gave you perfume as a present and although it smells nice, it's just not your bag. Instead of using it on yourself, use it to freshen rooms in your home. Squirt a small amount near light bulbs, and when you turn on the lights you'll turn on a lovely scent with them. You can also use perfume as a refill for a bottle that contains aromatherapy sticks.

Do You Play Guitar?

If so, you never need to buy a pick again! Instead, use the plastic fasteners found on bread bags. They work just as well, and they're free!

Cheesecloth

After you've used a piece of cheesecloth, don't throw it away. Throw it into a load of laundry, then use it as a dust rag. It will trap small particles in its weave, and won't leave behind a bunch of lint.

—*Fanny Lassiter, Pine Bluff, AR*

Get Creative with Wallpaper Scraps

You've just finished a big wallpaper job, and have at least a half a roll left. Use your extra wallpaper scraps to decorate accessories in the room. Cover the fronts of drawers or cabinets, even the backs of chairs! Wallpaper can also be used to cover notebooks, pencil cases, and other office supplies.

Yet Another Use for Packing Peanuts

Packing peanuts will take several decades to decompose, so you can make better use of them than throwing them away. Place them at the bottom of flowerpots before covering with soil and planting flowers and other plants. They'll keep the pot well drained and much lighter than if you had used rocks.

When a Pin Is a Button

Every now and then, we or our kids will receive a round pin with a removable back to commemorate an event, membership in an honor society, or an award. We never knew what to do with these pins (which look like tie tacks), until we discovered they can be used as a "replacement" button on jeans and other pants that have become too loose. If you've lost weight and your pants no longer fit, affix one of these pins to your pants next to the usual button that keeps them closed (you may want to secure the back with a bit of duct tape). You can then pull the other side of the fly tighter, looping the button hole through the new "button" that's farther away than the real one.

How Tennis Balls Can Keep Your Pool Clean

Tennis balls can keep your pool clean, but not in the way you might think. Throw a few old tennis balls into the pool, and they'll absorb any oil that floats to the surface. In the summertime, that means plenty of sweat and sunscreen.

Matchbook Substitution

Your chipped fingernail is driving you crazy, but you don't have an emery board on hand (no pun intended). Luckily, you can use a matchbook instead! Just rub your nail on the part that you would use to strike a match—problem solved!

Second Use for a Peppermint Tin

It seems like we can't think of second uses fast enough to use up all our empty peppermint tins. Here's one that will at least use up one or two: Clean the tin thoroughly, then fold up some tissues to keep with you on-the-go. It's much cheaper than a tissue "purse pack," and the tissues will be kept safe from any spills in your bag...meaning that you can use them for spills in your bag if necessary!

An Unlikely Home for Your Curling Iron

You're about to leave on a trip, but your curling or flat iron is still hot. Make sure you don't scorch your clothes or the inside of the your suitcase with an oven mitt. Just slip the iron inside (leaving the cord free) and you can be on your way.

Make Use of That Puffy Paint

Your kids were really into decorating T-shirts for a while, so you bought a dozen tubes of puffy paint. Now that their obsession has ended, what do you do with it all? Put it to good use by slip-proofing socks. Just dab several lines of dots on the bottoms of your and your children's socks, and they'll be just like store-bought "slipper socks" at a fraction of the cost.

Towel Rod Turned Organizational Tool

If you're replacing the towel rods in your bathroom, don't throw the old ones away. They're perfect for organizing spray bottles! Just install the rod in your laundry room, on the door to a cabinet, or wherever else you store your cleaning supplies. Then hook the spray triggers over the rod.

A Place for Your Pens

Do you have a bulletin board with a calendar, notepad, or something else your family regularly writes on? Instead of tying a pen to the bulletin board with a string, use this easy solution: Tack the sheath that came with your umbrella (you know, the one that's been littering the bottom of your coat closet) to the bulletin board, then store as many pens, markers, and pencils as you'd like inside.

Keep Your Wine Safe

Bringing two bottles of wine to a party? You're welcome at our house anytime! Make sure they don't bang against each other in the bag with the help of some sweat bands (the kind you'd wear on your wrist or forehead). Wrap one around each of the bottles, and they can safely clink together. Better yet, they'll soak up any condensation, making the bottles easy to hold and pour from.

Condiment Cuteness

If you're like us, you received a bunch of baby spoons at your baby shower—but what do you do when your kid is grown up enough to use a "big spoon"? We've repurposed ours as spoons to condiments like mustard and mayonnaise. They look adorable, and they're great conversation-starters at the table.

Using Up Those Baby Food Jars

If you have a baby, you probably have lots of baby food containers lying around. In addition to making great organizational tools for drawers, baby food jars are also great for painting projects. When you have quick touch-ups to do on your paint job, just pour a bit of paint into a baby food jar and take it with you around the room. It's much easier than carrying around the whole can or a tray.

CHAPTER 16

Managing Your Money and Lowering Your Bills

Reduce Your APR

Ask and you shall receive! It sounds too simple to be true, but one of the first things you should do when attempting to reduce your debt is call up your credit card company and ask them to reduce your interest rate or annual percentage rate (APR). If you have had the card for a while and have routinely made payments on time, the company is usually happy to take this piece-of-cake step to keep your business.

Planning for the Future

When you get a bump in salary, put a higher proportion of it into your savings account. For instance, if you get a 4 percent raise, add 1 percent to your household budget and set aside the other 3 percent for your retirement account. You'll thank yourself later!

Make Sure You Know the Facts

Always read the terms of a credit card agreement before you sign up for the card. The fine print may be boring, but you owe it to yourself to make sure you're not getting a bum deal. Highlight any passages you don't understand, and find out what they mean by asking a lawyer or accountant; or simply look the phrase up in an internet search engine. Some agreements will try to scam you—one recent ploy is for companies to buy up your bad debt, then trick you into signing up for a card that already has the bad debt tacked onto the balance. (If this happens to you, you should insist on getting documents that prove that you are accountable for that debt or the interest, so don't agree to anything until you speak with that lawyer or accountant). Be especially careful if the offer seems too good to be true.

Neighborhood Changes Can Mean Lower Insurance

A big factor in how much you're charged for homeowners insurance is where you live. So if there have been improvements to your neighborhood or subdivision, such as storm drains being installed or a fire hazard being cleared away, make sure to alert your insurance company and see if they will lower your rates.

Which Cell Plan Should You Be Using?

Do you end up with lots of unused cell phone minutes at the end of the month? Visit BillShrink.com, where you can enter the amount you talk and text to find the best plan for you in your area. We found a plan that saved us $10 per month!

● Who Knew?

According to the Federal Reserve Board, Americans have $2.56 trillion in consumer debt.

Bring It Together: Debt Consolidation

Debt consolidation is a smart and relatively painless way to ease some of the hardship of having lots of debt. With debt consolidation, you can lower your monthly payments, and you may also be able to lock in a lower interest rate. The easiest kinds of consolidations to obtain are for student loans, but many banks also offer consolidation services for mortgages, and (if your credit score is good) credit card debt. There are different types of debt consolidation services, so make sure you know what you're getting into. Some services—often non-profits—contact the financial institutions you owe the money to and try to get your interest rates lowered. Then you pay them one lump payment each month, and they pay the companies for you. Other types of debt consolidation—usually through banks—basically just give you a loan to pay off all your other loans. Either way, debt consolidation can make your finances a little more manageable.

When Insurance Isn't a Good Idea

When purchasing a cell phone, never sign up for insurance or a warranty—and if you're paying a monthly fee for insurance, cancel it immediately. The insurance plan of many cellular providers has a deductible of up to $50 that you are responsible for paying, and the phone you'll usually receive as a replacement will be an already-outdated model from last year. The cost of taking your chances and buying a cheap replacement if necessary is much less than what your cellular company is offering you.

Better Budgeting

Trying to get a handle on budgeting? Visit FrugalMom.net/blog/?p=364, which will not only walk you through how to better budget your money, but will also give you free, downloadable forms like a spending tracker to help get you started.

Up Your Credit Score

It's a tough time to get credit, so make sure your rating is as good as possible. Here are a few easy ways to raise your credit score.

✦ If you haven't already, get a free credit report by going to AnnualCreditReport.com or calling 1-877-322-8228. Don't be fooled by other "free credit report" sites, which often require you to pay a membership fee.

✦ Check your report for accuracy. On the internet, you can often click the item directly to dispute it. Make sure all of the addresses listed are current or former addresses, and that all loans and lines of credit listed are yours. If you're unsure, contact the customer service number on the report and ask for more information.

✦ Get rid of credit cards you never use anymore. See three or four credit cards for stores you don't frequently shop at? Even if you don't carry balances on these cards, one of the things that can lower your credit rating is the amount of available credit you have. Call the number on the back of the cards and cancel them!

✦ If you are listed as a secondary card holder for an account of someone who's racked up a lot of debt on the card, this can negatively impact your credit rating. If it isn't necessary for you to be on this credit card account, call the company and get your name taken off.

✦ You can request a free credit report once a year. Try to make a regular habit of requesting it and reviewing it as closely as you would your bank statement. The more quickly you notice a discrepancy, the easier it will be to get it removed from your report.

Meds by Mail

Before you reorder a prescription, find out if your insurance provider offers a pharmacy-by-mail service. Though it's not as easy as going to your local pharmacy, you can save up to 30 percent on some medicines.

—*Emme Boutin-Robertson, Cambridge, MA*

Smile: You're Saving Money on Dental Care

It's true: you can get that root canal you've been putting off *and* keep your retirement account. Find a dental school in your area to visit for regular cleanings and check-ups, and you'll save big. Be prepared, however, for crowded waiting rooms, long visits, and less privacy. While you're waiting, start dreaming about that cruise to Alaska.

Automatic Debit

Nothing's worse than getting socked with an unfairly enormous late fee for paying your bills a couple of days late. Say goodbye to late fees forever by setting up an automatic debit from your checking account. You can usually set up automatic debit by calling the company the account is with or visiting their website.

Gas Cards

Take an extra-careful look at credit cards offered by gas companies—most have a higher interest rate than average credit cards. Before you sign up, make sure to ask about their fraud protection, which is usually pretty weak. You may be better off using a "regular" credit card that offers rebates on gas purchases. Two good choices are the Discover Platinum Gas Card and the Chase Cash Plus Card.

Good Guidance

If you feel like you're in over your head with your debt, or if you simply want some answers about the most efficient way to pay it off and manage a budget, there is free counseling available to you. These one-on-one sessions are offered by organizations across the country who want to help people who are struggling with money problems. They also often offer consolidation loans and debt management programs. To find an agency that will work with you in person, over the phone, online, or via mail, call the National Foundation for Credit Counseling at 1-800-388-2227. This organization makes sure its members are accredited, not-for-profit, and generally on the level.

How Many Minutes Do You Have Left?

There are easy ways to keep an eye on how many minutes you've used on your cell phone each month. If you are a Verizon Wireless customer, dial #BAL (#225) and press call to check your balance. To check minute usage, dial #MIN (#646) and press call. To check text messages and data usage, dial #DATA (#3282) and press call. If you have AT&T, dial *BAL# (*225#) and press call. For minutes, dial *MIN# (*646#) and press call. Now you'll always know when you're about to go over your allotted minutes.

Entertainment Spending

The point of making a budget isn't getting rid of your entertainment spending, it's just prioritizing what you like to spend your money on.

Decide what your favorite activities are (as a family, couple, and by yourself or with friends). Then make sure you save enough to spend on the things you really enjoy. For instance, you may decide you'd like to give up going to the movies a few times a month so you can go to a concert. Or you might prefer to spend your money on a nice dinner rather than a couple of trips to the bar.

Make the Bank Switch

It may be a pain, but if you're getting socked with fees for your checking or savings accounts, it's time to switch banks. You should never have to pay monthly service charges, and many banks are now even offering cash for opening a new account. Make sure to visit several banks in your area and ask about their fees, interest rates, opening bonuses, and other perks like free checking.

Don't be Fooled by a Sneaky Bank

Many banks are desperate for your money these days, and they like to offer free stuff. Don't take their advertisements at face value, and make sure to read the fine print carefully. One major bank is currently touting, "Access to over 35,000 free ATMs! Never pay a fee again!" The fine print? Their offer is just a link to AllPointNetwork.com, where you can, in fact, get access to 35,000 free ATMs—without joining anything at all!

Are You Sure You Know What's on Your Phone Bill?

Phone companies are notorious for automatically enrolling you in a calling package filled with services you never use. Make sure to check your phone bills for extra charges such as voicemail, three-way calling, and call forwarding. If you don't use these services, cancel them to save! If you use your cell phone more than your home phone, you might want to consider stripping your land line down to the bare minimum or canceling your service outright.

A Must-Visit Site!

At LowerMyBills.com, you'll find a way to reduce just about any bill. Whether you're looking to refinance your home, consolidate your credit card debt, or just lower your phone bill, this site will give you the tools you need to compare different companies and calculate your costs. You can also sign up for an email newsletter filled with tips and deals.

Double Pay

Credit card interest is calculated based on your average daily balance over the month, which means you can reduce your charges by making more payments. Instead of paying, say, $300 at the end of the month, split that up into two $150 payments. That way, your average daily balance will be lower, and therefore your finance charges will be, too.

Cut the Cable

You can save money by disconnecting your cable TV service during the times of year that you don't need it. Going on a long vacation? Have a summer ahead filled with time-consuming activities? Just get rid of the cable during the time you won't be using it, and who knows, you might even be offered an enticing deal when it's time to re-subscribe.

Lead the Way for Your Friends

You're trying to keep your socializing budget under control, but your friends are constantly inviting you on expensive outings you can't afford! Instead of having to turn down invitations, take the initiative and be first to invite everyone out. This way, you can decide the place—something more in your price range. Better yet, host a potluck or movie night at your home.

A Visual Debt Reminder

If you're having trouble paying down your debt, try making a chart or graph of what you want to accomplish. Place it somewhere you'll see it often, and update it as you send in checks. Being able to track your progress will help keep you motivated!

—*Linda Everett*

Who Knew?

Seventy-seven percent of Americans say they "hate" financial planning. OK, I guess we did know that one.

Stop Paying For Unused Cellular Minutes

If you find yourself under-using your mobile minutes each month, consider canceling your current plan when your contract runs out and paying as you go instead. With pay-as-you-go phones, you pay an amount of money up front instead of getting a bill each month. Most plans will charge you 5–10¢ a minute, and offer discounts if you put a large amount of money—usually $100—on the phone. The good news is that you can also send and receive text (and sometimes picture) messages, and even surf the web on some phones. The bad news is that the minutes usually expire after a certain amount of time. Pay-as-you-go phones are great for phones that you pretty much only use in an emergency, and for giving to teens so that you can make sure they don't overspend. Ask at a cell phone or electronics store about pay-as-you-go phones and promotions.

Save Automatically

To help you save on a monthly basis, make it easier to contribute to your savings account. Banks allow you to set up recurring transfers, so set one up for each time you get paid. Putting even $50 into your savings account each time you get a paycheck will quickly add up, and you'll be glad you have it on a rainy day or when vacation time rolls around.

Be Vigilant about Your Car Insurance

When your auto insurance renewal comes in the mail, don't just write a check and send it in. Review your policy and make sure it's still the type of coverage you need as your vehicle ages year after year. When it gets to the point where your collision coverage premiums (plus the deductible) are almost the same as the value of the car itself, drop that portion of the coverage—you're only flushing money down the toilet.

When Health Insurance Goes Wrong

Those of us lucky enough to have health insurance love having to pay less for health care—as long as the system works. If (OK, *when*) you have problems with your health insurance reimbursing you for a claim, it can be so frustrating and even demoralizing that you're tempted to give up. Here are some steps you can take to make sure you get the money you deserve.

✦ Stay organized. Take notes when you are disputing a claim, and refer to them when you call the company. The representative will be more likely to take you seriously if you can state the dates you spoke to someone, what the claim or reference number is, and the amount it was for. Also make sure to have the date the service was performed and the date the claim was submitted on hand.

- ✦ Ask your doctor for help. If the insurance company is telling you the procedure wasn't necessary or "reasonable or customary," have your doctor's office write a letter or call the company to explain why it was.

- ✦ If you have a group plan, see if you can get the administrator of the plan (usually in your HR department) to help you complain to the company.

- ✦ Contact your state's department of insurance. If they won't help you go after the company, they can usually at least provide you with important information about your rights.

- ✦ Don't be afraid to go to court. If you feel you are unjustly being denied a claim, a court will probably think so, too. If the claim amount is less than $500, you will most likely not need an attorney, but if it is higher than that, many attorneys will take the case on a contingency basis (meaning they only get paid if you do) if it seems strong. Bring any literature from the company that seems to contradict why they have been telling you the cost wasn't covered—in most states, judges have ruled that policies have to be straightforward enough for a layperson to read them, not an insurance agent or lawyer.

Cheaper Tooth Care

Many companies don't offer dental insurance, but you can join a plan on your own for discounts ranging from 10–60 percent off. Check out DentalPlans.com or call 1-888-632-5353 to find a plan and dentist in your neighborhood. Certain plans may be used in combination with dental insurance you already have.

Waive It Off

It sounds too simple to be true, but you can often just ask credit card companies, utilities, landlords, and others to waive late fees. If you're a longtime customer with a good history, companies will often re-credit your account, especially if it was your first offense.

Share More Than Cookies with the Neighbors!

Do you and your neighbors both use wireless internet? A great way to save is to go in on an internet plan together. If you already have a plan, ask a neighbor you trust if they'd like to pay you for half the cost if you give them the password to your network. Especially if you live in an apartment building, you should be able to use the wireless internet hub you currently own, but if your homes are particularly far apart you may need to extend your network with a second hub or router.

Phone Cards: A Must for Overseas Dialing!

When making international phone calls, never dial directly. Instead, buy an international phone card at your local convenience store. Most specialize in a particular country or continent, and will allow you to talk for only pennies a minute. You can also go to AITelephone.com, which works pretty much the same way, but gives you the option of prepaying online or being sent a bill.

Choosing the Card That's Right for You

Even if you're in the market for a new credit card, the amount of offers that show up in your mailbox can be daunting. And whether you anticipate your relationship with the card to be long and prosperous, or quick and a little irresponsible, how do you know which card is right for you? Here are some questions to ask before you decide.

✦ How long is the introductory period? Most cards start you off with a good deal, like a low APR or free balance transfers. But make sure to check how long the promotional rates last.

✦ What perks does it have? If you fly a lot, cards with air-mile programs can save you hundreds. Other cards offer insurance on purchases or car rentals. Figure out how much you think these extras will save you, and take this into consideration when you pick a card.

✦ What will your credit limit be? Most companies don't like to tell you what your credit limit is until you apply for the card, but before you sign, first ask them how much you are going to be able to spend. If you're good about paying your bill off, having a high percentage of credit left will help your credit score. But if you have trouble keeping yourself from maxing out, ask if you can lower the card's limit.

✦ What's the best deal you can get? Compare card offers and don't be afraid to negotiate. Visit CardWeb.com, where you can find hundreds of cards sorted by types of rewards, your credit history, and their brand. Call the phone number listed to see if you qualify for cards that fit what you need.

Negotiate Your Way to Savings

If you're lucky enough to live in an area that has more than one company providing phone, cable, or other utilities, use this to your advantage by lowering your payment amount—without having to switch companies! Find out what the competitors are charging by calling them or visiting WhiteFence.com, then call and ask for your rates to be lowered. If the first person you talk to says no, don't be discouraged and don't be afraid to ask to speak to a supervisor. If you call between 9 a.m. and 5 p.m. you'll be more likely to get an experienced supervisor on the phone who's willing to bargain.

Who Knew?

Most banks are FDIC insured, but you should still make sure yours is. With an FDIC-insured bank, even if the financial institution fails your money will still be insured for up to $200,000.

Raise Your Deductibles to Lower Your Costs

You can save hundreds each year on your home and auto insurance by raising your deductibles. If you have more than one type of insurance with the same carrier, you may also qualify for bundled discounts. It's not in your insurance company's best interests to keep you informed about the lowest rates, so make sure you call them and ask.

Take Advantage of Employer Discounts

Your employer may offer more perks than just weak coffee in Styrofoam cups and free filtered water. In addition to the traditional retirement accounts and health care options, many employers—especially companies that have a national presence—offer many more benefits on a small and large scale. Check with your HR department to see if you can get pre-tax money for transportation or "flex-spending"—funds that you can spend on medical or other specified expenses. Many employers often have agreements with businesses and are able to offer their employees discounted movie and amusement park tickets, savings on cell phones and computer equipment, and cheaper rates at nearby gyms.

Change Your Due Dates

Here's an easy solution if you keep getting socked with late fees, or neglect to pay more than the minimum on your credit cards because the payment is always due at the same time as your rent. Ask your credit card company to change the date your payment is due. It might take a few months to kick in, but you'll be able to pay down the card more easily during the part of the month that isn't as much of a crunch.

It May Be Time For a Transfer

If you owe lots of money to one credit card and not-so-much to one with a lower interest rate, ask your credit card company if you can do a balance transfer. You may incur a fee, but you often end up saving in the end, and many cards offer them for free during the first year of your agreement. If you have two cards from the same company, ask if the card with the better deal allows "credit reallocation," which would let you transfer not only the balance from the other card but its credit limit as well, without even submitting you to another credit check.

What To Do When Collection Agencies Call

Nothing feels worse than having collection agencies calling you to try to collect on a debt. If you have old debt, it's time to stop feeling bad about it and confront the collection agencies or credit card companies head-on. Here are some tips for dealing with debt in collections, one of the worst kinds in terms of your credit report.

+ The first step is to stop ignoring phone calls and letters. It's hard, but you know it must be done!

+ It's important to remember the person you're talking to is just doing his or her job. If you're polite during the entire call, he or she will be more likely to help you out. Whatever you do, don't lose your cool.

+ The first tactic of most collection agencies will be to try to get you to pay the total amount at once. You should be aware that you can always set up a payment plan. Only pay as much as you think you can each month—never commit to more than you can pay and risk being unable to make payments.

+ Most collection agencies will settle for 40 to 60 percent of the total amount you owe. The more you can pay them immediately as a lump sum, and the higher you can make your monthly payments, the better! Don't be afraid to negotiate.

+ In local and state courts in many areas, lawsuits from collection and credit card agencies have been overturned. If you are being asked to pay more than 60 percent of the debt, the agency has been unable to show you proof that you owe the debt, or you otherwise feel like you're getting a raw deal, don't be afraid to go to court with the collection agency. Not only do you deserve to go in front of a neutral arbitrator, it will make the other party more likely to settle (because they won't want to pay lawyer's fees). However, it is vitally important that you stay apprised of court dates and show up to every one of them.

✦ Stay empowered! Remember the important thing: you're taking care of your bad debt. You deserve to be able to work toward clean credit, and to have the agency you owe money to be polite and respectful. Don't settle for less!

Save Money Fast On Homeowners Insurance

Did you know that most homeowners insurance policies will deduct 3–5 percent of your cost for adding simple security features such as a smoke alarm or dead bolts? You can often save a lot more if you're willing to install a more sophisticated security system. These systems can get expensive, but the savings (not to mention the security) may be worth it. Before you choose one, make sure to call your insurance company to see what kind of system they recommend. You may also be able to save if you are 65 or older.

Who Knew?

Although households with no landline use an average of 332 more minutes per month on their cell phones than those with a landline, they still spend an average of $33 less per month on phone service.

CHAPTER 17

Energy-Saving Solutions

A Smarter Power Cord

One of the easiest ways to save money on electricity is to turn off electronics when you're not using them. To make it easier, get a power strip like the SmartStrip, which powers down devices based on one device's usage. For example, when you switch off your computer, the SmartStrip will cut the power to your monitor, printer, and scanner as well.

Quick Lesson in Refrigeration

You can make your refrigerator more energy efficient by understanding how it works. Refrigerators use energy to reduce the humidity inside, which helps cool foods. Therefore, any time you leave an open container of liquid inside, you're wasting energy. Make sure all your pitchers have lids, and make sure dressings and moist leftovers are well-covered. You should also always let hot foods cool before placing them in the refrigerator, so it doesn't have to use extra energy to bring them down to room temperature. Of course, be careful with cooked meats, eggs, and poultry—they shouldn't stay out for more than an hour.

Be a Night Owl

You may not realize that most electric companies charge more for power during the day than at night. Contact your local utility to find out whether this is the case in your area. If it is, make sure to do all your laundry, dishwashing, internet surfing, and other power-intensive tasks during off-peak hours. We noticed the difference on our electric bill, and you will, too.

Hand Wash Separately

Having an Energy Star dishwasher is energy efficient, but not when you are running it twice a day. Cut back on the amount of space you take up in your dishwasher by washing large pots and pans the old-fashioned way in the sink. By spending a little extra water to wash these items separately, you'll save a lot of water in fewer loads washed.

Look For Leaks!

According to the Environmental Protection Agency, a well-sealed home can be up to 20 percent more energy efficient. Most leaks occur in the basement or attic—look where you feel a draft or around wiring holes, plumbing vents, ducts, and basement rim joints. You'll be able to seal lots of leaks with a simple caulking gun, but for instructions on how to plug larger holes go to EnergyStar.gov and search for "plug leaks."

Shut Out the Lights

One of the easiest ways to waste money is by leaving lights on that aren't being used. Save your hard-earned cash by buying motion-activated lights for your home, especially for bathrooms and hallways. It may seem expensive at first, but they'll pay for themselves soon enough. You'll love seeing a smaller electric bill each month!

—*Kitty Lubin Rosati, Crested Butte, CO*

Keep It Humid

It's true that it's not the heat that makes you feel warm, it's the humidity. Humid air feels warmer than dry air, so in the winter, instead of cranking the heat, run a humidifier. This allows you to turn down the heat, save energy, and still feel comfortable. Live, leafy plants also help raise humidity levels.

Does Your Teenager Take 45-Minute Showers?

If you have teenagers, try giving them an incentive to take shorter showers—like five minutes added on to their curfew for every minute they shave off their showering time.

—Salina Gonzalez, Minden, LA

Easy Fix for a Stuck Thermostat

If your furnace and AC don't seem to be paying attention to your thermostat, don't call the expensive repairman just yet. It could be a simple case of your thermostat's connectors being dirty. Take off the casing, and run the point of an index card through the connectors to remove any crud. Stand back and cross your fingers, and your thermostat may be as good as new.

Keep Cold Appliances Cold

It may be time to rearrange your kitchen for energy-efficient savings. Keeping appliances that heat things up (like a stove, oven, or toaster) away from your refrigerator will make it easier for your fridge and freezer to stay cold, which can save you lots of money in the long run.

Know Your Hot and Cold Water Levels

Quit fiddling with the knobs on your shower when trying to get the water just right before you hop in. Find your favorite setting, then mark where the knob is pointing on the tile with a dab of nail polish. This water-preserving trick is great for kids, who can take a long time adjusting the water before they get in.

Use Lighter Paint

If you're trying to decide between deep or baby blue for your walls, you should know that lighter colors of paint will help you use less energy. They reflect the light and heat in a room better than darker hues.

Make Sure That Lint Screen Is Clean!

Removing the lint from the screen in your dryer may not be enough to make sure it is running as efficiently as possible. The fabric softener used in dryer sheets can get caught in the mesh, even if you can't see it. To be sure you're completely cleaning the screen, remove it and clean it with warm, soapy water and a brush. Leave it out to dry completely before placing back in your dryer.

The Easiest Way to Save on Water

If you pay for water, make sure to never use more than you have to. Only wash full loads of laundry and dishes, and don't leave the tap running.

Fuel Co-Ops

A fuel co-op is an organization that negotiates lower rates for your heating gas by buying in bulk. Even though you normally have to pay a membership fee, you can save big bucks on your heating bill by joining a fuel co-op, and you often don't even need to change from your current gas company. Most co-ops will offer you discounts if you're a senior citizen or on a fixed income. To find one in your area simply type "fuel co-op" and your geographic location (e.g., "New Jersey") into Google or another search engine.

A Hot Attic Means a Hot House

When running your air conditioner, make sure your attic isn't hot, which will warm up ceilings and make it much more expensive to cool your home. Open any attic windows, and invest in a fan that will suck hot air out during the day and pump cool air in at night.

Leaky Fridge?

If your refrigerator is more than a few years old, the rubber lining that runs around the door (also known as the gasket) could be loose. To find out, close the door on a piece of paper. If you can pull it out without it ripping, your gasket is loose. To figure out where, turn on a battery-powered lamp or flashlight and place it in your fridge. Turn the lights off in your kitchen and close the door. Wherever you see light peeking through, cold air is leaking! Try regluing your gasket or buying a new one from wherever you purchased your fridge.

Close Some Vents

Close the heating and air-conditioning vents in rooms in your home you don't frequently use, like a guest room or laundry room. If your vents don't have closures, simply seal them off with duct tape.

—*Barbie Rodgers, Wilmington, NC*

Buy Your Water Heater a Jacket

A water heater insulation jacket costs $15–$35, but it can cut the cost to heat your water dramatically. By insulating your water heater, you'll cut in half the amount of energy it needs to heat standing water, also cutting down on the amount you need to pay. To find out if you need a water heater jacket, touch the side of it. If it's warm, it's leaking energy.

The Venetian Secret

Be smart when using your heating or air conditioning. When the heat's on, open the blinds on windows that are exposed to the sun, and use a little solar heat to help out your furnace! When you have the AC going, close as many blinds as possible, so that the sun won't get in and warm your house more than necessary.

Fabulously Full Freezer

Your freezer is more energy efficient when it's full of stuff, so don't be shy about stuffing it as much as possible. When you're running low on food items, just fill a few empty juice cartons with water and use them to fill up the space.

Ensure Accurate Temperature

For accurate temperature readings, make sure to place your thermostat away from sources of artificial heat, like ovens, appliances, computers, or direct sunlight. An inaccurately high temperature at the thermostat will cause the rest of the house to be colder than you want it to be. Similarly, make sure that cold air, such as that from windows or wiring holes, isn't making its way to the thermostat either. Also, make sure your thermostat is reading the inside room temperature and not the outside temperature.

Savings with Each Flush

A great way to save water is to fill a plastic bottle or two with sand and put them in your toilet tank. You'll use a lot less water with each flush. Just make sure you place them away from the operating mechanism. Also, don't use bricks—they disintegrate and can damage your toilet.

—Brad Elgart, Winters, TX

Replace Those Shower Heads!

If the shower heads in your home were installed before 1994, you should seriously consider replacing them with their modern, energy-saving equivalents. Check out your local hardware store for low-flow alternatives, and remember that just because it's low-flow doesn't mean it has to be weak!

Who Knew?

According to the US Department of Energy, electronics account for 15 percent of the average household's energy bill.

Finding a Water Leak

If you suspect you might have a water leak in your home, take a look at your water meter before you and your family leave the house on an all-day excursion. Write down the reading, and look at it again when you return. If any water has been used, you know you have a problem.

Defrost It!

A frosty freezer can make a tough job for your freezer's motor, which not only makes it less energy efficient, but can also lead to the motor burning itself out! If you have a quarter of an inch of frost build-up or more, it's time to defrost your freezer. Here's the easiest way how: Turn off your freezer, then turn a hairdryer on it. Use a wooden spoon to dislodge any large chunks of ice and throw them in your sink or potted plants. Once it's free of ice, wash it down with warm water with a bit of dishwashing liquid mixed in. Before you move back your perishables, first spray the entire freezer with non-stick cooking spray. It will make frost less likely to form, and ice a breeze to dislodge.

Lock Your Windows

In the winter, don't just keep windows closed, make sure they're locked for the tightest possible seal. This could greatly reduce drafts.

Let Your Computer Rest

Leaving your computer on all day can be a real energy drain, but with a program called Edison, you can program it to go into "sleep" mode to save you money. Visit Verdiem.com/edison to download the free software (sorry, PCs only), which lets you set up a schedule for when you normally use your computer and allows you to decide how deeply you want your computer to sleep. Then it does the rest of the work for you, making sure that your computer isn't using energy when it doesn't have to.

A Pain in the Drain

Make sure to drain your water heater once a year to get rid of sediment. Left too long, this grit can build up until you're using energy to heat sludge. To find out how to complete this simple home maintenance trick, type "how to drain a water heater" into Google or another search engine. And start to save!

● Who Knew?

If your faucet is leaking, it can add up to more than water running down the drain. One drop per second can add up to 165 gallons a month—that's more water than the average person uses in two weeks!

Brrrr!

When using your oven this winter, don't let all that warm air go to waste! As long as it won't pose a safety hazard to children or pets, keep your oven door open after cooking to help heat the house. A little goes a long way!

Leaky Toilets Mean Higher Water Bills

Does your toilet have a leak? To find out, put a drop of food coloring in the tank and see if it shows up in the bowl. If it does, fix the leak to save up to 73,000 gallons of water per year!

Keeping Extra Cool

It may feel like a waste to keep the fans on at the same time as the air conditioner, but it's not. You'll actually save money, because you can keep the thermostat higher once you've created an internal breeze that will make you feel several degrees cooler (think of how much the wind outside affects how cool you feel, regardless of the actual temperature). Keep the fan on only while people are in the room, though, and remember to regularly vacuum both fan and air conditioner vents for optimum efficiency.

Don't Throw Money Down the Pool Drain

Save money and electricity by running your pool pump and filter for the minimum amount of time necessary. Experiment by decreasing the amount of time you run it until you find where that point is. You should also set it for off-peak electricity times (morning and evening).

Water-Saving Secret

The easiest way to lower your water usage (and utility bill) is to screw low-flow aerators into your faucets. Aerators are easy to install, cost a dollar or less, and can save you $50 or more per year.

Make the Light Bulb Switch

If you know about going green, you've probably heard about compact fluorescent bulbs. If you haven't changed out your regular light bulbs yet, do it today! Not only will they last 10 times longer, they use up to 75 percent energy, bringing your electricity bill down.

Set It and Forget It

If you've ever turned on a sprinkler or soaker hose and then forgotten about it, the mechanical water timer is the gadget for you. Available at your local hardware store, these hose attachments work like egg timers and turn off the water supply after the amount of time you specify, usually between 10 minutes and two hours.

If You Were a Tree, Where Would You Be?

One way we save money on our electric bill is by providing our house with natural shade. Planting trees and shrubs so that they shade the sunny side of your home will help cut down on the amount of air conditioning needed.

Cold Is Better

Did you know that 80 to 90 percent of the energy used by a washing machine is to heat the water? When doing laundry, always use cold water to wash your clothes. Due to advances in detergents and washing machines, the only time you really need to use warm or hot water is when you need to get a really bad stain, like red wine or oil, out of an article. Not only will you help the environment, you'll save money on heating the water, too.

Who Knew?

New washing machines use about 20 fewer gallons of water per load than older machines.

Heat Less Water

You never use your water on full-blast hot anyway, so it's worth it to lower the temperature of your water. You can save up to $125 per year by simply lowering the thermostat on your hot water heater from 140° to 120° F.

A Cleaner Gasket

To save energy and keep your food cooler, clean your refrigerator door's gasket (that rubber lining that goes around it) with a little water and vinegar, then rub it with petroleum jelly to ensure a tighter seal.

Decorative Heat Saver

Here's a neat trick for keeping your house warm without spending a cent in the fall and spring. Pour water into mason jars or glasses (we use cleaned-out salsa jars with their labels removed) and line them up along your windowsill. During the day, the sun will warm the water, which will gently warm any air getting through your window at night. To make the jars even more decorative, add ribbons and bows! You can also add food coloring to the water for some pretty windowsill reflections.

—*MaryAnn Wenke, Foster, NH*

● Who Knew?

Brrr, it's cold in here! Wrap a very large piece of corrugated cardboard in aluminum foil (shiny side out), and place it behind your free-standing radiator. The foil will reflect the heat, and you won't have to keep telling your landlord to turn up the boiler.

Leaking Fix

If your toilet runs for a long time after each flush, you're wasting water! If the problem is that valve gets stuck open when the flapper chain gets tangled, here's an easy fix: Simply cut a straw so it's about 6 inches long, then thread the chain through it. It will keep the chain from tangling, ensuring that the valve closes properly.

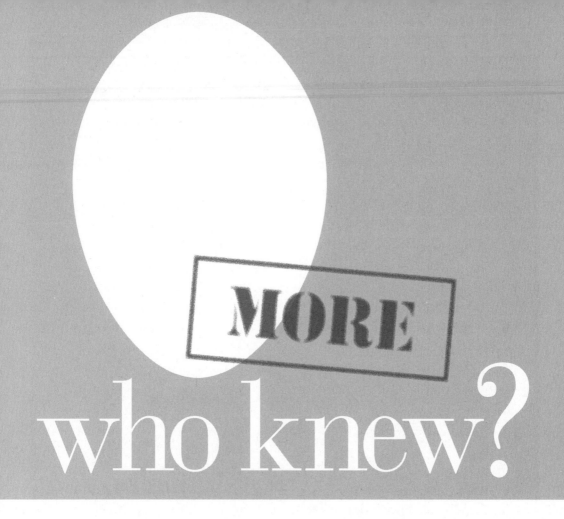

MORE
who knew?

Bruce Lubin & Jeanne Bossolina Lubin

PART THREE

CHEF'S SECRETS

Whether you're preparing a huge meal for a holiday get-together or just whipping up a snack for the kids, cooking conundrums can be some of the most frustrating. Mix your pancake batter just a bit too much and the pancakes will be flat; add the barbecue sauce too soon, and your ribs will burn. Simple mistakes like these can turn cooking into a chore. But in this section, we'll not only give you the how-to for improving your favorite dishes, we'll also provide tips and tricks to make the little things (and few of the big ones) quicker and easier, such as helping your food last longer, turning every mealtime into a success, and making the most out of your trips to the grocery store.

CHAPTER 1

Cooking Basics

What Is Meal Planning?

Meal planning is as simple as it sounds. Figure out what you're eating for dinner a week or two in advance, then plan your meals around similar ingredients so that they are quicker, easier, and cheaper to prepare. To make life even less stressful, try to make several meals at one time, so you can freeze or refrigerate them for later. Here are some tips to get you started.

✦ Begin with what you know: pick five to seven meals your family love and that you could make with your eyes closed. Try to include some that you can easily stretch to two meals—for example, a giant pot of soup or chili, a large casserole, or a big batch of pasta.

✦ Write your meals for the week (even if they are leftovers or if you have plans to eat out) on a white-erase board or a post-it note tacked to the wall. You'll not only be more motivated to follow through, but you'll hopefully get your family more involved.

✦ Make a list of the ingredients you'll need and buy them all in one shopping trip. As meal planning becomes ingrained in your everyday routine, you'll be able to plan your meals around what's on sale at the grocery store or what you have on hand.

✦ The more meals you can make out of the same ingredients, the better. Cut up a bunch of veggies, for instance, and use them in both a casserole and a stew.

✦ It's ideal to make a whole dish and freeze or refrigerate it ahead of time, but unfortunately, you won't always have the time or the space. So think about little things you can do to make preparing dinner quicker and easier later. For example, roast a whole chicken, then break apart the meat into bite-sized pieces that can easily be thrown into pastas, soups—or anything, really!

✦ Save your menu and use it again later. This will save you some thinking time, and will be especially handy when the meats you used last time are on sale again.

✦ One of the great things about meal planning is that it makes it easier to accomplish your food-related goals. Want to eat healthier, organic, or less meat? With these meal ideas ready to go, you'll be less like to resort to your usual less-than-healthy options.

Learn to Love Home Cooking

If you're used to eating out a lot, it's hard to break the habit. Since dining out eats up a lot of money (please excuse the pun), it's worth it to try to cut back. Make it easier on yourself by doing your shopping on a different day than when you actually prepare the food—that way you aren't stacking up the chores of buying groceries and making dinner. Plan ahead and try to make enough food to take to work with you for lunch the next day, thus saving even more. Encourage yourself by inviting over a friend for dinner; then have dinner at her house the next week. Once you see all the money you save, it will be much easier not to order in.

Save on Heat

When meal planning, think about multiple dishes that you can cook simultaneously in the oven, such as a roast and a casserole. Better yet, turn a pot lid upside-down while cooking, then place veggies wrapped in foil on top. This will save time—and money on your gas or electric bill!

Your Freezer Is Your Friend

Remember, your freezer can be used for more than just frozen casseroles and steaks. Every time you make something, ask yourself if it's worth it to double the batch and put it in the freezer. Examples of foods that can be frozen are cookie dough, pancake batter, cooked French toast, spaghetti sauce, pizza dough, and burritos. See the "Making Your Food Last Longer" chapter for more ideas!

Putting Parsley Through the Ringer

Unfortunately, when you're chopping parsley ahead of time, you'll find it quickly wilts. Solve this problem by getting out as much of the water as you can. This is easily accomplished by wringing it in a kitchen towel.

Who Knew? Readers' Favorite

Before using a measuring cup for a sticky liquid like honey, coat the inside with vegetable oil or nonstick cooking spray. The liquid will pour out easily.

Prepare for the Unexpected While Cooking

Professional cooks keep small plastic bags nearby in case both hands are covered with dough or food and they need to answer the telephone. Or, you could put your hands in plastic bags before mixing meatloaf or kneading dough, and then take them out to answer that urgent call.

Conserve Cooking Utensils by Planning Ahead

To use the fewest cooking utensils possible, first measure out all the dry ingredients, then the wet ingredients. This way, you can reuse the measuring spoons or cups without having to wash and dry them first.

Improvised Spoon Rest

Who needs a spoon rest when you're at the stove cooking? Just rest your spoon on a piece of bread; it will catch all of the juices and bits of food. Toss the bread when you're done cooking.

Tidy Tongs

You've figured out that putting tongs on a spoon rest often creates more mess than it saves. We got this idea from a barbecue party we went to last summer. Use a mug. So perfect and easy you're sure to have an "A-ha, why didn't I think of that?" moment.

Make the Kitchen Towel Switch!

If you use them a lot, paper towels can end up being one of your most expensive (and wasteful) grocery items. To encourage yourself to use a kitchen towel rather than its paper cousin, install a hook above the counter that you can hang a towel on. Having it close by will remind you of this cheaper, greener alternative and will cut down on your paper towel usage.

Dental Floss in Your Kitchen

A must-have for your kitchen tool-kit is unwaxed dental floss! (No, really.) Not only is it useful for trussing a turkey, but it's also great for baking. Dental floss is perfect for cutting a cake without making too many crumbs, and if your freshly baked cookies are stuck to the baking tray, simply hold a length of dental floss taut and slip it underneath the cookie. It works better than a spatula!

Who Knew? Readers' Favorite

We love hot-pressed sandwiches! And we were tempted to buy an expensive sandwich press to make ours at home until we learned this ingenious trick. Simply fry the sandwich in a pan as you would a grilled cheese, but place a piece of foil on top and weigh down the entire sandwich by pressing a kettle full of water on top.

Cuts Like a Knife

You've finally saved up enough to buy a brand new knife set (or, better yet, you're compiling a gift registry). So which knives should you get? The three basic knives everyone should own are a chef's knife, for chopping and slicing; a paring knife, for deseeding and other small jobs; and a boning knife, for cutting meat and poultry. Additional cutlery items you may want to have are a serrated knife for slicing bread, a cleaver, a fish-filleting knife, and a pair of kitchen scissors.

Storing Knives

Two of the best places to store knives are on a magnetic rack or in a wooden countertop knife block. Never store knives in a drawer with other utensils. Not only do you risk injury, but the knife blades may become nicked and dented.

On the Chopping Block

Studies continue regarding the safety of plastic cutting boards versus wood ones. Most cooks have their favorite, and many use both. No matter what kind of cutting board you prefer, here are some safety and cleaning tips.

- ✦ Reserve one cutting board for raw meats, poultry, and fish; use other cutting boards for prepping vegetables, cheeses, and cooked meats.

- ✦ Wash all cutting boards immediately after use in very hot, soapy water. If you have a plastic cutting board, run it through the dishwasher, which reaches higher temperatures than the water in your sink does. To make sure you get every last bacterium, you can also wash the boards in a weak bleach solution.

✦ Remember that it's harder to scrub bacteria out of nooks and crannies, so you should discard cutting boards whose surfaces have deep knife marks.

✦ Avoid setting hot pans on wood cutting boards or butcher-block countertops. Bacteria love heat, and the hot pan may serve to activate them or draw them to the surface of the wood.

✦ To quickly disinfect a plastic cutting board, wash it thoroughly, rub half a cut lemon over it, and microwave it for a minute.

✦ Another way to make sure you're getting the germs out of a wooden cutting board is to cover it with a light layer of salt to draw out any moisture from the crevices. Leave the salt on overnight before scraping it off. Then treat the wood with a very light coating of mineral oil. Make sure it is only a light coat, because mineral oil may affect the potency of a number of vitamins in fruits and vegetables.

✦ Do you have a cutting board that has a lingering odor that just won't quit? Remove the smell by rubbing the board with very salty water or some white vinegar.

Clean Cutting Boards

Cutting boards and breadboards need only simple soap and water to get clean, but you can make them look newer by rubbing salt over them with a wet cloth. After you rinse, plastic ones can be left to dry, but wooden ones do best if you towel them dry so they don't warp.

Fridge Hygiene

Store cooked foods above uncooked meat in your fridge. This minimizes the risk of food poisoning caused by drips from uncooked meat and other foods. Wrap any food with strong odors and avoid storing it close to dairy foods, which can become easily tainted. And throw away that slimy lettuce at the back of the vegetable drawer!

Who Knew? Readers' Favorite

The next time you defrost your freezer, spray it with a thin layer of cooking oil afterwards. The oil repels water (and ice), which will prevent it from frosting over. If it does ice up, you should easily be able to chip away the ice without having to defrost the entire freezer.

Freezer Facts

You can freeze any food except canned or preserved food and whole eggs. Some foods, however, do not freeze well. High-fat products like cream and mayonnaise tend to separate when defrosted, and high-water content vegetables such as lettuce and cucumbers will go soggy. Freezer temperature is critical for maintaining the quality of foods. Keep it set at 0°F.

Ice Rinsing Remedy

When ice cubes stay in the freezer tray more than a few days, they tend to pick up odors from other foods you have stocked away. Give them a quick rinse in cold water to avoid altering the flavor of your beverage.

Cook It Through

Contrary to popular belief, freezing doesn't actually kill bacteria or other food microbes, but what it does do is put them in a dormant state so they won't be active or reproduce until the food is thawed again. This is why it's important to cook food thoroughly after defrosting. If you defrost raw meat and then cook it, you can freeze it again, but remember you should never reheat foods more than once. If you want to use a meaty sauce like Bolognese for several meals, reheat individual portions when you need them rather than the whole pot.

The longer a food is frozen, the more nutrients it loses. Seal all foods to be frozen as tightly as possible to avoid freezer burn and the formation of ice crystals. Ice crystals cause thawed food to become mushy.

Slow Cooker Safety

Many people question whether a Crock-Pot is safe for cooking foods, or if it's a breeding ground for bacteria because it cooks at low temperatures. Most slow cookers have settings that range from 170–280°F, and most bacteria die at 140°F, so you should be safe. However, to minimize the risk of food poisoning, follow these tips.

- ✦ Don't attempt to cook frozen or partially thawed foods, and don't use the cooker to reheat leftovers. (Uncooked foods at refrigerator temperature are safe to use.)

- ✦ Cook only cut-up pieces of meat—not whole roasts or poultry—to allow the heat to penetrate fully.

- ✦ Make sure that the cooker is at least half to two-thirds full or the food may not absorb enough heat to kill bacteria.

- ✦ Cover the food with enough liquid to generate sufficient steam.

✦ Always use the original lid, and be sure it fits tightly. Never use the cooker with the lid off.

✦ When possible, cook on the highest setting for the first hour, then reduce it to low if necessary.

Deodorize the Disposal

A quick and easy way to deodorize your in-sink garbage disposal is to grind an orange or lemon peel inside it every so often. It will get rid of grease and smell wonderful!

Vanquish Smells with Vinegar

To help control unpleasant cooking aromas, dampen a cloth with a mixture of equal parts vinegar and water. Drape it over the cooking pot, taking care that the edges are far from the flame or intense heat.

Who Knew? Readers' Favorite

Remove strong food smells from your hands by running them under cold running water while rubbing them with a stainless steel spoon. Rinse with soap and water.

Toothpaste Trick

You've been cooking with garlic, and now you can't get the smell off your hands! To get rid of this or any other kitchen odor, just rub some white toothpaste between your hands and wash off.

Stop the Stink

Don't throw away used coffee grounds—instead, keep them in a can near the sink. Rub a small amount over your hands after handling fish, or chopping garlic or onions to get rid of odors on your hands.

Check the Temperature without a Thermometer

If you suspect your oven's temperature isn't in line with what it reads on the dial, but don't have an oven thermometer to test it, use this simple trick. Put a tablespoon of flour on a baking sheet and place it in a preheated oven for five minutes. If the flour turns light tan, the temperature is 250–325°F. If the flour turns golden brown, the oven is 325–400°F. If it turns dark brown, the oven is 400–450°F. And an almost a black color means the oven is 450–525°F. Figure out the disparity between what the temperature is and what it reads, and make sure to set your oven accordingly in the future.

Who Knew? Readers' Favorite

Save a lot of cleanup time by lining the bottom rack of your oven with aluminum foil when cooking something messy. But beware—you should never line the bottom of your oven with foil, as it could cause a fire.

Foil Foible

Never wrap foods that contain natural acids—like tomatoes, lemons, or onions—in aluminum foil. The combination of the foil and the acid in the foods produces a chemical reaction that affects the taste of the food.

Protect Silver from Acidic Foods

Some foods are particularly harsh on silver: Olives, salad dressings, vinegar, eggs, and salt will all cause silver to tarnish quickly. Wash your silver as soon as possible after it's had contact with any of these items.

Cooking with Wine

When cooking with wine, try not to use too much, or the taste may well overpower the dish. Wine should only be used to improve the flavor. If you want to assure that you taste the wine, just add it to the recipe about five to seven minutes before completion. And don't forget a little sip for the cook!

Avoid a Boiling Blunder

To keep a pot from boiling over, stick a toothpick between the lid and the pot. Other tricks include placing a wooden spoon across the top of the uncovered pot or rubbing butter around the inside lip of the pot.

Perfect Pasta Water

Stop your pasta water from spilling over with this trick: Add a long metal spoon to the pot, and it will absorb the excess heat and let your pasta cook at the correct temperature.

Canola Cure

To sauté or fry with butter, margarine, or lard, add a small amount of canola oil to raise the smoke point. This will keep the solid fat from breaking down at higher temperatures.

Who Knew? Readers' Favorite

When sautéing or frying, always heat your pan for a couple of minutes before adding butter or oil to ensure that nothing sticks and that the food will cook evenly. It's also a good idea to sprinkle a little salt in your pan before frying—it will keep the oil from splattering.

Important Tips for Deep-Frying

Sometimes food sticks together when you're deep-frying it. To prevent this, lift the basket out of the oil several times before leaving it in for good. And don't try to fry too much at once—the oil may bubble over from the temperature difference of the cold food and the hot oil. And speaking of hot oil, be sure it's 300–375°F before you add the food.

A Lighter Coat for Fried Foods

When making a batter for foods for deep-frying, try adding ½ teaspoon baking powder for every ½ cup flour. The coating will be lighter.

Frying Temperatures Are Critical

Oil needs to be at the proper temperature whether you're sautéing or deep-frying. If the temperature is too low, the food will absorb too much oil and become greasy, not crispy. If the oil is too hot, the food may burn on the outside and not cook through. Most breaded foods are normally fried at 375°F, but check the recipe. Chicken should be fried at 365°F for 15–20 minutes for white meat and 20–25 minutes for dark.

When Cooking with Oil

In terms of fat content, less oil is always better than more! So if you have to coat food with oil before sautéing or baking it, use a spray bottle rather than a brush to reduce the amount of fat that ends up on your food.

Unsalted Butter Is Best

If you sauté with butter, be sure you use the unsalted kind. When salted butter melts, the salt can separate from the butter and impart a bitter taste to the dish.

Tips for Breading

Keeping breading on foods can be a challenge, but there are a few tricks to try (other than using superglue, which we don't recommend). First, make sure that the food to be breaded is very dry. Use eggs at room temperature, and beat them lightly. If you have time, refrigerate the breaded food for an hour, then let it sit at room temperature for 20 minutes before cooking. Homemade breadcrumbs adhere better than the store-bought kind because of their uneven texture.

Who Knew? Readers' Favorite

When changing the yield of a recipe, don't increase the seasonings proportionately, or the recipe will taste wrong. If you're doubling the recipe, increase the seasonings only by one and a half; if you are tripling the recipe, double the amount of seasoning.

Crushing Spices

Don't have a mortar and pestle? A great way to mix and crush spices is to place them in a pan and press with the bottom of a smaller pan. A coffee grinder works well, too.

Herbal Flavor Booster

Crushing dried herbs before using them will boost their flavor, as will soaking them for a few seconds in hot water. This technique also works well with dried herbs that have lost their flavor.

Great Garlic Tips

Garlic is one of our favorite seasonings, and we find it's much better fresh than in powdered form. If you love garlic too, here are some tips for cooking with this delicious ingredient.

✦ To make garlic easy to peel, soak it in very hot water for 2–3 minutes, or rinse it under hot water to loosen its skin.

✦ If your head of garlic sprouts, some of the flavor will go into the sprouts; however, the sprouts can be used for salads.

✦ If you have added too much garlic to your soup or stew, add a small quantity of parsley and simmer for about 10 minutes.

✦ Mincing garlic can be a sticky mess, but it doesn't have to be. Sprinkle the garlic with a few drops of olive oil beforehand. The oil will prevent the garlic from sticking to your hands or the knife.

More Than One Way to Skin...Garlic?

Here's another easy way to remove the skins from garlic! Just break the cloves off from the head and place them in a bowl or mug. Place another bowl on top and shake heartily. The skins will start to come off, making the garlic easy to peel.

Save Some Zest for Later

Don't discard the rinds of limes, lemons, oranges, or other citrus. Grate them, then store in tightly covered glass jars in the fridge. They make excellent flavorings for cakes, and can be sprinkled over chicken and fish as well.

Make Seasoning Easy

Keep a shaker filled with a ratio of 75 percent salt and 25 percent pepper (or whatever ratio you usually use) next to the stove or your food-preparation area, and it will be even easier to season foods.

Who Knew? Readers' Favorite

If you're preparing a recipe that calls for crushed ginger, don't bother with your knife. Simply peel the ginger and put it through a garlic press.

The Baking Powder Test

Did you know that baking powder loses potency over time? If you can't remember when you bought yours, test it before using it. Here's how: Put ½ teaspoon baking powder in a small bowl, then pour in ¼ cup of hot tap water. The more vigorously it bubbles, the fresher the baking powder. Try this test first on a fresh box of baking powder so you will be familiar with the activity level of fresh powder. Once opened, baking powder will remain fresh for about a year.

The Baking Soda Test

If you are not sure how old your baking soda is, you can test its activity level. Stir ¼ teaspoon baking soda into about 2 teaspoons of white vinegar; it should bubble vigorously. If it doesn't, throw it out.

Cooking Substitutions

Preparing a recipe and realize you forgot one essential ingredient? Use the chart below to find a proper substitution. Unless otherwise noted, use the substitution in equal measure to the ingredient called for in the recipe.

INGREDIENT	SUBSTITUTE
Active dry yeast (one ¼-ounce envelope)	1 cake compressed yeast
Allspice (for baking only)	1 part ground cinnamon + 2 parts ground cloves or ground nutmeg
Anise seed	fennel seed
Apples (1 cup chopped)	1 cup firm chopped pears + 1 tablespoon lemon juice.
Arrowroot	use 2 tablespoons flour for every 4 teaspoons arrowroot
Baking powder (1 teaspoon, double-acting)	⅝ teaspoon cream of tartar + ¼ teaspoon baking soda *or* ¼ teaspoon baking soda + ¼ cup sour milk or buttermilk (lessen other liquid in recipe)

Basil (dried)	tarragon *or* summer savory *or* thyme *or* oregano
Bay leaf	thyme
Black pepper	cayenne pepper (use much less; start with a pinch)
Brandy	cognac *or* rum
Bulgur	cracked wheat *or* kasha *or* brown rice *or* couscous *or* quinoa
Butter	hard margarine *or* shortening *or* oil if it is not a baked good
Buttermilk (1 cup)	1 cup milk + 1¾ tablespoons cream of tartar *or* 1 tablespoon lemon juice + milk to make 1 cup (let stand 5 minutes) *or* sour cream
Cake flour (1 cup)	1 cup minus 2 tablespoons unsifted all-purpose flour
Capers	chopped green olives
Caraway seed	fennel seed *or* cumin

Cardamom	cinnamon *or* mace
Chervil	parsley *or* tarragon *or* ground anise seed (use a bit less)
Chives	onion powder (small amount) *or* finely chopped leeks or shallots (small amount) *or* scallion greens
Chocolate, baking, unsweetened	3 tablespoons unsweetened cocoa powder + 1 tablespoon (one ounce or square) butter *or* 3 tablespoons carob powder + 2 tablespoons water
Chocolate, semisweet (6 ounces)	9 tablespoons unsweetened cocoa powder or squares + 7 tablespoons sugar + 3 tablespoons butter
Cilantro	parsley and lemon juice
Cinnamon	allspice (use less) *or* cardamom
Cloves (ground)	allspice *or* nutmeg *or* mace
Club soda	sparkling mineral water *or* seltzer
Cornmeal	polenta
Cornstarch	flour, as thickener

Corn syrup, light (1 cup)	1¾ cup granulated sugar + ¼ cup more of the liquid called for in recipe
Crème fraîche	sour cream in most recipes *or* ½ sour cream + ½ heavy cream in sauces. Note that crème fraîche can be boiled but sour cream cannot.
Cumin	1 part anise + 2 parts caraway or fennel seed (grind if necessary)
Dill seed	caraway *or* celery seed
Egg (1)	1 tablespoon cornstarch + 3 tablespoons water *or* 3 tablespoons mayonnaise *or* ½ mashed banana + ¼ teaspoon baking powder
Evaporated milk	half-and-half or cream
Flour	cornstarch *or* instant potato flakes *or* pancake mix
Garlic (1 medium clove)	¼ teaspoon minced dried garlic *or* ⅛ teaspoon garlic powder *or* ½ teaspoon garlic salt (omitting ½ teaspoon salt from recipe)
Ghee	clarified butter
Herbs, fresh (1 tablespoon)	1 teaspoon dried herbs

Honey (1 cup, in baked goods)	1¼ cups granulated sugar + ¼ cup more of the liquid called for in the recipe
Lemongrass	lemon juice *or* lemon zest *or* finely chopped lemon verbena *or* lime zest
Lovage	celery leaves
Marjoram	oregano (use small amount) *or* thyme *or* savory
Masa harina	cornmeal
Mascarpone	8 ounces cream cheese whipped with 3 tablespoons sour cream and 2 tablespoons milk
Milk (in baked goods)	fruit juice + ½ teaspoon baking soda mixed in with the flour
Milk (1 cup)	½ cup evaporated milk + ½ cup water *or* ¼ cup powdered milk + ⅞ cup of water
Milk, whole	same as above + 2½ teaspoons melted and cooled butter
Milk, evaporated	half-and-half OR cream
Molasses	honey
Nutmeg	allspice *or* cloves *or* mace

Oregano	marjoram *or* thyme
Pancetta	lean bacon (cooked) *or* very thinly sliced ham
Polenta	cornmeal *or* corn grits
Poultry seasoning	sage + a blend of any of these: thyme, marjoram, savory, black pepper, rosemary
Rosemary	thyme
Saffron (⅛ teaspoon)	1 teaspoon dried yellow marigold petals *or* 1 teaspoon safflower petals
Sage	poultry seasoning *or* savory *or* marjoram
Self-rising flour (1 cup)	1 cup all-purpose flour + 1½ teaspoons baking powder + ⅛ teaspoon salt
Shallots	scallions *or* leeks *or* yellow onions
Shortening (baked goods only)	butter *or* margarine
Sour cream	1 tablespoon white vinegar + milk (let stand 5 minutes before using) *or* 1 tablespoon lemon juice + evaporated milk *or* plain yogurt
Tahini	peanut or almond butter

Tarragon	anise (use small amount)
	or chervil (use larger amount)
	or a pinch of fennel seed
Tomato paste (1 tablespoon)	1 tablespoon ketchup
	or ½ cup tomato sauce
	(reduce some of the liquid in recipe)
Turmeric	mustard powder
Vanilla extract (baked goods only)	almond extract
	or any other extract
Vinegar	lemon juice for cooking and salads
	or wine in marinades
Yogurt	sour cream
	or buttermilk
	or mayonnaise (in small amounts)

Who Knew? Readers' Favorite

Casseroles and baked goods should always be cooked at the temperature specified in the recipe, with one notable exception: If you are using a glass baking dish, reduce the oven temperature by 25°F. Glass heats more slowly than metal, but it retains heat well. Failing to lower the temperature can result in burned bottoms.

Greasing the Pan

When you need to grease a baking pan, choose vegetable shortening. Butter has a low smoke point and burns easily, and salted butter can cause food to stick to the pan.

Wax Paper Prescription

When braising or stewing meat or poultry, always place a piece of waxed paper under the lid. It will collect the moisture that would otherwise dilute your dish.

Defrosting in the Microwave

If you've ever defrosted meat or fish in the microwave, you probably know that the "defrost" or low-power settings are your best bet for ensuring that the outer edges of the food don't cook before the middle can defrost. But here's something you might not know: Arranging loose pieces of meat in a single layer with thickest parts or largest pieces toward the outside will also ensure more even defrosting.

Meat Market Primer

Wish you could always pick the most tender cuts of meat? These hints will help. When purchasing a chuck roast, look for white cartilage near the top of the roast. If you can spot a roast with cartilage showing, you've found the first cut, which will be the most tender. When purchasing an eye of round roast, try to find the one that is the same size on both ends. For round steak, look for uneven cuts, which are the ones closest to the sirloin.

Look for Lines

As you probably know, white streaks running through meat are fat. But even if you're diet-conscious, you should always choose well-marbled meat, which will be the most tender, since the animal didn't exercise those muscles very much. Fat is a storage depot for energy, and for meat to be well-marbled, an animal must be fed a diet high in rich grains such as corn (which is where we get the old saying that corn-fed beef is best). The fat imparts flavor and provides moisture that helps tenderize the meat.

The Wrapping Is Everything

When choosing meat or poultry in the supermarket, look out for liquid on the bottom of the package. If it's there, it means the food has been frozen and thawed; the cells have ruptured, releasing some of their fluids. To store meat in the refrigerator, wrap it in clean plastic wrap or waxed paper. The supermarket wrapping often contains residue.

Green Ham and Eggs?

Have you ever purchased a ham that has a greenish, glistening sheen? This effect occasionally occurs when a ham is sliced and the surface is exposed to the effects of oxidation. It isn't a sign of spoilage, but is caused by the nitrite modification of the meat's iron content, which tends to produce a biochemical change in the pigmentation.

Who Knew? Readers' Favorite

To easily slice meat or poultry, partially freeze it beforehand and your knife will glide right through.

Meat Miracle

All meat (except organ meats and ground beef) should stand at room temperature for a few minutes before cooking. This allows it to brown more evenly, cook faster, retain more juices, and stick less when frying.

Fish Safety

Seafood is responsible for a lot of food poisoning, but it's perfectly safe and very healthy if treated correctly. If you can't use a fish immediately, remove it from its original wrapping and rinse in cold water. Wrap it loosely in plastic wrap, store in the coldest part of the refrigerator, and use within two days.

Egg Safety

Because eggs can contain bacteria before they're even cracked, when preparing a hollandaise or béarnaise sauce, it might be best to microwave the eggs briefly before adding them to the sauce. To do so, first separate the egg yolks completely from the whites (do only two eggs at a time). Then place the two yolks in a glass bowl and beat them until they are well combined. Add 2 teaspoons lemon juice and mix thoroughly again. Now cover the bowl and microwave it on high until you see the surface of the mixture beginning to move. Cook for 10 seconds past this point, remove the bowl, and beat the mixture with a clean whisk or fork until it's smooth. Return the bowl to the microwave and repeat the previous step: Cook 10 seconds past when the surface starts to move, remove, and whisk till smooth. Let the mixture stand (covered) for 1 minute. Your yolks are now free of salmonella and will still be usable in your sauce!

A Good Temper

When adding raw eggs or yolks to a hot mixture, be sure to mix part of the hot mixture into the eggs, and then gradually add this new mixture to the hot mixture. Called "tempering," it may be extra work, but it makes the eggs less likely to curdle and separate.

Cracks Are Whack

Bacteria love eggs, so if you find a cracked egg in the carton, throw it out; it is probably contaminated. The refrigerator shelf life of eggs is about five weeks from the "sell by" date.

Egg White Wisdom

When beating egg whites for a recipe, remove all traces of yolk from the bowl with a Q-tip or the edge of a paper towel before trying to beat the whites. The slightest trace of yolk will prevent the whites from beating properly, as will any trace of fat on the beaters or bowl.

Who Knew? Readers' Favorite

For perfectly peeled hard-boiled eggs, crack the eggs slightly on your counter, then place them in a bowl of cool water. The water will seep in and loosen the egg from its shell, making sure you don't accidentally take off half the white when you're trying to peel it.

Washing Winner

When washing vegetables, place a small amount of salt in a sink full of cold water to draw out any sand and insects.

Bag the Baking Soda

You may have heard the old household tip that baking soda added to the cooking water will help vegetables retain their color, but it will also cause them to lose texture and vitamins. To help veggies keep their color, forget the baking soda and simply cook them for no more than 5–7 minutes.

Make It Hot

If you need to add more water to vegetables as they are cooking, make sure the added water is as hot as possible. Adding cold water to already-cooking veggies may affect their cell walls and cause them to toughen.

Carrot Can-Do

If you only have a few carrots to peel, a standard vegetable peeler will get the skins off. But what if you have a whole bunch? To slip the skin off carrots in one giant batch, drop them in boiling water, let them blanch for 5 minutes, then place them in cold water for a few seconds. The skins will slide off easily.

Peeling Potatoes

The easy way to peel a potato is to boil it first, then drop it into a bowl of ice water for a few seconds to loosen the skin.

Potato How-To

A new (red) potato has more moisture than other potatoes. Use new potatoes in dishes such as potato salad; they absorb less water when boiled and less mayonnaise when prepared, allowing your salad to have better flavor and less fat. They'll also break apart less easily when you mix the salad. Russet and Yukon gold potatoes are better for baking and making french fries. They are drier, meatier, and starchier, so they have a lighter texture when baked. Their lower water content means the oil will spatter less when you fry them. When baking a potato, make sure you pierce it so steam can escape; otherwise, it may become soggy.

Who Knew? Readers' Favorite

Hot potato or cold, it's hard to keep them from slipping out of your hands as you peel them. Screw a corkscrew partway in to keep a raw potato steady— one hand on the corkscrew handle, one on the peeler. For a cooked potato a fork easily does the job.

Cruciferous Cooking

When you cook cruciferous vegetables like broccoli, cabbage, and cauliflower, never use an aluminum or iron pot. The sulfur compounds in the vegetables will react with the metal. For instance, cauliflower will turn yellow if cooked in aluminum, and brown if cooked in iron.

Onions Go First

When sautéing onions and garlic together, sauté the onions first for at least half of their cooking time. If you start the garlic at the same time as the onions, it will overcook and possibly burn, releasing a chemical that will make the dish bitter.

Creating Caramelized Vegetables

Caramelized vegetables have nothing to do with caramel candy, but they taste almost as good. Caramelizing is the process of oxidizing the sugar content of a vegetable, which produces a sweet, nutty flavor and a brown color. To easily caramelize an onion or other vegetable, toss the slices in olive oil and roast them in a 400°F oven for 10–30 minutes, or until golden brown. You'll love the flavor for stir-fries and on top of pizza.

Pitting Practice

This trick is for adults only: To easily remove an avocado pit, thrust the blade of a sharp knife into the pit, twist slightly, and the pit will come right out.

When It's Good to Add Sugar

Cooking fruit? To make sure it doesn't get mushy, always add sugar to the cooking syrup. The sugar will draw some of the fluid back into the cells to maintain equilibrium in the sugar concentration, and the fruit will retain a more appealing texture.

Frozen Berry Delight

Frozen berries are filled with just as many healthy antioxidants as fresh ones, and in winter they are an excellent source of vitamin C and small amounts of vitamin A and calcium. If you're not going to enjoy the berries while they're still frozen, thaw them in the refrigerator. The fruit will have time to reabsorb its sugars as it thaws.

Mango Mission

If you slice open a mango and it tastes too acidic, place it in warm (not hot) water for ten minutes. This will speed up the process of its starches turning into sugars, and it will be sweet in no time! Just make sure not to leave it in the water for more than ten minutes, as it might begin to shrivel.

Who Needs a Juicer?

Instead of purchasing a handheld juicer (also known as a reamer) for fruit, simply use one blade from a hand mixer instead. Halve the fruit and twist the blade into it for easy juicing.

Shelling Secret

The easiest way to shell pecans, walnuts, and other nuts? Freeze them first. It shrinks the nut away from the shell and makes the job a breeze. Another easy way to shell nuts is to soak them in boiling water for 15 minutes.

The easiest way to clean a cheese grater is to spray it with vegetable oil before grating any cheese, which will make it less sticky. Afterward, rub the crusty heel from a stale loaf of French bread over the dirty end, and your cleanup is finished!

Grating Soft Cheese?

It's easier to grate Cheddar and other softer cheeses if you place them in the freezer for 10–15 minutes before grating. If the cheese is really soft, don't even bother with the grater. An easier method is to just push it through a colander with a potato masher.

Grater Priorities

Here's a chef's secret for keeping a grater clean so you can use it repeatedly without washing: Simply grate the softest items first, then grate the firmer ones.

CHAPTER 2

Breakfast and Lunch

Fresh-Tasting, Reheated Coffee

When you keep coffee warm in a coffeepot, it will only stay fresh for about 30 minutes after brewing. If your morning pick-me-up needs tastes stale, add a pinch of salt to your cup before reheating it. You won't taste the salt, but your coffee will taste like it's just been brewed.

Who Knew? Readers' Favorite

Who doesn't enjoy an iced coffee on a sultry summer day? To make sure melting ice doesn't dilute your drink, make ice cubes using the small amount of coffee left at the bottom of your coffee pot each morning. Use them in your iced coffee, and it will never taste watered down. This is also a great tip for iced tea!

Easy, Sweet Coffee

If you love sweetened, flavored coffee, simply mix ¼ fresh vanilla bean or 1 teaspoon cinnamon with 1 cup sugar in a food processor until well-blended, then add a little scoop to your next cup. It's usually much cheaper than buying flavored coffees or creamers, and it tastes better, too.

Coffee Combos

If you're like us, you know it's worth it to spend the extra money on high-quality coffee. The great thing about buying coffee in bulk is that you can easily mix the premium stuff with the not-so-premium stuff. We use 3 parts gourmet coffee with 1 part of the cheap stuff, and even we can't tell the difference!

Incredible Iced Coffee in an Instant

If you love iced coffee in the summer, make it even better with the help of a martini shaker or capped thermos. Pour in the coffee, milk, ice, and any flavoring, then cover and shake. The shaking will add lots of air to the mixture, making it light, frothy, and delicious.

How to Save Your Cream

If your cream or half-and-half has begun to develop an "off" odor, but you desperately need it for your coffee, try mixing in $\frac{1}{8}$ teaspoon baking soda; it will neutralize the lactic acid that is causing the cream to sour. Before you use the cream, however, taste it to be sure the flavor is still acceptable.

The Most Important Meal of the Day

For a quick and healthy breakfast, make waffles and pancakes ahead of time, then freeze them. When you and your family are ready to eat, pop them in the toaster to reheat. This tip saves both time and money.

Don't Pucker Up

It's surprising, but true: A small amount of salt will make a grapefruit taste sweeter.

Breakfast Bar Saver

Don't have time to eat anything but a breakfast bar in the morning? Store it in a glasses case to make sure it doesn't get smushed in your purse or bag on the way to work.

Toasty Treat

For a different type of toast, lightly butter a slice of bread on both sides and cook it in a waffle iron. Your kids will love it!

With Eggs, Your Bowl Matters

Aluminum bowls and cookware tend to darken eggs. The reason? Aluminum reacts chemically with the egg protein. A copper bowl, if you happen to have one, is best for beating eggs. The copper will release ions during the beating process that cause the protein in the whites to become more stable. The next best material to use is stainless steel; however, we recommend adding a pinch of cream of tartar to stabilize the whites.

Save Your Yolks

Believe it or not, you can save egg yolks for later use. If you have leftover yolks from a recipe that uses egg whites, slide them into a bowl of water, cover with plastic wrap, and store them in the refrigerator for a day or two. It beats throwing them out!

Poaching Eggs

The fresher the egg, the better it is for poaching. The white will be firmer and will help to keep the yolk from breaking. In addition, salt, lemon juice, and vinegar will make egg whites coagulate faster. Add a dash of one of these ingredients to the poaching liquid to help eggs keep their shape.

Sunny Side Secrets

When frying eggs, make sure the butter or margarine is very hot—a drop of water should sizzle. However, the heat should be reduced just before the eggs are added to the pan. Cook them over low heat until the whites are completely set. Add a couple drops of water and cover the pan just before the eggs are done to get a perfect white film over the yolks.

A Surprising Use for That Old Cappuccino Maker

Use your cappuccino maker for a speedy breakfast treat. Place the foamer (not the milk-uptake valve!) into a mug with a beaten egg inside. The steam will cook it into a scrambled egg in seconds!

For the Best-Ever Omelet

To make a great omelet, be sure the eggs are at room temperature (take them out of the fridge 30 minutes beforehand). Cold eggs are too stiff. For a super fluffy omelet, add ½ teaspoon baking soda for every three eggs. Also, try adding a drop or two of water instead of milk. The water increases the volume of the eggs at least three times more than the milk does.

Who Knew Readers' Favorite

Cleaning up after a yummy scrambled egg breakfast? Use cold water. It cleans dried egg off pans and utensils better than hot water, which causes the protein to bind to surfaces and harden.

Pancake Secrets

Short-order cooks and chefs have a host of tricks to make the lightest pancakes. Here are a few we've learned:

✦ Don't overmix the batter—you don't want the gluten in the flour to overdevelop and allow the carbon dioxide that creates the little air pockets to escape. It's better to leave a couple of lumps in the batter.

✦ Refrigerate the batter for up to 30 minutes. This further slows the development of the gluten and the leavening action.

✦ Always stir the batter before you ladle it onto the griddle. The ingredients can settle; stirring recombines them and aerates the mixture.

✦ Make sure you flip pancakes as soon as air bubbles appear on the top, then flip them back over if necessary to finish cooking them. If you wait until the bubbles break, gas escapes, and your pancakes won't be as light and fluffy.

✦ If you like brown-on-the-outside pancakes, add a little extra sugar. The sugar caramelizes, giving a browner color to the pancakes. Also, some people swear by the addition of a tablespoon of pure maple syrup (the real stuff—no imitations!) to your pancake batter.

✦ For perfectly formed pancakes, use a meat baster to squeeze the batter onto the griddle. It gives you so much control you'll finally be able to make those animal-shaped pancakes your kids have been begging you for!

Key to a Clean Griddle

When cooking on the griddle, you'll get better results if you clean it between each batch of pancakes or whatever you happen to be making. Do this easily with coarse salt wrapped in a piece of cheesecloth. The salt will provide a light abrasive cleaning and won't harm the surface if you're gentle.

Gauge Your Griddle

Pancakes and other griddle treats often require a precise temperature to cook to their best. But how do you know when the surface has reached the right temperature? Flick a few drops of water on the heated griddle. If the surface is 325°F (the perfect temperature for pancakes), the droplets will skitter and dance—steam causes the drops to rise, but gravity brings them back down. If the griddle is 425°F or hotter, the water drops will be propelled right off the griddle.

Who Knew? Readers' Favorite

Here's a trick to keep waffles from sticking to the waffle iron: Beat a teaspoon of white wine into the batter. You'll never taste the wine, but it will keep the batter from adhering to the hot surface.

Syrup Substitute

Out of maple syrup and still want waffles this morning? Make this delicious substitute. Combine 1/3 cup butter, 1/3 cup sugar, and ½ cup frozen orange juice concentrate in a saucepan. Cook over medium heat, stirring constantly, until the sugar has dissolved and the mixture is syrupy.

Wax Your Waffle Iron?

Waffle day is so much less fun when we have to beg and plead with the waffles to come out of the iron. Here's a quick fix if the "nonstick" material on your waffle maker has worn out: Place a sheet of wax paper in the iron, close, and heat up. Remove and now give it a try: thanks to the transferred wax, the waffles should pop out.

Another Chopstick Trick

Seems like the most-fun kitchen gadgets are the most annoying to clean. Here's a trick for the waffle maker—put a paper towel over a chopstick and go to work on the grid. Idiot reminder: Wait 'til it cools first!

Splattering Solution

To keep bacon from splattering, soak it in ice-cold water for 2–4 minutes, and then dry it well with paper towels before frying it. Or try sprinkling the bacon with a bit of flour before cooking.

Bacon Wrapper

If you're cooking less than a full package of bacon, how do you store the extra slices? Just roll each slice into a tight cylinder, place in an airtight plastic bag, and freeze. Simply thaw and unroll when you're ready to cook!

Stop Sausage Splitting

Keep sausages from splitting by piercing the skin in one or two places while they are cooking. A quick dredging in flour before cooking will reduce shrinkage.

Soggy Lunch?

If your kids complain that the sandwiches you make in the morning are mushy by lunchtime, put the mayonnaise (or any condiment) in a Ziploc bag, and stick it in the lunch box. This way, the kids can season their own sandwiches at lunchtime by turning the bag inside out and rubbing it on the bread.

Who Knew? Readers' Favorite

Kid's lunchbox starting to smell funky? Freshen it up with bread and vinegar! Just moisten a slice of bread with white vinegar and let it sit in the closed lunchbox overnight. In the morning, any bad odors should be gone.

Lunchbox Lesson

Freezing juice boxes is an excellent way to make sure your child's drink will still be cold at lunchtime. Plus, it keeps everything else in the lunchbox cool!

Be Prepared

Make school-day mornings a little less crazy by preparing a few days' worth of the kids' sandwiches at the same time (without condiments), then freezing them. Each morning, just toss the pre-made sandwich in their lunchboxes, add a small container or plastic bag with the condiments, and by lunchtime, the bread will be soft and fresh-tasting.

Forget About Refreezing

When any type of meat or lunchmeat is refrozen, the fat content may cause the food to go rancid. And this is only one reason why meats should not be frozen again after they've been thawed—the texture of the meat can suffer, and improper thawing can promote bacterial growth. Instead, refrigerate leftover meats; they can be stored safely for four days.

Mixed Nuts

If you buy all-natural peanut or almond butter, you know that it doesn't take long for the oil to separate from the rest of the spread. Solve this problem by storing your nut butter upside-down when you first buy it. When you flip it over, the oil will be evenly distributed throughout.

Stab That Potato!

When baking potatoes, pierce the skin with a fork to allow the steam to escape. Your reward will be a wonderfully fluffy texture.

Oil, Not Foil, for Baked Potatoes

Did you know that wrapping a potato in foil won't actually make it bake faster? Rubbing it lightly with vegetable oil, however, will.

Quick Quiche Tip

Quiches, especially those made with onions and mushrooms, should not be allowed to cool. Both of these vegetables have a high water content, which will be released into the quiche as it cools. The result: a soggy crust and runny filling. If buying a pre-made quiche, look for ones that don't have onions or mushrooms, and when making your own, make sure to serve after letting it sit for 10 minutes (which will prevent oozing).

Tomato Soup Tip

Cream-of-tomato soup can be tricky to make from scratch. To keep it from curdling, add the ingredients in the right order: Pour the tomato base into the milk instead of the milk into the tomato. Stirring a small amount of flour into the milk also helps.

A Smoother Finish for Soups

When serving creamed soups from the can, beat or whisk the soup 10–15 seconds before heating for a silky smooth texture.

Warm Sandwiches

Who doesn't love a warm sandwich? Luckily, you don't need an expensive sandwich press to make delicious heated sandwiches—just use your microwave! When heating a sandwich in the microwave, you'll get the best results using firm, textured bread such as French or sourdough. The filling should be heated separately. If the filling is heated in the sandwich, be sure to spread it evenly over the bread and very close to the edges. Wait a few minutes before eating the sandwich, as the filling may remain very hot even if the bread is cool to the touch.

Ring Around the Onion Ring

Cooking onion rings? Make sure you fry only a few at a time to prevent them from sticking together and to ensure even cooking.

Fantastic Fries

For the best french fries, soak cut potatoes in ice-cold water in the refrigerator for an hour; this will harden them so that they absorb less fat. Dry them thoroughly, then fry them twice. First cook for 6–7 minutes, drain well, and sprinkle them lightly with flour (this step makes them extra crispy and crunchy). Then fry them again for 1–2 minutes, until golden brown.

Who Knew? Readers' Favorite

Salt homemade potato chips by putting them in a paper bag with salt and shaking. This way, the salt is evenly distributed—and the paper absorbs the excess grease. Save calories wherever you can!

Salad Starter

Who doesn't love perfect carrot peels on top of salads? Getting this great look is easy. Just peel off slices of carrot with a vegetable peeler, then drop them into a bowl of ice water.

Quickie Salad Dressing

If you want to make a quick and unique salad dressing, just place a small amount of olive oil and wine vinegar inside an almost-empty ketchup bottle. Shake it up and drizzle over your salad. Voilà!

Salad Saver

For the crispiest salad, prepare it in a metal bowl and then place it in the freezer for one minute before serving.

Stop Soggy Salad!

Avoid wet, limp salads by placing an inverted saucer in the bottom of the salad bowl before you throw in all your veggies. The excess water that is left after washing the vegetables and greens will drain under the saucer and leave the greens high and dry.

Hard-Boiled How-To

Who doesn't love a hard-boiled egg? Great for snacks or a light lunch, these tasty treats are easy to prepare—especially with our hard-boiled-egg tips and tricks.

✦ You can prevent boiled eggs from cracking by using lemon. Just cut a lemon in half, then rub the cut side on the shells before cooking them. You can also add a pinch of salt to the water before to prevent cracks.

✦ If an egg does crack during boiling, remove it from the water and, while it is still wet, pour a generous amount of salt over the crack. Let the egg stand for 20 seconds, then put it back into the boiling water.

✦ Boiled eggs should be cooled at room temperature before refrigerating.

✦ To easily remove the shell from a hard-boiled egg in one piece, exert gentle pressure while rolling it around on the counter, then insert a teaspoon between the shell and the egg white and rotate it.

✦ Always cool a hard-boiled egg before you try to slice it; it will slice more easily and won't fall apart. Your best implement if you don't have an egg-slicer? Unwaxed dental floss makes slicing hard-cooked eggs easy.

✦ Using your hard-boiled eggs for egg salad? The fastest way to chop eggs is to peel them, place them in a bowl, and run a pizza cutter through them several times.

CHAPTER 3

Dinner

For the Best Roasted Chicken and Turkey

Who doesn't love chicken and turkey? Poultry is not only a popular choice for dinner, it's also inexpensive! Make cooking easier with these tips.

✦ Chicken and turkey must be thoroughly cleaned inside and out before cooking, in order to remove any residue that may be left from the slaughtering process. If you detect a slight "off" odor when you open the package, rinse the bird under cool water, then submerge it in a solution of water plus 1 tablespoon lemon juice or vinegar and 1 teaspoon salt per cup of water. Refrigerate 1–4 hours before cooking.

✦ Try basting your bird with a small amount of white zinfandel or vermouth—it will help crisp the skin, and the sugar in the alcohol will impart a brown color and glaze to the outside of the meat. Or brush the skin with reduced-sodium soy sauce during the last 30 minutes of cooking to produce a beautiful burnished color.

✦ A chicken or turkey cooked at a constant 375°F will be juicier than one cooked a higher temperature because more fat and moisture will be retained.

✦ Have a V-rack? Try cooking your next bird breast-side down on the V-rack for the first hour. The juices will flow to the breast and make the meat moist and tender. Then remove the V-rack. After trying this method, you will never buy another commercially prepared self-basting bird!

✦ If your roasted chicken or turkey tends to be too dry, try stuffing a whole apple inside the bird before roasting. (Just toss the apple afterward.) You can also line the bottom of the pan with lemon and onion slices. They'll give the bird a lovely flavor and ensure it stays moist.

✦ For the most tender bird you've ever eaten, try submerging the chicken or turkey in buttermilk and refrigerating for two to three hours before cooking.

✦ Once poultry has finished cooking, it should be allowed to rest for about 20 minutes before carving. As with other roasts, this standing time allows the proteins in the meat to reabsorb the juices, so they stay in the meat rather than spilling onto the cutting board.

Rack It Up

A V-rack is one of the best ways to roast a chicken or turkey, but if you don't have one, here's a free and easy substitution. Remove the grates from your gas stove burners and wrap them in foil. Poke a few holes to let juices through, then rest them against the sides of the roasting pan. Voilà: impromptu V-rack!

Dark Versus Light

Chicken breasts cooked with the ribs intact stay moister than the boneless variety. But if you're cooking chicken parts separately, remember that dark meat takes longer to cook than white meat does because of its higher fat content. Start the dark meat a few minutes before the white, so that the white meat doesn't dry out.

Skinning a Bird?

The easiest way to skin poultry is to partially freeze it first. The skin will come right off the bird with almost no effort.

Stock-Making Secrets

One mistake people frequently make when preparing stock is to place soup bones in the water after it has come to a boil. This tends to seal the bones and prevent all the flavor and nutrients from being released into the stock! The bones should be added to the cold water when the pot is first placed on the stove to allow the maximum release of flavors, nutrients, and especially the gelatinous thickening agents that add body to the stock.

Who Knew? Readers' Favorite

Make your own bouillon cubes by freezing leftover chicken broth in ice-cube trays. Once frozen, the cubes can be kept in resealable plastic bags until needed. They are easily defrosted in the microwave—or just toss them directly into a soup or sauce, and they'll melt quickly.

The Best Breaded Breasts

Always refrigerate chicken breasts after flouring, but before cooking. The coating will adhere better that way. Also, for a delicate coating, try adding a teaspoon of baking powder to your batter and club soda instead of water.

Common-Sense Breading

When breading chicken cutlets, make sure you don't bread your fingers, too! Always use one hand for wet ingredients and the other for the breadcrumbs.

For Super-Tender Pork

When roasting a pork loin, cook it with the fat-side down for the first 20 minutes, so that the fat begins to liquefy. Then turn the roast over for the balance of the cooking time, and the fat will baste the meat.

Ham Purchasing Secrets

If you're going to buy a canned ham, purchase the largest one you can afford. Most smaller canned hams are made from bits and pieces glued together with gelatin. Cured hams are injected with a solution of brine salts, sugar, and nitrites. The weight of the ham will increase with the injection, and if the total weight goes up by 8 percent, the label will usually say "ham with natural juices." If the weight of the ham increases by more than 10 percent, the label must read "water added."

Perfectly Sliced Ham

If ham is on the menu, ask your butcher to slice it when you buy it. When it's time to cook, just secure the ham slices together with unwaxed dental floss, and bake as usual. When it's done, you won't have to slice it, and the slices will look perfect. Slicing it ahead of time will also allow the glaze to penetrate the meat a little more deeply.

For Less Salty Ham

To make your ham less salty, pour a can of ginger ale over it, then rub the meaty side with salt at least an hour before baking it. This will cause the salt water in the meat to come to the surface, which will reduce the saltiness of the ham. Discard the mixture, but tdon't rinse the ham before cooking.

Ham Bone Help

To easily remove a ham bone, slit the uncooked ham lengthwise down to the bone before placing it in the pan—but leave the bone in place. While the ham is baking, the meat will pull away and the bone will come out easily after the ham is cooked. Leaving the bone in will also lead to moister meat.

"Shanks" for the Tip

When purchasing a lamb shank, be sure it weighs at least 3 pounds. If the shank is any smaller, the percentage of bone will be too high in relation to the amount of meat.

When you are preparing meatloaf, try rubbing the top and sides with a small amount of water instead of tomato sauce. This will stop the meatloaf from cracking and drying out as it cooks—and who wants a dry meatloaf? If you like a tomato flavor, add tomato sauce 15 minutes before the meat is fully cooked.

Hamburger Helpers

If you are preparing hamburger (or meatloaf) with very low-fat meat, mix in one well-beaten egg white for every pound of meat. This egg white will give the meatload a richer flavor without adding a lot of fat. Add a package of instant onion-soup mix to a pound of meat for tons of flavor, and mix in some cottage cheese or instant potatoes to keep it moist and make less meat feed more people!

Easy-Greasy

If you wet your hands with cold water before shaping sausage or hamburger patties, the grease won't stick to your fingers.

No More Meat Funk

When you refrigerate cooked beef, its fat oxidizes quickly, which will often give day-old burgers an "off" taste. If you know you'll be eating tonight's meal tomorrow as well, discourage fat oxidization by not cooking the beef in iron or aluminum pans, and by not salting the meat until you are ready to eat it.

Beef Up the Dark

The best-tasting beef should be a dark red color with slightly yellowish fat. If the fat is too white or the meat is bright red, the beef hasn't been hanging long enough and will be tough and not as tasty. It's better if there's some fat marbled throughout, as this makes it tender.

Meatballs for Health

When eating pasta, try to balance the meal with some protein to allow for balanced blood-sugar levels. Maybe that's why Grandma always made spaghetti with meatballs!

Who Knew? Readers' Favorite

Want the fastest way to make meatballs? Well, here it is! Shape the meat mixture into a log and then cut off slices, which then roll easily into balls.

Moister Meatballs

If you insert a small piece of cracked ice into the center of your meatballs before browning them, they will be moister. But be careful—you'll need to experiment to make sure the centers don't remain raw. Cut open a meatball and check the doneness to determine the proper browning time.

When Should You Season A Steak?

The jury's still out on which stage in the cooking process you should season a steak. One authority says to salt before cooking, another equally respected one says to salt after cooking. If you salt before, you get the benefit of a nice salty flavor through-and-through, but the salt tends to draw liquid from the meat, so make sure you're replenishing its juices. Whether you decide to salt before or after, you should never use ground pepper on any meat that is to be cooked in a pan with dry heat. Pepper tends to become bitter when scorched in a dry pan.

Press for Doneness

When cooking steak, it's good to know that the internal temperature of a rare steak is 135°F, medium-rare is 145°F, medium is 160°F, and well done is 170°F. However, an experienced chef rarely whips out a meat thermometer. Meat has a certain resiliency at different temperatures, and a chef can just press the steak with a finger to tell whether the meat is rare, medium-rare, medium, medium-well, or well done. As meat cooks it loses water, and the more it cooks, the firmer it becomes. Try pressing on your steaks to get a sense for how they feel at different stages of doneness, and you'll never need to cut them open to find out again.

Against the Grain

Here's a simple tip to make your meat more tender. When it's ready to slice, make sure to cut it against the grain (look for slight lines on the surface).

A Great Use for Stale Bread

If you're broiling steaks or chops, save a few slices of stale bread and set them in the bottom of the broiler pan to absorb fat drippings. This will eliminate smoking fat, and it should also reduce any danger of a grease fire.

Let the Air Flow for Roasts

Always use a shallow pot for cooking roasts. This will allow air to circulate more efficiently. Elevating the meat by cooking it atop celery ribs, carrot sticks, and thick onion slices also helps get the air underneath the meat (and gives it a great flavor!).

Timing Roasts

Don't have a roasting chart nearby? Then follow this rule of thumb: Beef roasts will take about 20 minutes for the first pound and about 15 minutes for every pound thereafter. The USDA recommends cooking beef to an internal temperature of at least 145°F.

To Cover or Not to Cover:
That Is the Question

The two methods normally used for cooking a roast are dry heat (without liquid) or moist heat (with liquid). When the meat is covered, steam is trapped in the pan. Many cooks use this method to prevent roasts from drying out. Dry heat (with the lid off) will brown the outside of the roast, and, if you wish, you can baste it every 15 minutes to provide the desired moisture. If you go the moist heat route, lower the temperature by 25°F, and make sure to turn the roast or cook it on a rack so its underside won't get mushy.

Let the Roast Rest

Let a roast stand at room temperature for about 15 minutes before you carve it. This gives the juices time to be reabsorbed and distributed evenly. When you cook a roast, the juices tend to be forced to the center as those near the surface are evaporated by the heat. Resting the roast also allows the meat to firm up a bit, making it easier to carve into thinner slices.Meat gets tougher as it cools on your plate, because the collagen, which has turned to a tender gelatin, thickens. The best way to eliminate this problem is to be sure you serve steak on a warmed or metal plate. After carving a roast, keep it in a warmer or put it back in the oven and leave the door ajar.

Perfect Leftovers

When storing a cooked roast in the fridge, place it back into its own juices whenever possible. When reheating sliced meat, place it in a casserole dish with lettuce leaves between each of the slices. The lettuce provides just the right amount of moisture to keep the slices from drying out.

Break It Down

To tenderize a tough steak, salt it generously for an hour before cooking to break up tough proteins. Then just wipe off the salt before cooking.

Sugar and Salt for Meat

Before sautéing meats, sprinkle a tiny amount of sugar on the surface. The sugar will react with the juices and then caramelize, causing a deeper browning as well as an improved flavor.

Who Knew? Readers' Favorite

Wine corks (the natural kind, not plastic) contain a chemical that, when heated, will help tenderize beef stew. Just throw in three or four corks while cooking your stew, and don't tell anyone your secret!

You Can't Spell "Tender" without "T"

The tannic acid in strong black tea can tenderize meat in a stew, as well as reduce the cooking time. Just add ½ cup strong tea to the stew when you add the other liquid. It will also give your stew a great brown color.

Let Stews Sit

The perfect "leftover" meal, stews are usually best prepared a day in advance to allow the flavors to blend—or, as the romantic French say, marry.

Stew's Secret Ingredient

Cooking a lamb or beef stew? Try this secret ingredient: Add a few tablespoons of black coffee and your stew will have a nice dark color and a rich taste. This tip also works well for gravies.

Quick Thickeners

An easy method of thickening stews, soups, or creamed vegetables is to add a small amount of quick-cooking oats, a grated potato, or some instant mashed potatoes. Never add flour directly, as it will clump. However, you can mix flour with melted butter and add that mixture to your dish.

For Tender, Tasty Chili

Marinate the meat for your chili in beer. It's a great tenderizer for tough, inexpensive cuts of beef, and it will add great flavor. All you need to do is soak the meat for an hour before cooking, or marinate it overnight in the refrigerator.

Seasoning Removal Remedies

Here's a great tip when cooking with whole garlic cloves that you plan to remove before the dish is served: Stick a toothpick firmly in the garlic so it will be easy to take out. Put herbs that fall apart during cooking in a tea infuser to make them easy to remove.

The Goods on Gravy

If you're like most people, you probably use flour or cornstarch to thicken gravy. Because flour thickens somewhat slowly, make sure you don't use too much! Gravy thickens as it cools, so if you use too much flour, the gravy can become unappealingly congealed by the time you're ready for seconds. It can also taste "floury" rather than having the flavor of the meat juices it's made with. To dispense with the flour entirely, deglaze your roasting pan with water, then add a small amount of butter before reducing the mixture over high heat while stirring frequently until it is the right consistency.

It's in the (Fish) Eyes

If you're buying whole fish, check out the eyes, which should be clear, and the gills, which should be transparent and bright red in color. Don't be afraid to ask the fishmonger to show you the fish close up—they might give you a fresher fish if they think you know what you're looking for!

Tipping the Scales

If you're gutsy enough to scale your own fish, rub white vinegar on the scales, let the fish sit for about 10 minutes, and they'll rub right off. Put the fish in a large plastic bag first (hold it by the tail) to keep the scales from flying all over your kitchen.

Get Rid of Fishy Smells

Before handling fish, rub your hands with lemon juice, and you won't smell of fish for the rest of the day! After frying fish, put a little white vinegar into the pan to help get rid of the odor on the surface.

Testing Fish for Doneness

To test fish for doneness, insert a thin-bladed knife into the thickest part of flesh. If it's done, it will be just barely translucent in the center. Even though it might not look quite ready, the fish will continue to cook after you remove it from the heat.

Who Knew? Readers' Favorite

If you're grilling or broiling thick fish steaks, marinate them for 15 minutes in lemon or lime juice before cooking. The acid from the juice "cooks" the flesh a bit, cutting down on the time it needs to stay on the heat—so your fish is less likely to dry out.

Cornflake Your Fish

For added crunch with fewer calories, use cornflakes instead of breadcrumbs to coat fish fillets. Not only do cornflakes contain fewer calories than breadcrumbs, they are less absorbent and give a lighter covering, so the fish will absorb less oil.

Dry Fish Fries Better

When frying fish, be sure the surface of the fish is dry before putting it in the oil. Moisture can cool the oil down and make the fish cook unevenly.

Quick and Easy Fish

Our favorite way to prepare fish is also super quick and tasty. Wrap your fillets individually in foil, adding a bit of chopped onion, salt and pepper, a sprig of dill, and a drizzle of olive oil. Bake for 30 minutes in a 350°F oven, then unwrap for a tender, flavorful dinner.

Frozen Fish Fix

Pining for fresh fish but stuck with frozen? Try this: Cover the frozen fish in milk until it thaws, then cook. It will taste fresher, and your family will never know it was frozen.

Serving Fish

Fish tends to cool very quickly, so it's best served on warm plates or a warmed platter. Garnish your fish with a wedge of lemon or other citrus.

To steam fish fillets in the microwave, place them in a shallow microwavable dish (a glass pie plate is ideal) with the thinner parts overlapping at the center of the dish. Sprinkle with lemon juice or herbs if you like, season with salt and pepper, then cover the dish with plastic wrap (making sure it doesn't touch the fish) and cook for 3 minutes per pound. If your microwave doesn't have a turntable, rotate the dish about halfway through the cooking time.

All About Anchovies

You can reduce the saltiness of anchovies by soaking them in ice water for about 15 minutes. Because of their high salt content, anchovies will keep about two months under refrigeration after the jar is opened, and up to a year without refrigeration in a sealed can. Once opened, they should be kept covered with olive oil in the fridge.

The Skinny on Shrimp

Shrimp are low in fat, delicious, and one of the most inexpensive kinds of shellfish you can buy. For the most tender shrimp, cool them down before cooking by either place them in the freezer for 10–15 minutes, or setting them in a bowl of ice water for five minutes. If you're boiling them, drop them into boiling broth or court bouillon for one minute, and then turn off the heat and let stand for 10 minutes. Sautéed shrimp are done when they are firm and pink, in just 3–5 minutes. Grilled shrimp cook in about seven minutes. No matter how you're cooking them, shrimp cook fast! So make sure to keep a close eye on them. As soon as they turn pink, they're done. (If they are already pink when you purchase them, they've been cooked, and all you have to do is heat them up.) To make sure you don't overheat shrimp, plunge them in cold water once they've turned pink to immediately stop the cooking process.

Full and Frozen

Frozen shrimp can make for a quick and easy meal, but try to avoid shrimp that have been peeled and deveined before freezing, which usually causes a loss of texture and flavor.

For Lobster You'll Love

It might sound crazy, but the taste, texture, and color of microwaved lobster is far superior to boiled or steamed, and microwaving produces an evenly cooked, tender lobster. Unfortunately, you can only cook one lobster at a time, so put your oven on the lowest heat and use it to keep already-cooked lobsters warm until your entire meal is done. To cook a lobster, place it in a large, microwavable plastic bag with ¼ cup water, and knot the bag loosely. A 1½ pound lobster should take five to six minutes on high, providing you have a 600–700 watt microwave. If you have a lower wattage oven, allow about eight minutes. To be sure the lobster is fully cooked, separate the tail from the body. The tail meat should be creamy white, not translucent. Even when microwaved, the lobster must still be cooked live because of the enzymatic breakdown that occurs immediately upon its death. To stop the lobster's movements, put it in the freezer for 10 minutes before cooking to dull its senses.

Eating a Lobster

If you're eating a whole lobster and bibs aren't really your thing, cover the lobster with a napkin or towel before twisting off the legs and claws. This will keep the juices from squirting out.

Crayfish Know-How

Like lobsters and crabs, crayfish (also known as crawfish or crawdads) are always cooked live. However, all the meat is found in the tail. To remove the meat easily, gently twist the tail away from the body, then unwrap the first three sections of the shell to expose the meat. Next, pinch the end of the meat in one hand while holding the tail in the other, and pull the meat out in one piece.

Who Knew? Readers' Favorite

The most effective way to get rid of sand and grit from clams is to soak them in water with a bit of cornmeal stirred in. It irritates the clams, and they expel the sand while trying to eliminate the cornmeal.

Opening Shellfish

Cooking shellfish at home can be a lot of fun (not to mention, delicious), so don't be intimidated by the task of opening the shells! First, wash the shells thoroughly. Hold the clam or oyster in your palm and slip the tip of an oyster or butter knife between the upper and lower shells. Run the knife around the edge of the shell and pry until you hear a pop at the hinge. Loosen the clam or oyster and remove any shell fragments.

Oyster Answers

Store live oysters for up to two days in the refrigerator in a single layer with the larger shell down, covered with a damp towel. Oysters are easy to overcook, so cook them carefully. If you are poaching them, take them out as soon as their edges start to curl.

Mussel Madness

Mussels are a succulent seafood treat, and they're not hard to make. Here are some tips to make delicious mussels.

+ When purchasing, make sure they're alive by tapping their shells, which will snap closed. Any mussels that don't close are probably dead and shouldn't be eaten.

+ Live mussels will keep in the refrigerator for two to three days if placed on a tray and covered with a damp towel. Spread them out; never pile the mussels on top of one another.

+ Clean them with a brush under cold running water, and discard any that have a non-clear liquid coming out of them. If they have a visible "beard," brush it off just before cooking, as removing it will kill the mussel.

+ To cook them, all you have to do is boil them in a pot. Mussels are ready when their shells open, and any mussels that aren't open should be discarded. Serve over pasta or with french fries, and enjoy!

Clam-Cooking Know-How

The shells of healthy clams should be closed when you buy them. They will gradually open as the clams cook. (If you keep the clams on ice, they will also probably relax and open their shells.) Like mussels, if a clam's shell doesn't open by itself when the clam is cooked, it should be discarded.

Prevent a Clam Calamity

Once clams are dug up, they must be cleansed of sand and debris. To accomplish this, the clams should be allowed to soak in the refrigerator in a solution of one part salt to 10 parts water for several hours or overnight. If you're pressed for time, rinse them in a bowl of fresh water, changing it frequently, until no sand remains.

The Truth About Clam Chowder

Chefs always add clams to their chowder during the last 15–20 minutes of cooking. If added too early, clams can become either tough or too soft.

Who Knew? Readers' Favorite

If you like dry, fluffy rice, try this trick as soon as the rice is done cooking: Wrap the lid with a cotton dishtowel and set it on the pot for about 15 minutes. The cloth will absorb the steam.

Secrets for Perfect Mashed Potatoes

No matter how long we spend cooking a delicious cut of meat, we find that the mashed potatoes are always more popular at our dinner table. Here are some of favorite tips for perfect mashed potatoes.

✦ Never pour cold milk into cooked potatoes. It will change the taste of the starch, giving it an unpleasant flavor, not unlike cardboard. The milk should be warmed in a pan (preferably with a small amount of garlic or chives for flavor) before being added.

✦ Buttermilk will give the potatoes a great flavor.

✦ If you're watching your weight, save some of the cooking water from the potatoes and use that instead of butter or cream.

✦ A pinch or two of baking powder will give mashed potatoes extra fluff. Never put baking soda in potatoes; it will turn them black.

✦ Don't overmix or overcook potatoes. The cell walls will rupture, releasing an excess of starch and resulting in gluey potatoes. Potatoes should be mashed with a vertical motion, not stirred in a circular motion, to minimize the damage that occurs by crushing the cells on the wall of the bowl.

- ✦ Try adding powdered milk or instant potato flakes for extra-fluffy mashed potatoes.

- ✦ Squeeze some fresh lemon juice into your mashed potatoes instead of butter or oil. Season with freshly ground black pepper for a no-added-fat mash that is flavorful and goes fantastically well with roast chicken.

Pasta Perfection

Cook pasta only until it is slightly chewy (what the Italians call al dente, or "to the tooth"). Always use plenty of water, and keep the water at a rapid boil—the pasta needs to move around as it cooks, to keep it from sticking together. Some cooks like to salt the water, but we find it tends to toughen pasta. Use a pinch of sugar instead, and salt just before serving. After it's cooked, don't rinse it. The sauce will cling better to the residual starch, and the noodles will retain more nutrients.

Stuffing Secrets

- ✦ Never stuff a turkey or other fowl and leave it overnight, even in the refrigerator. Cooking the bird may not kill all the bacteria, and hundreds of cases of food poisoning occur every year because birds are stuffed and then left for too long before roasting.

- ✦ If you plan to cook your stuffing in the turkey, consider this tip: Pack it into a piece of cheesecloth before placing it in the bird. When you're ready to remove the stuffing, simply pull the cheesecloth out, and none of the stuffing will be stuck inside the turkey. You can also seal the opening of the bird with a slice of raw potato.

✦ If the stuffing inside the bird is never enough (or if your family picks at the turkey and trimmings before the meal is served), try this. Fill some buttered muffin pans with additional stuffing and bake in a very hot oven. You'll have a stuffing treat that's crunchy on the outside and moist on the inside. Yum!

Lentils Done Easily

Lentils are delicious—and great for you! When cooking them, make sure to add a few teaspoons of oil. It will prevent the pot from spilling over, and actually helps in the cooking process.

A Bean Bonanza

Beans are as delicious as they are nutritious. Here are a few tips for preparing them.

✦ To tell whether a bean is fully cooked, squeeze it. There should be no hard core at the center. Be aware that cooking the beans with an acidic ingredient, such as tomatoes, will slow down the cooking time.

✦ If you're making beans as a side dish, add a small amount of brown sugar or molasses at the end of cooking for a delicious flavor.

✦ You can make dry beans less gassy by soaking them overnight with fennel seeds. Use a teaspoon of fennel per pound of beans.

Vegetarian Protein Powerhouses

It's important to make sure your family gets the appropriate amount of protein each day. However, the protein doesn't need to come in complex forms like meat, fish, and poultry, which are the biggest contributors to a costly grocery bill. Try substituting combinations of simple proteins like beans, tofu, mushrooms, and even nuts in your meals at least once a week to save money and boost nutrition.

Who Knew? Readers' Favorite

You don't have to avoid baked beans because you fear they'll make you gassy. Instead, just add a dash or two of baking soda to the beans when they're cooking, and their gas-producing properties will be dramatically reduced.

Cooking Corn

Never add salt to the water when boiling corn; table salt contains traces of calcium, which will toughen the kernels. Instead, add a little milk, which will bring out the sweetness of the corn.

Easy Eggplant

Fried or roasted eggplant is delicious, but if you try preparing it as-is it will normally come out quite bitter. Luckily, it's easy to remove this bitter taste. Before cooking eggplant, cut it into thick slices. Salt the slices, and let them drain on a wire rack or in a colander for 30 minutes. Then rinse them well and pat dry. This procedure will also reduce the amount of oil they absorb during frying.

Mushroom Maker

Mushrooms can be kept white and firm during sautéing if you add ¼ teaspoon lemon juice for every 2 tablespoons butter or olive oil.

Getting Rid of Celery Strings

For the most part, celery is easy to cook—the pectin in its cells breaks down easily in water. However, celery strings, which are made of cellulose, are virtually indestructible and won't break down under normal cooking conditions. Even the body has a difficult time breaking the strings down, and many people can't digest them at all. Remove the strings before preparing celery with this simple trick: Once you remove a stalk from the bunch, place it curved-side up on the counter or a cutting board, then grab hold of the very bottom (white part) of the stalk and quickly bend it up. It will crack off the bottom of the celery, but the strings will still be attached.

Better Brussels Sprouts

Brussels sprouts are an excellent source of vitamins A and C, and although they get a bad rap, our kids adore them. Store them in the fridge to prevent their leaves from turning yellow. Cut an X on the stalk end of each sprout to ensure even and quick cooking.

Get Choppin'!

Trust us, no one hates the tedium of chopping vegetables more than we do. However, it's absolutely essential when you're trying to save money on groceries. No more baby carrots and pre-minced garlic! Invest in a good knife, and the job will go much more quickly. If you've got teenagers, teach them how to safely cut up fruits and veggies and put them to work. If you can manage to chop up all the vegetables you need for a whole week and put them in containers in the fridge, cooking dinner every night will be unbelievably more manageable.

Perfect Peas

Here's a quick tip for one of our favorite vegetables: When cooking shelled fresh peas, add a few washed pods to the water. They will improve the flavor and give the peas a richer green color.

Who Knew? Readers' Favorite

Baking stuffed apples, tomatoes, or bell peppers in a well-greased muffin tin will help them to hold their shape—and make sure they don't tip over when you take them out of the oven.

Sprightly Spinach

Always cook spinach in an uncovered pot. The steam that builds up when a pot is covered causes the plant's volatile acids to condense on the lid and fall back into the water. Keeping the lid off will make sure your spinach keeps its lovely green color.

Cauliflower Cooking

Cauliflower cooks in 10–15 minutes, and overcooking will cause it to turn dark and tough, so make sure to keep an eye on the pot. Add a small amount of lemon juice to the cooking water to keep it white, and to reduce the odor replace the hot water when it's halfway done. Never cook cauliflower in an aluminum or iron pot, because contact with these metals will turn the vegetable yellow, brown, or even blue-green!

Beet Red

To make sure beets keep their red color through the entire cooking process, cook them whole with at least two inches of stem still attached, and add a few tablespoons of white vinegar to the water.

Rescuing Lost Veggies

Cooking Thanksgiving dinner and your vegetables turned to mush? Simply add some herbs along with tomato sauce or cream. Then top with cheese and/or bread crumbs and stick in the oven for 30 minutes. Your family is sure to be impressed with your new recipe for "vegetables gratin"!

Simple Garlic Trick

Chopping your own garlic instead of buying it pre-minced can be a real pain but a huge money saver. Use this simple trick to make it a little easier on yourself: microwave the garlic for about eight seconds to make it easy to peel. Once the cloves are peeled, drizzle a tiny amount of oil over them to make them less sticky when you're trying to chop them.

Fixing a Hot Mess

Ow! If you or your child bites into a piece of pizza that's too hot to eat, reach for a glass of milk. Milk will soothe the roof of your mouth better than cold water because the protein in milk will create a protective film over any burns. Now let the pizza cool a bit before you take another bite!

The Knife Test

You've had a hectic day, but luckily you had a frozen casserole in the freezer! Unfortunately, you were in such a rush you have no idea how long ago you popped it in the oven. To tell if your casserole is heated through, insert a butter knife into the center, lift it out, then slowly and carefully press it to your wrist. If the knife is hot, you'll know the casserole is too.

CHAPTER 4

Desserts

Make a Great Cake

For the best-tasting cakes ever, always bring the eggs, milk, and butter to room temperature before you make your batter.

For the Sake of the Cake

If a cake recipe calls for flouring the baking pan, use some of the dry cake mix instead. The cake will absorb the mix, and you won't have a floury mess on the outside when the cake is done.

Who Knew? Readers' Favorite

To keep the frosting from sticking to your knife as you cut the cake, dip your knife into a glass of cold water between each cut.

Egg Substitution

When baking a cake, try substituting two egg yolks for one whole egg. The cake will be very rich and dense, because the yolks won't hold as much air as the whites. This isn't exactly a healthy tip, but it sure tastes good!

Keeping Your Cake Light

For a light, moist cake, enhance your cake flour by adding 2 tablespoons cornstarch to every cup of flour, then sifting them together before you add to the mix. You may be surprised by the results!

Popping Your Cake's Bubbles

Make sure you get rid of any bubbles in your cake batter before baking it. This is easily accomplished by holding the pan an inch or two above the counter and tapping it two or three times to release any air pockets. Just be careful—the batter might spatter.

We Heart Cakes

A heart-shaped cake is easier to make than you might think. Simply divide your cake batter between one round pan and one square one. When the cakes are cool, cut the round cake in half. Turn the square cake so it looks like a diamond and set the half-rounds on the two top sides. Voilà!

Piece of Cake!

If you're about to show off your cake prowess by cutting up baked cakes and re-assembling them in an impressive configuration, try freezing the cake first. Fresh cakes, especially those made from a box mix, often crumble easily, but freezing will make your knife glide right through. Freezing detracts little from the taste of your cake, as long as you don't frost it first.

Cake Magic

If you find icing too sweet or too rich, try this cake topping: Set a paper lace doily on the cake, and then dust lightly with confectioners' sugar. Carefully lift the doily off the cake, and admire the beautiful design. Try colored confectioners' sugar or a mixture of confectioners' sugar and cocoa powder.

Here's a new twist on transporting frosted cakes. Don't just insert toothpicks and cover in plastic, because the sharp ends can puncture the plastic and result in a gooey mess. Instead, attach miniature marshmallows to the toothpicks before covering. Strands of spaghetti can also be used instead of toothpicks.

Keep a Cake from Sticking

Does your cake stick to the plate? Sprinkle a thin layer of sugar on a plate before you put a cake on it. Not only does it prevent the cake from sticking, it also makes the bottom delightfully crunchy.

Stale Cake Cure

If you need to store a cake more than a day or two, put half an apple in the container. The apple will provide just enough moisture to keep the cake from drying out too soon.

Frost in Translation

Want to freeze a cake, but don't want the frosting to stick to the plastic wrap? Here's a handy tip for doing just that. First, put it in the freezer without any wrapping. Once the frosting is frozen, cover the cake with plastic wrap. The cold frosting won't stick to the wrap.

Awesome Icing Hints

Even if you've just made the most delicious cake ever, it still won't be a hit unless your finishing touch—the icing—holds its own. Here are a few of our favorite tips for perfect icing.

✦ If you sprinkle a very thin layer of cornstarch on top of a cake before you ice it, the icing won't run down the sides.

✦ To keep icing from hardening, just add a very small amount of white vinegar after it is whipped. You can also add a pinch of baking soda to the confectioners' sugar. This will help the icing retain some moisture and it will not dry out as fast.

✦ If you're making your own chocolate icing, add a teaspoon of unsalted butter to the chocolate while it is melting to improve the consistency.

✦ Here's a great bakers' trick to make it easier to decorate the top of a cake: With a toothpick, trace the pattern, picture, or lettering before you pipe the icing on. This will give you a guide, so you'll make fewer mistakes.

✦ If you're having a problem keeping a layer cake together when you're icing it, stick a few bamboo skewers into the cake through both layers; remove them as you're frosting the top.

✦ To keep the cake from sliding around on the plate as you're icing it, place a dab of frosting in the middle of the plate before you place the cake on top. The icing will keep the cake in place, and by the time you've served all the slices, no one will notice the little bit of extra frosting on the bottom.

Who Knew? Readers' Favorite

To give the icing that silky look that professionally made cakes always seem to have, ice it as usual and then blow air from a hairdryer over the top of it for a minute. It will melt the icing slightly, giving it the shiny appearance you're looking for.

Keep Leftover Cake Moist

If you have leftover cake, you have more self-control than we do! To keep the inside of the cake (where you made the last slice) moist, place a piece of white bread next to the exposed surface. The bread can be affixed with a toothpick or a short piece of spaghetti.

Three Cures for Domed Cakes

Unfortunately, part of baking is always trial and error. If your cakes "dome" when baked, the problem may be caused by one of these common errors: the oven temperature was too high, your pan was too small, or the balance of liquid, egg, flour, and fat was off. Time for a new trial!

The Big Fat Truth

The texture of a cake depends on the type of sweetener and fat used. These ingredients affect how tender the cake will be, so be sure you use the right ones. Never substitute granulated sugar for confectioners' sugar and vice versa. Cakes made with oil are very tender and moist—oil doesn't hold air as well as butter or shortening, so eggs and other thick ingredients must trap the air.

Angel Food Aid

Never bake an angel food cake on the top or middle rack of the oven. It will retain moisture better if baked in the lower third of the oven, and always at the temperature specified in the recipe.

Angel Food Fact

An angel food cake can be left in the pan and covered tightly with foil for up to 24 hours or until you are ready to frost it.

Say Cheesecake!

When preparing a cheesecake, go exactly by the recipe and don't make any substitutions. You'll have a much better chance at success. Here are some other pointers for perfect cheesecake.

✦ Be sure that the cream cheese is at room temperature before using it.

✦ When you bake a cheesecake at a low temperature, there's less chance of it shrinking from the sides of the pan.

✦ Don't open the oven for the first 30 minutes when baking cheesecake! The cheesecake may develop cracks or partially collapse.

✦ Cheesecakes will develop cracks when they are overcooked. They're done when the center of the cake is still wobbly and shaky—which may look underdone to you.

✦ Flourless cheesecakes need to be baked in a pan of water (called a bain-marie, or water bath) to keep the eggs from coagulating.

✦ Cheesecake cracks can be repaired with whipped cream cheese or sweetened sour cream, but you'll be able to see the repair. It's better to top the cake with berries if it has too many cracks.

Who Knew? Readers' Favorite

It's always disappointing when you remember you have one last bit of ice cream in the freezer, only to open it and find it's covered in ice crystals. To keep this from happening, store your ice cream container in a sealed plastic bag in the freezer. It will stop ice crystals from forming. You can also cover the top of your ice cream with aluminum foil before you put the lid on top.

Perfect for a Summer Day

You'll never buy a box of popsicles again after you learn this easy recipe for the homemade variety. Simply pour juice into waxy paper cups, then add a small plastic spoon or tongue depressor to the middle once they are half-frozen. When they're completely solid, peel away the cup for an icy treat.

Cool Sundae Station

Repurpose a plastic ice cube tray by making it into a sundae station to talk about. Use the various compartments for nuts, crushed cookies, candy, and other toppings, then serve with ice cream and let the kids make their own sundaes. (Don't be surprised if they dump everything on top.)

Banana Fun

A great and healthy summer treat for kids is to cut a banana in half (horizontally, not vertically), put a popsicle stick in the flat end, dip it in some melted chocolate or sundae topping, and freeze it for a few hours on waxed paper. Your kids will love you for these banana treats! (At least for a little while.)

Who Knew? Readers' Favorite

Keep your ice cream cones leak-free with this simple tip: Place a miniature marshmallow or chocolate kiss in the bottom of the cone before adding the ice cream. Either of them can help prevent the cone from leaking—and they're a delicious treat at the end!

Shimmering Pies

Do you want your pies to glisten like those in the bakery? It's easy with this trick: Just beat an egg white and brush it over the crust before baking. This works especially well for a pie that has a top crust, like apple pie.

When It's Good to Be Flaky

Even if your pie's filling is near perfect, you won't win any accolades for your creation unless its crust is up to par. Here are a few tips for making perfectly flaky piecrusts.

✦ Be sure the liquid used in your piecrust dough is ice cold. In fact, anything hot going into a piecrust will affect it.

✦ Add a teaspoon of vinegar to the water for an even flakier crust, or substitute sour cream or whipping cream for the entirety of the water.

✦ Low-gluten flour such as pastry flour is your best bet. Cake flour is too soft and won't give the crust the body it needs, and bread flour has too high a gluten content and would make a tough crust. As a substitute for pastry flour, combine two parts all-purpose flour and one part cake flour or instant flour.

✦ Replace the shortening or butter with lard. Lard has larger fat crystals and three times the polyunsaturates as butter, making the crust flakier.

Pie Dough Know-How

Never stretch pie dough when you are placing it in the pan. Stretched dough usually shrinks from the sides.

Pie Serving Secret

Pies with graham cracker crusts can be difficult to remove from the pan. However, if you dip the bottom of the pan in warm water for 10 seconds, the pie will come right out without any damage.

Pumpkin Pie Loves Marshmallows

For a unique pumpkin pie, put small marshmallows on the bottom of the pie, just above the crust. As the pie bakes, the air in the marshmallows expands and the marshmallows rise to the top.

Who Knew? Readers' Favorite

Making graham cracker crust can turn into quite a mess—particularly when pressing the crumbs into the pie plate with greasy, buttered hands. Stop the crumbs from sticking by putting your hands into a plastic bag before the pressing begins!

Get Rid of Soggy Bottoms

It's always disappointing when you slice into your carefully prepared pie only to find that the bottom is soggy. If you have a problem with fruit or fruit juices soaking the bottom of your piecrust, brush the bottom crust with egg white before adding the filling. This will seal the crust and solve the problem. If your fruit filling is simply too wet, thicken it up. The best thickener is 3–4 tablespoons of minute tapioca. Just mix it with the sugar before adding to the fruit. Other solutions for soggy pie bottoms include prebaking the piecrust, partially cooking the filling, or brushing the crust with jelly before you fill it. When using a cream filling in a pie, sprinkle the crust with granulated sugar before adding the filling to keep the crust flaky.

Cutting a Creamy Pie

Spray a small amount of vegetable oil on your knife before cutting a pie with a cream filling. This will stop the filling from sticking to the knife.

For Extra Tasty Tarts

Here's a pastry chef's trick to add flavor to a lemon tart or pie: Rub a few sugar cubes over an orange or lemon, then include the cubes in the recipe as part of the total sugar. The sugar tends to extract just enough of the natural oils from the peels of the fruits to add some flavor.

Tender Pastries

Add some sugar to your pastry recipe to help tenderize the dough. Pastry dough should look like coarse crumbs after you cut in the fat (butter, shortening, etc.).

Store your rolling pin in the freezer. It's much easier to roll out pastry dough and piecrusts with a frozen rolling pin.

Fire up Your Flambé

If you're making a flambéed dish, you have more guts than we do! Just be warned that you may have trouble igniting brandy when it's not hot enough. Some chefs warm the brandy gently before adding it to food to ensure that it will light. If it's too hot before being adding it to the dish, however, it may ignite too soon. Serving a dessert that's flambéed? Try soaking sugar cubes briefly in a lemon or orange extract that contains alcohol, then set them on the dessert and carefully ignite.

A Lower-Cal Cookie

If you're making cookies, choose the soft drop, more-cakey versions rather than the rolled variety—they generally contain more air per serving and therefore, fewer calories.

Dough To-Do

When you mix cookie dough, only stir as much as you must to fully combine the ingredients—over-stirring can cause the cookies to become tough. Unbaked cookie dough may be frozen and thawed when you're ready to bake. Wrap the dough tightly in a freezer bag, try to resist eating any, and stick in the freezer for up to one month.

Chilly Dough

Cold cookie dough will not stick to the rolling pin. Refrigerate the dough for 20 minutes for the best results.

I Want Cookies!

If you give your kids cookies as treats, you can save a lot by making a batch of cookies every week or two rather than buying them at the store. This is a great activity for the parent who doesn't do most of the cooking. Have him or her (OK, it's probably a him) spend twenty minutes making cookies with the kids on the weekend, and you'll have enough to last you until next time.

Avoid Heavy Baked Goods

To keep cookies or butter cakes from becoming too heavy, be sure the butter is at room temperature before you cream it with the sugar. Try to avoid softening butter in the microwave, as it's likely to melt.

Margarine Mayhem

When making cookies with margarine, be aware that the firmness of the dough will depend on the type of margarine used. Be sure to use stick margarine, not margarine from a tub. Note that margarine made from 100 percent corn oil will make the dough softer. When using margarine to make cookies, you may need lengthen the chilling time or place the dough in the freezer instead of the refrigerator. If you're making cutout cookies, the chilling time should be at least one hour in the refrigerator. Dough for drop and bar cookies doesn't have to be chilled.

Maintain the Moisture

Keep soft cookies, cakes, and pancakes deliciously moist by adding a teaspoon of jelly to the batter.

Who Knew? Readers' Favorite

Our favorite part of oatmeal cookies, is—naturally—the oatmeal! Boost the oatmeal's flavor by toasting it lightly before adding it to the batter. Simply sprinkle the oatmeal on a baking sheet and heat it in a 300°F oven for about 10 minutes. The oats should turn a golden-brown.

Burned Bottoms?

If you've ever burned the bottoms of your cookies when baking a number of batches, the baking sheets may be to blame. Let the baking sheets cool between batches—when you start with too hot a surface the cookies may burn. Two to three minutes cooling time is usually long enough. Another alternative is to line the baking sheets with parchment paper—simply lift the cookies, still on the parchment paper, right onto the cooling rack.

Cookie Cooling

Cookies can go from beautiful to burned in no time. To lessen the chance of this happening, take the cookies out of the oven when they are not quite done, but don't transfer them to the cooling rack right away—let them sit on the hot pan for a minute or two to finish baking. Then transfer to the rack to cool fully.

An Improvised Cooling Rack

If you're baking cookies or pies and don't have a cooling rack, simply line up a bunch of butter knives in alternating directions (first with the blade towards you, then with the blade away from you), and put the baking sheet down on top of them. You can also use old egg cartons.

Browning Cookies

If your cookies typically don't brown enough, bake them on a higher rack in the oven. Other techniques to boost browning include substituting a tablespoon or two of corn syrup for the sugar, using egg for the liquid, and using unbleached or bread flour in the recipe.

Who Knew? Readers' Favorite

Dye your cookie dough, not your hands, by dropping food coloring into a bag with the dough. Knead a bit and roll around to even out the color. You can use right away or keep in the freezer. Either way, you'll have fun, colorful cookies, and save lots of time on hand cleaning.

Cookie Dough Spoon Saver

Is your cookie dough sticking to everything? It's easy to get a spoonful of cookie dough to drop to your baking pan if you first dip the spoon in milk.

Nonstick Mixing

Making cookies? Spray the beaters with a little vegetable oil or nonstick cooking spray and you won't have to stop every few seconds to scrape the batter off the beaters and back into the bowl.

Cookie Cutter Tip

To get a sharp edge on your cookies when using cutters, dip the cutter in flour or warm oil occasionally during the cutting process.

Crisper Cookies

If crisp cookies are what you're after, be sure your cookie jar has a loose-fitting lid. This allows air to circulate and evaporates any moisture.

Storing Cookies

Rinse out coffee cans and store cookies in them. Use the original lids, or stretch plastic wrap across the top and seal with a rubber band.

Who Knew? Readers' Favorite

To keep your cookies chewy, add half an apple or a slice of white bread to the cookie jar. This will provide just enough moisture to keep the cookies from becoming hard.

Getting Your Brownies Out of a Sticky Situation

If your baked goods are stuck to the pan, wrap the bottom of the pan in a cold, wet towel for a few minutes. Once the pan is cooler, your brownies or bar cookies may come out more easily.

Whip It Good

Whipping up some cream? Heavy cream will set up faster if you add seven drops of lemon juice for each pint of cream. But you don't necessarily need heavy cream to make whipped cream. Light cream can be whipped to a firm, mousse-like consistency if you add a tablespoon unflavored gelatin dissolved in 1 tablespoon hot water for every 2 cups of cream. After whipping, refrigerate it for two hours.

How to Get the Creamiest Custard

Making perfect custard takes time and patience, but these tips should help. For a super-rich custard, add 2–3 egg yolks in addition to your usual amount of eggs. For a custard that is creamy rather than solid, stir the mixture continuously over low heat to keep the protein from setting too quickly. The milk helps separate the egg proteins from one another, which allows the custard to coagulate at a higher temperature and reduces the possibility of curdling. Never replace the milk with water, because your custard will not set. You should also never try to speed up the cooking process by increasing the heat.

Meringue Magic

Not only is homemade meringue delicious, but it will also impress your friends—especially if you use these tips for getting the best meringue and the highest peaks.

- ✦ Make sure that your egg whites are at room temperature. As you beat, add 2–3 tablespoons of superfine or granulated sugar for each egg used. Keep beating until the peaks stand up without drooping.

- ✦ For the fluffiest egg whites, add a pinch of salt before whipping, and use a copper bowl if you happen to have one.

- ✦ To keep the peaks firmer for a longer period of time, add 1/8 teaspoon of white vinegar per egg white while beating. To get more meringue per egg white, add 2 teaspoons cold water for each egg white before beating.

- ✦ How do you know if beaten egg whites are stiff enough? Just run a knife through the middle of the bowl—if they whites stay separated, they're ready.

- ✦ Remember, if it's rainy (or even damp) outside, the meringue peaks will not remain upright! It might be better to save your baking for a drier day.

◆ Occasionally, meringue will develop small droplets of water on its surface shortly after being removed from the oven. This beading is caused by overcooking, so to prevent this, bake meringue at a high temperature (between 400°–425°F) for a short time—four to five minutes.

Who Knew? Readers' Favorite

When boiling syrup, one of the more frequent and annoying problems is that it crystallizes. The easiest way to avoid this is to put a pinch of cream of tartar in the syrup while it's cooking. This adds a small amount of acidity—just enough to prevent crystals from forming but not enough that you should taste it.

The Candyman Can

Cooking up your own candy is as delicious as it is fun. Experienced candy makers know that it's tricky to keep the sugar from crystallizing during cooking. A simple solution? Heat the sugar over low heat, without stirring, until it's completely dissolved. To eliminate the sugar crystals that inevitably cling to the sides of the pan, cover with a tight-fitting lid and continue cooking the syrup for three to four minutes. The steam that's generated will melt these pesky crystals.

Can-Do Candy

Making candy? Not only do we recommend using a larger pot than specified in the recipe to keep the hot, bubbling syrup safely away from your hands, we also recommend using your heaviest pot. Pots made out of thinner material tend to heat unevenly, which will make it harder to properly heat the syrup.

Egg Secret

When making a soufflé, it's best if you use egg whites from eggs that are at least a week old (but not yet expired). Why? Very fresh eggs contain more water, which can make your soufflé taste grainy.

The Collapsible Soufflé

Be careful when you're making a soufflé. Air bubbles are trapped when you beat the egg whites, and when a soufflé is placed in the oven, the air expands, causing the soufflé to rise. If the soufflé is punctured or shaken, however, the air will be released too early and the soufflé will collapse. It's also true that a soufflé must be served as soon as it is removed from the oven. Soufflés begin to collapse as soon as they start to cool down. So it's best to serve them right in the baking dish.

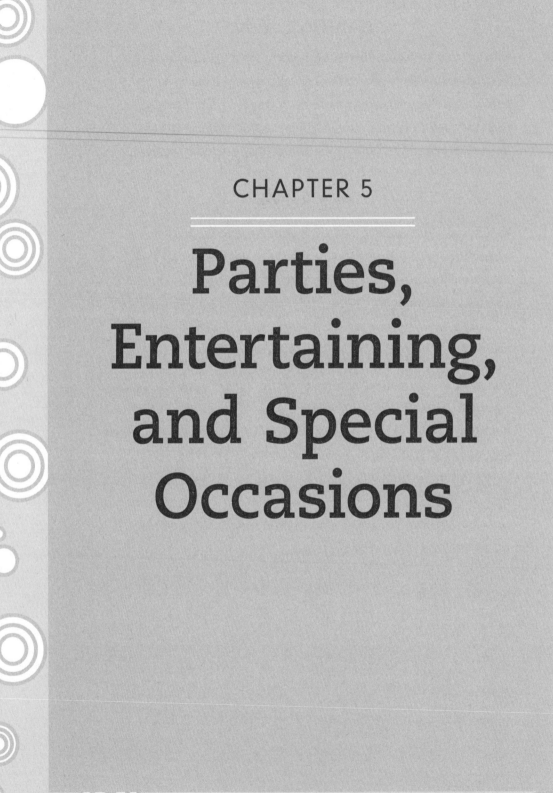

CHAPTER 5

Parties, Entertaining, and Special Occasions

Hot Cross Buns

Having a dinner party? Here's a great tip for keeping dinner rolls warm long after they've come out of the oven. When you put the rolls in the oven to bake, put a ceramic tile in, too. By the time the rolls are done, the tile will be (very!) hot. Place it in the basket and put your rolls on top. The tile will keep them warm. You can also use aluminum foil instead of the tile, but it won't retain the heat as long.

For Cheese Plate Praises

Always bring cheese to room temperature one hour before serving it. Even if the cheese becomes a little melty, the flavor will be much better.

Who Knew? Readers' Favorite

To keep meat or cheese hors d'oeuvres moist, cover them with a damp paper towel, then cover loosely with plastic wrap. Many fillings (as well as bread) dry out very quickly, but with this tip, you can make these simple appetizers first and have them on the table when guests arrive.

Creative Fruit Display

For a fun display on your buffet table, hollow out a melon, orange, or grapefruit and fill it with cut-up fruits (and maybe even some miniature marshmallows). For an even more attractive holder, you can scallop the melon edges or cut it in the shape of a basket.

Booze Clues

Having a party? Instead of buying "wine rings," which go around the base of wine glasses to mark whose drink is whose, simply keep a dry-erase marker on hand and have guests write their names (or a funny message) right on their glass.

Rubber Bubbly

Having a New Year's party? Put your child's inexplicable Silly Bandz obsession to good use! These rubber bands in fun shapes are perfect for putting around the stems of champagne glasses so your guests can tell whose bubbly is whose.

For a Sweet Sparkle

For a snazzy New Year's treat, color some granulated sugar by adding a few drops of food coloring to it. Then wet the rim of each champagne glass and press into the sugar to give it a sweet, colorful rim—perfect for guests who find champagne a little too dry.

Don't Stick a Cork in It!

Nothing kills a party like a stuck cork. Old method: Shove the cork all the way into the bottle and apologize to guests for the tiny pieces floating in their Cabernet. New method: Soak a washcloth in hot water and fold around the bottle's neck. When the glass expands, it will release its death grip on the trapped cork.

Fast Filter

The next time you attempt to open a bottle of wine only to have cork end up in the bottle, reach for a (clean) comb! Just hold the comb over the spout and pour, and it will catch any bits of cork.

Who Knew? Readers' Favorite

Wondering what to do with leftover wine (besides drinking it, of course)? Keep it fresh by putting whatever is left in a small container such as a jam jar. This limits the amount of air the wine is put in contact with, keeping it fresh. Which is the same thing those expensive "wine vacuum sealers" do!

Leprechaun-Worthy Lager

Even wondered how bars turn their beer green on St. Patrick's Day? It's as easy as adding 3–4 drops of green food coloring to a pint glass of beer. This trick will work best with light-colored beer.

Shaken, Not Stirred

Who needs a martini shaker? Instead of buying this expensive bar tool, simply use a stainless steel thermos with a screw-in lid. If there's no way to close the sipping hole on the top, make sure to cover it with your thumb while you shake!

A "Cool" Idea

To keep ice cubes from melting at a party, put them in a bowl, and then set that bowl in a larger one filled with dry ice.

Keep Your Punch Cold

Drinking punch that's half water is never fun, but ice cubes can melt so quickly when left out in a bowl. One of the easiest ways to keep a large punch bowl cold is to make larger ice cubes, as it will take one giant ice cube much longer to melt than many little ones. To make a long-lasting, large cube, fill a rinsed-out milk or juice carton half-full with water. Then peel off the cardboard when it's time to use.

Ice Cube Math

If you run out of ice at a party, you're in trouble! But how do you know how much to buy? Use this simple metric. If you're serving mostly cocktails, the average person at a party will go through 10–15 cubes. When you buy ice cubes in the bag, you will get about 10 cubes per pound.

Who Knew? Readers' Favorite

Champagne lost its fizz? Place a raisin in the glass and the last bits of carbon dioxide that remain will cling to the raisin, then be released again as bubbles. You can also try throwing a few raisins into the bottle before you make the final pour.

Better Than the Bathtub

If you're having a party and have run out of space to cool beverages, don't go buy a Styrofoam cooler. Instead, fill your washing machine with ice and store bottles and cans inside. The lid will keep everything cool, and once the ice melts you can simply run the rinse cycle to get rid of the all the water.

Back On the Wagon

For the spring and summer picnic seasons, use your kids' wagon or wheelbarrow as a drink cooler: Just fill it up with ice, add your cold beverages, and enjoy your days in the sun.

Party Time!

Here's a cute way of sending out unique party invitations. Write the invite on a blown-up balloon with a permanent marker, then deflate it and put it in the mail. Your guests will have to blow up the balloon to read the invitation.

Harvest Party Lights

We love this festive-for-fall decoration: Cut a slice off the side of an apple so it lays flat on a saucer or candleholder. Then cut a hole out of the top and you have an instant votive or tea light holder! Coat the hole with some lemon juice to keep the apple from turning brown.

Eliminate the Drip

Don't spend extra for dripless candles—you can make "regular" candles dripless with this simple procedure. Place the candles in a shallow pan and add enough water to cover them. Then add 2 tablespoons salt per candle, and mix or agitate until the salt dissolves (you might want to take the candles out while mixing, then put them back in). Let the candles soak in the saltwater for two to three hours, then rinse them and let them dry. Wait at least 24 hours before using them and they'll be virtually dripless. The salt water hardens the wax, which makes it burn more slowly and cleanly, reducing the chance of messy drips onto linens or furniture.

A Must for Candles

Bringing out the candles for your party? Put them in the freezer the night before, and they'll burn more slowly and drip less when you take them out.

Who Knew? Readers' Favorite

You just had a great dinner party, except now your candlesticks left wax drippings all over the place. To remove candle wax from just about anything, simply put the item in the freezer. Leave for a couple of hours and the wax will peel off easily.

Tin Can Candle

Having an outdoor party? Washed-out tin cans make great holders for votive candles around your garden. They'll give off a shimmering, silvery glow, and you won't mind if they get dirty!

Marshmallow Candleholders

To add a little color and whimsy to a birthday cake, make natural candleholders from small marshmallows, thus protecting your cake from melting wax. Keep them refrigerated for best results. The best part is that you can give them to guests to eat after the candles are burned out, as long as they don't have any wax on them.

A Thoughtful and Thrifty Gift for a Bride-to-Be

Here's a wonderful, one-of-a-kind gift for a bridal shower: Buy a blank hardcover book, add dividers, and create a family cookbook. Just ask the bride and groom's families to provide their favorite treasured recipes.

Two-for-One Bridal Gift

Turn your gift packaging into part of the gift itself. For a bridal shower, wrap your gift with a pretty bath, kitchen, or tea towel. Write a recipe on the gift tag, or use a recipe card for the tag, and tie a bow with a beautiful ribbon and a kitchen utensil, such as salad tongs, inserted inside.

Cupcakes for Kids' Parties

Having a birthday party for your child? Consider serving cupcakes instead of one large cake, which will eliminate the need for forks and paper plates—and save you money. (Just serve on napkins.)

Put a College Student to Work

If you're hosting a party that requires you to hire someone like a clown, face painter, or bartender, head to your local college first. There you'll find hundreds of young people who will do the job for a lot less than a pro. Put up at ad near the cafeteria, and stop by the career office to see if they have an online "bulletin board."

Who Knew? Readers' Favorite

Little kids usually end up eating cake with their hands anyway, so try this fun dessert treat: Place flat-bottomed ice cream cones in a high-sided baking pan and fill them two-thirds full with cake batter. Bake at 325°F for 30 minutes, and once they cool you can hold your cake and eat it, too!

So the Wind Won't Blow It All Away

If your picnic is windier than you expected, keep your tablecloth in place with the help of some nonskid shelf liners. Lay them out in strips at the corners of the table and the tablecloth will stay put!

Impromptu Trash Can

Having a party and need an extra trash bin for your guests? Just repurpose your hamper. (Your dirty clothes will be fine in a garbage bag in the closet until tomorrow.)

CHAPTER 6

The Perfect Barbecue

Get Your Grill In Shape for BBQ Season

When Memorial Day rolls around, make sure your outdoor grill is prepped for the first barbecue of the season. Clean the grates by placing them in the tub and covering them with very hot water and one cup each ammonia and dishwasher detergent. Cover with old fabric softener sheets and soak overnight. The next day, don your rubber gloves, scrub away, and watch the grease dissolve.

Who Knew? Readers' Favorite

A great way to clean your barbecue grill is with wet newspaper. After cooking, just place it on a warm grill for one hour with the lid closed. You'll be amazed how easily the grime comes off!

A Grill-Cleaning Trick

Save on expensive grill cleaners by simply using WD-40 instead. Get rid of charred food by removing the grates from the barbecue and spraying them with the oil. Let sit for five to ten minutes, then wipe off and clean with soap and water.

Alliums to the Rescue!

Your BBQ chicken was a hit, but your grill is a mess. What to do? Dip half an onion in vegetable oil, put it on your grill fork, and scrub it over the hot grates. There are enzymes in onions that break down grime, and the oil will help softer the grilled-on gunk.

Just Say No to More Lighter Fluid

When the coals start to die down on your grill, don't squirt them with more lighter fluid, which not only costs money, but can also leave your food tasting bad (not to mention, burn the hair off your arm). Instead, blow a hair dryer on the base of the coals. The hairdryer acts as a pair of bellows, and your fire will be going again in no time.

Great Grilling

Spraying your grill with a bit of vegetable oil before you start grilling will make cleaning even easier, and your grill even hotter (which will put those cool "grill marks" on your meat and veggies). For the easiest clean-up, coat the grill with vegetable (or canola) oil before starting the fire, then wipe it with a wet rag shortly after you are through. Never spray the oil on the grill after the fire has started—it may cause a flare-up.

A Tasty Grill

To help reduce smoke and improve the flavor of food on your grill, use an onion! Cut a red onion in half, pierce it with a fork, and dip in water. Then use the onion half to wipe down the grill rack.

Tongs Are Terrific

Always use tongs when turning meat on the grill. When a fork pierces the meat, it releases some of its juices, making it dry out more quickly.

Keep Chicken from Stickin'

When grilling chicken, always grease the rack well. Why? Because as the bird cooks, the collagen in the skin turns into a sticky gelatin, which will in turn stick to the grate. Another way to solve the problem is to sear the chicken on the grill, and then finish it in a preheated oven for 15–20 minutes, breast-side up.

Who Knew? Readers' Favorite

If you're grilling a steak on a closed barbecue, here's a neat trick to impress your friends. Open a can of beer and place it on the hottest part of the grill. It will boil and keep the meat moist, while adding flavor, too.

Prevent a Barbecue Blunder

Remember that barbecue sauces contain sugar, and high heat can burn the sugar as well as some of the spices in the sauce. Wait to apply the sauce until about five minutes before your meat is fully cooked. Another secret is to use low heat and leave the meat on the grill for a longer period.

The Hubbub About Rubs

Applying a rub is a common method of seasoning the surface of meats and poultry. A dry rub is simply a blend of various herbs and spices that doesn't penetrate the meat. The rub provides a tasty coating, which usually forms a brown crust of concentrated flavor. (Yum!) Rub on the seasoning before you begin to grill the meat, and let it sit awhile for the coating to take hold.

Burger Buzzkill

While undercooked burgers may pose a risk of E. coli poisoning, well-done burgers may contain a potentially harmful carcinogen called heterocyclic aromatic amine (HAA). This compound is formed when meat is cooked at too high a temperature. To avoid HAA, try these tips:

✦ Choose lean cuts of beef. Sizzling fat creates smoke, which creates HAA.

✦ Place the ground beef in a microwave oven on high power for 1–3 minutes just before you cook it. HAAs form when browning occurs, but precooking meat before it goes onto the grill reduces the amount of time HAAs have to form.

✦ Reduce the amount of meat in your burgers by adding mashed black beans, cottage cheese, or cooked rice and you will have a safer—not to mention delicious—medium-well burger.

For a Juicy Steak

You may think that searing a steak at a high temperature will keep the juices in. Nonsense! Searing does cause the browning that creates a good flavor, but it doesn't seal in the juices. A steak cooked slowly and at a lower temperature is more tender and juicier than one cooked at an extremely high heat. If you want to sear a steak, only do it for a minute or two on each side, then lower the temperature and let it cook more slowly.

Speedier Grilling

When you are grilling for a crowd, and your grill isn't big enough, you can save time by utilizing your oven, too. Place a few layers of hamburgers between sheets of foil on a cookie sheet and bake them in a 350°F oven for 15 minutes. Then throw them on the grill for 5–10 minutes more, and they'll be fully cooked but still have that grilled taste. Hot dogs may be done the same way, but only bake them for 10 minutes.

Thick Is the Trick for Grilling Fish

If you plan on grilling fish, be sure to purchase steaks that are at least one-inch thick. Fish dries out very quickly on the grill, so the thicker it is the better. The skin should be left on fillets while grilling and removed after they are cooked.

Lemon Aid

Grilling fish is always a drag because the skin inevitably gets stuck to the grate—particularly when cooking salmon. Avoid this by placing a few thin slices of lemon or lime on the grill, and then the fish on top. Not only will your cleanup be easier, but the citrus flavor will also taste great with the seafood.

Who Knew? Readers' Favorite

When grilling shrimp, always thread them onto the skewers lengthwise, so they won't curl on the grill. They'll also be less likely to fall into the fire.

Perfect Grilled Corn

Doing some grilling? Impress your guests by barbecuing fresh corn to perfection this way: Before grilling, peel all but the innermost layer of husk from the corn, and trim the excess silks as well. Place on the grill and as soon as the husk darkens enough that the outline of the kernels is visible through it, remove the corn. It will be perfectly cooked and have a wonderful, smoky flavor.

Veggies on the Grill

When grilling vegetables in aluminum foil on the grill, try placing a sprig of fresh herbs within each foil wrap. Marjoram is the most popular choice, but almost any herb will do: try tarragon, Italian parsley, sage, chives, dill, chervil, oregano, and thyme. It will give your veggies a fresh, wonderful taste.

Potato Salad Trick

If you would like a richer color to your potato salad (and who doesn't?), try adding a small amount of mustard when you are mixing it.

For Divine Deviled Eggs

To keep yolks centered when boiling eggs for deviled eggs, stir the water while they are cooking. And to keep them from wobbling on the platter when they're done, cut a thin slice off two sides of the egg before you halve it lengthwise. This will give each egg half a flat base.

The Coal Truth

Though they may be more work than a gas grill, charcoal grills impart an amazing smoky flavor to meats and veggies. Here are a few tips to get the most out of your charcoal grill.

✦ To add flavor to barbecued foods, place dried herbs on the hot coals. Some of our favorites are savory, rosemary, and basil.

✦ If the coals become too hot or flare up, squirt them with water from a mister or a bulb baster.

✦ Store charcoal briquettes in airtight plastic bags— they absorb moisture very easily and won't be as easy to light if exposed to air.

Who Knew? Readers' Favorite

To keep your cooler fresh and odor free, throw in 10–15 charcoal briquettes, close the top, and leave it overnight. In the morning, clean the cooler with soapy water, and it will smell like new.

Plain Vanilla

Before you put your cooler away, wipe the inside down with a paper towel or rag that has been dampened with water and a few drops of vanilla extract. The alcohol in the vanilla works as a disinfectant and your cooler will smell great!

For the Fastest Cold Beer

The best way to chill beer or soda rapidly is to fill a cooler with layers of water, ice, and salt, then plunge the beers inside. In about 20 minutes or less, the beer will be ice cold! Even if the ice water is warmer than your freezer, it will still absorb the warmth from the bottles or cans more rapidly and efficiently than the cold air of the freezer does. Just remember that premium lagers should be served between 42°F and 48°F and ales between 44°F and 52°F, so don't let them get too cold.

Frozen Grapes

If you want to keep your wine (or other beverage) cool on hot summer days, use frozen grapes instead of ice cubes. They'll keep the drink cold and they won't dilute it or change the taste as they thaw. Just make sure you wash them before freezing!

Perk Up Your Tabletops

Linoleum or vinyl floor tiles are excellent for covering picnic tabletops. You can also use linoleum on kitchen shelves, instead of contact paper. It will last a long time and is easy to keep clean.

How to Save S'More Marshmallows

Rock-hard marshmallows don't have to be thrown out. You can soften them up in a resealable plastic bag placed on top of warm water. Now go get that grill fired up again.

Ultimate Frisbee Plates

Having a barbecue? Super-power your paper plates by placing them on top of Frisbees. Or cover your Frisbee with foil and it's perfect for serving food right off the grill.

'Cue Tool Holder

It might not be a great Father's Day present, but an old oven mitt makes an ideal holder for barbecue utensils. Use its hanging loop to attach it to your grill and insert tongs or anything else you need.

Who Knew? Readers' Favorite

Before you light up your Weber grill, put a little bit of cat litter in the grease tray. It not only will prevent any flare-ups, it will keep the tray from overheating and warping.

Keep It Clean

Make sure to remove the ashes from the bottom of your grill after each use, because the ashes can retain moisture and cause your grill to rust. Before you remove the ashes, try sprinkling them with used coffee grounds. The grounds will keep the ash from blowing up into your face.

CHAPTER 7

Baking Tips

Your Level Best

The next time you get chopsticks with your Chinese take-out, keep a few for your kitchen. Even if you haven't mastered the art of eating with them, they're perfect for leveling off cups of flour and other dry goods.

Warm for Cakes, Cold for Pastries

When baking cakes and cookies, the ingredients should always be at room temperature. For pastry, it is just the opposite—the ingredients should be cold.

Who Knew? Readers' Favorite

Electric stand mixers are a boon for bakers, because the dough hook attachment reduces or eliminates the need to knead. To keep the dough from climbing up the hook, spray it with nonstick cooking spray or vegetable oil before turning the mixer on. This is also a great tip for when you're using a hand mixer.

Don't Skip the Salt

Although it may be tempting for health reasons, never omit the salt from your bread recipe. Salt strengthens and tightens the gluten, keeping bread from becoming crumbly.

Moldy Bread?

You may know that you can usually just cut mold off of cheese, but the same does not hold true for bread. If you see the slightest sign of mold on baked goods, throw the item out. Mold sends out "feelers" that often can't be seen.

Yeast Saver

Where should you store yeast, you ask? Always keep it in the refrigerator, because the cold will slow down deterioration. Bring the yeast back up to room temperature to help it dissolve at the normal rate.

Weak Flour?

Adding a bit of ascorbic acid (vitamin C) to flour when baking bread can help to strengthen weak flour. For every 6 cups flour, add a pinch of powdered ascorbic acid to the yeast. Ascorbic acid is easiest to find in the form of vitamin C tablets in the vitamin or cold remedy section of your drugstore.

Who Knew? Readers' Favorite

Consider keeping a clean powder puff in your flour container. It's a great way to dust flour onto rolling pins or pastry boards. And remember, always store your flour in the freezer to prevent any sort of bug infestation.

Perfectly Greased and Floured Pans

Recipes for baked goods often call for greased and floured pans, a process that involves oiling a pan down, then sprinkling flour inside and shaking the pan until it's equally distributed. However, professional bakers don't often use this method because it can leave flour on your baked goods or make them cook unevenly. Instead, they mix up a batch of "baker's magic," and now you can, too. Mix ½ cup room temperature vegetable shortening, ½ cup vegetable oil, and ½ cup all-purpose flour. Blend the mixture well and use it to grease pans. It can be stored in an airtight container in the refrigerator for up to six months.

Bread Pan Pandering

It's never good to be dull...unless you're a bread pan. For the best results when baking, avoid a shiny bread pan. A shiny pan reflects heat to such a degree that the bread may not bake evenly. However, a dark pan may cook the bread too quickly, resulting in burned bottoms. Your best bet? A dull aluminum pan.

Who Knew? Readers' Favorite

Making cupcakes or muffins and don't have enough batter to fill the tin? Before sticking them in the oven, fill the empty holes in the tin halfway with water. It will extend the life of the tin and make sure the other muffins bake evenly.

Blending Basics

When baking, it is important that all the ingredients be blended well, without being mixed too much. If you need to sift flour, add the other dry ingredients (such as leavening and salt) to the flour before you sift.

Kneading Know-How

Don't skimp when kneading bread—it's what distributes the yeast and other ingredients evenly throughout the dough. If dough isn't kneaded properly, it won't rise evenly. Electric bread machines, stand mixers, and food processors make short work of this important task, but if you're kneading dough by hand, rub a small amount of vegetable oil onto your hands before you begin, which will make kneading thick dough easier. A wooden cutting board is your best bet for kneading bread, but other surfaces will work. Just be sure to flour the board adequately.

A Proper Cool-Down

After you've removed bread from the oven, cool it on a wire rack. This will allow air to circulate around the bread and should prevent any soggy areas from developing in the loaf.

Dough Won't Rise?

One of the most frequent problems bread bakers encounter is yeast dough that doesn't rise adequately. If your dough won't rise, check out the following tips to see if you can pinpoint the cause.

✦ Your dough may be too cool, which reduces the level of yeast activity. Dough can rise at lower temperatures—even in the refrigerator—but it takes several hours or overnight to attain the same volume that it can in an hour or two at 80–90° F.

✦ The yeast may have been prepared with water that was too hot, which can kill it. The water must be under 120°F for optimum results.

✦ The yeast may have been too old. Proof your yeast before using it to be sure it's not ready for retirement. Dissolve a little sugar in some warm water, then sprinkle in the yeast. The mixture should begin bubbling within 5–7 minutes. If it doesn't, the yeast is too inactive to provide proper leavening and should be thrown away.

Who Knew? Readers' Favorite

We love this secret for a perfect loaf of bread, given to us by a baker friend: Put some ice cubes in a shallow pan and put it in the oven with your loaf of bread. This ice cubes will produce a dense steam, and as the water evaporates, the crust becomes hard and crispy. The steam also will allow the bread to rise more evenly, giving you a crumb that's firm and chewy.

(Not Too Much) Garlic Bread

Want a hint of garlic without a too-garlicky taste? You can make a lightly scented garlic bread by adding 1 teaspoon of garlic powder to the flour when you're making white bread.

Flavored Crusts

The next time you make a pie, add a little flavor to the crust by tossing a pinch of ground spice or a few minced herbs into the flour. Use cinnamon or ginger with an apple or other dessert pie, and try finely chopped parsley with a quiche or meat pie.

Buttermilk: Not Always Bad for You

Buttermilk can be substituted for 2 percent or whole milk in most pastry or bread recipes. Buttermilk is less than 1 percent fat, almost equal to skim milk, but it has a thicker consistency.

Creamy Cream Cheese

When baking a recipe that calls for cream cheese, be sure it's at room temperature before you start, and make sure you beat it so it's light and fluffy before adding any other ingredients, especially eggs.

Flour the Fruit

Bread, muffins, and other baked goods are fun (and delicious) to make with dried fruit, but the fruit often sinks to the bottom because it doesn't have a lot of moisture and becomes more even solid during baking. If you coat it with a little flour, though, it'll stay put.

Go Gently

If you make bread with 100 percent whole-wheat flour, it will be moister if you add the flour to the water slowly and mix gently. Whole-wheat flour absorbs water at a slower rate than do other types of flour. Reserve ¼ cup flour and knead in a tablespoon or so at a time as needed.

Who Knew? Readers' Favorite

When bread dries out, it hardens. But to make hard bread as good as knew, wrap the loaf tightly in a damp paper towel for 2–3 minutes, then remove the towel and heat the bread in a 350°F oven for 15–20 minutes. When French or Italian bread hardens, sprinkle the crust with cold water and heat at 350°F for 8–10 minutes.

What Kind of Crust Do You Want?

Different liquids will impart different characteristics to the crust of your bread. Water, a common choice, will cause the top of the bread to be crisp, and will significantly intensify the flavor of the wheat. Save some of the water you've used to boil potatoes and it will add a unique flavor, make the crust smooth, and cause the dough to rise faster due to the high starch content. Milk gives bread a rich, creamy color and leaves the bread with a fine texture and a soft, brown crust. Eggs will provide a moister crust. A liquid sweetener such as molasses, maple syrup, or honey will cause the crust to be dark brown and will also keep it moist.

Vegetable or meat broth will give the bread a special flavor and provide you with a light, crisp crust. Alcohol of any type will give the bread a smooth crust with a flavor that may be similar to the alcohol used, especially beer; just don't use too much or you'll kill the yeast. Coffee and tea are commonly used to provide a dark, rich color and a crisp crust. But our favorite tip may also be the easiest not to mess up: A couple of minutes before you bread is done, just brush some apple cider vinegar onto the crusty. It will be a lovely brown color, and nice and shiny!

For Perfect Popovers

If you want the lightest popovers every time, puncture them with a fork when you remove them from the oven to release the air inside.

Puff Pastry Perfection

Puff pastry dough is made from flour, butter, and water. A small amount of butter is layered between dough that is folded several times to form as many as 700 layers. When you cut puff pastry dough, be sure to use a very sharp knife and cut straight down; never pull the knife through the dough or cut the dough at an angle. Doing so will cause the ends to puff up unevenly as the pastry bakes.

Removing Muffins

To easily remove muffins or rolls from a pan, set the pan on a damp towel for about 30 seconds. Use an old towel, because the pan might stick.

Stale Muffin Trick

If the delicious muffins you slaved over have gone stale, here's an easy trick to make them fresh again: Place them in a brown paper bag and squirt them with water two or three times from a spray bottle. Then place the bag in your oven with just the pilot light on overnight. By morning, they'll be ready for breakfast!

Beautiful Biscuits

Who doesn't love a tasty biscuit? Not only are they delicious, but homemade biscuits are also a great way to spruce up a leftover or frozen meal. Here are some tips and tricks for making the best-tasting biscuits.

✦ Handle the dough gently. Overworking the dough and re-rolling the scraps makes for tough biscuits.

✦ If your biscuits are heavy and dense, check your baking powder for freshness and make sure that you are properly sifting all the dry ingredients together. Even blending of the ingredients is key, so if you don't have a sifter, put the dry ingredients into a large sieve and shake them into the mixing bowl, or whisk them together.

✦ If you like your biscuits to be a rich golden color, add a teaspoon of sugar to the dry ingredients. It helps the crust to caramelize (and only adds 16 calories to the whole batch!).

◆ If you're using a cutter to cut your biscuits, dip it in flour first so the dough won't stick to it. Be sure to press the cutter straight down—don't twist it even slightly. Doing so seals the edges of the biscuits and they won't rise as high.

◆ Shortening is the preferred fat for biscuits. Butter makes for more solid biscuits, and oil makes them greasy.

◆ For super-soft biscuits, brush them with milk or melted unsalted butter before baking, then arrange them in a cake pan so the sides touch one another.

Glazing Over

Before you put rolls in the oven, make a delicious glaze for their tops that your guests are sure to appreciate. Lightly beat an egg white with a tablespoon of milk and brush on each roll. You'll love it!

Who Knew? Readers' Favorite

When you're done with an afternoon of baking, sprinkle your messy countertop with salt, and the doughy, floury mess that you've left behind can be easily wiped away with a damp sponge.

Reheating Rolls

The quickest way to reheat biscuits or rolls? Sprinkle them lightly with water and wrap them in foil. It should take about five minutes in a preheated 350°F oven.

Best Croutons Ever

If you really want to impress your dinner guests, make some homemade croutons for your salad. Here's how: After cutting your leftover bread into cubes, fry the pieces in olive oil and a little garlic powder (not garlic salt), a pinch of parmesan cheese, and parsley until golden brown, then let cool on paper towels. They freeze well, too!

Save Those Bread Bags

Don't forget to save your store-bought bread bags for the times when you bake bread. They are perfectly sized for homemade breads.

For the Best Baked Sale Item

For your next bake sale, write out the recipe for your baked good on an index card and tape it to the serving plate or box. That way, if buyers find your goody to their liking, they'll know they can make it themselves in the future. They may also be more likely to buy your item if it comes with a free recipe!

CHAPTER 8

Making Your Food Last Longer

Know Your Terminology

When shopping, only the term "use by" means that you shouldn't eat the food after the date indicated. "Sell by" dates are only an indication for the store, and foods will usually keep one to two weeks after. "Best before" is only an indication of food quality, not of food safety, so again, your perishables may still be good to eat.

The Best Ways to Freeze Food

Freezing food is vital for being able to save money, because it allows you to buy food when it's on sale, make it when you have time, then save it for later. It seems like it should be as easy as just shoving food in the freezer, but there are a number of tips that will make your food taste better after defrosting.

+ Never use quick-cooking rice in a dish that will be frozen, as it becomes mushy when reheated. Use regular or long-grain rice instead.

+ Don't add toppings to dishes to be frozen; add when serving.

+ When preparing most vegetables for freezing, they should be blanched, not fully cooked. This will lessen the enzymatic activity in the vegetable, and reheating will complete the cooking process. To blanch, simply steam or boil vegetables for about half the time you normally would cook them, then plunge them into ice water and drain. Potatoes and squashes are the exception to this rule—they should be fully cooked.

✦ Freezing causes russet or Idaho potatoes to fall apart; if you need them to stay whole or in chunks, use potatoes with red skin or waxy flesh.

✦ Freezing tends to intensify the flavors of certain foods, such as garlic, peppers, and cloves. Use less in a dish that you will freeze, and when reheating, taste and add more as needed.

✦ On the other hand, use more onion than you would otherwise, because freezing tends to cause onion to lose its flavor. Herbs and salt also tend to diminish in flavor, so it's best to add them after freezing, when you're reheating the dish.

✦ Avoid freezing sauces. Egg-based sauces and those high in fat tend to separate when reheated, and cheese- or milk-based sauces are prone to curdling. Don't try to freeze mayonnaise, salad dressing, or jam. Most gravies will thicken considerably when frozen, but they can be thinned when reheated.

✦ Artificial sweeteners do not freeze well, so don't substitute them for sugar.

✦ Don't freeze any bakery item with a cream filling because it will become soggy. Custard and meringue pies, for example, don't freeze well. The custard tends to separate and the meringue becomes tough.

✦ Cool already-cooked foods in the refrigerator before freezing. Cooling them quickly prevents bacterial growth.

Prepare to be Frozen!

When you freeze foods, evaporation continues and fluids are lost. The entire surface of meat must be protected from this process with a moisture-resistant wrap. The best way to wrap meats for freezing is in plastic wrap covered by a protective freezer paper or aluminum foil. This will not eliminate evaporation entirely, but it will reduce the risk of oxidation and rancidity.

Consume It or Freeze It!

Small cuts of meat will spoil more quickly than larger cuts and should not be kept in the refrigerator for more than a day or two. Liver, sweetbreads, and cubed meats should be cooked within one day or be kept frozen.

Meatless Mondays

Never buy meat from the supermarket on Monday morning. It's likely that those packages for sale were not sold over the weekend, and most shipments of fresh meat arrive on Monday afternoon or on Tuesday.

How Long Does Raw Meat Keep in the Freezer?

Buying meat when it's on sale and keeping it in your freezer is a great way to save on groceries. Unfortunately, you can't keep it in there forever! Here is a helpful guide to how long different kinds (and cuts) of raw meat will keep at 0°F, the optimal temperature for your freezer.

MEAT	MONTHS	MEAT	MONTHS
Bacon	1	Ground pork	2–3
Beef	9	Ham	3
Chicken (in parts)	9	Pork (chops or ribs)	6–9
Chicken (whole)	12	Pork roast	9
Cold cuts	1	Rabbit	6–9
Duck	4–6	Sausage	2
Fish (fatty)	3	Shellfish	4–6
Fish (lean)	6	Turkey (in parts)	6
Goose	4–6	Turkey (whole)	12
Ground beef	2–3	Venison	6–12

You'll find it's well worth your time to cook an entire turkey every now and then, especially after Thanksgiving and Christmas when the prices drop dramatically. Stuffing is one of our favorite foods, so we love having "fake Thanksgiving" every once in the while. Then we chop up what we don't eat, throw it in the freezer, and use in soups, stir-fries, casseroles, and tons of other meals.

A Meat Freezing Secret

When slicing up beef or pork into bite-sized pieces to save for later, first partially freeze the meat by placing it in the freezer for 1–2 hours. You'll find it's much quicker and easier to slice.

Score One for Easy Thawing

Use this trick to make unfreezing a portion of ground meat easier. Place the meat in a resealable plastic bag, flatten, then score into sections (like a tic-tac-toe board) by pressing a butter knife into the bag. Seal the bag and stick it in the freezer, and when you need just a little ground meat you'll easily be able to break off a chunk.

Lemons at the Ready

If you have a bunch of lemons that are about to go bad—you guessed it, freeze them! First cut in slices, then freeze on a baking sheet or in between pieces of wax paper. They're perfect for adding to glasses of water.

Fruity Freezes

Blueberries and cranberries are two more foods that are easy to buy when in abundance and freeze for later. Place them in a single layer on a cookie sheet and place the sheet in the freezer. Once they're frozen, you can transfer them to a resealable plastic bag. Frozen berries are great in smoothies, pies, and even eating cold!

Getting Rid of Tomato Paste Waste

When we used to clean out our fridge, the thing we'd end up throwing away every time was half-empty cans of tomato paste. Even though tomato paste doesn't cost that much, we still felt like we were throwing away money. So now, when we've used a couple of tablespoons of tomato paste, instead of putting the rest of the can in the fridge, we separate out the unused portion into plastic bags—usually about 2 tablespoons per bag—and freeze. When our next recipe calls for tomato paste, we simply turn the bag inside out and plop the frozen paste right into the pot. If you don't want to use the plastic bags, you can also accomplish this using an ice cube tray!

Who Knew? Readers' Favorite

Keep raw ginger in a sealed plastic bag in the freezer, and it will last pretty much forever. Best of all, you don't need to defrost it before you grate it into stir-fries, sauces, or whatever else you're making.

Deep Freeze

The freezing process can decrease the flavor of some foods, which is why all the foods in the freezer section of your grocery store have been flash frozen in seconds (usually with the help of some liquid nitrogen). It's important that frozen foods don't thaw and refreeze before you eat them, so on hot days make sure to visit your store's freezer section last. That way, your purchases have less time to thaw.

Stock Up

When carving a chicken or turkey, it's easy to make a stock at the same time. Place all unused parts in a pot with celery and onion (using the skins of the onion will give the stock a nice, rich color), then heat up to boiling. Reduce the heat and simmer while you make dinner. Then turn off and skim the fat when cooled. Stock can be used for gravies, soup (naturally), and to add flavor to rice, potatoes, and tomato sauce. This free and easy seasoning would have cost you up to $5 for a quart at the grocery store!

Freezing Stock

To easily freeze the delicious stock you've just made into smaller portions, line a drinking glass with a resealable plastic bag. Pour the stock into the glass until it's about three-quarters full, then seal the bag and lay flat on a baking pan. Repeat until you've used up all your stock, laying the bags on top of one another. Once they're frozen, you can move them anywhere in the freezer that there's room.

Making Condiments Last

It's frustrating to have to throw out condiments like sour cream, mayo, yogurt, and mustard because you didn't use the entire container before it went bad. However, you can easily combat this by changing containers as you use up the item. Using a smaller container exposes the condiment to less air—and fewer bacteria. The trick, of course, is making sure you successfully transfer every bit of mayo possible from the jar to the tiny Tupperware. We usually do our container downsizing right before we're about to use the condiment on something. That way, we can scrape out what we don't transfer onto our sandwiches.

Say Cheese

Believe it or not, you can successfully freeze many varieties of cheese without sacrificing taste or texture. Cut it into small blocks, place in sealed plastic bags, and then keep it in the freezer for when you need it. Cheese varieties that can be frozen successfully include Brick, Cheddar, Camembert, Edam, Gouda, Mozzarella, Muenster, Parmesan, Port du Salut, Swiss, Provolone, Mozzarella, and Romano. Small cheeses, such as Camembert, can even be frozen in their original packages. When removed from the freezer, cheese should be put in the refrigerator and used as soon as possible after thawing.

A Great Tip for Noodle Soups

If you can't already tell, we freeze practically everything. Two frozen items that sometimes take our friends by surprise are cooked rice and cooked noodles. If you accidentally make too much, simply put them in an airtight container in the freezer. Though they won't hold up well enough to eat plain, they'll be perfect for soups!

Spice Saving Secret

Make dried herbs and spices last last longer by putting half of the amount into a sealed, airtight container when you purchase them. Label the container and keep it in your freezer. When the spice on-hand loses its aroma, replace it with your stash in the freezer, and you'll never have to be irritated about throwing away that unusable mustard seed or marjoram again.

The Life of Spice

If you're using McCormick brand spices, and you're not sure if they're past their prime, just go to McCormick.com/Spices101. aspx. There you can type in the code on the bottom of the container and find out if the spice is still good. And don't forget to transfer your spices to smaller, airtight containers as you use them. Air makes them stale!

What You Never Knew About Milk

When you know your milk is going to go bad before you can use up the rest of it, separate it out into a few sealable containers and put them in your freezer. That's right, milk can be frozen! If you use skim milk, it can be thawed and drunk later and you'll never be able to tell the difference. For other varieties of milk, use for sauces or baking after thawing. This is a great strategy when you find milk at a deep discount. Buy as much as you can and freeze for later!

Don't Always Ditch the Fat

It might sound counterintuitive, but buying fattier meat can actually help your food go further—and keep your waistline intact. You're likely to eat less, assuming you cut off the fat when it's on your plate. And fattier meat generally has a better taste, so a little bit goes a long way.

Who Knew? Readers' Favorite

To avoid the absorption of refrigerator odors, always store eggs in their original carton on an inside shelf of the refrigerator. Before you put away the carton, though, turn each egg upside down. Storing eggs with the tapered end down maximizes the distance between the yolk and the air pocket, which may contain bacteria. The yolk is more perishable than the white, and even though it is more or less centered in the egg, the yolk can shift slightly and will move away from possible contamination.

Egg-cellent!

For eggs that last practically forever, separate them into whites and yolks, then freeze them separately in a lightly oiled ice-cube tray. When frozen, pop them out and store in separate Ziploc bags in the freezer. These frozen eggs are perfect for baking, and will last longer since they're separated.

Leftover Rice

Rice can be stored in the fridge for a longer amount of time if you store a slice of toast on top of it. The toast will absorb excess moisture and keep the rice fluffy and fresh.

Should Produce Be Refrigerated?

Refrigerating your produce can help it keep longer, but not all produce does well in the cooler temperatures. The majority of fruits and vegetables handle cold fairly well, but naturally enough, the exceptions are tropical fruits, whose cells are just not used to the cold. Bananas will suffer cell damage and release a skin-browning chemical, avocados don't ripen when stored below 45°F, and citrus fruit will develop brown-spotted skin. These fruits, as well as squash, tomatoes, cucumbers, bell peppers, melons, and pineapples, are best stored at 50°F—so keep them out of the fridge unless you've already cut them and need to keep them fresh. Most other vegetables, including lettuce, carrots, and cabbage, will do better in your refrigerator, as will fruits like apples and pears. Garlic, onions, shallots, and potatoes should never be refrigerated because the cold will cause sprouting, loss of flavor, or conversion of their starch to sugar. Keep these foods out of the refrigerator (at a little cooler than room temperature, if possible) and in a dark cabinet. Humidity is also an important factor, so fruits and vegetables should always be stored in the refrigerator crisper bins, which will prevent them from drying out.

For Happy Peppers

If you're only using half of a bell pepper for a recipe, make the other half last longer with this simple trick. When you're slicing the pepper, make sure to leave the seeds and membrane intact on one side. Then store this side in a sealed plastic bag or container in the fridge. Leaving the seeds intact will make the pepper last longer.

Let Your Produce Breathe

Wrap all produce loosely; air circulation around fruits and vegetables reduces spoilage. A sealed perforated plastic bag is ideal—make your own by simply poking several holes in an ordinary sandwich or freezer bag.

Why There's a Sponge in Our Fridge

The next time you buy a pack of kitchen sponges, throw one in the fruit and vegetable drawer of your fridge. The sponge will absorb moisture before it can work its way into your produce, meaning it will last longer. Most kitchen sponges are also treated with anti-bacteria agents, giving your fruits and veggies even extra protection. Replace the sponge when you replace the baking soda in your fridge, a couple of times a year.

A Home for Your Potatoes

Never refrigerate potatoes, because that tends to turn potato starch to sugar. Potatoes will last longer and remain solid longer if they are stored away from light in a cool, dry spot, preferably at 45–50°F. If white potatoes are stored below 40°F, they tend to release more sugar and turn sweet. Air must circulate around potatoes; otherwise, moisture will cause them to decay.

Keep Potatoes for Longer

It is best to purchase potatoes in bulk bins—not in bags, which make it hard to determine which are bruised. If you store fresh ginger with potatoes it will help keep them fresh longer. Half an apple stored with potatoes will stop the sprouting by absorbing moisture before the potato does.

Don't Toss Those Potato Peels!

If your family loves mashed potatoes as much as ours does, here's a great way to use the nutritious skins in their own dish the next night. In a bowl, sprinkle the potato peelings with salt and pepper, mix with a bit of Italian dressing, and then stick them in the oven at 400°F until crispy (about 20 minutes).

Who Knew? Readers' Favorite

It is always a good idea to line the crisper bins of your refrigerator with a few paper towels or sheets of newspaper to absorb excess moisture. Mold spores love moisture, but the towels will keep it away.

Separate Your Onions and Potatoes

Potatoes hate onions…at least until they're cooked together. Onions should never be stored with potatoes because moisture from the onions can cause potatoes to sprout. Onions also release gases that will alter the flavor of a potato.

Onion Color Counts

Yellow and white onions can be kept for a longer amount of time than red ones, as they have a lower sugar content. Store in an open space that's cool and dry, and away from bright light, which can make them bitter. Don't store them anywhere that may become damp.

Keep Onions Fresh

The sugar content in yellow onions makes them spoil quickly if they are stored closely together—who knew? The solution is to store your onions in an old (clean) pair of pantyhose, making knots in the legs so the onions can't touch. It might look a little weird, but it works!

An Onion's Better Half

If you need only half an onion, use the top half first, because the root half will store longer in the refrigerator (it won't sprout).

A Second Life for Your Onion

If you have an onion that starts to sprout, place it in some soil in a pot on a windowsill and, as it continues to sprout, snip off pieces of the sprouts to use in salads. These tiny greens are flavorful and mild.

Water Your Asparagus!

To make asparagus last longer in the refrigerator, place the stem ends in a container of water, or wrap them in a wet paper towel and put in a plastic bag. Like flowers, the asparagus will continue "drinking" the water and stay fresh until it's ready to use.

Spinach Saving Solutions

Spinach will keep in the refrigerator for 2–3 days, as long as it's stored in a sealed plastic bag. To preserve its shelf life, don't wash it or cut it before you are ready to prepare it. Want to freeze fresh spinach? Remove the stems, blanch the leaves in boiling water for two minutes, then run under cold water and dry before you freeze. Removing their stems will allow the leaves retain more of their moisture. Spinach will keep in the freezer for 10–12 months.

Who Knew? Readers' Favorite

The best way to store celery is to wrap it in aluminum foil and keep it in the fridge. It will last for weeks and weeks.

Save Your Celery Leaves

Don't throw away celery leaves—while they don't work well with dips, they still have a wonderful flavor. When chopping celery, set the leaves aside on a paper plate, let them dry, and throw them in stuffing, salads, and soups for great extra flavor.

Cucumber Rules

When storing a cucumber, keep it away from apples and tomatoes, which will shorten its life. Cucumbers stay fresh for up to a week, when the water content starts to drop.

Avoid Frosted Vegetables

When shopping in the freezer aisle, avoid packages of frozen vegetables that have frost on them. It's a sign that the food has thawed and been refrozen, and a percentage of moisture has already been lost.

Lettuce Abuse?

To make sure iceberg lasts as long as possible, you should remove the innermost core before you store it. An easy (and admittedly fun) way to do this is to hit the lettuce against a hard surface and then twist the core out.

Revive Wilted Greens

To crisp cut-up greens like lettuce, cilantro, or anything else that wilts, soak them in ice water for 15–20 minutes. This also works for limp asparagus and carrots!

Lasting Lettuce

Iceberg lettuce remains fresher longer than any other type of lettuce because of its high water content. Iceberg will keep for 7–14 days, whereas romaine lasts for 6–10 days, and butter (or Boston) lettuce for only 3–4 days.

Don't throw away the outer leaves from a head of lettuce! They come in handy when you need to cover foods in the microwave. You won't have to use a paper towel, and the leaves will keep your food moist.

Overcooked Overtures

If you've overcooked broccoli, asparagus, or any other vegetable, don't throw it away. Save it for later, when you can cut it up into small pieces and add to a soup, sauce, or stew. It'll cook down even further, so you won't notice anything but the taste.

Give Your Veggies a Haircut

If you've purchased a vegetable with a leafy top, such as beet greens or carrots, remove the green top before you store it in the fridge. The leafy tops will leach moisture from the root or bulb and shorten the vegetable's shelf life.

Storing Corn

Always store corn in a cool, dry location, and keep the ears separated in order to prevent them from becoming moldy. Remember that as it warms up, the sugar in corn converts to starch very quickly. (In fact, when corn is piled high in supermarket bins, the ears on the bottom will be less sweet because of the heat generated by the weight of the ones on top.) To freeze corn, blanch the ears for a minute or two in boiling water, drain, and immediately flush with cold water to stop the cooking. Freeze the ears on a tray, leaving room between them so the kernels aren't crushed and will hold their shape. Once the corn is frozen, place the ears in a sealed plastic bag. Frozen corn will keep for one year.

A Sweet Tip for a Sweet Pepper

If you eat pimientos, make sure to cover them in vinegar before storing them in the fridge. They'll last much longer!

Mushroom Musts

Ever wonder why mushrooms are usually sold in Styrofoam or cardboard containers? Plastic containers tend to keep the mushrooms too wet, and they go bad quickly. Fresh mushrooms have a shelf life of only 2–3 days and must be stored in the refrigerator in an open container. The original container or another paper product will work best. Never wash mushrooms before storing them—they'll retain the water and become soggy. If you must keep them for a few days, place a single layer of cheesecloth on top of the container. (If they do become shriveled, they can still be sliced or chopped and used in cooking.) To freeze mushrooms, wipe them off with a damp paper towel, slice them, sauté them in a small amount of butter until they are almost done, allow them to cool, and place them in an airtight plastic bag and freeze. They should keep for 10–12 months.

Separate Drawers

Store fruits and vegetables in separate drawers in your fridge. Even when chilled, fruits give off ethylene gas that shortens the shelf life of other fruit and vegetables by causing them to ripen more quickly.

Who Knew? Readers' Favorite

Broccoli will keep longer in the fridge if you store it like a bouquet of flowers. Cut about an inch off the stems, then submerge the stems in a bowl of water. This tip also works for asparagus, chives, and other stemmed vegetables.

Kill Two Birds with One Stone

If you have kids who don't like vegetables, you'll love this clever way to get more nutrients into them. If you have too many fruits and vegetables to use before they go bad, puree them in a blender with a little bit of lemon juice, then freeze. Defrost and add to sauces, soups, stews, enchiladas, and more—your kid won't be able to taste the difference! The key is making sure you don't dramatically alter the color of the dish you're serving. So if you're making a white sauce, for instance, try a puree of cauliflower and summer squash. Tomato-based sauces can usually handle one part "green puree" for every four parts tomato sauce. Pureed fruit works great in muffin recipes or mixed into ice cream. So grind up that broccoli and spinach and get going!

Tomatoes at the Ready

It's easy to make your own version of whole, peeled tomatoes that you would normally buy in a can. Buy a bunch of tomatoes when they're cheap, then core them and freeze them in an airtight container. When you're ready to use them in soups, sauces, or stews, hold each frozen tomato under warm running water and the skin will peel right off.

Making Tomatoes Last

For the best storage, keep tomatoes stem-side down in a cool place. If they're still attached to the stem, try to space them so that they're not touching.

High and Dry

The moisture content of fresh berries is high, so make sure to thoroughly dry them before you stick them in the fridge, or wait until you're ready to eat them before you wash them. Otherwise, they can easily rot. Also make sure to store berries, especially strawberries, loosely covered in the refrigerator.

Who Knew? Readers' Favorite

Never throw out overripe bananas! Stick them in the freezer once they get completely brown, and you can still use them later for banana bread and other baking projects.

"Orange" You Glad?

We hate throwing anything away, so you can imagine how delighted we were when we heard this great use for orange rinds. After you've peeled an orange, stick a small piece of the rind in a sealed container with brown sugar, fresh herbs, or anything else that easily dries out. The moisture in the orange is just enough to keep it fresh.

Keeping Grapes

Grapes will stay fresh only for three to five days, even if refrigerated. They keep best in a plastic bag in the coldest part of the refrigerator, but they must be washed very well before eating. If you do wash them before storing, make sure to dry them thoroughly, as they'll easily absorb the water. Grapes can be eaten frozen (they're especially tasty treats), and frozen grapes can be used in cooking; however, they become mushy when they're thawed because of the high water content. They'll keep in the freezer for about one year.

Long-Lived Lemons

Lemons will stay fresh for up to three months if you store them in a bowl of water in the fridge. Just change the water every week. Who knew?

Long-Lasting Raisins

Raisins will last for several months if they are wrapped tightly in plastic wrap or a plastic bag and kept at room temperature. They will last even longer (up to a year) if you place the plastic bag in the refrigerator.

Some of That "Can Do" Spirit

A wonderful and—dare we say it?—fun way to make your fruits and veggies last longer is to try home canning. You may think canning is just for country folk, but it's becoming more and more popular as a way to save money and make sure you're eating foods with the least amount of preservatives possible. Buy foods when they are in season, or better yet, grow your own and can to save for later. The biggest trick in canning is to make sure that no air (which contains bacteria) gets into your jars; this is achieved with a pressure canner or a boiling-water canner. Find out what these contraptions are and how to safely can fruit, vegetables, pickles, meat, poultry, seafood, salsas, pie filling, jams, and more from the USDA's extensive free Guide to Home Canning, available at Uga.edu/nchfp/publications/publications_usda.html.

Who Knew? Readers' Favorite

Don't spend money on store-bought bread crumbs. Set aside a special jar and pour in the crumbs from the bottom of cracker or low-sugar cereal boxes. Also add crumbs from leftover garlic bread and a few dried herbs, and soon you'll have seasoned bread crumbs! The great thing is that homemade bread crumbs are even better than store-bought, since their uneven texture helps make them stick.

Keeping Bread

Bread stays fresh for a longer time if you place it in an airtight bag with a stalk of celery. If you are going to freeze a loaf of bread, make sure you include a paper towel in the package to absorb moisture and prevent it from becoming mushy when thawed.

What to Do with Stale Bread

There are many uses for stale bread other than feeding the ducks at the pond! Spread with butter, minced garlic, and whatever dried herbs you have, then toast in the toaster oven and cube to make croutons. You can also cut the bread into smaller pieces, then chop in a blender or food processor to make bread crumbs (you may have to cut off the bottom crust first). If you find that your bread often goes stale before you use it, slice it and store in the freezer. Separate out slices and let sit for about five minutes at room temperature to defrost, or stick directly in the toaster. Frozen bread is also great to use for grilled cheese sandwiches— it's much easier to butter and it will defrost as it cooks in the pan.

Who Knew? Readers' Favorite

Never pay for aerosol cooking sprays. Instead, buy a giant jug of vegetable oil and add it to a clean spray bottle as needed. It's the same thing and will cost you a fraction of the price.

Herbal Remedies

Fresh herbs are a wonderful addition to any dinner, but they go bad quickly and are hard to freeze. To keep herbs fresh longer, loosely wrap them in a damp paper towel, store in a plastic bag, and keep in the vegetable crisper of the refrigerator. If you have more fresh herbs than you can use, hang them upside down to dry. (Tie them together and hang them from a peg.) In about a week, you'll be able to crumble off the leaves. The flavor won't be quite as wonderful as that of fresh herbs, but it will still be much better than commercial dried herbs. Another simple solution is placing chopped, fresh herbs in ice-cube trays. Fill the trays with water and then freeze. When it's time to add herbs to soups and sauces, simply pop as many cubes as you want out of the tray and throw them in the pot.

Tea Saver

Want to get more for your money when it comes to tea? Always buy the loose variety, and then use one-third of what's recommended. Just let the tea steep a little longer, and it will taste exactly the same.

Storing Dairy Products

It's better to store milk on an inside shelf—not on the door—toward the back of the refrigerator. Why? All dairy products are very perishable. The optimal refrigeration is actually just over 32°F; however, few refrigerators are ever set that low or hold that low a temperature. Most home refrigerators remain around 40°F, and the temperature rises every time the door is opened. Store cheese near the bottom of the refrigerator, where temperature fluctuations are minimal.

Adding a teaspoon of baking soda or a pinch of salt to a carton of milk will keep it fresh for a week or so past its expiration date. Just remember that leaving milk at room temperature for more than 30 minutes can reduce its life span.

Better Butter

Where you store butter will affect how long it lasts. It will keep for around six months in the freezer, but if you're storing it in the fridge, it will start to lose its flavor after three weeks. Butter tends to absorb odors and flavors more rapidly than other foods, so make sure to wrap it in a few layers of plastic wrap or foil before storing, especially in the freezer.

Save Those Butter Wrappers

After finishing a stick of unsalted butter, hold on to the wrapper. It'll come in handy when you need to grease a pan: Simply wipe the pan with it. But don't use wrappers from salted butter, since they may cause foods to stick.

For the Last Bit of Shortening

Here's a great tip for the really thrifty. If you want to get all the shortening or lard out of a can, pour 2 cups boiling water into the container and swirl it gently until the fat melts. Refrigerate the container until the shortening solidifies on the water's surface, then just lift or skim it off with a knife blade or a sharp-edged spoon.

Extend the Life of Your Cheese

To keep cheese mold-free longer, place a piece of paper towel that has been dampened with white vinegar in the bottom of a plastic container with a tight-fitting lid. Add three or four sugar cubes, which will attract the mold if some does form. Make sure to use a clean knife whenever you cut the cheese.

Keep Your Cheeses Longer

Before you store semi-hard cheeses like Cheddar, Swiss, or Gruyère, rub the cut edges with a little bit of butter. You'll never notice the taste difference, and the cheese will be less likely to dry out or become moldy.

How to Soften Cheese

To soften a piece of hardened (but not moldy) cheese, submerge it in a bowl of buttermilk for one minute. If it's still not soft, cover the dish and refrigerate it overnight.

Revive Moldy Cheese

Believe it or not, cheese with a little mold on it is still perfectly safe to eat once you remove the offending areas. The easiest way to do this is to take a knife or cheese grater, dip it in vinegar, and slice the mold off. Dip the knife in vinegar after each slice—it kills the mold and prevents it from coming back.

Cheese, Please!

A little bit of delayed gratification will pay off on pizza (or pasta) night. Grate a wedge of Parmesan or Romano cheese all at once, then store it in a Ziploc bag (one inside the other, if you need it to stay fresh for longer). Two benefits: you only have to wash the grater one time and you won't be tempted to buy that expensive pre-grated cheese.

Cottage Cheese Care

Because of its high water content, cottage cheese doesn't last as long as other food products in the refrigerator. To extend its life, store it in the container upside down. This will also work for other dairy products like mayonnaise and sour cream.

A Cottage Cheese Shortcut

When making meatballs, meatloaf, or hamburger patties, try adding ½ cup cottage cheese for every pound of ground meat. Not only does it add flavor and protein, but it will stretch your recipe to serve a few more people. You can also use cottage cheese as a substitute for sour cream. If your dip recipe calls for sour cream but you're out, cream some cottage cheese in your blender instead. The low-fat variety works best.

For Long-Lasting Marshmallows

In case you've always wondered where to store marshmallows, the answer is the freezer! To separate the frozen marshmallows later, just cut them with scissors dipped in very hot water.

Sweet Savings

To save money, purchase solid chocolate candy (usually in bunny or Santa form) after major holidays when it's gone on super sale. Store the chocolate in the freezer, then shave off bits with a vegetable peeler to use on top of desserts.

Keep Christmas Going Until Valentine's Day

After Christmas is over, snag a bag of tiny candy canes that are on sale and use them for these heart-shaped cupcake toppers. Flip one cane over and place against another one ("hooks" and bottom edges touching). Bake on a nonstick baking sheet at 325°F for 3–5 minutes. Pinch together to seal, then remove with a spatula.

Cake Keeper

This one you won't believe until you try it. Cubes of sugar can keep cake nice and moist for those rare occasions when you don't finish it all the first night. Make sure the container is airtight.

CHAPTER 9

Kitchen Problems Solved!

For Clean Knives Every Time

When trying to remove stubborn food debris from a knife, don't use a scrubber, which can ruin its finish. Instead, rub a cork over the knife, then wash it in warm water.

For a Clean Cookbook

To keep a cookbook clean, open, and still easy to read while preparing your meal, just place it under a glass pie plate—unless you're making pie, of course!

A "Cookmark"

Making dinner and need something to mark your page in the cookbook? Try using a single strand of raw spaghetti!

Keep Your Remote Clean While Cooking

If you like to channel surf while cooking, place your remote control in a plastic bag or plastic wrap. The buttons will still be visible, and the control will stay clean.

Kill a Kitchen Fire in Two Seconds Flat

If there's a grease fire in a pan, cover the pan immediately with a lid. You'll cut off the oxygen supply and the fire will go out. Baking soda is one of the best fire extinguishers. Always keep an open box next to the stove to dump onto grease fires—and never use water!

If you lost the knob to a pot lid, don't throw out the pot! Place a screw into the hole, with the thread side up, then attach a cork to it.

Stubborn Lid?

Have you ever left a covered pot on the stove only to find that the lid is stuck on? If this happens to you, just try setting the pot over moderate heat for a minute or two. Why? When you cook a food in a covered pot, the air inside the pot increases in pressure, raising the lid ever so slightly so heated air can escape. When you turn off the heat, the air pressure decreases (along with the temperature) and may become lower than the air pressure outside the pot. This decrease in pressure, combined with the water from the steam, creates a vacuum around the lid and seals it tight. The longer the lid is left on, the tighter the seal. Turning the heat back on will increase the air pressure, loosening the lid's seal.

Open a Stubborn Stuck Jar

An easy way to open a tight jar lid is to cover the top in plastic wrap to create a firm grip. Rubber kitchen gloves or rubber bands work well too. If the jar lid still won't budge, set it in a bowl with a little hot tap water for a few minutes, and then try again. Still stuck? Try this trick with a puncture-type can opener: Carefully work the pointed tip under the lid and gently loosen the cap. This should release enough pressure to allow you to open the jar.

Fixing Low-Flow Ketchup

Can't get the ketchup out of a stubborn bottle? Just stick a straw inside. Now when you turn it upside-down, the airflow through the straw will make the ketchup flow right out.

Get Rid of Food Smells

If your plastic storage containers smell of garlic, onions, or another potent food, wash them thoroughly, then stuff crumpled newspaper inside before snapping on the lids. In a few days, the smell will be gone.

Tame Tupperware Odor

Washing a plastic container with a stale smell over and over won't get rid of the sour odor, but this will. Wipe inside with tomato juice, wash as usual, dry completely and place in freezer (top and bottom separately). In a few days it will be as good as new.

Keep Wrap in Line

Plastic wrap loves to hug itself. Avoid this by keeping the box in the refrigerator. The cold keeps the wrap from sticking to itself.

Who Knew? Readers' Favorite

To lessen your cleanup time when using a food processor, protect the lid by first covering the bowl of food with a piece of plastic wrap. The lid will stay clean and you can toss the plastic wrap in the trash when you're finished.

Make Your Own Ziploc

If your plastic bags are not resealable, you can seal them yourself with this quick trick: Fold a small piece of aluminum foil over the end you'd like to seal, and iron it so both ends of the foil close over the plastic. This will ensure that the plastic doesn't melt.

Fuss-Free Blender Cleaning

Wash your blender in less than a minute with this simple trick! Just fill it halfway with hot water, then add a drop of dishwashing liquid, cover with its lid, and hit blend for 30 seconds. Suds will fill your blender and clean it without you having to disassemble the whole contraption.

Stop Syrup from Running

Frustrated with syrup running down the sides of the bottle, making a disgusting mess? Try this trick: Rub the threads at the neck of the bottle with a small amount of vegetable oil. The oil will prevent the syrup from running and the cap from sticking next time you open it. This also works for molasses and honey containers.

Making Coffee More Drinkable

If you're sensitive to acidity in coffee, but love the pick-me-up in the morning, here's a tip to reduce the acid level: Just add a pinch of baking soda to the drink! You can also use this tip to decrease the acid in other high-acid drinks and foods.

For Mugs That Look As Good As New

To remove coffee or tea stains from a ceramic mug or pot, gently wipe them with a lemon sprinkled with salt. The salt will act as an abrasive, while the acid will get rid of the tannins.

Cure Cloudiness in Iced Tea

Cloudiness is common in brewed iced tea, but it can be easily prevented. Simply let the tea cool to room temperature before refrigerating it. If the tea is still cloudy, try adding a small amount of boiling water to it until it clears up.

Easier Iced Tea

Is there anything more refreshing than iced tea in the summer? When making a big pot of tea, here's a tip to easily add and remove your tea bags. Just wrap the strings around a chopstick, then place the chopstick over the top of the pot.

A Fizzy Fix

Have you ever had the problem of soda fizzing over the top of an ice-filled glass? Here's a quick trick that will make the cubes fizz less. Put them in the glass first, then rinse them for a few seconds. Pour out the water and add the soda. Since the surface tension of the ice will have changed, the soda won't fizz over.

Make Flat Soda a Thing of the Past

When you pour a warm soft drink over ice cubes, the gas escapes from the beverage at a fast rate because the ice cubes contain more surface area for the gas bubbles to collect on, thus releasing more of the carbon dioxide. This is the reason that warm beverages go flat rapidly, and warm drinks poured over ice go flat even faster. To slow down the process, add ice after you've poured the drink and the bubbles have dissipated.

Slow Down Soda Bubbles on the Go

Yes, there is a way to keep open soda from going flat. Not for a month, but for an hour or so. Leave an open can or bottle inside a sealed Ziploc bag while you run out to do your errands, and it will still be bubbly when you get back.

Who Knew? Readers' Favorite

Wine sediment is harmless, but it doesn't always look too nice. Get rid of sediment, and any bits of cork, by pouring your wine through a coffee filter and into a decanter before you serve it.

Add Flavor and Fun

Here's a neat trick to save the last bit of wine at the end of the bottle. Freeze it in ice cube trays, then store the cubes in a freezer bag. Use them in wine coolers and any dish that calls for wine.

Salt Shaker Shakeup

When your salt gets sticky in high humidity, keep it flowing freely by adding some raw rice to the shaker to absorb the moisture. Rice absorbs moisture very slowly under these conditions and lasts for a long time.

Two Glasses Stuck Together?

The next time you find two drinking glasses stuck together, try this: Fill the top glass with ice water and then place the bottom one in a few inches of hot tap water in the sink. It should only take a few seconds for them to come unstuck.

Loosen Up

Our little guys are great about emptying the dishwasher, but here's what we often have to do when reaching for a glass afterward—unstick them, by putting ice in the top one and setting the bottom one in a bowl of warm water. Remember high school chemistry? Heat expands. Cold contracts.

An Amicable Parting

End the tug-of-war over glasses that are stuck one inside the other. Instead, use vegetable oil as a lubricant around the attached part. Works for glass bowls as well.

Who Knew? Readers' Favorite

Make your own version of sippy cups using real glassware you already have. If your glasses are slippery, put a wide rubber band around them so children can get a better grip.

Unstick Stuck Ice Cube Trays

If your ice cube trays stick to the bottom of the shelf, try placing a piece of waxed paper underneath the tray. Freezing temperatures do not affect waxed paper.

Freezer Freeze Up

A common problem with icemakers is that they freeze up. Next time this happens, just use a blow-dryer to defrost it. (For safety's sake, keep the dryer away from any pooling water.) To prevent this problem in the first place, release a few ice cubes every few days.

Microwave Mishap

If someone accidentally turns on the microwave when it's empty, it can damage the oven. To avoid any problems, just keep a cup of water in the microwave when it is not in use.

Make Cooking with Olive Oil Easier

Olive oil is healthful as oils go, but it has a low smoke point, which means that it will break down rapidly when exposed to heat. You can increase the smoke point of olive oil by adding a small amount of canola oil, which has a very high smoke point. If your recipe calls for tablespoon of olive oil, use 2½ teaspoons olive and ½ teaspoon canola oil and sautéing will be easier.

How to Save a Burned Meal

If you accidentally scorch dinner, set the pot or dish into cold water immediately. This will stop the cooking action and minimize the damage. Carefully remove any unharmed food—don't scrape it—then discard whatever is unsalvageable. When you reheat the edible leftovers, set a fresh piece of white bread on top to remove the burnt odor. Alternatively, there's always pizza delivery!

Burned a Roast?

There are few kitchen disasters more disheartening than burning a roast. But there's help! First, remove the roast from the pan and cover it with a towel dampened with hot water for about five minutes, which will stop the cooking. Then remove or scrape off any burnt areas with a sharp knife, and put the roast back in the oven to reheat if necessary.

Ham Too Salty?

A little salt in ham is a good thing, but if your ham slices are too salty, place them in a dish of low-fat milk for 20 minutes before heating, then rinse them off in cold water and dry them with paper towels. The ham won't pick up the taste of the milk, but it will taste much less salty.

Defrost in a Flash

The best way to thaw turkey is on a shallow baking sheet in the refrigerator, in its original packaging, allowing 24 hours for every five pounds of bird. But if it's Thanksgiving morning and you've forgotten to stick the bird in the fridge, the fastest, safest method of thawing frozen poultry fast is to place it—still wrapped in plastic—in a bowl (or bucket) of cold water. Check the water regularly and change it as the water warms up—you should never use hot water, as it will promote bacterial growth.

Zap Microwave Odors

Fresh fish is a summertime treat, but fresh fish smell in your microwave is not. Get rid of fish or other microwave odors by putting a quartered lemon or a small bowl of vanilla in your microwave for a minute or two on high.

Who Knew? Readers' Favorite

The odor from cooking fish and other pungent foods can linger over your kitchen for hours. To make it quickly disappear, place a bowl of white vinegar on the counter near the stove while cooking. The vinegar will absorb the smell.

Get Rid of That Fish Smell

If you've been preparing fish and want to remove the smell from your hands, try washing them with water and a bit of toothpaste. Lemon juice and a little salt will also work well.

Stop Separation Anxiety in Gravies

Does your gravy separate? If so, simply add a pinch or two of baking soda to emulsify the fat globules in a matter of seconds.

Gravy Savers

Gravy is so delicious, yet so easy to mess up. To help prevent lumpy gravy, add a pinch of salt to the flour before using any liquid. If lumps persist, use your blender to smooth it out. If your gravy burns, just stir in a teaspoon of peanut butter to cover up the burnt flavor without altering the meaty taste.

Skimming the Fat without the Refrigerator

You can de-fat soup or gravy easily even if you don't have time to refrigerate it. Remove it from the heat for 5–10 minutes. Put four or five ice cubes in a piece of cheesecloth and swirl it around the soup or gravy. Fat is attracted to the cold, and should stick to the cheesecloth. It will also be attracted to lettuce leaves—stir a few leaves into the soup for a few minutes, and then discard them. Another method is to add a slice of fresh white bread on top of the fat for a few seconds. After the bread absorbs the fat, it should be disposed of—if you leave the bread on the soup too long, it will fall apart.

Too-Salty Solutions

If your soup or stew is too salty, use one of these methods to make it less so. If it won't affect the taste, add a can of peeled tomatoes or a small amount of brown sugar. Alternatively, stir in a slice or two of raw apple or potato, let simmer a few minutes, then discard the apple or potato.

Spicy Salves

Overspiced your dinner? Just add a bit of sugar, honey, or maple syrup. The sweet flavor allows your tastebuds to handle more hot, saving your meal.

Egg Separation Made Easy

If you don't have an egg separator, the easiest way to separate yolks from the whites is to crack them into a funnel. The whites slide out, leaving the yolk behind.

Who Knew? Readers' Favorite

It's easy to tell whether an egg has been hard-boiled: Spin it. If it wobbles, it's raw—the yolk sloshes from one end of the egg to the other. Hard-cooked eggs spin evenly, because the yolk is held in place by the cooked egg white. Reduce your risk of spinning an egg right off the counter by adding a drop or two of food coloring to the water when you boil them. It will dye the shells so you can tell the difference between the two kinds.

Fishing Out Eggshells

If you've ever gotten eggshell in a bowl of cracked eggs and tried to fish it out with your finger, you know how hard it can be. A better tool than your finger—and even a spoon? An eggshell half that you were able to break cleanly. The edge cuts through the egg whites easier than other implements.

Don't OD on Mayo

Too much mayonnaise or salad dressing can ruin a dish. To fix the problem, try adding breadcrumbs to absorb the excess.

Unstick Your Rice

If your rice tends to stick together when you cook it, add a teaspoon of lemon juice to the water when boiling. Your sticky problem will be gone!

Rice Repair

If you burned the rice, fear not! It's white bread to the rescue. Get rid of the scorched taste by placing a slice of fresh white bread on top of the rice while it's still hot, and covering it for a few minutes.

Pizza Cutting Prescription

Pizza cutters are great—until they start to get dull. One of easiest ways to cut a pizza is to use clean scissors with long blades—you can cut from top and bottom, and then you can cut the pizza into slices quickly. Make sure the scissors are sharp and used only for food.

A Plan for Pizza-Making

Making pizzas at home is a great way to save money and get the kids involved in making dinner. But homemade pizzas often lack the crispness of pizzeria pies. Here's one tip that should help: Add the cheese before the tomato sauce. Cheese has a lower water content than tomatoes do, so the crust won't get as soggy.

Insta-Peel for Tomatoes

Need to quickly peel tomatoes for a recipe? The easiest way is
to place them in a pot of boiling water for a minute. The skins will
practically fall off.

Keep Tomatoes from Staining Your Plastic

Plastic containers are perfect for keeping leftovers and sauces,
but tomato sauce will often stain clear plastic. To keep this from
happening, simply spray the container with nonstick cooking
spray before pouring in tomato-based sauces. To remove a
plastic stain, cover the area with mustard and leave overnight.

Easing the Acidity of Tomatoes

Some people are unable to eat spaghetti sauces and other
tomato-based foods because of their high acid content. Adding
chopped carrots and cooking them with tomato dishes will
reduce the acidity without affecting the taste.

No-Sugar Sweetener

Carrots are a natural sweetener. To sweeten a soup, stew, or sauce without adding sugar, stir in a small amount of pureed carrots. Use one of the sweeter carrot varieties.

For a Guacamole Emergency!

If you bought a whole bunch of avocados for your guacamole and one or two are still not ripe enough to use, try this tip—which isn't ideal, but will do the trick. Prick the skin of the unripe avocado in several places, then microwave it on high for 40–70 seconds, flipping it over halfway through. This won't ripen the avocado, but it will soften it enough that you'll be able to mash it with ripe avocados and your guests won't notice the difference.

Keep Guacamole Looking Fresh

You may look good with a tan, but your guacamole sure doesn't! To keep the avocados from oxidizing (which causes the brown color), cut them with a silver or stainless steel knife, and leave the pit in the dip (until serving). Sprinkle lemon or lime juice on the surface of the dip, and cover tightly with plastic wrap until you're ready to eat.

Sippy Cup Redux

It's a beautiful, fresh, colorful salad until—no! Stop the floodgates! Someone over-dressed it and now it's barely edible. Titrate your vinaigrette with a baby sippy cup. Mix inside the cup, shake (covering the opening), and scatter over the salad with its perfectly sized spout.

Reduce Green Odors

Kale, cabbage, and collard greens are delicious to eat, but can sometimes smell stinky when they're being prepared. Make sure not to overcook them, which will make them release more odors. Also try placing a few unshelled pecans in the saucepan while cooking to help absorb any scents.

Peeled Potato Prescription

You've managed to talk your kids into helping you with tonight's scalloped potatoes, but now the potatoes are peeled long before you need them! To keep peeled potatoes from discoloring, place them in a bowl of cold water with a few drops of white vinegar, then refrigerate. Drain before cooking and add a small amount of sugar to the cooking water to revive some of the lost flavor.

Keep Fruit Looking Fresh

Even though the taste isn't affected, it's still disappointing to unveil your fruit salad only to discover a thin layer of brown oxidation all over the fruit. A common method for keeping cut fruit looking fresh is to add a bit of lemon juice. However, an even more effective method is to fill a spray bottle with water and a few dissolved vitamin C tablets (usually available in the vitamin and nutritional supplement section of your drugstore). Spray this mixture on the cut fruit and not only will you stop the oxidation, you'll also be getting added vitamins!

The Brown Bag Trick

Fruit normally gives off ethylene gas, which hastens ripening. Some fruits give off more gas than others and ripen faster. Other fruits are picked before they are ripe and need a bit of help. If an unripe fruit is placed in a brown paper bag, the ethylene gas it gives off does not dissipate into the air but is trapped and concentrated, causing the fruit to ripen faster. To get it to ripen even more quickly, add a ripe apple—one of those ethylene-rich fruits.

Perking Up Apples

If apples are dry or bland, slice them and put them in a dish, and then pour cold apple juice over them and refrigerate for 30 minutes. OK, so it's kind of a cheat, but it will make sure picky eaters get their nutrients!

Who Knew? Readers' Favorite

Making jam? If you add a small pat of butter when cooking fruits for preserves and jellies, there will be no foam to skim off the top. The fat acts as a sealant and prevents the air from rising and accumulating on top as foam.

Apple Botox

To prevent baked apples from wrinkling, peel the top third or cut a few slits in the skin to allow for expansion.

Juice for Juice

If you've been cooking with berries and your hands are stained, try removing the berry juice stains with a bit of lemon juice.

Raisin Rejuvenation

Sad-looking raisins? To plump them up to perfection, place them a small baking dish with a little water, cover, and bake in a preheated 325°F oven for 6–8 minutes. Or, pour boiling water over the raisins and let them stand for 10–15 minutes.

Chopping Dried Fruits

Raisins and other dried fruits won't stick to your knife (or anything) if you first soak them in cold water for 10 minutes.

Who Knew? Readers' Favorite

Chopping nuts in a blender? Try adding a small amount of sugar. It will keep the nut pieces from sticking together.

Quick-Rising Solutions

It's not always a good idea to artificially quicken the amount of time it takes your bread dough to rise (the flavor of the bread may not be as complex), but if you're in a time crunch, it's always nice to have a back-up plan. To speed whole-wheat bread dough's rising time, add one tablespoon of lemon juice to the dough as you are mixing it. When it comes to other breads, a little heat does wonders when it comes to cutting down on rising time. Set the dough (either in a bowl or a loaf pan) on a heating pad set on medium, or over the pilot light on a gas stove. You can also use the microwave to help speed up the rising process by as much as one-third. Set ½ cup hot water in the back corner of the microwave. Place the dough in a well-greased microwavable bowl and cover it with plastic wrap, and then cover the plastic wrap with a damp towel. With the power level set at 10 percent, cook the dough for six minutes, and then let it rest for 4–5 minutes. Repeat the procedure if the dough has not doubled its size.

Slow Down Browning Baked Goods

If you're having a problem with bread browning too fast, set a dish of water on the oven rack just above the bread. The added humidity in the oven will slow down the browning. This will work with cakes as well.

Double-Decker

If you don't have an insulated or a thick baking sheet, there's a simple solution: Try baking the cookies on two sheets, stacked one on top of the other. It will eliminate burned bottoms caused by a too-thin pan.

Rust Remover

To treat rust on metal baking dishes and cookware, sprinkle powdered laundry detergent on the spot, then scour with the cut side of half a raw potato.

Prevent a Pudding Problem

Lay a sheet of wax paper directly onto a custard or pudding while it is still hot to keep a skin from developing.

Is Your Brown Sugar Lumpy?

Brown sugar loses moisture rather quickly and develops lumps easily. To soften hardened sugar, place the sugar in a tightly covered dish with a slice of fresh white bread or half an apple, cover the dish tightly, and heat for 15–20 seconds in the microwave. Let it stand five minutes before using. The moisture from the bread or apple will produce enough steam to soften the sugar without melting it. Store brown sugar in the freezer to keep it from getting lumpy in the first place.

Who Knew? Readers' Favorite

Keep your brown sugar soft and lump-free with this simple trick: Just throw a couple of marshmallows into the bag with it.

More Tips for Lumpy Sugar

Granulated sugar clumps less than brown sugar, but it's still easy to get lumps. Keep this from happening by sticking a few salt-free crackers in the canister to absorb the moisture; replace the crackers every week.

Soften Hardened Marshmallows

If you find an old bag of marshmallows that have hardened, add a slice of very fresh white bread or half an apple to the bag to soften them. Unfortunately, it's not a quick fix: you might need to leave the bag for one or two days until the marshmallows absorb the moisture.

When Movie Night Goes Wrong

If you've ever burned popcorn in your microwave, you know that it stinks, and the smell likes to permeate the entire household. Make it smell fresh again by stuffing the microwave with crumpled newspaper for a few hours (but don't turn on the microwave!). Remove the paper, and boil water and baking soda in a glass bowl for five minutes, and the smell should be gone.

Who Knew? Readers' Favorite

Are your popcorn kernels too pooped to pop? It's probably because they have lost too much moisture, but they can be revived. Soak the kernels in water for five minutes, then dry them off and try again.

Perfectly Popped Popcorn

This simple trick will make sure almost every single kernel pops when you're making popcorn—and who doesn't want more popcorn? Just store your unpopped popcorn kenernels in the freezer, and pop them when they're still cold. (Unfortunately, this won't work for microwave popcorn.)

Perfectly Popped…Nuts?

Toasted nuts are often an essential (and delicious) part of recipes. Want to know how to make sure your nuts won't burn, even if you aren't looking at them? Toast them in a popcorn air popper! Just add ¼ cup nuts, plug it in for 60 seconds, and your nuts will be a perfect golden brown.

Simple Spout

It's silly to buy a spout for oil when you have one practically built in! When you first purchase a bottle of oil, poke a small hole in the protective seal with a chopstick or paring knife. Keep it stored with the cap on.

Cut Down on Paper Towels

When preparing a recipe that requires you to dry something you've just cooked on several layers of paper towels to absorb the grease, use this trick. Lay down several sheets of old newspaper, then place a single layer of paper towels on top.

Rolling Pin Replacement

If you don't have a rolling pin on hand, reach for a zucchini. The dough won't stick, and it's not as unseemly as using a shampoo bottle.

Keep Your Eye on the Recipe

In our house, recipe cards are always sliding under permission slips, falling into the sink, or just plain vanishing. A new trick we learned: Use a fork in a medium-sized glass as a recipe card stand. The card goes between the tines, and the recipe will be easy to see when you need it.

Thawing Cheesecakes

One of our kid's groups sells frozen cheesecakes as a fundraiser, so we always end up with several cheesecakes in our freezer each year! If you're eating a frozen cheesecake, thaw it in the refrigerator instead of at room temperature—we've found they end up much creamier this way, even though it might take a little longer.

Picture Perfect Pasta

If you still have old 35mm film canisters hanging around your house, use them in the kitchen! These canisters are ideal measuring tools for pasta: fill one with uncooked spaghetti to measure out the proper amount to make. One canister of spaghetti will feed two people.

The problem: You love store-bought butter spreads, but you know the trans fats inside aren't good for you. The solution? Make your own at home! Just combine a stick of butter and ¼ cup canola oil with a hand mixer. It will be soft and easy to spread!

Lightning Grease Remover

If you're cooking at the stove and grease splatters onto your clothes, think fast. Grab some baking soda from the cupboard and rub it into the spot to absorb as much grease as possible. This will make it more difficult for the stain to set, and it will soak up most of the grease before it works its way into the fibers of your clothes.

Just Cool It!

Make sure you let your pots and pans cool before you wash them. Drastic changes in temperature can cause them to warp, meaning they won't heat evenly and will be harder to cook with.

Supercharge Your Dishwasher

Keep a spray bottle filled with water and a bit of dishwashing detergent near your dishwasher. If a dish is heavily soiled, spray it down before you put it inside. The detergent gets working on the food immediately, so you won't have to rinse your dishes before putting them inside, or run a separate "rinse" cycle before you do your dishes.

Doing Dishes?

Sprinkle a little baby powder onto your hands before placing them inside rubber gloves. They'll come off more easily, and your hands won't get that clammy feeling from too much sweat while you're doing the dishes.

Cook Your Dishes Clean

Here's a terrific way to make your post-dinner clean up a breeze: Remove cooked-on food from pots and pans effortlessly by filling them with water, adding a tea bag, and simmering. The tea's acid will break up food.

Great Grater Cleaning Tip

What's the easiest way to clean a messy cheese grater? Reach for a lemon! Just rub the pulp-side of a cut lemon across a grater and it will clean off any stuck-on cheese.

Who Knew? Readers' Favorite

Where do you keep your scouring pads? Believe or not, we keep them in a plastic bag in our freezer. That way, we don't have to worry about them rusting, and they'll last a lot longer.

Make Your Own Bowl Scraper

Have you ever seen those bowl scrapers in kitchen stores that sell for $3 to $10? These circular, plastic tools are easy to make at home. Simply take the lid of a round take-out container, cut it in half, then remove the rim. Instant savings!

Cheap Clips

Instead of buying those clips for fastening cereal and chip bags, simply buy a box of large binder clips from an office supply store. They're the exact same thing at less than half the cost.

The Ice Trick

When you go away on vacation, fill a sealable plastic bag with a few ice cubes and put it in the freezer. If a power failure occurs while you are away, the ice will melt and refreeze in a solid block, alerting you that your frozen food has been defrosted.

For a No-Scratch Stack

Stacking fine china? Insert paper plates between the real plates before stacking to prevent scratches. You can use the same trick for stacking nonstick pans.

Who Knew? Readers' Favorite

When you're preparing a big meal and need more counter space, try this clever quick fix: Simply open a drawer in your kitchen and cover it with a heavy-duty cutting board. Voilà!

CHAPTER 10

Secrets of the Supermarket

The Gift of Groceries

Need a little help budgeting your trips to the supermarket? Many chains now offer prepaid gift cards. Buy one for yourself and think of it as a portable checking account that you "withdraw" from it every time you shop. With a dedicated grocery "account," you'll find it's easier to keep a tighter rein on your spending.

Work for It!

If you have a few spare hours each week, you can get huge savings on your groceries by joining a food co-op. Co-ops are run completely by neighborhood volunteers, and in turn offer gigantic discounts to their members. Most co-ops allow you to choose what job you do (stocking, cash register, billing, cleaning, etc.), and many allow you to work a different number of hours depending on what job you do (the person cleaning up for the butcher will work fewer hours than someone doing paperwork, for instance). To find out if there is a co-op in your area, visit CoopDirectory.org/directory.htm.

For the Freshest Food Around

Have you ever heard of community-supported agriculture? Known as CSAs, they connect local farmers with their communities by offering people a "share" in the farm. You sign up for shares, then each week during the farming season you receive a box of seasonal produce—and sometimes even staples like milk and eggs. The downside is that you usually don't have much choice in what you're getting. But if you like to buy locally grown foods, the prices can't be beat. To find out if there is a CSA program near you, visit LocalHarvest.org.

Meet You at the Meat Locker

If you live in the Midwest, you are lucky to have access to the best meat in the country. You are also lucky to be able to purchase meat from the farmers themselves, in the form of stores called meat lockers. At your local meat locker, you can buy large packages of meat cut into different portions—for instance, one package may include skirt steaks, rib eyes, half a dozen ground patties, pork chops, spare ribs, and more. Packages usually come out to $1.50–$2.00 per pound, which can be a substantial savings when you're getting choice cuts of meat. If you don't have the room to store so much meaty goodness, split it with a friend!

Go Native

Especially in cities, stores by and for immigrants abound. Whether it's a Mexican, Indian, Ethiopian, Chinese, or Korean grocery, you'll find cheap deals on foods that are native to that country. Bulk spices can be especially cheap, and you'll also find items such as inexpensive tortillas and avocados. We never buy rice unless it's from an ethnic market, as it's usually up to 80 percent cheaper than buying it at the grocery store.

Who Knew? Readers' Favorite

Many dollar stores have more than just easy decorations, cheap toys, and fake flowers—they have food! Make sure to check the prices for canned goods and other staples in your neighborhood dollar store. You may be surprised at the deals you find.

Come for the Cough Syrup, Stay for the Soup

You may not think of CVS, Walgreens, and other drugstores as good places to buy food, but many of them carry weekly specials on staples and snacks such as soup, spaghetti sauce, and soda. It's worth it to take a walk down their food aisle while you're in the store, and always check the circular to see if anything you use is on special.

New Stores Spell Savings

Whenever a new grocery store opens up in our area, we always stop by to take a look. It may be a pain to navigate differently laid-out aisles, but new supermarkets always offer big sales and the lowest prices possible in their first few weeks and months of business as an incentive to get customers to switch stores. Many stores also offer contests and giveaways to celebrate their grand opening, so plan a visit during that first week.

Leaner Isn't Always Better

Even if you want to prepare low-fat meals, you don't always have to buy the leanest (and most expensive) ground beef. If you're preparing hamburgers on a grill or on a broiler rack, most of the fat will be lost during the cooking process, so stick with the less-lean (and more affordable) varieties.

Memorize This Meat Chart

You're at the supermarket, and both boneless chicken breasts and whole chickens are on sale! The whole chicken seems cheaper, but it also has skin, bones, and other parts you don't want to eat...so how do you know which to buy? Use the list below to see how many servings are in each cut of meat, and then figure out your unit price from there. The column on the left indicates the type of meat and the cut, and the column on the right indicates the number of servings per pound.

MEAT	SERVINGS PER POUND	MEAT	SERVINGS PER POUND
Chuck roast	2.5	Chicken, Leg quarters	2
Cubed steak	4	Chicken, Whole	2
Ground beef	4	Fish, Dressed, (scales head, and tail removed)	2
Rump roast	3		
Strip steak	2	Fish, Fillets	2
T-bone steak	2	Steaks, Whole (bone-in)	2.5
Top loin steak	3	Bacon	6
Chicken, Boneless breasts	4	Pork, Boneless top loin	3
Chicken, Boneless thighs	3	Ham	5
Chicken, Bone-in breasts	2.5	Pork chops	3
Chicken, Bone-in thighs	2.5	Pork roast	2

 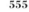

MEAT	SERVINGS PER POUND	MEAT	SERVINGS PER POUND
Sausage	4	Turkey, Legs	2
Turkey, Bone-in breasts	3	Turkey, Whole	2.5
Turkey, Ground	4		

Freezer Patties

Never buy meat that's already been shaped into patties (unless it's on sale). Instead, buy your own, and shape it into patties yourself. Place a sheet of waxed paper between each, then place the entire stack in a resealable plastic bag in the freezer.

Market Watch

Supermarkets have started using their own wording on meat packages to make you think the meat you are buying is a better grade than it really is. Most of the major chains are buying more select-grade beef, but may call it by any number of fancy names such as "top premium beef," "prime quality cut," "select choice," "market choice," or "premium cut." Be aware that these titles don't actually mean anything!

More Meat Tips

Grocery stores make a lot of money on meat, so it's not surprising that they display the priciest cuts in the case! Get dramatic savings by asking the butcher to slice different cuts for you from the same primal (or section) of the cow or pig. These cuts can be as little as one-fifth the cost of the expensive, pre-packaged cuts, and they'll be just as tender and tasty. Here's what to ask for.

✦ If you're looking for rib eye steak, request chuck eye. You may need to ask the butcher to cut a 4-inch roast off the front of the boneless chuck, then to peel out the chuck eye and cut it into steaks.

✦ Instead of pork tenderloin, buy an entire loin roast and ask the butcher to cut it up for you.

✦ When cross rib roasts are on sale (which is usually quite often), ask your butcher to carve a flatiron roast for you from the cross rib, and ask him to cut it into boneless ribs. Don't be put off by this unattractive cut—that seam of what looks like gristle down the middle is actually a gelatin that will cook off. Meanwhile, these ribs will cut up just as well as short ribs, and they're boneless, so you'll get more for your money.

✦ Instead of buying ground beef, ask the butcher to grind up a bottom round roast for you.

✦ If you like Italian sausages, try asking for ground pork shoulder butt. It's also a great substitute for ground beef.

✦ Whenever you see cut-up beef for stir-fries or stroganoff, know that you're not getting the most for your money. Simply buy a rump roast and slice it (or ask the butcher to do it for you).

Get a Knife and Go For It!

Meat is expensive enough, but a big part of the cost is the price you're paying the butcher to cut it up for you. Buy the largest cuts of meat you can, then cut it up, wrap in foil, and put it in a plastic bag in your freezer. Here are some more tips for butchering meat.

✦ Many stores will butcher big cuts of meat for you for free, so ask before doing it yourself!

✦ Use the sharpest knife you have, and never use a serrated knife, which will shred the meat.

✦ If you're working with a cut of beef or pork with a bone in it, the first thing you will need to do is remove the bone. Using a filet knife, cut along the bone until the meat is loosened and you can pull it away.

✦ With a cut of beef like a sirloin tip, you can just cut it into portions that are the correct size for what you'd like to use them for. Start with the thickest portion and slice along the grain (muscle strands that all run in the same direction).

✦ Once you cook and eat a pork shoulder, you'll be so hooked you'll wonder why you never bought a huge slab of pig before. These may be hard to find at your local supermarket, but try requesting one at the butcher counter or checking at a local ethnic store. Marinate the pork shoulder overnight in your favorite seasonings, and cook on 400°F for a half hour, then on a very low temperature (around 250°F) for about five hours. The meat will come right off the bone, and it will be so juicy and tender everyone will want to know your secret.

✦ To cut up a chicken, turkey, or duck, first remove the legs, then separate the drumstick from the thigh by placing it skin-side-down on your cutting board and slicing right through the joint with a sharp knife (you should be able to feel where the knife will slide through). Place the bird on its back, then cut off the wings. Turn the remaining meat on its side and cut through the cavity of the bird starting from the tail end. Cut parallel to the backbone and slice the bones of the rib cage. Repeat on the opposite side of the backbone. Now all that's left is removing the breast from the backbone. Slice the breast in half if desired.

✦ To fillet a whole fish, make a vertical cut just behind the head and a horizontal cut on the top of the fish from the head to the tail. Use a metal spatula to lift out the fillet, running it over the bones from head to tail. Repeat on the other side of the fish.

✦ For illustrated instructions on how to cut any piece of meat, type the word "butchering" along with the type of meat into a search engine online. There are many tutorials (some including video) online.

Get It While It's Hot!

While perusing the cereal aisle, you'll quickly realize that hot cereals are cheaper than cold ones. Though they may not be as popular with your family, try saving money by making hot cereal at least once a week. It's often more nutritious, so it's worth it to make the switch.

Break Free From Brands

When you've been buying the same brand for as long as you can remember, it's hard to make the switch to generics. However, you'll be surprised when you find many generic and store-brand products taste exactly the same (or better!) for less than half the cost.

✦ Always buy generic baking ingredients such as flour, oil, and sugar. These generics are indistinguishable from their more-expensive counterparts. Frozen and canned vegetables are also usually exactly the same.

✦ As for products such as cereals, cookies, and crackers, basic is better—we've had good luck with plain granola, potato chips, and wheat crackers.

- No matter what the product, it never hurts to try. If you end up having to throw away one can of soup, you've wasted a dollar or two, but if you like it, you can save a lot over the course of a year.

- Save the boxes from name-brand products your kids are attached to, then empty the generic products into them. Your picky eaters won't know the difference if they can't see it on the outside.

Never Pay a Dollar For a Lemon Again

It may be a pain, but the best way to save on groceries is to shop at more than one market. You'll soon find that one store will have cheaper produce, one will have cheaper meat, and so forth. Explore grocery stores you've never shopped at—perhaps one that is closer to your workplace or gym rather than by your home—and you may find even lower prices. We've even found cheaper products at stores that are the same chain, just a different location. Write down the prices of your most frequently purchased items, or bring a receipt from an average grocery trip with you. That way you can be sure to remember where the prices are the most reasonable.

Shop Smart at the Grocery Store

Shop later in the day to take advantage of markdowns in your grocery store's bakery and meat departments. Also make sure to keep an eye on the prices at the salad bar. If you only need a few artichoke hearts or croutons, they may be cheaper to buy there by the pound than elsewhere in the store.

Know Your Store Brands

What is the name of the store brand at your local grocery store? What about at the store the next town over? Many stores have names for generic brands, like "White Rose, " "Equate," or "Kirkland," so make sure you're aware of what they are so you can keep an eye out for savings.

Buy Dry Beans

If you can help it, never buy beans, peas, or lentils in cans, unless they're significantly marked down. These items are much more cost-effective if you purchase them dry. You'll have to plan ahead in order to soak them overnight, but once you get used to this extra step, it will seem routine.

Who Knew? Readers' Favorite

Never, ever let us catch you buying sundae toppings in the ice cream aisle! These nuts and mini candies are up to 50 percent cheaper in the baking aisle, which often even has sprinkles, too. Melt some chocolate chips in a double boiler, then let them cool a bit, and add to the top of ice cream for your own "instant shell."

Mix It Yourself

Frozen, concentrated juice is almost always less expensive per glass than juice you buy in a bottle. Find a brand that says "100% juice" and mix with a pitcher of water for savings.

Weighing In

If you're buying produce that is priced by the item rather than by the pound (such as a head of lettuce, lemons, or avocados), take advantage of the store's scales and weigh the item to find the heaviest. This way, you'll be sure you're getting the most for your money.

Go for the Heavyweight

When considering prices of pre-packaged produce at the supermarket, weigh them first to make sure you're getting the best deal. I've found that bags of things like carrots, apples, and potatoes are often heavier than their package specifies.

—*Karen Hall, Lexington Park, MD*

Shake It Up

Supermarkets are continually misting their produce with water. That's because this keeps it fresher and makes it look more appealing to customers. Make sure you're not paying for all this moisture, however! When buying fruits and vegetables by the pound, give herbs, leafy greens, and other produce a good shake before you bag it.

The Lifespan of Your Produce

Tomatoes are on sale, and they'd be great to use in that fresh salsa you want to make for next week's picnic. But will they still be good? The handy list will give you a rough timeline of how long your ripe fruits and veggies will last once you get them home from the market.

UP TO THREE TO FOUR DAYS

Apricots

Artichokes

Asparagus

Avocados

Bananas

Cherries

Corn

Cucumbers

Eggplants

Grapes

Greens (lettuce, spinach, chard, etc.)

Mushrooms

Pineapples

Strawberries

String beans

Summer squash

Watercress

ONE WEEK OR LESS

Blueberries

Broccoli

Brussels sprouts

Cauliflower

Cranberries

Grapefruit

Leeks

Lemons

Limes

Oranges

Peaches

Pears

Peppers

Plums

Tomatoes

Watermelons

....

Apples	Garlic
Beets	Onions
Cabbage	Potatoes
Carrots	Winter squash
Celery	

Snack Assembly

It's easy to turn bulk foods into convenience foods, ensuring that you don't get frustrated and start buying those always-expensive prepackaged snacks. Invest in a big box of sandwich bags and spend some time at the beginning of the week filling them with carrot sticks, strips of mozzarella cheese (which is the same thing as string cheese), or granola. It's also easy to make trail mix by purchasing nuts, seeds, and dried fruits and combining them.

Don't Fall for This Trick

Did you know that when an item is on sale, most customers are 14 times more likely to buy items that complement it at full price? Make sure you're not falling into this trap—the next time peanut butter is on sale, don't buy jelly; when laundry detergent is on sale, don't buy fabric softener; and when strawberries are on sale, don't buy those delicious sponge cakes! You get the picture.

Beware of Sneaky Supermarkets!

It's important to know that not all products are cheaper when you buy bigger sizes. Make sure to compare unit prices carefully at the store, because we have found that some items—like cereal and prepared frozen foods like french fries—are less expensive in smaller sizes. This is probably because the store knows these items are more likely to be purchased in bulk.

Who Knew? Readers' Favorite

If you love instant soups in single-serving sizes, it's easy to make your own at home rather than buying the more expensive versions in the store. First, purchase disposable, microwaveable cups made for hot beverages (if they have lids, all the better). After making your favorite soup, pour into the cups and cover with foil or plastic wrap if you don't have lids. Then when it's time for lunch, simply take out a cup and stick it in the microwave (of course, removing the foil first if you used it!).

Buy the Giant Juice

If you've been paying attention to prices at all, you know that buying a big jug of juice or soda is five or even ten times cheaper than buying one-serving bottles. When packing school lunches, use a thermos or reusable bottle instead of juice boxes or bottles. Make sure to have several, in case your child leaves one at school or you don't have time to wash it every evening. And if you simply can't work reusable bottles into your routine, consider buying empty bottles in bulk. The website Bottles.us sells plastic water bottles for about 50¢ per bottle, and while filling them and letting your child recycle them at school won't save as much as a thermos would, it's still much cheaper than buying Snapple from a vending machine.

Low-Cost Take-Out

If you're considering take-out for dinner, think first of your grocery store. Supermarkets often offer pre-made foods at a low cost to attract shoppers; you'll often find good prices on rotisserie chickens, french fries, coleslaw, pasta salad, and more. Just make sure you don't make any impulse purchases once you're in the store!

Can It

Save at the store by going canned—all recipes except for salads can be made with canned vegetables instead of the fresh ones. As long as you check the ingredients to make sure sugar hasn't been added, any vegetable in a can will taste nearly indistinguishable from a fresh one you cooked yourself, especially if it's going into sauces or casseroles.

Convenience Is Key

Remember the cardinal rule when it comes to saving money on food: If it's "convenient," it's probably costly. For example, pickles cut flat for sandwiches, juice in single-serving bottles, pre-shredded cheese, and "baby" carrots. Think carefully about what you're buying and if the convenience is worth it!

Sugar, Sugar

Don't buy colored sugar for your baking projects! Instead, buy a big bag of regular granulated sugar and add coloring at home. Just put the sugar in a resealable plastic bag and add a few drops of food coloring. Shake up the bag until the color is distributed, and add more food coloring if necessary. You'll get the exact same result at a small fraction of the cost.

Head to the Baking Aisle

Buying toppings for Sundae night? Stay away from the dessert aisle for your nuts, candy, and other toppings. These toppings can be found for much less in the baking aisle, and all you'll have to do is a little chopping. Also don't forget that a banana makes a cheap, delicious, and nutritious topping for ice cream!

Stick to the List

To make sure we don't impulse purchase things that aren't on our grocery list, we keep it right in front of us: taped to the cart! Slip a tape dispenser into your purse so you have tape handy. You'll not only make sure you stick to your list, you'll be much less likely to lose it midway down the aisle.

Deli Discount

Ask the folks at the deli counter if there's a discount for "bulk ends." These end bits are too small to slice in the machine, but can be sliced or cubed at home. They're often offered at half off!

Any Day's a Holiday

After major holidays, go to your grocery store and grab bargains on things like turkey, stuffing, canned pumpkin, and baking supplies. Then freeze the turkey and store the rest. When you're craving holiday food, you'll have a bunch already in your cabinet, all bought at a bargain price.

Who Knew? Readers' Favorite

Does your coffeemaker require cone-shaped filters? Save some cash by purchasing the less expensive round filters in bulk. You can buy a 500-pack for cheap, then shape the filters into cones so they fit your machine. With a few simple folds, they work just as well as the pricier alternatives.

Traveling with Food

When transporting perishable food from the supermarket, don't put it in the trunk. Always put it in an ice-filled cooler inside the air-conditioned car. If possible, you shouldn't leave food in a cooler for longer than an hour.

PART FOUR

Cleaning and Organizing Room by Room

Saving money starts at home, and the tips in this section will give you simple ways to make your money go further both inside and outside your home. As you move from room to room, you'll discover how to affordably clean your home using all-natural, homemade cleaners; get rid of any kind of stain on the planet; organize like a whiz; keep your car at its best; and perform simple household repairs. You'll be amazed by some of our surprising solutions for your most stubborn problems.

CHAPTER 1

Your Living Room

Minimize Broom-Swept Dust

The trail of dust that your broom leaves behind can be eliminated: Just fill a spray bottle with three parts water and one part liquid fabric softener, and spray the broom before sweeping. The spritz makes the broom strands more pliable and helps it collect dirt more efficiently.

Quick Dusting

Instead of using a rag, wear a pair of old socks on your hands when dusting. It's efficient (you're using both hands), cheap (remember, these are old socks), and you can reuse them.

Get a Lampshade Dust Free

The trick to cleaning a pleated lampshade is to find the right tool. Stroke each pleat from top to bottom with a dry, clean paintbrush. Or use a rolling lint remover for a quicker clean.

Forget that Pricey Dustcloth

Don't bother buying fancy dustcloths that are treated to attract dust. Instead, simply sprinkle a piece of cheesecloth with a few drops of lemon oil. Let the cheesecloth air dry, and it will be just as effective as an expensive cloth.

A DIY Duster for Hard-to-Reach Spots

Wrap a paper towel around the broad end of a kitchen spatula and secure with a rubber band. Use this to reach dust trapped between radiator coils. Spray the paper towel with all-purpose cleaner to get rid of sticky spills and stains.

For a Shiny Chandelier

There's no need to buy special chandelier cleaners. When it's time to tackle this difficult job, use a cloth dripping with a solution of two parts rubbing alcohol and one part hot water. Just slop it on, and be sure to hang an umbrella upside down from the chandelier to catch the mess.

Got Old, Smelly Books?

If your books stink, try this tactic for wiping out mildew. Dust mildewed pages with corn flour, French chalk, or talcum powder. Leave it inside the closed book for several days, then brush it off.

Out of Furniture Polish? Check the Pantry!

Vegetable oil works wonderfully on wood furniture. A very light coat will nourish the wood and help protect the finish, but be sure to rub it in well so it doesn't leave a residue. Leftover brewed tea (at room temperature) can also be used on wood furniture.

Keep Wood Wonderful

Preserve the beauty of wood by rubbing the surface with boiled linseed oil. Wipe away the excess with a soft cloth.

Prevent Sun Stroke on Wood Furniture

Don't keep your good wood furniture in direct sunlight, especially during the hot summer. It damages the finish and can bleach the wood.

Prevent Polish Buildup

Excess polish can build up and leave a dull finish on wooden furniture. To remove it, mix together 2 tablespoons white vinegar and 2 tablespoons water. Apply to the surface and wipe off at once. Alternatively, cornstarch will also do the trick: Sprinkle a little on the furniture and polish with a soft cloth.

Mask Scratches in Wood Furniture

If you notice a scratch, try this crafty (and delicious!) solution. Find a nut that matches the color of the wood; the most common types for this purpose are pecans, walnuts, and hazelnuts. Rub the scratched area gently with the broken edges of the nuts—using the insides, not the shells. When you're all done, enjoy a snack break.

Coffee Stains to the Rescue

Cover up scratches in wood furniture or floors with coffee! Just brew a very strong pot, and then use a cotton ball or rag to apply the coffee over the scratch. It works as a stain, and the scratch will blend in with the floor in no time!

Another Prescription for Scratches

Repair scratches in your wood furniture with shoe polish. A crayon also works. Just find a color that's a close match to the wood, then rub the crayon or polish into the scratch. Wipe off any excess wax with a credit card edge, then buff with a cotton cloth.

Who Knew? Readers' Favorite

You've probably seen those little cushions with the sticky material on the back that can be placed on the bottom of furniture legs or the backs of picture frames to keep them from scratching floors and walls. Rather than spending the money for these expensive items, buy cushions for corns and bunions instead! As long as they aren't medicated, they're the exact same thing, and usually much cheaper.

Say "Vamoose" to Water Stains on Wood

Does your wood furniture have white rings left from wet glasses? Remove them with a mixture of 2 tablespoons corn oil and enough salt to make a paste. Apply the paste to the rings and let stand for at least one hour before rubbing the area gently. If the finish on your furniture is very delicate, you can substitute baking soda for the salt (it's less abrasive). If neither of those mixtures works, give mayonnaise a shot: Rub a tiny bit (½ teaspoon) on the ring with a paper towel and let it sit overnight. In the morning, just wipe with a damp cloth and the ring should be gone! Cover with furniture polish to get the shine back.

Slipcover Secret

When washing a slipcover for a couch or chair, you should put it back on your furniture while the cover is still damp. Not only will the slipcover be easier to get on, but it won't need to be ironed. It will help keep it from shrinking, too!

A Clean Home for Your Fish

The easiest way to clean a fish bowl is to wipe the inside with a cloth soaked in white vinegar, which will help remove mineral deposits. Just make sure you rinse the bowl thoroughly before putting your fish back in.

Cure for Cat Clawing

Here's something you probably didn't know: Cats hate hot sauce. So if you can't get your cat to stop clawing at your woodwork, just rub in a little hot sauce, buff it thoroughly, and your cat will stay clear.

Easily Clean Up Pet Hair

Pet hair all over the house? The easiest way to clean it up is to rub the furniture, carpet, or any other shedding victim (including the pet himself!) with a fresh dryer sheet.

Sponge Solution

If you don't have a lint roller and just realized your couch is absolutely covered in pet hair, use a clean, dry kitchen sponge instead. Just run it slowly across the couch and the fur will cling to it!

Who Knew? Readers' Favorite

The easiest way to keep your dog or cat off of your good furniture when you're out is to place a piece of aluminum foil on it. They hate the feeling under their paws and will stay away.

Another Quick Pet Hair Remover

Uh-oh, guests are on their way and you've just realized that your beloved cat has made a cat-fur nest all over your couch. For a quick and easy way to remove pet hair from furniture, turn to your rubber dishwashing gloves. Just slip them on, then rub the offending furniture with them. The hair will stick to the gloves and you can quickly throw it away.

Sponge Bath for Soot Marks

If your beautiful candle is staining your walls with black soot marks, don't try to scrub them away—that'll only make more of a mess. Instead, remove those unsightly spots by sponging them with rubbing alcohol.

Homemade Air Fresheners

You don't have to spend hard-earned cash to keep your house smelling nice. Freshen it up with these crafty odor-fighting tricks.

✦ Make a great homemade air freshener with an orange: Just cut the orange in half, remove the pulp, and fill with salt. It's effective, easy—and cheap!

✦ If you're not a great baker, but love the smell of fresh baked goods, try this trick: Dab a few drops of vanilla extract on a cool light bulb, then turn it on. When it heats up, the smell will fill the room.

✦ To keep the house smelling fresh during the dog days of summer, tape fabric softener sheets onto your air conditioner filter under the grate. Not only will they exude a lovely smell, but they'll also make the filter last longer.

Refresh Potpourri

If your favorite potpourri loses its scent, it's easy to revive—with vodka. Just pour a little vodka into a spray bottle and spritz the potpourri, mixing it up so each piece is saturated.

Stop Smoky Smells

Did you know that a bowl of sliced apples will remove the smell of cigarette smoke in an enclosed space? The next time you have a smoky party, cut up some apples and leave them around the house before you go to bed.

Vacuum Off Odors

To rid your house of pet, cooking, or other smells, add a cotton ball soaked in vanilla or lavender oil to your vacuum cleaner bag, and vacuum away. It's a great way to rid your home of an offensive odor by creating a nice scent instead.

Who Knew? Readers' Favorite

Water can collect in umbrella stands. Prevent this by cutting a large sponge to fit in the bottom. Remove it and wring it out as necessary.

Clean Up Sooty Bricks with Cola

Try an old masonry trick to brighten up soot-stained brick. Mix a can of cola with 3½ fluid ounces all-purpose household cleaner and 7 pints water in a bucket. Sponge onto sooty bricks and leave for 15 minutes. Loosen the soot by scrubbing with a stiff-bristled brush. Sponge with clean water. For a stronger solution, add more cola.

Candle Scandal

Removing candle wax from your wood floors is easy if you soften the wax first with a blow dryer, then peel off. Wipe any excess with a paper towel, and then clean with a mixture of half white vinegar and half water.

Candle Cleaning

If you have some beautiful candles that have begun to get dusty, cleaning them is easy. Just ball up some old pantyhose and rub them down. Its microfiber is perfect for picking up the dirt without harming your candle.

Drop a Glass? Sacrifice a Sandwich.

If your post-party cleanup involves collecting the shattered remains of Champagne glasses—or if you've merely dropped a glass on the floor—try out this crafty tip. Dampen a piece of white bread, and dab it on the glass fragments. It's much more effective than using a broom.

Get Gleaming Wood Floors

There's no need to buy a special cleaner for your wood floors. Simply mix equal parts vegetable oil and white vinegar in a spray bottle, and apply. Then shine with a clean cloth until the solution is gone.

A Recipe for Clean Wood

Save money on wood cleaners by making your own at home. It's simple: Just combine the juice of one lemon with 2 cups vegetable or olive oil. Use it just like you would use a store-bought cleaner!

Patch Up Carpet Burns

Here's how to eliminate cigarette burns in your carpet: First, cut away the burn mark. Then, cut a bit of carpet from an area that's covered by a piece of furniture (e.g., under a couch), and glue it carefully over the burnt spot. Finally, smack the person who dropped the ashes.

Salt Does the Trick on Carpet Stains

If you spill red wine or anything else with a bright pigment on your carpet, pour salt on the area as soon as possible and watch it absorb the wine almost instantly. Wait until it dries, then vacuum it up. Salt tends to provide a special capillary attraction that will work for most liquids. Baking soda, with its high sodium content, works with wine, too. Salt also works on mud stains.

Remove Pen Marks from Leather

If your kid has decided to write a novel on your favorite leather chair, don't panic. Just blot the stain with milk until the ink disappears, then wipe it clean with a damp sponge. You can also try using egg whites.

Crayon Cleanup

Have your little Picassos taken to the walls with their crayon masterpieces? Don't fret! A great way to clean off the Crayola is by using a car paste wax: Apply it to the affected area, let it sink in and soften the crayon, then buff it off. Wipe the wall with an all-purpose cleaner and it'll look like new. If you child has drawn on your furniture with crayon, run the warm air from a hair dryer over the marks. The heat will melt the waxy marks a bit, making them easy to remove.

Spruce Up Satin and Gloss Finishes

Clean painted walls with a solution made of 4 fluid ounces white vinegar, 1 ounce washing soda, and 1 pint water. Or mix 7 ounces ammonia, 1 teaspoon dish soap, and 7 pints water.

Breathe Easy

Purify the air without an air filter by buying potted plants that naturally clean your air. Some good choices are rubber trees, corn plants, bamboo palm, ficus, mums, gerbera daisies, English ivy, peace lily, and philodendrons.

There Really Is a Use for Dryer Lint!

Use dryer lint to prevent dirt from falling out of your potted houseplants when you water them: Place some dryer lint in the pots so it covers the holes. The water will drain out, but the dirt will stay in!

Shinier, Prettier Plants

If your houseplants are dusty, gently wipe the leaves with a soft cloth and a damp sponge. If you want your plants' leaves to really shine, rub them (gently!) with a cotton ball dipped in either mayonnaise, diluted mineral oil, or a solution of half baking soda and half water. Wipe off any excess with a soft cloth.

Got Stale Milk? Use It!

Stale milk will do a great job of cleaning plant leaves. The protein in milk called "casein" has a mild cleansing effect on the plant cell walls.

Clay Flowerpot Caveat

Never place a clay pot on wooden furniture, unless you use a coaster. Clay is porous, so water will seep through and possibly damage the wood finish.

Protect Your Soil (and Your Shirt!)

To keep mud from spattering when you water plants in window boxes, top the soil with a half-inch layer of gravel. Do the same for outdoor plants to prevent mud bombs during heavy rainfalls.

Window Washing 101

If the sun is shining on your windows, wait until they are in the shade to wash them. When they dry too fast, they tend to streak.

What Works on Your Windshield, Works on Your Windows

For light window cleaning, pick up a gallon of windshield washer fluid for less than a dollar. Although it's not as pungent as Windex, it'll spiff up spotty glass for less money.

Grease Up Your Windows

Don't pull a muscle trying to shove open a stuck window. Windows will open and close more easily if you occasionally rub a bar of soap across the track.

Dusting Your Blinds

Is there any chore more annoying than dusting your Venetian blinds? Luckily, you don't have to buy one of those "blinds cleaners" found in stores. Instead, use bread crusts. Just hold a piece of crust around each slat, then run it along the length of the blinds. An old paintbrush will also do the trick, or use the brush attachment on your vacuum cleaner.

Don't Let Dust Find Your Blinds

Dusting the blinds is always a pain, so after you're done make sure you won't have to do it for a while: Spray Static Guard (usually used for clothing) onto your blinds to repel dust!

Quickly Clean Mini-Blinds

Give mini blinds a good clean by simply throwing them in a bathtub filled with water and white vinegar, or your favorite cleanser. Just give them a good shake, and hang them up wet. There may be a few streaks once they've air-dried, but they're nearly impossible to spot.

Cleaning Aluminum Blinds

Aluminum blinds are great for keeping out light, but they can be hard to clean! The easiest way to clean smudges is with a pencil eraser. Dust will come off with a few swipes of a fabric softener sheet.

For Cleaner Shades

Stubborn smudges and stains on your window shades? Lay the shades on a table or countertop and rub the spots with an art-gum eraser (which can be found at art- or office-supply stores). It will take the smudges away!

If it feels like the minute you're done dusting your glass or coffee tables you have a layer of dust covering them again, use fabric softener for a different purpose. Mix a few teaspoons in a spray bottle of water and wipe the glass surface with it. Buff with soft, dry towel, and it will keep dust away.

Clean Those Piano Keys

Don't get upset if you find your toddler wiping the piano keys with mayonnaise. It's actually a great, gentle way to get them clean. (Just make sure she doesn't move on to the sofa!)

Diaper Wipe Double-Duty

For an effective alternative to wood cleaners and polishes, use baby wipes to whip your wood furniture and paneling into shape.

No Need for Febreze

Sprinkle rugs, the couch, and upholstered chairs with baking soda before you vacuum. Give it an hour to work its magic and go to work. It will keep rugs and furniture cleaner and fresher over the long haul.

In a Minute

Alcohol wipes will easily clean off any sticky substances on your phone, stereo, or computer (surface only). This is an easy chore to tackle on commercial breaks or whenever you only have a minute.

Just Suck It Up

Trying to clean super-small spaces around the house? Don't buy additional vacuum equipment if your attachments are too big. Instead, grab a straw—preferably one of those giant straws from a fast-food chain—and insert part of it into the smallest attachment you have. Tape it in place, and you'll be able to suck up dirt and dust in the tiniest of spaces.

Clean Out the Cobwebs

Here's an easy way to clean cobwebs from corners: Cover the head of your mop or broom with a pillowcase dampened with water, vinegar, or your preferred cleaning solutions, then secure it with a rubber band and go to it.

Be a Bag Lady

When vacuuming your home, it's always annoying to find bits and pieces that are too big for your vacuum. Instead of ending up with all those icky bits in your hand, tie a plastic grocery bag to your belt loop. That way, you'll have a portable garbage can with you at all times!

Who Knew? Readers' Favorite

When sliding heavy furniture across a wooden floor, put socks on the legs. It will make for a much smoother ride and you won't scratch the floors.

Sliding Doors

If your sliding glass door is sticking, simply spray the tracks with furniture polish. It will remove dirt and give the tracks the lubrication they need to keep the door moving smoothly.

Mending Marker Mishaps

If your kids (or you) get a permanent-marker stain on furniture or the floor, don't despair! There may be hope in the form of rubbing alcohol. Test an inconspicuous area first to make sure it won't harm the finish, then apply directly to the stain with a rag or paper towel. Rub until it disappears, then wipe with a clean cloth moistened with water.

Need More Storage Space?

If your living room sofa has a skirt that reaches the floor, you have storage space you didn't even know about. Underneath the sofa is a great place to store a bin of wrapping paper and accessories, old photo albums, and other skinny items you reach for often.

The Key to Finding Keys

Always misplacing your keys around the house? Tie a brightly-colored ribbon to your keychain. It'll be much easier to spot.

Gum? Gone!

Here's another way to get gum out of fabric or upholstery (taught to me by my great aunt). Beat an egg white, rub or brush it into the gum, and let it sit for up to a half an hour, then wipe off. The egg white breaks down the gum and makes it easy to remove.

Wonder Bread

If you have a precious oil painting in your home, it's important to keep it clean without damaging it. Our surprising cleaning tool of choice is a piece of white bread! White bread has the perfect amount of moisture to pick up dust easily, without being so wet that it will ruin your painting.

Easy Electronics Cleaner

If your MP3 player has seen better days, give it a quick clean. Our favorite method? A bit of rubbing alcohol or astringent on a clean make-up sponge. Just rub it over the player and it will look as good as new!

Citrus for Ceramic

The easiest way to clean ceramic figurines is to rub them with the cut side of a lemon wedge. Leave the lemon juice on for 15 minutes, then polish up with a soft, dry cloth.

The Answer for Artificial Flowers

To clean silk flowers, try blowing off the dust with a hairdryer set on cool. You can also put the flowers in a paper bag, add some uncooked rice, and shake. The dirt will transfer to the rice. You can also clean silk flowers easily by placing them "bloom" end down, in a plastic bag with 2 tablespoons salt. Hold onto the stems, close the bag, then shake vigorously. The salt will attract the dust, leaving your flowers looking as good as the real thing!

CHAPTER 2

The Kitchen and Dining Room

The Clean Stove Trick

Save on household cleaners by keeping your stove neater. How? When cooking, cover unused burners with a baking sheet or pizza pans. The pans will catch all the splatter, and they're easy to just stick in the dishwasher afterward!

A "Hair"-brained Idea

If you're having trouble cleaning the baked-on grease and grime on your range's hood or other areas around your stove, don't resort to harsh commercial cleaners. Instead, warm it up by blasting it with your hair dryer. Once the dirt is warm, it will wipe right off with a damp cloth.

Sticky Trick

To get a pantry even your mother-in-law won't criticize, store honey and other bottles with sticky drip-potential in little bowls or all together in a baking pan that you can easily take out, wash, and replace.

Bag the Bags

With so many free plastic bags for the taking at drugstores and supermarkets, we never buy garbage bags. Instead, we use the smaller bags for all of our trash cans, and make it even easier for ourselves by affixing two self-adhesive plastic hooks upside-down on the outside of the bin. These hooks easily hold the handles, so the bags won't slip down inside.

Clean a Dusty Dust Mop

Always clean dust mops after using them. To avoid making a dust cloud, cover a dry dust mop with a damp paper bag before you shake it out. If your mop has a removable head, put it in a large mesh lingerie bag and toss it into the washer.

Naturally Deodorize Garbage Cans

Wash and deodorize trashcans with a solution of 1 teaspoon lemon juice mixed with 1 quart water. Sprinkling baking soda into the base of every garbage bag will also help keep odors at bay.

Eau de Trash?

It's easy to keep your trashcans from stinking up your home. We like to rip out those perfume strips from magazines and place one at the bottom of every trashcan throughout the house. Or try dryer sheets: They make your clothes smell fresh and wonderful, so they'll work miracles in stinky garbage pails too.

Who Knew? Readers' Favorite

There's no need to throw out your stinky old sponges. Just soak them in cold salt water, rinse, and they're good to use again.

Stretch the Life of Your Sponge

To make your kitchen sponges and brushes last longer, wash them once a week in the utensil compartment of your dishwasher with a load of dishes. This will ward off any bacteria and mildew.

Odor Eaters

All sorts of nasty odors lurk in the kitchen, whether it's expired food, a lingering trash bag, or a mix of flavors still hanging around after a meal. Next time you've got a persistent stink, try out one of these quickie odor-killing tips.

- ✦ Keep a few washed charcoal briquettes in a shallow dish on top of the refrigerator.

- ✦ To eliminate refrigerator odors, leave a small cup of fresh coffee grounds on two shelves.

- ✦ Deep-fry a small amount of cinnamon to chase all odors from your home.

Make Your Home Smell Sugar-and-Spice Nice

For a great DIY home fragrance, simmer apple cider with a cinnamon stick and a few whole cloves. Also add a bit of orange peel if you like. Isn't this what Martha Stewart smells like?

Freshen Up the Garbage Disposal

Keep your garbage disposal running at its best with this simple once-a-month trick: Grind about a dozen ice cubes made from white vinegar. The ice sharpens the blades while the vinegar deodorizes the drain.

Saline Solution

Salt will clear out the gunk that collects in the garbage disposal and the smell that goes along with it. Pour a few spoonfuls in and flush with cold water, then run the disposal.

Quick Fix for a Stinky Microwave

Microwave odors? Cut a lemon in quarters and put it in a bowl of water, then put in the microwave on high for two minutes.

Nuke the Popcorn Smell

Too bad you didn't know about this back in college when you made popcorn in the dorm lounge. A tea bag in water (even a used one) placed in the microwave for a minute is all you need to eliminate that unidentified stale smell in there.

Orange Oven

A self-cleaning oven can leave an odor after it's done its work. Eliminate the lingering smell by turning down the oven to 350°F when it's finished, then putting orange peels on a baking sheet inside. Cook the peels for a half an hour, and not only will the oven smell fresh, but your whole kitchen will, too!

Admit It, Your Fridge Sometimes Smells

Besides baking soda, a number of other foods are capable of removing odors. Pour a little vanilla extract into a bottle cap and set in the refrigerator to absorb odors. One of the best ways to eliminate odors is to hollow out a grapefruit or orange, fill it with salt, and place in the back of the fridge. Leave it there until the salt gets completely damp, and then throw the whole thing out and replace.

Time to Clean Out Your Refrigerator?

When cleaning your refrigerator, don't use chemicals that can linger on your food and produce nasty odors. After emptying the fridge, simply dissolve a cup of salt in a gallon of hot water and wipe away. Squeeze in the juice of a lemon for a nice scent.

Spruce Up Your Stainless Steel Sink

Nothing makes a kitchen look better than a shiny kitchen sink, and luckily, there are a lot of ways to clean and shine stainless steel!

✦ Club soda is a terrific way to clean stainless steel sinks, dishwashers, ranges, and other appliances.

The least expensive club soda works just as well as the pricey brands; and flat club soda works, too. Add a little flour for really stubborn stains.

✦ You've scrubbed it twice, but you can't seem to get those water spots out of your stainless steel sink! The solution? A little white vinegar. Just rub it into the spots and they'll disappear.

✦ Stainless steel can also be quickly and easily cleaned with vodka. Place a little on a sponge or paper towel and wipe. Your faucet, sink, and other stainless steel will soon be sparkling again, so pour yourself a little glass to celebrate!

✦ Instead of using a rag or a paper towel, use newspaper, which will get it even shinier. A tougher option is aluminum foil. Just crumple it up, and scour with the shiny side.

✦ For a spectacularly shiny finish on a stainless steel or aluminum sink, rub a liberal amount of baking soda in a circular motion all over its surface with a damp sponge.

✦ For the shiniest sink you've ever seen, finish off your cleaning session by buffing the sink with a touch of baby oil on a soft cloth.

Oven Cleaning Made Easy

A simple way to clean your oven is to place an oven-safe pot or bowl filled with water inside. Heat on 450°F for 20 minutes to loosen dirt and grease with the steam. Once your oven is cool, wipe off the condensation and the grease will come with it. After you're done, make a paste of water and baking soda and smear it on any enamel. The paste will dry into a protective layer that will absorb grease as you cook.

Not a Fan of Oven Fans?

Oven fans are magnets for grease. The simplest way to clean the resulting mess is to pop out the fan filter, then run it through your dishwasher on the top shelf.

Who Knew? Readers' Favorite

To clean your electric can opener, run a piece of paper towel or waxed paper through it. This will pick up the grease and some of the gunk.

Clean Your Coffee Maker

For the best tasting coffee, make sure to clean your coffee maker regularly. Just add several tablespoons of baking soda to your pot, fill it with water, and then run your coffee maker as usual. It's a good idea to run it again with just water. You can also use a denture-cleaning tablet instead of baking soda.

Now Clean Your Coffee Grinder!

Even your coffee grinder needs a good cleaning every now and then, and uncooked rice can do the job. Simply mill a handful of rice as you normally do to your coffee beans. The chopped rice cleans out the stuck coffee grounds and oils, and absorbs stale odors to boot. Afterwards, throw away the rice, wipe the grinder clean…and brew fresh coffee.

Lube Up Your Blender

To keep your blender and mixer in top working order, be sure to lubricate all moving parts every three months with a very light coating of mineral oil (not vegetable oil).

Getting Rid of Counter Stains

Stubborn stains can be removed from your countertop by applying a baking soda paste and rubbing with a warm, damp cloth. If the stain still remains, consider using a drop or two of bleach, but be careful—bleach can fade your countertop along with the stain!

Cease Grease!

Forget about buying those expensive stove cleaners to get rid of cooked-on grease stains. Just wet the stains with vinegar and cover with baking soda. After watching the fun foaming reaction, wipe with a damp sponge and buff with a dry, clean cloth.

Make a Gross Chore Easier

Eventually, it's time for one our least-favorite cleaning chores: cleaning the top of the fridge (vinegar usually does the trick). After you finish, place an old placemat on top. When it gets gross, either replace it or throw it in the washing machine for a quick clean.

Who Knew? Readers' Favorite

Ammonia is a no-nonsense cleaning essential for your kitchen. To clean a really greasy pan, add a few drops of ammonia to your soapsuds.

Great All-Purpose Cleaner

For a perfect all-purpose cleaner, mix together 1 gallon hot water, 3½ fluid ounces ammonia, 3½ fluid ounces white vinegar, and 7 ounces (1¼ cups) baking soda. Store in a tightly sealed bottle and use on glass, silver, and countertops.

Perk Up Your Floor

If you have black scuffmarks on your linoleum or vinyl flooring, you can remove them with a bit of white (non-gel) toothpaste. Simply rub the toothpaste over the scuff vigorously until it disappears.

A No. 2 Will Do

The easiest way to remove black scuffmarks from a vinyl floor? Just use a pencil eraser! It really works.

Mopping Up

If you own a mop that requires replacement cloths, substitute baby wipes instead of buying packs of those pricey cloths. Rinse the wipes off before using, and they'll get your floors just as clean. Sturdy paper towels are another solid option for ready mops—just rip small holes in the towel so the cleaning liquid still sprays through the mop.

No More Tears!

The secret to shiny laminated floors is baby shampoo. Just mix a spoonful with a gallon of warm water and mop as usual!

A Two-for-One Deal

You can save cash and storage space with this quick-fix cleaning alternative: Use a small, plastic garbage can as your mop bucket and you'll not only clean the can, but you'll never have to buy a bucket!

Make Your Ceramic Floors Gleam

There are tons of commercial cleaning products for ceramic or vinyl floors, but they're costly, toxic, and liable to irritate your skin. Luckily, they can be easily replaced with this safe, effective homemade alternative: Combine 1 cup white vinegar and 1 gallon warm water, and mop till those floors sparkle.

If your vinyl tile has loosened, simply put it back in its original place. Lay a piece of aluminum foil on top, and run a hot iron over it. In no time at all, the glue will begin to adhere. Then just stack a few books on top of the tile until the glue hardens again.

Shiny Chrome

What is chrome for, if not to be shiny? To bring back dull chrome fixtures, dampen them, then rub them with newspaper. You can also shine them up with a paste of vinegar and cream of tartar.

For the Best Potholders

Your potholders don't have to look stained and dirty. Wash frequently, and after each time you wash them, spray them with starch. Spray starch repels grease, so your potholders will stay unstained.

Conserve Steel Wool Pads

It's easy to keep your wet, soaped steel wool pads from rusting: Just wrap them in aluminum foil and store in your freezer. But before you do, cut them in half. It's economical, because they won't wear out as fast, and the frozen half will stay rust-free. And as a bonus, it's a great way to sharpen your scissors.

Handle with Care

If you've ever experienced the frustration of breaking a dish while washing it, you'll love this tip! Prevent breakages by lining your sink with a towel or rubber mat before washing.

Stuck-On Substances

If you've given up hope of ever removing stuck-on food from your pots and pans, help is on the way—in the form of a fabric softener sheet! Just cover the stain with hot water, and float a fabric softener sheet in it. Leave overnight, and in the morning, the food should wipe off easily.

Who Knew? Readers' Favorite

There's no need to buy expensive dishwashing liquid. Buy the cheapest brand you can find, then add a few tablespoons of white vinegar to the water while you're washing, and your dishes will shine. The same is true for dishwashers—just buy the least expensive detergent, and add some white vinegar to the machine. Vinegar will remove spots from glass in a flash.

Cast Iron Cure

The best way to clean cast iron pans is to cover any stain with a paste of cream of tartar and white vinegar. Apply liberally, let it sit, then scrub with a damp, soft cloth.

What if Your Nonstick Pan Sticks?

For the most part, coated pots and pans are easy to keep clean, but they do stain, and over time grease and oil may build up. This will adversely affect the efficiency of the nonstick surface, so it's important to clean and re-season any stained areas. To do so, simply mix 1 cup water, 2 tablespoons baking soda, and ½ cup white vinegar in the pot, set on the stove, and boil for 10 minutes. Wash the pot as usual, then rub vegetable oil on the surface to re-season it.

Burnt Food Be Gone

Here's another great way to remove burnt food from pans. Sprinkle baking soda, salt, and dishwasher detergent over the crusty bits, then cover with water and boil for a half an hour. Even the toughest baked-on food will wipe off easily.

For a Sparkling Coffee Pot

To remove coffee stains from inside a glass coffee pot, add 1 tablespoon water, 4 teaspoons salt, and 1 cup crushed ice. Gently swirl until it is clean, then rinse thoroughly. (Just make sure the coffee pot is at room temperature before cleaning.)

Get Rid of a Smelly Thermos

The easiest way to remove smells and stains from a thermos is by filling it with hot water and ½ cup baking soda, then letting it sit overnight. In the morning, just rinse well, and it should be good as new! Next time, place a few whole cloves or a teaspoon of salt inside before closing it up.

Remove Stubborn Stains

Get rid of really tough stains on your metal and ceramic pots, pans, mugs, and dishes by filling them with boiling water and adding a denture tablet. Let it sit overnight, and the stain should disappear.

This Cup Has Seen a Lot of Coffee!

If the inside of your coffee cup is stained from coffee or tea, it's not too late to get it to look like new. Mix a paste of coarse salt (or baking soda) and water. Scrub the mug with this, then rinse well.

Who Knew? Readers' Favorite

Cleaning a cheese grater will never be a problem if you grate a small piece of raw potato before trying to wash it out. Sometimes an old toothbrush also comes in handy for cleaning graters.

Crystal Clean

Use a paste of lemon juice and baking powder to remove small stains from crystal. Treat tougher stains by placing 2 teaspoons uncooked rice inside the crystal piece, adding water, and swirling. The small amount of abrasive action from the rice will remove the stains—perfect for vases with narrow necks.

Camouflage a Crack in Your China

Antique dealers use this trick to hide hairline cracks on china plates and cups. Simmer the piece in milk for 45 minutes. Casein, a milk protein, may fill in the crack, depending on its size. If your china is old or fragile, though, this could backfire—heat can cause pieces to expand and crack.

Nix the Nicks

Buff away a nick on the rim of a glass or your china with an emery board. Don't use a nail file or sandpaper; both are too coarse and will scratch the glass.

Everything You Need to Know to Care for Your Silver

Even if you didn't get it as a wedding present, you probably have silver cutlery that has been passed down from generation to generation. This beautiful silverware is always a nice treat on a special occasion. But as you've probably discovered, silver will eventually tarnish if exposed to air for an extended period of time, turning duller and darker as time goes on. However, you can keep your silver shiny and beautiful by polishing and storing it wisely.

✦ Never combine silver and stainless steel cutlery in the dishwasher—the silver will turn black. Any contact with dishwasher detergent will also result in black spots. Remove silver cutlery from the dishwasher immediately after the cycle ends, and dry at once to avoid stains and pitting.

✦ Sulfur compounds in the air cause silver to tarnish; to prevent this, store your silver in airtight containers, or wrap it in tarnish-proof cloths or papers. (Never wrap silver in plastic food wrap. It will keep air away, but it can also cause stains and corrosion.)

✦ If your silver does develop spots, dissolve a little salt in lemon juice, then dip a soft cloth into the mixture and rub it onto the cutlery. Rinse in warm water and finish by buffing to a shine with a chamois.

✦ You can also rub off tarnish with toothpaste. Place some white (non-gel) toothpaste on a soft cloth and use it to rub solid silver (not silver plate). Then rinse it off gently. Don't use whitening toothpaste—it can damage the surface.

✦ To remove tarnish from the tines of a fork, coat a piece of cotton string with toothpaste and run it between the tines.

✦ Polishing silver is never a neat chore, but an old sock can make it easier. Slip the sock over your hand; use one side to apply the polish and the other to buff it out.

✦ If you have large silver items that are not used with food, consider having them lacquered by a jeweler to prevent tarnishing. Candelabras, vases, and trophies are good candidates for this treatment.

✦ If you place a small piece of chalk in a silver chest, it will absorb moisture and slow tarnishing. Calcium carbonate (i.e., chalk) absorbs moisture from the air very slowly. Break up the chalk and expose the rough surface for the best results.

Who Knew? Readers' Favorite

Believe it or not, a great way to polish copper is to rub it with ketchup and let it stand for an hour. Rinse off the ketchup with hot water, then buff to an incredible shine.

Lemon for Brass and Copper

One of the best cleaners for brass and copper is a simple lemon! Cut a lemon in half, sprinkle the cut side with salt, and rub over the surface you're cleaning. Rinse with cold water and watch it shine.

For Tablecloth Blunders

If you spill wine on a tablecloth, blot up as much as you can as soon as you can with a cloth, then sponge with cool water. Wash immediately. If the fabric is not machine washable, cover the stain with a small cloth dampened with a solution of detergent, water, and vinegar, then rinse. Get the cloth to the drycleaner as soon as you can.

Keep Candleholders Clean

To prevent wax from sticking to a candleholder, rub a thin coat of olive oil on the base of the holder before lighting the candle. If your holder already has some wax buildup, mix olive oil with dish soap to clean it out.

Candlestick Fit

Most taper candles won't fit perfectly into standard candlesticks, so you'll have to do a little work to ensure your candle fits securely. (Do not light the candle and melt wax into the base— this is messy and dangerous!) First, try placing the candle base under hot water; this softens the wax and allows it to mold to its new surroundings. If this doesn't do the trick, whittle down the wax around the base of the candle with a paring knife, checking the fit as you go. Stop when you get it narrow enough to fit the holder. Apply wax adhesive around the base of the candle, and place it in the candlestick.

Who Knew? Readers' Favorite

Accidentally drip candle wax on a tablecloth? Remove it by rubbing with an ice cube and then scraping with a dull knife. Another way to remove candle wax from a tablecloth or other fabric is to place some brown paper (not newspaper) over the top and iron it on a low heat. The wax will transfer to the paper!

Cardboard Tubes for Tapers

Here's a great way to store tapered candles: Use paper towel tubes to protect them. Just wrap two candles at a time in tissue paper, then slip them into the cardboard tube. Keep tubes together with rubber bands if necessary.

Try This Tip and Call Us in the Morning

When your toddler spills your iced tea, and you don't want to waste a bunch of paper towels mopping it up, use pages ripped from last year's phone book instead. The thin (free!) pages are perfect for minor drips and spills.

A Tidy Toaster Oven

How will you get the toast just right if you can't see through the toaster oven window? Mix four parts white vinegar with four parts hydrogen peroxide and two parts dishwashing soap. You can clean directly with paper towels or else spray on first, let it go to work, and wipe clean an hour or so later.

Mended Mug

Broke a mug? Pour sand into the bottom of a little tray (Tupperware will do) to hold broken china while you line the edge with glue and stick the other piece (also lined with glue) on top. Leave the repaired cup balanced on its side to dry so the break won't have to fight gravity before the glue takes hold.

De-Gunk Your Griddler

Here's the easiest way we've found to clean a countertop grill: Unplug the grill, and put a wet paper towel inside (with the lid closed) for 10 minutes. The grease loosens up and is easy to clean off.

A Pint-Sized Space Saver

Those plastic baskets that berries come in are perfect for small items in your dishwasher. Just wedge in place and throw bottle tops, lids, and small utensils inside.

Who Knew? Readers' Favorite

You know you're not supposed to use "regular" dishwashing liquid in your dishwasher, but...what do you do when you're out of powdered detergent and company is on its way? The truth is, you can use some of the liquid kind—use only a few drops, and fill the rest of the detergent container with baking soda. It will stop the soap from producing too many suds.

For Clean Cabinet Shelves

Instead of using contact paper on your kitchen shelves, use some peel-and-stick vinyl floor tiles (cut to size if necessary). They're super easy to clean, and they're usually cheaper, too—some stores will even give you a free sample.

Liquor Is Quicker

If you're having trouble removing a pesky label, just soak the spot in rubbing alcohol. Leave on for up to a minute, then wipe right off. Don't have any rubbing alcohol? The kind of alcohol you drink—like vodka, rum, or gin—works well, too.

Getting Rid of Grease

When flushing grease down the drain, don't use hot water (like many of us were taught). The grease coats the pipes, cools, and will collect bits of debris. Instead, use cold water. It will make sure the grease solidifies in chunks that will easily get flushed through the pipes. Better yet, empty your grease into a soda can and throw it away!

Thrifty Kitchen Storage

Save space by reusing an empty six-pack holder to store aluminum foil, plastic wrap, waxed paper, and other boxes of wrap. Stand the long boxes on their ends, insert them into the plastic rings, and put them under your sink. This'll free up a valuable kitchen drawer.

A Pantry Pointer

Keep packets of sauces and gravies in one easy-to-manage spot in your pantry—we suggest using a child's empty shoebox! Stand the envelopes upright in the box, so the labels are easy to read, and the shoebox should fit perfectly on a shelf in your pantry.

Free Up Shelf Space with Hanging Cup Storage

Under-the-shelf cup holders are a clever, super-efficient way to save space in your kitchen. You can buy a slip-on cup holder for less than $10, no tools required. You'll save tons of shelf space for plates and bowls, while your cups, mugs, glasses, and cooking utensils stay out of the way.

A System for All Those Plastic Lids

Are plastic lids taking over your kitchen? We feel your pain, and can offer a solution: Store a dish drainer in your cabinet, and file the lids on their sides in size order. You'll find the lid you need in seconds, and your kitchen will seem much more organized.

Who Knew? Readers' Favorite

Plastic grocery bags have a way of multiplying and taking over kitchen drawers. A space-saving solution is to stuff all of them into an empty tissue box. You'll be amazed how many fit, and you can easily remove them one at a time when you need to.

Another Use for Cardboard Tubes

Instead of trashing cardboard tubes from paper towels or toilet paper, create a cozy storage container for all those stray plastic grocery bags. Stuff the plastic bags inside, one by one, until the tubes are full. Then you can tie several tubes together with a rubber band, and store them in a drawer or on a closet shelf.

CHAPTER 3

The
Bathroom

Bathroom Quick Clean

If you can only clean one room before guests arrive, make it the bathroom. It's the only room where your guests will be alone (and possibly snooping around!), and a dirty bathroom is more unappealing than a cluttered living room. Here's how to do it in two minutes or less: Just apply a touch of baby shampoo to a wet sponge and wipe down your sink, fixtures, tiles, and bathtub. It cuts through oily residue, and smells good, too.

Steam Out a Nasty Bathroom

If you've let the bathroom get so dirty that it now resembles a gas station restroom, turn on the hot water in the shower for 10 minutes with the door closed. The steam will loosen the buildup of mildew and mold. Then get in there and clean.

Who Knew? Readers' Favorite

Looking for an easy mildew remover? Simply scrub the affected area with an old, damp toothbrush sprinkled with baking soda.

Another Use for Vodka!

For a great mold and mildew fighter, try vodka! It works especially well on the caulking around your tub. Just spray on, leave for 10 minutes, and wipe clean.

Ever-Useful Alcohol

Isopropyl alcohol, which is available at most supermarkets and drugstores, is a cheap and effective disinfectant. But it also belongs in your bathroom cabinet for more than just first-aid purposes. Use it, mixed with equal parts water, to clean the bathtub caulking and shine chrome and glass.

Clogged Showerhead?

Removing mineral deposits from a showerhead without harsh chemicals is easy. Just unscrew it and submerge in white vinegar overnight, and the clogs will disappear. It you can't unscrew it, fill a small, sturdy bag with vinegar and attach to the showerhead with duct tape. You can also brush the showerhead with vinegar using an old toothbrush to make it sparkle. To clean the screen in your showerhead, wash it with water with a dash of dishwashing liquid added.

Flour Fix

If your chrome faucets are less than sparkly, try rubbing them with flour. Rinse, then buff with a soft cloth, and they'll really shine. Vinegar also works well for cleaning chrome.

Who Knew? Readers' Favorite

Believe it or not, toothpaste makes a great polish for your faucets. Just rub on and buff off with soft cloth. The white, non-gel variety works best.

Mirror Miracle

Make your mirrors shine with a solution of equal parts vinegar and water. Use old newspapers to wipe the surface of mirrors with the mix, then add extra shine by rubbing with a clean dry-erase or blackboard eraser.

Shined to a "Tea"

Here's an all-natural way to clean your mirror that will also give a spotless shine: Wipe the mirror with a clean cloth dipped in strong, cool tea. Buff with a dry cloth and you're done!

Get Rid of Copper Stains

Removing blue-green stains caused by high copper content in your water can be challenging, even with the help of bleach. Instead, treat this stain on your shower or tub with a paste of equal parts cream of tartar and baking soda. Rub into the stain, leave for half an hour, and rinse well with water. Repeat, if necessary.

Toilet Bowl Cleaner

To remove hard-water deposits in your toilet bowl, pour 1 cup white vinegar into the bowl and allow it to sit for several hours or overnight before scrubbing. A fizzy denture tablet works well, too!

Plop-Plop, Fizz-Fizz

Oh, what a relief it is to clean the toilet this easily. Throw in two Alka-Seltzer tablets and let them soak for a half hour. Give a quick brush and follow with a flush.

Who Knew? Readers' Favorite

Nothing says bachelor pad faster than using cola to clean your toilet, but it actually works! Pour a can into the bowl, let it sit for an hour, and clean as usual.

Scouring Powder Substitute

The best thing about scouring powder is its abrasive action. The worst is the harsh chemical smell. Get all the benefits without the caustic chemicals by using baking soda instead. In most instances, baking soda will work just as well as scouring powder.

Another DIY Alternative

Make your own all-natural scouring powder by combining 1 cup salt with 1 cup baking soda. Store in a closed jar or can, and use it to scrub off hard water stains on your porcelain sinks and bathtub.

Soap Scum Solution

Clear soap scum away effortlessly from shower doors by wiping them with a used (dry) dryer sheet. It gets the job done quickly!

Spic-and-Span Shower Doors

Need to clean those dirty glass shower doors? You can wipe down the doors with leftover white wine (if you haven't finished it off!). Wipe the wine on with a damp sponge, leave for five minutes, then rinse off. Finish by quickly buffing with a clean, dry cloth.

Cleaning Your Shower Curtain

If your shower curtain has seen better days, wash according to the care label attached, but add a cup of vinegar to the water and it will look like new. Remove as soon as the cycle is complete and hang back in position to drip-dry without any creases.

Shower Curtain Savvy

Avoid leaving a shower curtain bunched up after use, especially in a small bathroom—the steam encourages mildew. Always close the shower curtain after use, and if small spots of mildew do appear, dab with baking soda on a damp cloth. Wash larger areas in hot water, rub with lemon juice, and dry in the sun, if possible.

Who Knew? Readers' Favorite

Need to remove mildew from a plastic shower curtain? Try washing the curtain in the washing machine with two large, white bath towels. Add a little bleach in with your usual detergent and 1 cup white vinegar to the rinse cycle to prevent future mildew growth.

In the Pink

If you have a pair of pinking shears (scissors with a zigzagging edge used in sewing), put them to good use in the bathroom. Use them to cut the bottom of your shower curtain liner: The uneven hem allows water to slide off more easily, making bottom-of-the-curtain mildew a thing of the past.

Smooth Move

Do the rings on your shower curtain squeak as they run along the rod? The solution is simple: Just rub some petroleum jelly or car wax along the rod and they'll slide right along it.

Save a Shower Curtain

Our family used to go through shower curtains like toilet paper, until we learned how to prevent the nasty culprit: mildew. Simply soak a new shower curtain in salt water for a few hours before hanging it up.

Ceramic Care

To keep them sparkling, wipe ceramic tiles regularly with a sponge dampened with water and a splash of vinegar. Avoid soapy or oily cleaners and never use abrasives, which will dull the finish and make glazed tiles more prone to dirt.

Perfect Porcelain

Steel wool and scouring powders will scratch porcelain, so if your tub or sink is made of this material, rub a freshly cut lemon around the surface to cut through grease, then rinse with running water.

Stubborn Tub Stains

No matter how hard we scrub, we never seem to get the corners of our tub clean. Luckily, we have a clever solution! Soak cotton balls in your favorite tub cleanser (or just some rubbing alcohol) and leave one in each corner of your tub overnight. By morning, they'll be as clear as day.

Fabric Softener Sheets to the Rescue (Again)

To clean chrome-plated fixtures in your bathroom instantly, always keep fabric softener sheets handy. Just wipe, and the chrome will sparkle. Rubbing alcohol also does the trick.

Grout-Buster

If you've tried milder grout cleaners and you still have black stains on your grout, it's time to bring out the big boys. Make sure to wear protective gloves and that the area is well ventilated, soak some paper towels in bleach, and place them around the grout. Leave for at least an hour, then remove the towels and enjoy your clean, white grout.

Who Knew? Readers' Favorite

When the grout stains in your bathroom have you throwing up your hands, bring on the sandpaper. The folded edge will slide into the space between tiles and around the edge. This is still a delicate job—steer clear of the tiles themselves or they'll scratch.

Get Rid of Caked-On Hair Spray

If your beauty routine includes spraying your entire 'do to keep it in place, you probably have a film of hair spray on your bathroom vanity and walls. Easily remove it with a solution of two parts water and one part liquid fabric softener. Wipe on with a damp cloth, then rub off with a clean one.

Cut Down on Cleaning

You've just spent what seemed like an entire day cleaning your bathrooms. Now keep them that way by applying mineral oil all over shower doors and tiled surfaces. This will delay build-up and cut down on future cleaning time.

Drain Maintenance

Don't wait until your drain gets clogged before you flush out grime, grease, and hair. Perform monthly maintenance with the help of a little yeast. Pour two packets of dry yeast and a pinch of salt down the drain, then follow with very hot water. Wait half an hour, then flush again with hot water. The yeast reproduces and expands, which breaks up stubborn grime and hair clogs and saves you from calling the plumber.

Down the Drain

If you have a clogged drain, try this before springing for expensive drain cleaners that are harmful to your pipes. First, remove all standing water so you can access the drain. Then pour 1 cup baking soda down the drain, immediately followed by 1 cup table salt, and then ½ cup white vinegar. Let stand for five minutes, and pour 1–2 quarts boiling water down the drain. The baking soda, salt, and vinegar will dissolve any organic matter (like hair or grease), while the water will flush it out.

Get the Most from Your Plunger

Add a little petroleum jelly to the rim of your rubber plunger. It helps achieve great suction, so the disgusting job ahead is a little bit easier.

Bar Soap Solution

Always try to keep the soap in your soap dish dry. It will last much longer that way, and let's face it—picking up a soggy piece of soap to wash your hands is a bit on the disgusting side. Choose a soap dish that allows water to escape somewhere and your soap will stay solid!

Who Knew? Readers' Favorite

Stinky litter box? A great way to keep cat litter smelling fresh is to mix in a bit of baby powder each time you change the litter.

Give Your Toothbrush a Bath

A great way to keep your toothbrush clean is to soak it overnight, every few weeks, in a solution of equal parts water and baking soda. Rinse well before brushing again.

Bring Back Your Brushes

Revive hairbrushes and combs by soaking them in a pot of warm water and 1 tablespoon baking soda or ammonia.

Frost a Window to Keep Out Prying Eyes

To create a temporary "frost" for a bathroom window, mix a solution of 1 cup beer and 4 tablespoons Epsom salts. Then paint the mixture onto the window. The paint will wash off easily.

Defogging Glass

What household item will cause mirrors or eyeglasses to stop fogging? Shaving cream! It's weird but true: just rub glass with the cream, leave on for a couple of minutes, then rub off for a fog-free finish.

Newer Nail File

Ever wondered if there's a way to clean dirty emery boards? Just press transparent tape onto them, smooth over a bit, and peel off. Metal files can be cleaned with soap and water.

Who Knew? Readers' Favorite

To create an automatic air freshener in the bathroom, we blot a bit of perfume or scented oil in the center of the toilet paper roll. Whenever someone uses it, the roll releases a pleasant whiff to keep the room smelling fresh.

Bag That Soap Scum

Keep soap scum off the walls of your shower with this easy trick: Just rub wood furniture polish onto the tile and doors, and soap scum and mildew won't stick.

Soften Up Scum

Fight soap scum in your bathroom by using a granulated water softener (such as Calgon). Water softener is a cheap, gentle, skin-safe product that is also an excellent additive for your washing machine water.

A Shining Sink

Here's a quick and easy way to clean your bathroom sink: Just dampen a cotton rag or a bit of toilet paper with hydrogen peroxide and give it a few swipes! It's even great for sink stains, too.

One Soap, Two Uses

These days, most dishwashing liquids have moisturizers in them to keep your hands smooth even after doing the dishes. They work so well that you can use dishwashing liquid as a stand-in for hand soap! Just fill an old soap dispenser with 2 tablespoons dishwashing liquid and top off with water. Shake to combine and you'll have hand soap at a fraction of the cost.

Keep Cords Tidy

From hair dryers and blenders to electric shavers, most small electrical appliances have cords that can get a little unwieldy. Keep them neat and out of the way with ponytail holders or rubber bands, or fold them up and store them in paper towel tubes—label the tubes to remind yourself which cord belongs to which appliance.

Who Knew? Readers' Favorite

If your bathroom drawers are a jumbled mess, invest in an inexpensive plastic silverware tray. It's a great way to organize the little things you've got rattling around in there.

Small-Item Storage

If you need extra storage space in your bathroom, try one of our favorite fixes: an over-the-door plastic shoe storage container. Available at home stores, these organizers are perfect for make-up, lotion, and even small appliances like curling irons.

Mirror, Mirror on the Wall

Rather than purchase a bulletin board or whiteboard for your home, write messages with dry-erase markers on the mirror in your bathroom. The bathroom gets heavy foot traffic, so it's a great place to keep notes and reminders for everyone in your family.

CHAPTER 4

The Laundry Room

Whitening Whites

White fabrics can turn yellow for any number of reasons—detergents, plastic storage containers, the oils in your skin, or simply old age. To whiten old linens, boil a pot of water, then add ¼ cup dishwasher detergent and the linens and let sit for overnight. Rinse and wash as usual. The whitening powers of the dishwasher soap will restore the brightness to your whites.

Bringing Brightness Back

If you have a white linen tablecloth or other cotton item that has turned yellow over time, bring it back to its original brightness with baking soda and salt. Just bring a gallon of water to a boil, remove from the heat, stir in ¼ cup each baking soda and salt, and add the fabric. Let it soak for at least one hour. Then rinse and launder as usual.

The Order of Things

Without order, we have chaos! Make sure to add the detergent at the proper point when doing your laundry. Your clothes will get cleaner if you turn the washer on while it's empty and add the detergent immediately. Let it dissolve and mix with the water before you add your dirty clothes. Putting detergent onto clothes that are still dry can cause dyes to fade and stains to crop up.

Color Saver

Separates that go together should be dry cleaned together so the colors will continue to match. Slight fading can add up over time to turn an elegant suit into a sloppy one!

Don't Overdo the Dry Cleaning

Just when you're done patting yourself on the back for getting your dry cleaning done on time, here's a news flash: Don't overdo it or you'll risk damaging the fabric of your favorite outfits. Suit jackets, for example, usually only need to be dry-cleaned once every three months.

Cold for Clothes

No matter which temperature you choose to wash your clothes, always use a cold-water rinse. It will help the clothes retain their shape and color, and you'll save money and energy by not taxing your water heater.

Vinegar in Your Wash

If you suspect the rinse cycle isn't getting all the soap out of your clothes, add ½ cup apple cider vinegar while they are rinsing. The vinegar will dissolve the alkalinity in detergents as well as give the clothes a pleasant fragrance.

Who Knew? Readers' Favorite

Cut your dryer sheets in half (or in quarters). You won't be able to tell the difference in your clothes, but your pocketbook will.

Sock Sorting the Easy Way

Use a mesh lingerie bag or zippered pillowcase to launder each family member's socks separately. It's an easy way to keep them together, so they'll be easier to sort later.

Make White Socks White Again

Weird but true: Discolored socks will return to their original color if you boil them in a pot of water with a few slices of lemon.

Chalk it Up

One of our laundry room must-haves? A piece of chalk. That's because chalk is great at removing grease stains. Just rub it on the stain as soon as possible at it will absorb much of the grease. Chalk can also be used to prevent ring around the collar. Rub some white chalk on your collar before ironing and it will absorb sweat before it stains your shirt.

Stop Shrinkage

Jeans are usually tight enough as it is! To minimize shrinking, wash them in cold water, dry them on medium heat for only 10 minutes, and then air dry them the rest of the way.

Who Knew? Readers' Favorite

Add a big, dry towel to the clothes dryer when drying jeans and other bulky items. It will cut the drying time significantly. It will save you time and energy costs!

Add Scented Salts for Beautiful Linens

Salt is a miracle worker when it comes to removing linen stains, and if you use scented salts in your laundry, you'll get the extra bonus of lovely-smelling sheets. Add ¼ cup scented bath salts during your washing machine's rinse cycle. Not only will your sheets smell great, but the salt acts like a starch to keep them extra crisp. Just make sure not to use bath salts with dyes on light sheets.

Don't Dry-Clean if You Don't Have To!

If a clothing label of a silk garment doesn't specify dry-cleaning only, you can wash it by hand. Silk should be hand-washed using cool water with mild liquid soap. Always air dry silk—never place it in the dryer, even on cool—and iron it from the "wrong" side of the fabric.

Wily with Wool

Dry-cleaning wool can cost some major money. Try using your washing machine instead. Wash wool with mild dishwashing liquid in cold water on the gentle cycle. If it's a blanket, air fluff to dry. If it's a garment, handle with great care, since wool fibers are very weak when wet. When getting rid of excess water, don't pull, stretch, or wring out the garment. Instead, roll it in a towel, squeeze the excess water out, and then dry flat.

Inside Out

Washing corduroy can be a nightmare, thanks to the amount of lint it attracts. To keep corduroy garments from retaining lint, wash them inside out. This technique also will keep acrylic sweaters from pilling.

Stain Quickie

Here's a great use for a cleaned-out plastic bottle (of the ketchup or salad dressing variety). Pour in a mixture of water and laundry detergent or your favorite stain remover, and use it to quickly pretreat stains on your clothing.

Fight with Fizz

If your clothes are extra greasy, add a can of lemon-lime soda to your washing machine along with detergent. The acid in the soda breaks down the oil in the greasy clothes, and your wash will sparkle.

Oh, Baby!

Forget expensive stain pretreatments for your laundry—just reach for the baby shampoo! Use as you would a pretreater, and it will work just as well for a fraction of the cost.

Blame the Fabric Softener

Does it seem as though your clothes get greasy stains on them in the laundry? It may not be your imagination. One cause: adding undiluted fabric softener. Remove these stains by pretreating the fabric with a paste made of water and detergent, or use a commercial stain remover. Next time, dilute the fabric softener before you add it, or skip the stuff altogether and use vinegar instead.

Why the Sour Face for Lace?

If you own a lace tablecloth or doily that is beginning to turn yellow, let it soak in a bucket of sour milk for a few hours to return it to its former brilliant white. Just make sure to hand-wash it in mild detergent afterward!

Wrinkle-Free Curtains

Need to wash your sheer curtains but hate the thought of ironing them afterwards? Simply dissolve a packet of clear gelatin in the final rinse when laundering, and hang them up damp afterwards. The gelatin will remove almost all the wrinkles.

Treat Ties Tenderly

Never try to remove a stain from a tie with water or rubbing, or you may create a large, hard-to-remove watermark. Blot away excess stains (salad dressing, sauces, and gravy are popular ones) with a napkin or soft, white cloth. Take it to the dry cleaner as soon as possible: stains set after 24 to 48 hours.

The Best Stain Fighters

It's not necessary to buy expensive chemicals to treat stains on your clothing! Instead, use these all-natural remedies to remove drips and spills on fabric. To remove tough stains, you may have to apply a stain remover more than once—if all else fails, just keep the garment near your washing machine and wash it over and over (applying the stain-remover each time) until the spot is gone. Just make sure the stain is gone before you put the fabric in the dryer. The heat can further set the stain.

✦ **BERRIES.** Soak the stain overnight in equal parts milk and white vinegar. Launder as usual.

✦ **BLOOD.** Soak the stained area in club soda before laundering. If the blood is fresh (ouch!), make a paste of water and either talcum powder, cornstarch, cornmeal, or meat tenderizer. Apply it to the stain. Let it dry, and then brush it off.

✦ **COFFEE AND JUICE.** Stretch the garment over a bowl, cover the stain with salt, and pour boiling water over the stain from a height of one to two feet. (The gravity helps.) Of course, always test first that the garment can withstand hot water (unlike, say, cashmere). Repeat a couple of times if necessary, but some of the stain (especially if it's not fresh) may remain. If so, treat with your usual spray-and-wash stain remover.

✦ **COSMETICS.** Dampen the stain with water and rub gently with a white bar soap (like Dove or Ivory), then rinse well and launder.

✦ **DEODORANTS AND ANTIPERSPIRANTS.** Apply white vinegar, then rub and rinse. If the stain remains, repeat with rubbing alcohol, then launder.

✦ **DIRT.** Rub shampoo over the area and let sit for five minutes before washing. For tougher stains, try presoaking in a mixture of one part warm water, one part ammonia, and one part laundry detergent.

✦ **GASOLINE.** Removing gasoline stains from clothing can be tricky. The most effective way we know is to apply baby oil to the stain, then launder as usual. Since gasoline is an oil-based product, it takes another oil to pull out the stain and smell.

✦ **GRASS.** You can get rid of grass stains with toothpaste. Scrub it into the fabric with a toothbrush before washing. Or rub the stain with molasses and let stand overnight, then wash with regular dish soap by itself.

✦ **GREASE.** Grease is one of the hardest stains to remove from your clothes, but if you catch it before it dries, you can remove it with baby powder. Apply baby powder to the stain, let it sit for an hour or so, and then wipe off the powder.

✦ **GUM.** Rub with ice until the gum hardens, then carefully remove it with a dull knife before laundering.

✦ **INK STAINS.** Rub the area with a cut, raw onion, letting the onion juice soak in. Let sit for two to three hours before laundering.

✦ **KETCHUP AND TOMATO PRODUCTS.** Remove excess with a dull knife, then dab with a damp, warm sponge. Apply a bit of shaving cream to the stain, and let it dry before laundering as usual.

✦ **LIPSTICK.** If you have lipstick on your collar (or anywhere else), first try getting as much as you can off by pressing some Scotch tape over the area. Then, apply petroleum jelly to the spot and let sit for 15 minutes before laundering.

✦ **MUSTARD.** Hydrogen peroxide is effective at getting rid of mustard stains. After making sure the fabric is colorfast, apply a small amount to the stain and let set for several minutes before laundering.

✦ **NAIL POLISH.** Unfortunately, the only thing that can remove nail polish is nail-polish remover. If the fabric can withstand this harsh chemical, work it in from the inside of the fabric by pressing gently with a paper towel.

✦ **OIL.** The best way to remove stains from cooking oil (olive, vegetable, canola, etc.) is with regular shampoo. Just make sure it doesn't have a built-in conditioner.

✦ **OLD OR UNKNOWN STAINS.** If a stain is so old that it's set, try softening it up with vegetable glycerin. Glycerin can be found in health-food stores, vitamin shops, and online. Apply some to the stain and let set for an hour before laundering.

✦ **PAINT.** Treat the stain while it is still wet; latex, acrylic, and water-based paints cannot be removed once dried. While the paint is wet, rinse in warm water to flush the paint out, then launder. Oil-based paints can be removed with a solvent; your best bet will be to use one recommended on the paint can. If none is mentioned, blot with turpentine, rinse, and rub with bar soap, then launder.

✦ **PERSPIRATION.** A great way to remove perspiration stains from white shirts is to crush 4 aspirin tablets into ½ cup warm water, and apply to the stain. Soak for at least three hours, and launder as usual.

✦ **RUST.** Remove rust stains by wetting the spots with lemon juice, then sprinkling with salt. Let the fabric stand in direct sunlight for 30–45 minutes.

✦ **SCORCH MARKS.** Scorch marks will come out if you rub the area with a cut, raw onion and let the onion juice soak in thoroughly—for at least two to three hours—before washing. You can also try blotting the area with hydrogen peroxide.

✦ **SHOE POLISH.** Try applying a mixture of one part rubbing alcohol and two parts water for colored fabrics and just straight rubbing alcohol for whites. Sponge on, then launder.

✦ **TAR.** Rub gently with kerosene until all the tar is dissolved, then wash as usual. Like with all stain removers, make sure to test a small area first to be sure the fabric is colorfast. If you don't have kerosene, try petroleum jelly—just rub it in until the tar is gone. The jelly itself might stain the fabric, but it's much easier to remove with a spray-and-wash stain remover.

✦ **TOBACCO.** Moisten the stain and rub with white bar soap (like Dove or Ivory), then rinse and launder.

✦ **WINE.** Blot the stain with a mixture of one part dishwashing liquid and two parts hydrogen peroxide. If this doesn't work, apply a paste made from water and cream of tartar and let sit. You can also try using shaving cream.

Lipstick prints on silk seem like disaster, but it's almost as easy to lift them off as it is to get them on there. Use transparent or masking tape to pull off the stain. Any remnants can be sprinkled with talcum powder and shaken off.

Lipstick Stain?

Lipstick on your collar? To remove a lipstick stain from fabric, cover it with petroleum jelly for five minutes, then wash as usual. The glycerin in the jelly will break down the oils in the lipstick, making it easy to wash away.

A Silly Solution

If you happened to give the kids silly string yesterday, their clothes probably now have silly string stains all over them. Easily remove them by soaking the areas in vinegar before you throw them in the wash.

"Out, Damned Spot!"

Shakespeare's Lady Macbeth probably wishes she knew this trick for getting rid of bloodstains: Make a paste from cornstarch and water to rub the stain out and simply brush it off when dry. (Cornmeal mixed with water works equally well.)

Fight the Flu—and Fabric Stains

Hand sanitizer can fight germs and stains on fabric—we always keep it on hand in case of spills. If you've dropped something on your clothes, immediately rub a generous amount of sanitizer on the spot; blot with a soft cloth or tissue, and reapply as necessary. The alcohol in the sanitizer will quickly get to work breaking up the stain.

A Dirty Job

Kids came home with fresh mud stains on their clothes? Don't apply water! Instead, let the mud dry, then use a piece of packing or duct tape to lift all of the hardened dirt you can. Then wash as usual.

Tablecloth Tragedy Averted

Did your clumsy uncle spill gravy all over your best holiday tablecloth? Not to worry! Just blot up what you can with a paper towel, then sprinkle artificial sweetener or flour over what remains on the tablecloth. After dinner, soak the tablecloth in the washer with your regular detergent for half an hour, then wash as usual.

Perspiration Elimination

You don't have to throw out shirts with embarrassing yellow stains under the arms. Mix 2 tablespoons salt with 2 cups hot water and use a little elbow grease to rub the stain out.

Sick of Sweaty Stains?

If you're sick of the sweat stains on the armpits of your white shirts, use this pretreatment to get rid of them forever. Turn the shirt inside out and sprinkle the pits with baking soda, then press with an iron on medium heat for three seconds. The pressed-on powder will absorb sweat and keep the fabric clean.

A Zipper Fix

Stuck zipper? Rub a beeswax-based candle or lip balm on the zipper, and the problem is solved! You can also try rubbing the zipper with the lead from a pencil.

To Keep Your Thimble Nimble

Do you use a thimble to sew or sort papers? If so, wet your finger before you put the thimble on. This will create suction, so the thimble stays put.

Never a Knot

To prevent thread from getting knotted when sewing on a button, first run a bar of soap over the thread. The soap will stop knots!

Shoes That Stay Put

Have you been looking for a way to make your mules stay on your feet? Spray hair spray inside to provide more traction (just be sure to let them dry before you slip them back on)!

A Citrus Refresher

Smelly shoes? Make them a thing of the past with orange rinds. Place the inside of the rinds against the soles of your shoes and they'll absorb moisture and make them smell wonderful!

Shoe Freeze

Believe it or not, a great way to get rid of smelly shoes is to store them in a plastic bag in the freezer each night. The cold slows down the growth of bacteria, which causes the funky smell.

Sneaker Keeper

During the hot summer months, don't leave your sneakers for the gym in the car. The heat can partially melt the rubber, making your shoes less supportive.

Get Rid of Wrinkles

What's the secret to wrinkle-free pants? When hanging up your pants to dry, make sure to hang them by the cuffs at the bottom. (Either use a pants hanger with clips, or just add clothespins to a hanger.) Thanks to gravity, they'll dry with few to no creases!

Pantyhose Pleaser

The easiest way to clean suede? Simply ball up some old nylons and use them to brush to suede back to its original luster.

Iron Too Hot?

If you scorch a garment when ironing, cover the scorch mark with a vinegar-dampened cloth, then iron with a warm iron (not too hot). Presto! The burn is gone. For scorches on cotton garments, you can also use hydrogen peroxide or lemon juice instead. Just dab it onto the scorch and leave out in the sun to bleach away the stain.

Unclog Your Steam Iron

Another way to clean your iron is to pour equal amounts of vinegar and water into the water holder. Turn the dial to "steam" and leave it upright for five minutes. Unplug and let the iron cool down. Any loose particles should fall out when you empty the water.

Pumping Up Your Iron

The layer of starch that collects on your iron can be easily gotten rid of by ironing aluminum foil. Then put the used aluminum foil sheet under the cover of the ironing board for greater efficiency in ironing (it will reflect heat).

Sticky Iron?

If your iron is beginning to stick to fabrics, sprinkle some salt on a piece of waxed paper and iron it. The salt will absorb the stickiness.

Spring-Cleaning Prep

Get prepared for spring-cleaning by storing your cleaning products in a vinyl shoe holder, and hanging it on the back of your laundry room door. It's a great way to save space, and a reminder of the cleaning storm to come!

Who Knew? Readers' Favorite

You can make your own dehumidifier for the laundry room (or basement) without having to spend a lot in the process. Simply fill a coffee can with charcoal briquettes and punch a few holes in the lid. Place it in damp areas, and replace the charcoal once a month as it absorbs the humidity.

A Dab'll Do Ya

Are you using too much laundry detergent? Today's high-efficiency washers need a lot less detergent than you might think. To see if you're using too much, throw a clean towel into the washing machine by itself. After the wash cycle begins, take a look inside. If you see any suds, you're using too much.

A Blue Streak

Growth spurts don't have to mean new blue jeans, at least not right away. Take down the hem, then use a blue permanent marker to disguise the faded band.

Stop a Stain Before It Sets

Don't let a stain "set" even if you are running out the door. Instead, spray with stain remover or soak in water and store in a resealable plastic bag until you have time to deal with it. Once a stain dries, it's much harder to remove.

Make Your New Jeans Your Old Favorites

Got a new pair of jeans? To make them softer and more comfortable to wear, stick them in the wash with ½ cup salt in addition to your regular laundry detergent. The salt helps reduce stiffness and locks in the dye.

Break In Your Blue Jeans

New jeans are great, except for how stiff they are when you first put them on. Break them in without having to do some strange squats by throwing them into your dryer with a few tennis balls. After 15 minutes on low they'll be as good as...worn!

Breaking News! No Ironing Board Needed

Save room in your utility closet by forgoing an ironing board and using a pillowcase over stacked up newspapers. Make it as high or low as you find comfortable.

Dyeing to Make a Change

Not happy with the color of a handbag or pair of fancy shoes? Instead of buying new accessories, turn that unbecoming chartreuse into an elegant black with a can of shoe color spray. You can pick up an inexpensive can of color from a shoe repair shop, then revamp the item yourself instead of paying someone else to do it for you.

A Fresher Hamper

We feel bad throwing away used dryer sheets and now we don't have to. Instead, we place them at the bottom of the hamper to keep clothes smelling fresh (a relative term) until we're ready to wash them.

Lean on Me

If you have a toddler or pet safety gate that you no longer need, give it a new life in the laundry room! Lean it against the side of your washer or the wall to make the perfect drying rack for delicates and sweaters.

Extending Your Clothesline

If you love the smell of air-dried clothing, but never have enough room on your clothesline, you'll love this ingenious trick: Pull the fabric off an old umbrella with a hooked handle. Then open it up, hang it from the line, and you'll have a bunch of spokes on which to hang your laundry overflow.

A Delicate Matter

You don't need to spend money on detergents just for delicates. Instead, use this homemade solution: 1 cup baking soda mixed with 1 cup warm water. The baking soda will clean your clothes without harming their delicate fibers.

Pin the Spot!

If you spilled something on a tablecloth or blanket, make the stain easy to find in the laundry room by clipping a bobby pin or safety pin to the location. Find the pin and you've found the stain!

To Pick Up Pills

If you have a Velcro hair roller you no longer use, repurpose it as a lint roller! It's perfect for rolling over sweaters and other clothes to pick up any stray pet hair or pills.

Care for Cotton

Make your clothes last longer by taking your cotton clothing out of the dryer 20 minutes before the cycle is about to end and letting them air-dry the rest of the way. Excess dryer heat can break down the fibers in your clothes prematurely.

Who Knew? Readers' Favorite

Repurpose an old ice cube tray as an organizational tool for your laundry room. It's perfect for keeping buttons that have fallen off your clothes and other small items you may find in your pockets.

All-Natural Fabric Softener

Fabrics made of from natural fibers do not need fabric softeners; only synthetics do. Add ¼ to ½ cup baking soda to the wash cycle to soften synthetic fabrics.

CHAPTER 5

Bedrooms

Bed Pillow Know-How

Here's an easy way to start your spring-cleaning: Begin with your bed pillows. To make them fluffy and fresh, just place them in the clothes dryer with fabric softener and two clean tennis balls for a few minutes.

Refresh Drapes and Bedspreads

The easiest way to freshen draperies and heavy bedspreads is to place them in your dryer with a damp towel, on the delicate cycle, for 30 minutes. For extra freshness, hang them outside afterward if the weather allows.

Quick Fix for a Saggy Mattress

To keep your mattress from sagging, it's a good idea to reverse it once a month. If it dips in the middle, place a few folded sheets under the center to even it out.

The Pencil Is Mightier than the Sword?

Squeaky door hinges can be fixed with a pencil. Just rub the point over the hinge. Pencils contain graphite, which is an effective lubricant. Rubbing a pencil over the ridges of a stubborn house key will also help it slide into the lock more easily.

For Brass That Shines

Shining the brass hinges and knobs of your doors is easier than you think! Apply a white, non-gel toothpaste (a mild abrasive) to door fittings with a soft cloth, then rub. Use a fresh cloth to wipe clean, and your brass will sparkle! To protect brass between cleanings, apply a light coating of olive or lemon oil.

For Sweaty Summers

On sticky summer nights, cool down by sprinkling a little baby powder between your sheets before retiring for the night.

Smell the Roses Everyday

Clean laundry loses its fresh scent quickly when sitting in stuffy drawers and closets. To get your clothes, lingerie, and linens smelling freshly washed all the time, place fabric softener sheets in your dresser drawers.

Keep Drapes Fresh

Try this nifty trick to make sure your new or recently cleaned drapes stay crisp and fresh: Spray them with a few light coats of unscented hair spray before hanging them up.

Raise Matted Carpet

If a section of your carpet has been matted down by a piece of furniture, you can raise the nap back up with this simple ice cube trick. Let the cube melt into the matted area; wait until the next day to vacuum.

Time to Clean Teddy

To clean stuffed animals, just place them in a cloth bag or pillowcase, add baking soda or cornmeal, and shake. The dirt will transfer to the powder.

De-Grease Sticky Playing Cards

An oft-used deck of cards can get sticky and grimy from the oils on your hands. De-grease the cards by placing them in a plastic bag with a few blasts of baby powder. Give it a good shake before dealing the first hand.

Silence a Squeak

When a squeaky door needs grease, spray shaving cream on the offending hinge as a lubricant. Now open and listen—silence! Much easier to play hide-and-seek around the house this way.

Odors Vanish with Vanilla

Fight odors in smelly places throughout the house (closets, coolers, drawers, etc.), with this nifty trick. Place a damp paper towel in a cup and add a couple teaspoons of vanilla extract. Let it sit for a few days in the stinky spot, and the odor will vanish.

Stop a Stale Smell

Wondering how to get that stale odor out of old wooden dressers or chests? Soak a slice of white bread in a shallow dish of white distilled vinegar, and place it inside. It'll freshen up in no time.

Protecting Fine Linens

Use wax paper to separate lace handkerchiefs, doilies, and other linens in your drawers. It will block light and keep dyes from seeping between items.

Reorganize for More Storage Space

Move your bed sheets and linens from the hallway linen closet to a top shelf in your bedroom closet. That way, they'll be closer to where they're actually used, and if you fold them properly, they won't take up much room. The major bonus? You've now freed up a valuable hallway closet to store something else.

Classic Cedar Tip

Clothes moths are a pain in the neck to get rid of once they've invaded your closets. Since mothballs are toxic, pick up cedar chips at a craft store instead—cedar is an effective and safe moth repellent. Stick the chips in cheesecloth or an old nylon sock, tie it closed, and store in closets or drawers to keep the pests away.

Who Knew? Readers' Favorite

Cedar chests are wonderful because they not only look great, but their scent keeps moths away, too. But what to do when they begin to lose their scent? Get out some fine sandpaper and go to work! Gently sanding the inside of the chest will bring its scent back to life, making sure your clothes are safe and your room smells wonderful.

Keep That Candle Longer!

If your wonderfully scented candle is almost gone, it's easy to keep the smell with you! Carefully cut or break the remaining candle into pieces, then put them in an old sock or nylon and hang in your closet. The enclosed space will be filled with your candle's scent every time you open the closet door.

A New Use for Old Toys

Do your kids have lots of stuffed animals? This winter put those less-popular ones to good use: Line them up in front of their bedroom windows to prevent drafts from coming in underneath.

Hoard No More

Going through your closet or storage area and can't decide whether or not to get rid of something? Put it in a "Maybe" box and set it aside. If you haven't used it or thought about it after three months, it's a definite sign you should sell or donate it.

Alleviate Dresser Drawer Mayhem

Is your dresser drawer starting to look like someone ransacked it? Egg cartons and plastic ice cube trays make great organizational tools for jewelry, cuff links, and other trinkets, and they'll easily fit inside your drawer.

Art Supply Storage

Keep art supplies in a clear, vinyl shoe bag hung from the back of your child's door. It's a smart, space-saving way to hold paints, pens, markers, brushes, and more.

A "Cap"-ital Idea

Don't throw away caps to your hair spray, spray starch, and other cans! They make perfect organizing containers for your drawers.

Hanging Handbags

Here's a handy storage tip: Hanging purses to store them puts stress on the handles. You'll do better keeping them on shelves or in one big bag so they'll last longer.

Purse Cleaning Secret

You've cleaned out your purse, but it stills has crumbs, grime, and little pieces of god-only-knows-what at the bottom. Quickly clean it out with a lint roller. Just roll the inside and you're done!

Sage Advice

Break up a few leaves of sage and spread them around inside your shoes. They'll kill the bacteria that causes foot odor. To cut down on how much you perspire in the first place, try drinking sage tea. Herbalists say it will take several weeks, but you'll see results!

Perfume Perfection

You probably keep your perfume bottles on your dresser or wherever else you usually apply it. But we keep ours in the refrigerator! Why? The colder temperature makes the volatile chemicals in perfume evaporate less quickly, meaning that your perfume will not only last longer, it will retain the scent it had when you fell in love with it.

CHAPTER 6

The Home Office

Clean Up Your Keys

The easiest way to clean the gunk and dust between your computer keys is with transparent tape. Just slide a two-inch strip between the rows of your keyboard, and the adhesive will pick up any debris.

Delete the Dirt

Need to clean a computer keyboard? Simply dip a cotton swab or cotton ball in hydrogen peroxide and run it between the keys.

Who Knew? Readers' Favorite

Unless it's cracked, it's usually possible to fix a skipping CD. First, eliminate any dust and dirt by holding the CD under running water and rubbing with a soft, lint-free cloth to dry. To fix any scratches, rub a little white (non-gel) toothpaste into the scratch, then wipe with the damp cloth to remove any excess. The toothpaste won't repair the CD entirely, but it will at least keep it from skipping.

Label Madness

If you're like us, you receive free address labels in the mail from time to time. Put them to good use by labeling notebooks, kid's items, and anything else you'd like to personalize.

Lost Your Ruler?

If you need to measure something and don't have a ruler, grab a dollar bill instead. A dollar is exactly six and a quarter inches long.

Cuts Like New

Rehabilitate a pair of old scissors with these simple tips. First, remove any rust by applying a paste of salt and lemon juice, leaving for 15 minutes, and then rubbing thoroughly with a dry cloth. Then, sharpen the scissors by cutting a piece of steel wool or balled-up aluminum foil 20 times or so.

Substitute Staple Remover

Need to remove a staple and don't have a staple remover? Don't risk using your fingernail. Instead, use nail clippers. They work perfectly for removing stubborn staples.

Go-To Glue Remover

To remove glue residue on almost any surface, try vegetable oil on a rag. It's also an easy-breezy way to clean off residue from sticky labels. The vegetable oil neutralizes the glue's bonds.

Get Rid of Glue Fast

If your gluing project gets a little messy, use WD-40 to lift off dried glue spots. Wipe clean and now get back to arts and crafts.

How to Get Unstuck

It's a great feeling when you save the day by breaking out the extra-strong glue. Just remember not to stick your fingers to each other! If you forget, slink off to the supply closet while you pretend everything's fine. This is yet another instance where WD-40 comes to the rescue.

Goo Be Gone

You don't want to know whether the smooshed item on your magazine, book, or page-a-day-calendar is a raisin or something worse. You just want a fast way to get it off! Blow dry (on low). The gooey substance will melt so you can effortlessly wipe it clean.

Invisible Ink

If you have ink stains on your hands from a marker or pen, try this: Just add a bit of sugar to your hands when washing with regular soap, and the granules will act as a gentle abrasive to help wash the ink away.

Who Knew? Readers' Favorite

Use a thinner font to save when you print out documents. Thinner fonts like Times New Roman and Century Gothic will use up to 30 percent less ink than Arial.

Toner Tip

Need to print out some helpful but not super-important pages (such as a grocery, chore, or to-do list)? You can conserve ink by changing the font color to gray rather than using the heavier black ink.

Shake It Up, Baby

Here's a trick used by office workers everywhere: When your printer's out of ink, remove the cartridge and shake it up for a bit. Stick it back into the printer, and you'll find it's got enough ink left for at least a few more print jobs.

Full of Hot Air

You're trying to print out a document, but you just ran out of ink! This solution will save you a trip to the store: Take out the ink cartridge, then blow hot air on it with a hair dryer. Once it's warm, put it back in the printer. The heat loosens the ink that is stuck to the side of the cartridge, often giving you enough to finish the job.

Safely Store Important Papers

The school year is over, and you need a place to store the kids' artwork and diplomas. Try rolling them tightly in paper towel tubes so they won't crease, then label the outside, so you know what's inside. The tubes can also be used to store marriage certificates and other important documents.

Mail Safety Measure

Always put outgoing bills in a post office mailbox instead of the mailbox at your front door. A thief could get to your mail before the mail carrier does, and the information provided in your envelope could lead to identity theft.

Who Knew? Readers' Favorite

Never carry your Social Security card in your wallet—if it's lost or stolen, thieves can use it to access all sorts of information about you. In addition, make a copy of the front and back of each credit card you carry, and store them in a safe place at home. That way, you'll be able to cancel those cards quickly should your wallet be lost or stolen.

Mail Management

If you're mailing out invitations, stick them in the mailbox on Wednesday, so that they'll arrive on Friday or Saturday. People respond more quickly to mail received on the weekend—and you'll get your head count finalized sooner!

Minimize the Mail Pile

With such a busy family, it's hard to control the clutter in our house. So we try to prevent it before it even starts: We keep a small, inconspicuous trashcan near our usual mail-opening spot. That way, we can easily toss junk mail into the garbage without setting it on a table or countertop, where it will sit for weeks.

Send It "Media Mail"

Mailing books, CDs, or DVDs? The cheapest way to get them there is to take your package to the post office and ask for it to be sent "media mail." Though it will take a little longer to arrive, this low rate—reserved for mailing "media"—will save you a lot of money, especially if your package is heavy.

Postage Prescription

If you're sending a get-well card to a friend in the hospital, but aren't sure how long she'll be there, try this: Put the hospital's address on the front of the envelope, and your friend's address as the return address. That way, you're certain she'll get the card—at the hospital or once she returns home. (Just don't tell the post office!)

Unstick Stuck Stamps

If your postage stamps are stuck together, place them in the freezer for about 10 minutes. (Unfortunately, this doesn't work as well with self-adhesive stamps.)

Frozen Moments

If you discover a couple of photos stuck together, don't lose hope! They can be unstuck. Place them in the freezer for half an hour, then gently break them apart with a butter knife. You can also slowly unstick them by blowing air on them with a hairdryer set on low.

Saving Precious Memories

If a beloved book or photo album has gotten wet, it's not ruined yet. Try sprinkling baby or baking powder on each page, then placing it in a closed paper bag for up to a week. The powder should absorb the water while keeping your book safe.

Newspaper Mementos

To preserve special newspaper clippings, dissolve a milk of magnesia tablet in a shallow pan with a quart of club soda. Soak the paper for an hour, then let it lay flat to dry. Afterward, it's best to keep the paper under plastic in a photo album.

Who Knew? Readers' Favorite

If your windows or desk drawers are stuck, simply rub a candle or white soap on the runners and the problem should be solved.

Finally, a Use for Old Telephone Cords!

If your desk is a tangled mess of computer, printer, and internet cables, keep them tidy by running them through a coiled telephone cord. The coils will keep everything together neatly. You can also use a few cardboard tubes from paper towels instead of a telephone cord.

Bind Your Cords

You'll love this way to keep all the cords to your various electronic devices organized on your desk. Clasp several binder clips to the side of your desk, then slide the cord through the arms and let the plug be held by the narrower end. Instant organization!

Nonskid Drawers

A nonskid rug pad is a terrific liner for your office drawers. The tacky surface prevents paper clips, thumbtacks—anything!—from slipping around. It'll work well in your kitchen drawers, too.

Dry-Erase Board Substitute

Need a dry-erase board? Consider picking up white shower board instead—it does the job just as well, but it's less expensive. You can find it sold in sheets at most home supply stores. Just cut it down to the size you want and either frame it or hang it on the wall as is.

Cleaner Communications

The phone is a bacteria hotspot. Wipe yours down with alcohol wipes or plain alcohol on paper towels. (Don't forget the phone at work.) It not only helps the spread of colds, it will also cut down on acne along your jawline.

A Surprising Use for an Egg Carton

Forget bubble wrap and packing peanuts! For a cheaper and more environmentally sound alternative, hold on to old foam egg cartons, and use the egg cups as packing material. Store them stacked on a shelf in your closet, and you've got sturdy padding handy for your next fragile package.

Consider a Credit Union

Tired of all the fees and high interest rates at your bank? Consider joining a credit union instead. CUs are not-for-profit, member-owned institutions, thus allowing them to be more beneficial for every account holder—not just the ultra-wealthy ones. To find one in your area and to determine if it's right for you, visit NCUA.gov and select "Credit union data."

Internet Password Organizer

If you're in over your head when it comes to computer passwords, consider trying out RoboForm.com. This neat site keeps track of your passwords on one encrypted site, then enters them when you're at sites that require passwords.

Save Your Dying Cell Phone Battery

You've just realized your cell phone's battery is about to die, but you're at work at don't have your charger. Get a little more talk time by detaching the battery and placing it in your workplace's freezer, then allowing it to come back up to room temperature before you use it. The cold will keep your battery from losing any more juice.

If your electronic gadget starts to lose its juice, try this trick before you buy new batteries: Take the batteries out and rub their contacts with a pencil eraser. This will remove small particles of dust and dirt that keep the energy flowing. Put the batteries back in and you'll be surprised how much longer they last!

Hey, Watch This!

The next time someone at work asks you why you bother wearing a watch anymore, show them this: Put your watch face-up on your desk and your mouse on top of it. The reflective surface will confuse the optics inside your mouse, making your computer think it's still moving. If you have a work computer that makes you log in every five minutes when you're not "active," you know how helpful this is!

Sounds Great

Have trouble hearing music through your mobile device's speakers? Just place it in a bowl (preferably an aluminum or stainless steel one). The sides of the bowl will amplify the sound.

CHAPTER 7

The Great Outdoors

Bid Adieu to Oil Stains

Cleaning oil spots off the driveway is difficult, and the cleaners can be quite expensive. Instead, sprinkle baking soda over the stains, then rub with a scrub brush soaked with hot water. The baking soda breaks apart oil particles, so with a little elbow grease you can have your driveway spot-free in no time.

Get Rid of Grease

Another way to remove a grease stain from your concrete driveway is to rub kitty litter into the stain and let it stand for one to two hours before sweeping it up. The super-absorbent litter will soak up the stain.

Tidy Up the Driveway

You can keep paved areas looking spiffy with this trick. To remove unwanted grass or weeds from sidewalk and driveway cracks, squirt them with a solution of 1 gallon vinegar, 1 cup salt, and 8 drops liquid detergent.

Sidewalk Cleanup

Want to get rid of the grass growing in the cracks of your sidewalk or patio? Make a mixture of salt and baking soda, sprinkle it on and sweep it into the cracks. Problem solved.

Stains on Stones?

If you have stains on paving stones or a concrete patio, the solution is simple. Try pouring hot water from several feet above the stone onto the stain. Repeat several times, and your stain may just disappear. If this doesn't work, try rubbing some dishwashing liquid into the spot with a toothbrush, then rinsing off. For really tough stains, add a bit of ammonia to the water.

Algae Antidote

Your birdbath used to be a hot spot for the feathered folk, but ever since it became slimy with algae, they've stayed away! Make your birdbath as fresh as new by emptying the water, then covering it with bleach-soaked paper towels or newspaper. After letting the paper sit for 5–10 minutes, remove it and rinse the bath thoroughly. Then fill it with fresh water and watch the birds enjoy. To attract even more birds to your birdbath, just cover the bottom with multi-colored marbles.

A Better Birdbath

There's a chemical in lavender that inhibits the growth of algae. Make a bundle of lavender flowers and daylily leaves for your birdbath to keep it free and clear of algae. Change every few weeks.

Slip and Slide

This idea may conjure up a cartoon chase scene, but here's a safe, natural way to feed the birds and not the squirrels: Simply rub shortening on the pole leading up to your feeder to keep the uninvited guests from letting themselves in.

The easiest way to clean plastic or resin patio furniture? Just toss it in the swimming pool before going to bed, and in the morning it'll be good as new. Meanwhile, your pool's filter will clean up the dirt.

No Fungus Among Us

If you have mold on your faux wicker (plastic resin) furniture, get it summer-ready by mixing a paste of lemon and salt. Polish it on in a circular motion, rinse, and leave to dry in the sun. If your patio umbrella has mold, here's another easy fix: Fill a bucket with warm water, add 2 cups of white vinegar, and a couple of generous squirts of dishwashing liquid. Let soak for a half an hour, then scrub with a cleaning brush. Rinse with water and let it dry in the sun.

Get Your Wicker Ready for Spring

Make sure your wicker furniture is front-porch ready for the spring and summer months. Blow-dry off the loose dirt, then clean with white vinegar and warm salt water, and apply a coat of lemon oil.

A Little Lube

To keep your metal deck furniture free from rust and wear all winter long, reach for the petroleum jelly. Just apply a thin layer (especially in areas where the furniture tends to rust) after cleaning the surface with simple soap and water.

Stow Your Wicker for the Winter

Before the first freeze arrives, bring all your wicker furniture inside to protect it from the cold. Freezing will cause the wicker to crack and split, which unfortunately is impossible to repair.

Frugal Furniture Covers

No space to bring outdoor furniture inside in bad weather? Instead of buying pricey furniture covers, protect lawn chairs and tables by covering them with large plastic bags.

Store Your Hose Properly for Maximum Usage

Your garden hose will last twice as long if you store it coiled, rather than folded. Try coiling it around a bucket. Note that the hose will be easiest to work with when it's neither very cold nor very hot outside.

Who Knew? Readers' Favorite

If you have an old hose you're about to throw away, here's a great second use. Cut off a two-inch section, then cut a horizontal slit all the way through it. Slide onto the handles of buckets to make them easier to carry. Reinforce with duct tape if necessary.

Keep Your Trash Bag in Place

When you're raking leaves, nothing is more frustrating than a plastic trash bag that slips down into the garbage can. Rest easy, friends: All you need to do is secure the bag with a bungee cord (or two) and get to work. Fold the open end of the bag over the rim of the trashcan and wrap the cord around the outside to hold it in place.

Tiki Torch To-Do

If you have tiki torches lighting up your backyard, here's a trick that make them burn twice as long. Before you start them blazing, soak the wick of each torch in white or apple cider vinegar for an hour, then allow them to dry. The vinegar will make the wick burn more slowly.

Guard Outdoor Light Bulbs from Winter Wear

Before it gets too cold, consider applying a thin layer of petroleum jelly to the threads of all your outdoor light bulbs. It will prevent them from rusting and make them easier to replace when they blow out.

Shovel Snow Without Killing Your Back

Shoveling wet, heavy snow is a backbreaking job, but you can make it easier with a simple tip: Just coat your shovel with vegetable shortening, car wax, or cooking spray, and the snow won't stick. If you're using a snowblower, coat the inside of the chute.

Don't Stand On Icy Ground—Melt It!

Make your winter season safer by salting icy ground in the most effective way possible. Use a lawn seeder or fertilizer spreader to distribute salt or sand in a thin, even layer. And don't forget to watch your step!

Flag FYI

You may know there are particular rules governing how to keep and fly a flag, and that includes making sure it stays clean. To do so, simply wash with a bit of liquid dish or laundry detergent in the sink. Iron to get out any wrinkles. For vintage flags or flags with tassels, get them dry-cleaned.

Proper Pyrotechnics

Setting off fireworks this Fourth of July? Make sure you keep a bucket of water on hand in case of fire, and never try to relight a firecracker that malfunctioned or didn't go off for some reason. Only light fireworks on a smooth, flat surface away from others.

Who Knew? Readers' Favorite

If there is too much chlorine in your pool, don't buy expensive treatments that will just have you balancing and counter-balancing chemicals for the rest of the summer. Simply don't put the cover on the pool for several days. The sun will naturally lower the chlorine content, and after a bit of evaporation, you can add more fresh water.

Cleaner Containers

We haven't figured out why our storage containers always seem to be covered with a sticky substance when we take them out of the garage. But we have figured out a way to prevent it! Simply spray them with cooking spray and sticky substances will be less likely to cling.

A Clever Catch-All

When you're clearing out leaves this fall, make a sturdy leaf bag with this smart trick: Cut out the bottom of a hard plastic laundry basket, and stick the bottomless basket into your leaf bag. It'll hold the bag in place so you can dump leaves into it without worrying about spills. Just remove the basket when the bag is ready for the trash.

Proper Use of Paving Stones

Never use decorative paving stones near your home. Certain kinds of ants love to make their homes underneath them! Use them away from your house to be sure ants won't decide to come in for a visit.

Padlock Protection

Have a padlock on your shed or another outdoor structure? Keep it from rusting by protecting it from the elements. Slice open the side of a tennis ball (carefully!) and slip it over the lock.

CHAPTER 8

Home Repair

Thaw Frozen Pipes Before They Burst

When temps drop to freezing, be on alert for frozen pipes in your walls, attic, or basement. Should a pipe burst, you might be left with some serious and costly damage. If your pipes are frozen but haven't yet burst, find the suspected area (often in an exterior wall), turn on your faucets, and use a blow-dryer to thaw it out. As always, though, take care that the hair dryer doesn't get wet.

Moving Marble

If you're moving a large piece of marble, such as a tabletop, always transport it upright. If you carry it flat, it can crack under its own weight.

Repurpose Wine Corks

Slice old corks into thin disks, then glue them to the feet of your heavy furniture. It's a great way to protect your floors, and it makes moving the furniture a bit easier.

Walls Have Cavities, Too!

Small holes in your white wall? It's toothpaste to the rescue! Simply dab a small amount of white (non-gel) toothpaste into the hole, and you'll never notice it again—or at least your guests won't!

Who Knew? Readers' Favorite

Before driving a nail into a plaster wall, place a small piece of tape over the spot you're working on. This simple prep step will prevent cracking.

Got Grease Stains on Your Wall?

If grease is still visible on the wall after removing wallpaper, apply a coat of clear varnish to the spots. The grease won't soak through to the new wallpaper.

Wallpaper 101

Hanging wallpaper? Try using a paint roller to apply paste, instead of a sponge, and then use a separate clean paint roller to smooth it out afterward. You'll get more coverage per stroke.

A Sour Solution for Old Wallpaper

You're renovating the kitchen, and step one is taking down that old wallpaper. To make your job easier, use a sponge or spray bottle to saturate the wallpaper with vinegar first. Wait a few minutes and it will peel right off.

Border Patrol

Redoing a room with a wallpaper border? Easily remove it by blowing hot hair from a hair dryer on it. The heat will loosen the glue and it will peel right off.

Speed Up a Paint Job

Quicken your interior paint jobs by mixing a quart of semigloss latex paint into a gallon of flat latex paint. The finish won't shine more than it would with straight flat paint, but the paint will glide on and cover much more easily.

Don't Let Your White Paint Yellow

Some white paints can yellow in a matter of months, making a new paint job look much older and staler than it really is. Keep your white walls white by adding 7–10 drops of black paint to each quart. Also, when selecting your paint colors, note that white paint will age better if exposed to natural light.

Get Rid of Paint Smell

If you hate the smell of drying paint, fix it before you start. Simply add 1½ teaspoons vanilla extract to a gallon of paint, and your drying walls will smell delicious.

This Tip is Old News

When painting a windowsill, forget the edging tape: It's expensive, and it can pull up the paint you already have on the sill. Instead, use strips of newspaper. Dampen them and wring out as much excess moisture as you can without ruining the paper, then use them in lieu of tape. They'll stick as long as they're wet, but won't pull up any paint when you're done.

Remove a Painting Mistake

You've just painted your window trim and got a big glob of "country yellow" on the glass pane. There's no need to use a dangerous razor blade to remove the paint that spilled on the glass. Instead, remove the paint safely and easily with a pencil eraser. If the paint has dried, or is old, dab on some nail polish remover, wait a minute, then erase.

No Cleaning Necessary (for Now)

If you want to avoid cleaning a paint roller, wrap it in foil or a plastic bag and place it in the refrigerator. This will keep the roller moist and usable for a few days, so you can finish where you left off later.

The Art of Paintbrush Maintenance

Old, crusty paintbrushes put a cramp in our paint projects. To soften those bristles, we soak them in full-strength white vinegar and then clean them with a comb. To prevent brushes from hardening in the first place, rub a few drops of vegetable oil into freshly cleaned bristles to keep them soft.

Keep Your Paint Fresh for Longer

If you've got leftover paint, you can prevent it from drying up with this crafty maneuver: Blow up a balloon until it's about the size of the remaining space in the can. Then put it inside the can and close the lid. This will reduce the amount of air in the can, thus prolonging the paint's freshness.

Want your paint to last longer in the can? First, place a piece of plastic wrap under the paint can's lid, then make certain the lid is on tight before you turn the can over. The paint is exposed to less oxygen this way and will last much, much longer.

Avoid That Icky Paint Skin

If you've ever stored a partially used paint can, you've probably noticed that a skin of dried-up paint forms at the top of the can. To prevent this, place a piece of waxed paper the size of the opening on top of the remaining paint.

Strain Out Lumpy Paint

If you have lumps in your paint, cut a piece of window screen just slightly smaller than the circumference of the can. Place it inside the can and let it settle to the bottom. It'll carry the lumps with it.

Guard Your Work (and Your Shirt) from Dripping Paint

To catch drips while you paint, try this makeshift drip cup: Cut a tennis ball in half and slice a thin slot in the bottom bowl of one half. Then slide your brush handle through the slot so the bristles stick out of the open side. A small paper plate or cup works too.

Prevent a Dripping Paint Can

You know that little groove along the rim of a paint can that tends to fill up and spill paint all over the place? Using a nail or an awl, notch a few holes in there to create a drain for the paint, so it drips back into the can instead of dripping down the outside. Alternatively, you can place masking tape on the rim of the paint can before pouring—remove the tape later and the rim will be clean.

Who Knew? Readers' Favorite

Painting doors? Avoid getting paint on the hinges by coating them lightly with petroleum jelly before you start.

Paint Roller Pan Liner

There's no need to spend your money on disposable paint liners for your roller pan. It's just as easy to line the pan with aluminum foil—and a lot cheaper, too.

Perfect Pan Liner

Here's yet another use for larger plastic bags you get from the store: Put one over a roller tray whenever you're painting with a roller. When the job is done, just pull off the bag and turn inside-out to throw away, and the tray is ready to be used again!

Quick Clean for a Paintbrush

The fastest way to clean a paintbrush? Put ½ cup liquid fabric softener in a gallon of water and vigorously swirl the brush in it for 20 seconds.

Revive Old Paintbrushes

Don't throw out old paintbrushes. Just soak them in hot vinegar for 20 minutes, then wash with dish soap and warm water. They'll be close to brand new again.

For Paint-Covered Hands

It's hard not to get paint all over yourself when painting a room. And old household trick is to wipe turpentine on your hands to get the paint off, but there's a much less smelly way! Simply rub your hands with olive oil, let it sit a couple of seconds, then rub off with a damp, soapy sponge. Not only will the olive oil remove the paint, but it's great for your skin, too! For enamel or oil paint, rub your hands with floor paste wax, and then wash with soap and water.

Sticky Fingers (and How to Unstick Them)

If you glue your fingers together when working with a quick-bonding glue or epoxy, nail polish remover will do the trick. If you get stuck working with rubber cement, try lacquer thinner; you may need to let the thinner soak in for a few minutes before gently pulling your fingers apart.

Looking for a Stud? (In a Wall, That Is)

If you'd like to hang a heavy mirror or piece of art, you'll first have to locate a wall stud. Don't own a stud finder? No worries. Studs are normally 16 inches apart, so measure 17 inches from a corner to find your first stud. Keep measuring out by 16 inches until you find the stud nearest your desired spot. Alternatively, you can use a compass. Hold a compass level with the floor and at a right angle to the wall, and then slowly move the compass along the surface of the wall. When the needle moves, that's where you will find a stud.

When's Your Wood Smooth Enough to Use?

If you're sanding wood and want to know when it's smooth enough, use the pantyhose test: Slip an old nylon stocking over your hand and run it over the wood. You'll have no trouble finding the slightest rough spot. Just don't wear those nylons afterwards!

Aged Wood Absorbs Stains Best

If you allow wood to "weather" before you apply a stain, the stain will last years longer. It's a case where patience pays off.

For a Smooth Varnish

Stir varnish thoroughly from the bottom of the can, but don't stir vigorously. Stirring can create air bubbles, which can ruin a smooth finish. If you notice air bubbles, brush them out while the varnish is still wet. If it's already dry, gently buff them out with very fine steel wool.

Flour Power

If you're painting old woodwork and need to patch small holes, fill them with flour and then paint. It will harden without being noticeable.

Who Knew? Readers' Favorite

If you need to repair a hole in a piece of wood, add a small amount of instant coffee to the Spackle, or to a thick paste made from a laundry starch and warm water. The coffee tints the paste to camouflage the patched-up spot.

Window Screen Fix-Up

To repair small holes in window screens, cover them with a few of layers of clear nail polish. It will keep the hole from becoming bigger and prevent insects from coming through.

Tighten Droopy Cane Chairs

A chair's caning can loosen and begin to droop. If you let it go long enough, you might even fall through the seat and hurt your bum (not to mention your ego). But, no fear! You can tighten it easily and cheaply. Apply very hot water to the underside, then dry the chair in direct sunlight.

A Safe Ladder, with a Coffee to Go

Save up your used coffee cans for your next home-maintenance project. If you need to use a ladder on soft earth, set the legs inside those empty cans so they won't sink from your weight.

Saw Safety

Keeping your saws safely stored is easy. Use a split piece of old garden hose to cover the sharp teeth whenever they're not in use.

Nip Rust in the Bud

Prevent your tools from rusting now, and avoid the annoying rust-removal process later. Place a few mothballs, a piece of chalk, or a piece of charcoal in your toolbox—all three eliminate moisture and fight rust before it begins. If you've got nuts and bolts that are rusted together, just submerge them in cola for a day and they'll come apart easily.

Loosen a Rusty Nut or Bolt

To remove that pesky rusted nut or bolt, put a few drops of ammonia or hydrogen peroxide on it, and wait 30 minutes. If you're out of both, try a little bit of cola instead.

Squeak Tweak

Squeaky doors and cabinet hinges, as well as sticky locks, benefit from a light spritz of a nonstick cooking spray. And it's cheaper than WD-40, too!

Safely Remove a Busted Light Bulb

To remove a broken light bulb from the socket, first turn off the electricity or unplug the lamp, and then push half of a raw potato or small apple into the broken bulb's base. Turn it to unscrew the base. Just don't eat it afterward!

Fix a Glass Scratch

Don't tell the kids this, but scratches in the window and breakfront glass don't have to be permanent. Rub a little white toothpaste into the mark and buff. Wipe clean and coat with a solution of 1 tablespoon vinegar and ½ cup water.

Patch It Up

Patch up little holes and imperfections in your walls with a natural paste made from 2 tablespoons salt, 2 tablespoons cornstarch, and 5 teaspoons water. Sand first, then spread the paste over the areas you want to revitalize.

Careful Nail Removal

If you do more damage than good when removing nails with the claw of a hammer, you can use a spatula as a guard, holding it between the claw and the wall each time you yank.

Got a Screw Loose?

Are the knobs to your drawers and cabinets coming loose? To fix the problem forever, remove the knob and coat the end of the screw with nail polish (use clear if you're a bit messy), then screw the knob back on before the polish dries.

Chalk Talk

Chalk is good for more than just writing! If your kids have outgrown sidewalk chalk, or you happen to have some around, place it in the damp areas of your home (like your basement) to absorb excess moisture and repel mildew. Use a container that allows air to get through it, like a mesh bag, a coffee can, or a paper bag with holes poked in it.

Who Knew? Readers' Favorite

You need a Phillips-head screwdriver, but your search through your junk drawer was fruitless. A great replacement in a pinch is a metal potato peeler. The curved top edge will fit into the x-shaped groove of the screw.

A Nutty Idea

The next time someone sends you a box full of packing peanuts, save a few and throw them in your toolbox. They're great for getting screws into stripped holes. Just stuff the packing peanut into the hole, and then turn the screw into its dense Styrofoam. Cut away any pieces of the peanut that remain outside the hole.

Fix a Chip

If you've chipped a vase, stop swearing at yourself and go get your kid's biggest box of crayons. Then very carefully hold a flame under the tip of the crayon, letting the melted wax drip onto the chip. Once it has cooled but not hardened, smooth it out and your vase will be almost as good as new.

Open a Sealed Window

If humidity has sealed your window shut, here's how to get it open again: Hold a block of wood up against the frame, and tap it gently a few times with a hammer. Then move to a different place on the frame until you've tapped all the around the edges. You should now be able to easily pull it up.

Must Buster

Does your basement smell like, well, a basement? Try this: Cut an onion in half, and put it on a plate near where you smell the mildew. It will smell like an onion for a bit, but afterwards, the mildew odor will be gone!

There's a blackout, and you just realized your flashlight is out of D batteries. Even if you don't have any of these jumbo batteries around the house, there may be a solution: Place a couple of C-sized batteries inside and fill up the extra space with a ball of aluminum foil. You won't get as bright of a light, but it will help shine the way.

Temporary Screen Fix

Don't leave a hole in your screen door just because you don't have the right tools to fix it. Instead use rubber cement to affix a small piece of pantyhose around the area. It's easy to remove but will keep ugly flying things out of your house in the meantime (at least the ones that don't live there).

Light the Way

We were nostalgic about our boys' dinosaur nightlights, but—like many relics from their baby years—they were ready to toss them without so much as a backward glance. What to do? Turns out a nightlight on an extension cord can serve as a perfect work light for a small, dark space so we held on to all of them. Dragons do live forever!

CHAPTER 9

Your Car

For a Better Car Battery

The corrosion around your car battery posts can be cleaned easily with a thick solution of baking soda and water. Let it stand for 10–15 minutes before washing it off.

Is Your Car Winter-Ready?

Winterize your car battery so you don't get stuck in the cold. Pour a can of cola over the battery posts; let it sit for a half hour, then wipe it clean. Rub petroleum jelly on the posts before reattaching the battery cables. You should be good to go for the winter!

Tar on Your Car

It's easy to remove tar from the outside of your car. Make a paste of baking soda and water, then apply it to the tar with a soft cloth. Let it dry, then rinse off with warm water.

Clean Car with Cornstarch

To clean dirty windows or your car's windshield, mix a tablespoon of cornstarch to about ½ gallon of warm water, and dry with a soft cloth. It's amazing how quickly the dirt is removed—and no streaking, either!

Club Soda Saver

One thing that never leaves our cluttered trunk (except when we're using it) is a spray bottle filled with club soda. Club soda does wonders for getting grime, bird droppings, and bug guts off your windshield. Just spray on, wait a few minutes, and turn on the wipers.

Smeary Windshield Wipers

Messy wipers are a safety hazard, and they're also pretty annoying. To fix the problem, wipe the blades with some rubbing alcohol.

Make Car Cleaning Easier

One of the dirtiest parts of your car is usually the wheels, thanks to all the dark brake dust that accumulates there. Next time you clean your car's wheels, spray them with a light coat of vegetable oil when you're done. It will keep the dust from clinging, and you'll be able to wipe off the dust easily. Use steel wool pads for cleaning whitewalls.

Gross Grille?

Don't you hate the smashed-up insects that seem to cover your car grille in the summer? The only thing worse than looking at them is trying to scrape them off, unless you try this trick: Spray a light coating of vegetable oil or nonstick cooking spray on your grille, and the revolting bugs will wipe off easily.

Who Knew? Readers' Favorite

Got a bunch of bug guts on your windshield after a road trip? Easily remove them with a pair of old pantyhose and some vinegar. Just bunch up the hose and wet it with white vinegar, then easily scrub away.

Zap the Sap!

Tree sap dripping on your car is one of the hazards of summer, but you can remove it easily with butter or margarine. Just rub the butter onto the sap with a soft cloth, and it comes right off.

De-Rust Your Bumper

The best way to remove rust from your car's chrome bumper? Just rub the rusted area with a shiny piece of crumpled aluminum foil that has been dipped in cola.

A Surefire Way to Wipe Away Window Decals

Transparent decals may be easily removed using a solution of lukewarm water and white vinegar. Place the solution on a sponge and dampen the area thoroughly for a few minutes. If this doesn't work, saturate the decal with straight vinegar and let stand for 15 minutes.

Who Knew? Readers' Favorite

Is it finally time to get rid of your "Gore 2000" bumper sticker? Try this: Set your blow-dryer on high and run it back and forth over the sticker until the adhesive softens. Then apply a bit of vegetable oil. Carefully lift a corner with a credit card, and peel it off.

Make Dashboard Scratches Disappear

Got scuffs and scratches on your odometer? You can eliminate the marks on dashboard plastic by rubbing them with a bit of baby oil.

Got a Stink in Your Car?

Instead of buying a commercial air freshener, repurpose a dryer sheet to sweeten the air. Place sheets under the seats, in door pockets, or in the trunk to keep your car smelling fresh.

Forget the Ice Scraper

When the forecast calls for ice or snow, protect your car by placing two old bath towels across your windshield. When it's time to drive, simply pull off the towels and you're ready to go!

Ice Proof Your Windshield

If an ice storm is in the forecast, coat your windshield with a solution of one part water to three parts white vinegar. It will keep your windshield ice-free.

Ice Ain't Nice

In the winter months, the only thing worst than having ice all over your windshield is having to spend a lot for a windshield deicer. Here's an inexpensive, yet effective, alternative to deice your windshield and windows: 1 part antifreeze, 4½ parts alcohol, and 4½ parts water.

Prepare Your Car for Winter Weather

Before winter hits, fill a few old milk cartons with sand or kitty litter and keep them in your car's trunk. If you get stuck, sprinkle the sand on the ice to improve the tires' traction.

Who Knew? Readers' Favorite

If your car doors freeze shut during the frigid winter months, try this preventative measure: Rub vegetable oil on the rubber moldings around your doors. Since it's the rubber, not the metal, in your doors that freezes, lubing it with oil should do the trick.

Stuck in the Mud?

If you get stuck in snow or mud, try using your car floor mat for traction. Better yet, be prepared and keep a blanket in the trunk for this very purpose.

Be Careful with Cruise Control

Important safety tip! While cruise control is a great fuel-conserving feature on your car, make sure it's turned off when the roads are wet or icy. If your tires start to hydroplane, the cruise control may continue to accelerate, and you might end up skidding and losing control of the wheel when your tires catch the ground again.

Spend Less on Car Washes

Specialty items used to clean cars are often found in big box and hardware stores. However, you'll find the same items—squeegees, shams, and sponges—for much less in the cleaning aisle of your local grocery store.

And No One Will Be the Wiser

Misjudge how much room you had backing out of a parking spot? Just whip out a can of WD-40 and spray whichever car got left with a paint stain. Wipe with a clean cloth or tissue and the paint will come right off.

Safe from Spit Up

Taking a road trip? If your baby tends to lose most of her food on your car's upholstery, don't forget to guard it with a towel, tablecloth, or bath mat before you leave.

Fantastic Air Freshener

We love this cheap, environmentally friendly air freshener for the car. All you need is an old, burned-up candle with a strong scent. Chop the leftover wax into chunks, slip it into an unused (but clean!) sock, and tie the sock closed. Stick it in the side pockets of your car door or under the seat during cooler months.

When your car's keyless remote needs a new battery, don't head to the dealership for a replacement— depending on the kind of car you have, it could cost anywhere from $50 to $150. Instead, pry open your remote and check the size and type of battery you need. Then head to a hardware or electronics store for a much-cheaper alternative.

Boost Your Remote

Want to know how to increase the range of your car's keyless entry by 30 percent? Just press it against your head as you use it. It will conduct the (perfectly safe) radio signal through your body, giving its travel power a boost. Strange but true!

A Penny for Your Thoughts?

Does your car need new tires? To find out, put Abe Lincoln to work! Place a penny in your tire's shallowest tread, with Abe facing the hubcap. If you can see the hair on top of the president's head, the tread is worn down to the point that you should buy new tires.

Saved a Scorched Cell Phone

Left your cell phone in your hot car, and now it won't work? Just turn on the car's air-conditioner, and direct it at the phone. When you get home, continue cooling the phone until it is no longer hot to the touch, and then put it in an airtight bag in the fridge (not freezer) for five minutes. Your phone should work fine again now!

Control the Clutter

Your daughter is suddenly too cool for her Dora the Explorer backpack. It's not even worn out, but it's not really your look, either. A great way to repurpose it is to use it as storage in your car! It will easily hang on the back of one of the front seats to store all those odds and ends that usually litter the floor.

Who Knew? Readers' Favorite

Chips in your car's paint job can be expensive to fix, so before you head to the auto body shop, see if you can find a crayon that closely matches the color of your car. Fill in the nick with the crayon, and then buff gently. This works especially well with minor scratches!

Frugal Fueling

The cheapest days to refuel your car are Tuesdays and Wednesdays. People fuel up on Thursdays and Fridays for weekend trips, and on Monday for their workweek. Therefore, most gas stations do their weekly price changes on Tuesdays or Wednesdays.

Don't Tempt Fate

If you park your car on the street, make sure to remove any electronics from your car, as well as the holders. Thieves will often break into cars if they see a GPS holder attached to the windshield, assuming that the unit is in the glove compartment.

PART FIVE

MORE WAYS TO SAVE

In this section, we pull out all the stops to help you make the most of your budget—on your schedule. You'll find out how to get rid of pests that invade your home using ingredients you already have; get more goodies from your garden; haggle like a hero; beat the airlines at their own game; keep the kids under control, and much, much more. Whether you're a novice at saving money or you consider yourself scrimping royalty, you're bound to find lots of tricks and tips that will have you saying, "Who knew?"

CHAPTER 1

Getting Rid of Pests

Killing Roaches the Green Way

Nothing is more revolting than roaches, except perhaps the chemicals we use to kill them. Try this natural pesticide: Make a mixture of equal parts cornstarch and plaster of paris, and sprinkle it in the cracks where roaches appear. They'll soon be a thing of the past.

A Safer Roach Spray

Chasing, banging with a shoe, and squishing—none of these is a fail-safe method when it comes to getting rid of roaches. Go for the kill by zapping them with WD-40 instead of bug spray.

A Spoonful of Sugar...

Sugar and baking powder are a great one-two punch when it comes to getting rid of roaches. Mix in equal parts and shake over any area where you've had a sighting or suspect entry. Clean and replace at regular intervals. Sugar attracts, baking soda (strangely) kills.

Who Knew? Readers' Favorite

Another great method for eliminating cockroaches is to fill a large bowl with cheap wine, then place it under the sink or wherever you see the revolting little bugs. The pests drink the wine, get drunk, and drown.

Say Bye to the Flies

The easiest way to get rid of fruit flies is to limit their access to their favorite foods. Let your fresh fruit ripen in closed paper bags. Then when it's ripe, store it in the refrigerator.

Fruit Fly Formula

To eliminate fruit flies naturally, fill a spray bottle with 10 parts water and one part rubbing alcohol, and spray away. It's about as effective as an insecticide, but not nearly as harmful to your family.

Vengeance with Vinegar

Have a fruit fly problem? Add a couple of drops of dishwashing liquid to a bowl of apple cider vinegar and leave it where you see flies. The smell of the vinegar attracts the flies, while the dish soap breaks the surface tension of the vinegar and causes the little nuisances to drown.

Herbal Help

A number of herbs will ward off crawling insects. The most potent are fresh or dried bay leaves, sage, and cloves. Place any of these herbs in locations where a problem exists, and the critters will do an about-face and leave the premises. Ants, roaches, and spiders may be more difficult to get rid of. If these herbs don't work, try mixing 2 cups borax with an equal amount of sugar in a large container, and then sprinkle the mixture in areas that you know the pests frequent. When crawling insects cross a fine powder, they lose the waterproof layer from their bodies, causing water loss and, ultimately, death.

Repel Flying Insects

Basil is not just for pesto! If you have a problem with any type of flying insect, keep a basil plant or two around the house. You can also dry the leaves and hang them in small muslin bags to repel flying insects—they hate the sweet aroma.

Clove's the Way

Silverfish are disgusting, down to each and every one of their little legs. An effective, natural way to repel them is with whole cloves. Just sprinkle a few in drawers and other areas where you see them.

So Long, Silverfish

Silverfish like to hang around damp places, but they'll slither away if you decorate with spiced sachets. Try combining sage, bay leaves, and apple pie spice in fabric bags and hanging in the kitchen, bathroom, basement, and other moist areas.

Who Knew? Readers' Favorite

If you can figure out where ants are entering your house, you can keep them out. Simply sprinkle salt, cinnamon, chalk dust, or ashes on their path of entry, and they'll turn around and go elsewhere.

A Not-So-Happy Ending for Carpenter Ants

Get rid of carpenter ants naturally with this formula: Mix one packet dry yeast with ½ cup molasses and ½ cup sugar, and spread on a piece of cardboard. Leave this sticky trap wherever you see the ants; they'll come in droves to the sweet smell. Unfortunately for them, they'll also get stuck. Wait until your molasses mixture is covered with the creepy pests, then throw away. We've also had readers tell us they've used this method for catching wasps!

Mealworm Menace

Keep a few sticks of wrapped spearmint chewing gum near any open packages of pasta, and they'll never get infested with mealworms.

A Mouse's Favorite Food

Though cartoons would have us believe otherwise, mice love the flavor of peanut butter even more than cheese. If you're having problems trapping a mouse with cheese, try smearing peanut butter on the trap instead.

Mice Hate Mint

If you're suffering from a mouse infestation and can see the mouse holes, smear a bit of mint toothpaste nearby and the smell will deter them. You can also rub toothpaste along the bottom of your baseboards and anywhere else mice may get into your home.

Peppermint for Pests

In addition to mice, moles, squirrels, gophers, and rats also hate the aroma of peppermint. Try planting mint near your home—chances are you will never see one of these pests again! For a preexisting gopher problem, soak cotton balls in peppermint oil and then drop them down a gopher hole.

Who Knew? Readers' Favorite

If you're squeamish about having to pick up the remains of a rodent you've set a trap for, place the baited trap inside a brown paper lunch bag. Rodents like exploring small spaces, and once the trap has done its trick, you can scoop it right up and throw it way.

Keep Flies Away from Their Favorite Places

If you don't keep trashcans and compactors sealed tightly, you can quickly end up with a swarm of flies. Luckily, flies are repelled by lavender oil. Soak a few cotton balls with the oil and toss them into your garbage at the beginning of each week. The flies will stay away and your garbage won't smell as bad! Other natural repellents that will send flies in the other direction are oil of cloves and wintergreen mint sprigs.

Keep Plants Pest-Free

When watering outdoor plants, place a few drops of dishwashing liquid into the water, and make sure it gets on your plants' leaves. The detergent will keep bugs away, making sure your plants remain healthy and beautiful.

Do Battle with an Army of Ants

If your yard or garden is infested with pesky ants, sprinkle artificial sweetener (anything with aspartame) over the affected areas. Or try oats, cornmeal, instant grits, or cream of wheat. The ants will eat the dry cereal, which will then absorb all the moisture in their bodies and kill them.

Solve a Snail or Slug Problem

Need to get rid of snails or slugs in your garden? Find the cheapest beer you can, then pour it into several shallow containers (shoeboxes lined with aluminum foil work well). Dig a few shallow holes in your garden and place the containers inside so that they are at ground level. Leave overnight, and the next morning you'll find dozens of dead (or drunk) snails and slugs instead. These critters are attracted to beer (who isn't!), but it has a diuretic effect on them, causing them to lose vital liquids and die.

Clear Out Slugs with Cabbage

If you're having problems with slugs eating your flowers and nothing else seems to work, your best solution might be in the form of distraction. Slugs love cabbage, so planting a few in your garden will ensure they stay away from your flowers and go for the cabbage instead.

Save Your Plants

If you want to keep bugs off your plants, try spraying the leaves with a solution of 10 parts weak tea and one part ammonia. Try it first on a few leaves to test for damage, and make sure pets and children don't try to eat or lick the leaves (hey, they've done weirder things!).

For Crawling Critters

Sometimes, getting rid of insects is as easy as making it hard for them to get where they're going. Smear petroleum jelly around the base of plant stems, and ants and other crawling insects will slide right off, protecting your plants.

Buh-Bye, Bambi!

Hang small pieces of a deodorant bar soap on trees to keep deer from munching on them. Or, try a piece of your clothing that you've worn for several days—deer don't like the smell of humans.

Who Knew? Readers' Favorite

Spray your garbage cans with a mixture of one part ammonia and three parts water on a regular basis to keep squirrels, raccoons, dogs, and other critters from rummaging through the cans.

Rotten Eggs Are Good for Something!

It's a breeze to keep deer, antelope, elk, and other large animals away from your garden and trees by using eggs that have gone bad. Just break them open (outside of the house!) around the area that you want to keep the critters away from. The smell of hydrogen sulfide from the rotten eggs will keep them away long after the offending odor has dissipated.

Strip Tease

If birds or other critters are nibbling at your fruit trees, try hanging long strips of aluminum foil from the branches. They'll be attracted to its shiny surface, but once they bite it, they'll fly away.

Get Rid of Bothersome Bees

Don't you hate having to worry about a bee hijacking your soda while you're having a drink outside? So sip in confidence by covering the top of your drink with aluminum foil, then sticking a straw through the top.

Picnic Peace

To win the war against ants at your picnic, place the picnic table's legs in old coffee cans filled with water. The ants won't be able to climb up the table, and your food will stay safe.

Wasp Reduction

If you find a large wasp's nest, have it removed professionally. But for smaller numbers of these freaky fliers, fill a jar with half jam and half water. Cover with paper punctured with holes to attract, trap, and drown them.

Wary of Wasps?

Is there anything worse than coming upon a swarm of wasps when you're enjoying your garden? If you find that wasps are building a nest in the same spot year after year, spray the area with white vinegar several times in the beginning of the spring, and they'll find somewhere else to roost.

Great Trick for Window Boxes

If you keep plants in window boxes, paint them white first. The bright, reflective surface will deter insects and reduce the risk of dry rot. It looks great, too!

Give Flies the Brush-Off

If you prefer not to use chemicals to get rid of flies, and you're not the most accurate fly swatter, invest in a strong fan. Scientists say that flies' wings are unable to operate in a breeze above nine miles per hour, so open the windows, turn the fan to full power, and they'll soon buzz off. This is also a great trick for an outdoor party—just aim a few fans at the center of the action instead of spraying down your yard with awful smelling repellant.

Free a Bee, Don't Smack It

If a bee or other stinging insect gets trapped in the car with you, do not swat at it! Instead, pull your car off to the side of the road, open all the windows or doors, and let the critter fly out.

Moth Trap

Trap moths by mixing one part molasses with two parts white vinegar and placing the mixture in a bright yellow container. The moths will be attracted to the color and the smell, then drown inside.

Placing your woolen clothes in a well-sealed bag isn't always enough to keep moths away, as any eggs laid in them beforehand will hatch—and the new moths will have a field day. To make sure all the eggs die before you put your clothes in storage, place the airtight bag of clothes in the freezer for 24 hours.

Keep Clothes Safe with Soap

When winter rolls around, do your sweaters smell like mothballs? Ick. Mothballs work great, but leave a nasty odor. When you're storing winter clothes next year, put a few leftover soap slivers in a vented plastic bag, and add it to your closet or cedar chest instead of mothballs. The soap will keep moths from damaging your clothes, and it smells fresh, too.

Flea Flicker

Fleas can be eliminated from upholstery and carpets by using a high-powered vacuum cleaner (ideally one with a canister) with a bag that seals well. Remove the bag and dispose of it outside as soon as you finish.

A Good Night's Sleep for Your Pet

To ward off fleas from a pet's sleeping area, try sprinkling a few drops of lavender oil in the area. Fleas hate the smell of lavender oil and will find somewhere else to hide. Your pet, meanwhile, can enjoy a good night's sleep—and smell great in the morning.

Spray to Lead Bugs Astray

If flies or bees have invaded your home, and you want to get them away from you fast, squirt a little hair spray into the air. They hate the stuff and will go elsewhere.

Repel Bugs Naturally

Don't spend money on bug sprays. Their main ingredient is usually alcohol, so save some money by simply making a mixture of one part rubbing alcohol and four parts water, then spraying it on as you would bug spray. Another natural (and great-smelling) alternative is equal parts water and pure vanilla extract.

Dryer Sheet Wonder

Is there anything a dryer sheet can't do? Many people report that keeping dryer sheets in your pockets will help repel mosquitoes and other bugs. This may be because of a citronella-like ingredient they contain.

A Use for Pencil Shavings!

Add pencil shavings to your plants if they suffer from bug infestation. Bugs don't like the smell of the cedar in pencils. Just mix in with the soil, mostly at the bottom.

Fooled by Fake Flowers

If your child is being bitten by a lot of bugs this summer, it may be because of his or her colorful clothing. Believe it or not, bugs are fooled by bright colors and floral prints. They think they're real flowers, then bite your kids instead when they fly close.

Stopping Slugs

If slugs are finding their way into your container plants, cover the bottom hole with used sanding disks or circle of sandpaper. Slugs hate the scratchy surface and won't cross it.

Chalk It Up

Draw a line ants won't cross…with chalk! Ants think chalk is ash and won't cross it (because it may be a sign of fire). Use their tiny brains against them by drawing a thick line of chalk along windowsills, cabinets, or anywhere else they enter your home. You can even draw a line on your picnic table!

An Ace Solution for Aphids

If aphids are infesting your plants, here's an easy solution. Cover a tennis ball with petroleum jelly and leave it nearby. The bugs will be attracted to its bright color, and then get stuck on its side.

Can't You Smell That Smell?

Citronella candles are great for repelling insects, but they can be pricey. Get the same effect for much less by mixing garlic with water and spraying it near all your outdoor light bulbs. As the bulbs heat up, they'll spread a faint garlicky scent across your yard, which will keep mosquitoes and other bugs away.

Send Peter Rabbit Packing

Are rabbits overrunning your garden? Keep them away with the help of some vinegar. First poke a few holes in a pill bottle, then soak 3–4 cotton balls with vinegar and place them inside. Bury the bottle just under the soil and the smell will keep rabbits away.

CHAPTER 2

Energy-Saving Tips

A Truly Bright Idea

Dusting a light bulb can increase the light in a room by up to 50 percent.

Electrical Insulation

Did you know that you could be losing warm (or cold) air through your electrical outlets? We placed some fireproof foam insulation under our outlet covers and switch plates and saved several dollars a month on our utility bill.

Vacuum Those Vents

Make sure to vacuum your heating and air conditioning vents regularly. When the vents get caked up with dust, your furnace or air conditioner has to work much harder!

Slow and Steady with the Heat

When it's time to turn on the heat, be patient. Your house won't heat up any faster if you crank the thermostat way up, but you are likely to forget to turn it down, which can be a huge energy waster.

Who Knew? Readers' Favorite

Don't let your fan go to waste just because it's no longer hot outside. To stay toasty during the frigid days of winter, hit the reverse switch to push hot air down into your room.

Feed Plants from Your Fish Tank

If you have an aquarium, save the water each time you change it, and use it to water your houseplants. The fishy water contains nitrogen, potassium, and phosphorus—all three function as natural fertilizers for plants. You'll be amazed at the results.

Set Up an Efficient Kitchen

Organize your kitchen so your hot appliances (an oven or dishwasher) don't sit near your cold appliances (the fridge and freezer). Otherwise, they'll have to work harder to do their jobs. Also, make sure your refrigerator isn't exposed to direct sunlight or heat vents. These simple tips will help keep your kitchen in tip-top shape and your energy costs down.

Ease Your Energy Bill

Even when you're not using appliances, they still continue to use energy. So pull the plug when you're done with the blender, toaster, food processor, even your television—everything except appliances that need constant power to preserve a special setting.

Energy Saving Tips for Your Fridge

Clean the condenser coils on the back of your refrigerator twice a year, and you'll use less energy while increasing the life of the appliance. It's also important to keep your freezer packed—even with bags of ice if necessary—because a full freezer is much more efficient than a half-empty one.

Microwave Safety

Microwave doors may become misaligned, especially if you pull down on them when opening them. When the doors don't close properly, they can leak radiation, making your food take longer to cook. Check them periodically with a small, inexpensive detector, which can be purchased in any hardware store.

Battery Booster

Batteries will last longer if they're stored in the refrigerator. To boost their energy, place them in the sun for a day before you use them.

Warm-Weather Dishwasher Tip

Here's a terrific tip to use during warm weather: Turn off your dishwasher after the rinse cycle, open it up, and let your dishes drip-dry. You'll save a lot by avoiding the heat-drying cycle on your machine.

Keep a Tight Seal

If your refrigerator is more than a few years old, its seal is probably not as tight as it used to be. To save energy and keep your food cooler, first clean the door's gasket (that rubber lining that goes around it), then rub it with petroleum jelly to ensure a tighter seal.

Radiator Energy Saver

Here's a great energy-saving tip for cold winter nights: If you have cast-iron radiators, tape aluminum foil to a sheet of cardboard (shiny side out) and place it behind the radiator. The radiant heat will bounce back into your room instead of being absorbed into the wall.

Who Knew? Readers' Favorite

In the summer months, make sure to keep your closet doors closed. Otherwise, you're paying to cool your closets, which will increase your energy bill.

Lengthen Laptop Battery Power

If you clean the battery contacts on your laptop and cordless phone, the charge will last for a longer time. Use the tip of a cotton swab dipped in rubbing alcohol to clean the connection points.

Save Water in the Shower

When it comes to saving water, a short shower is better than a bath, but even still, lots of water gets wasted. Collect as much as you can with buckets to use for the lawn (or water play later on in the day, if you have young kids).

CHAPTER 3

The Art of Decorating

All Decked Out

When it's time to repaint your deck or porch, why not get creative and paint a piece of artwork? Try painting a "rug" by using a different color than the main base color for an inside rectangle, along with stencils for a border. If you skip the acrylic topcoat, you'll get a worn look that will add to the tromp l'oeil effect.

The Floss Fix

To hang lightweight artwork that's not in a heavy frame, there's no need to buy picture wire. Unwaxed dental floss will do the trick.

Picture This

Hanging a picture? Make it easy by first taping a thumbtack (pointy side out) to the back below the hanging bracket. Perfectly position your picture, then give it a bit of a push into the wall.

Bookshelf Decorating Done Easily

A pair of wine bottles, either full or empty, makes great bookends for your shelf—especially if there are cookbooks on it!

Who Knew? Readers' Favorite

When slipping curtains over a metal rod, first place a plastic freezer or sandwich bag over the metal end. This will help you avoid snagging the curtains so they go on easily.

If You Never Use Paper Napkins

If you have a set of pretty cloth napkins you never use, consider making them into an equally pretty throw pillow. Fill it with pillow foam, an old mattress egg crate, cotton stuffing, old fabrics, or nylon stockings.

Stuff It

Tired of the way your expensive valances seem to hang limply at the windows? Get that magazine look by stuffing plastic grocery bags into your draperies to get them to pouf out more.

Upright Candles

Do your candles slide around in their holders like a kid wearing his dad's pants? Wrap the bottom with tape to get the right fit.

Magazine Management

Are magazines piling up around your home? Make some decorative and functional magazine holders by cutting cereal boxes at angles and covering them with wrapping paper. Cover with some craft lacquer for a durable finish.

Everything in Its Place

Here's an unusual way to get a put-together look in your kitchen. Outline your small appliances with weather stripping to keep them stationary on the counter. This works well for the phone, blender, coffee machine, toaster oven—anything you permanently leave out.

From the Frying Pan

You treasure your grandmother's antique cast-iron pans, but you hate cooking in them! Repurpose these kitchen classics as magnet boards by hanging them from hooks and using some refrigerator magnets to hang recipe cards, postcards, artwork, and more.

Put on a Pedestal

Cake stands are perfect for displaying much more than cakes. Use them to show off trinkets or collections, or simply use as a just-in-the-door clutter catcher for keys and change. Now you finally know what to do with all those cake stands you got for wedding presents!

Do-It-Yourself Headboard

To perk up your bedroom with a splash of color, get crafty with a DIY faux-headboard. Find a colorful sheet that complements the décor of your room; any fabric will work, so consider cotton, linen, velvet, and even fur! First, consider the width of your bed; a headboard should be slightly wider than your mattress. Then decide what style of headboard you like best, and cut your fabric to the right size and shape. Either wrap your fabric around a foam base and hang it on the wall, or hang it up on its own.

A terrific way to hang posters in your kid's room without leaving holes or stains is with white, non-gel toothpaste. Just put a generous drop on the back of each corner, press to the wall, and watch it stick.

Your Poster Child

If your teenager loves tacking posters up on his bedroom wall, here's a great tip to keep the corners hole-free. Place a binder clip on each corner, then slip them over nails or thumb tacks. As an added bonus, get shiny or colorful binder clips.

A Great Use for Old Jewelry

Do you have too many brooches and pins to ever get around to wearing them all? Repurpose them by turning them into unique magnets that get noticed! Just use wire cutters to clip off the pin on the back, then glue a magnet (available at craft stores) on the back.

CHAPTER 4

Fantastically Frugal Kid Tips

Never Buy a Baby Wipe Again

If you have a baby, you know that one costly item that's impossible to use less of is baby wipes. When we had babies, we saved hundreds per year by making our own diaper wipes! They are easy to make and can be kept in an old baby wipes container, a plastic storage bin with a lid, or a resealable plastic bag. Here's how to do it: combine 2 tablespoons each of baby oil and baby shampoo (or baby wash) with 2 cups boiled and cooled water and 1–2 drops of your favorite essential oil for scent (optional). Remove the cardboard roll from a package of paper towels, then cut the entire roll in half (you can also tear off sheets by hand and stack them in a pile). Put some of the liquid mixture at the bottom of your container, then place the half-roll in the container. Pour the rest of the liquid over your paper towels and voilà—homemade baby wipes! Let the wipes sit for about an hour to absorb all the liquid, and your baby will never know the difference.

Freshen Up Stinky Diapers

If you get a nasty whiff every time you open the diaper pail, drop a few charcoal briquettes under the pail's liner. You'll be amazed at what you don't smell.

A Trick Worthy of the Lucky Charms Leprechaun

If you're one of those super-parents who don't let their kids eat sugary cereal, have you thought about using it as a reward? Kids not used to having a morning sugar fix normally like sugary cereal brands as much as they like candy, so why not use it instead? That way, when kids are getting a sugary treat for being good, they'll at least get it from a food that is also enriched with vitamins. And if you want to wean your children off the sugary stuff in the morning, this might be a good way to start!

An Idea You'll Love

Uh-oh, it's Valentine's Day, and you forgot to buy cards for your kid's class. Don't despair! Just head over to FreePrintableValentines.net, a site that gives you dozens of valentine designs to print out instantly.

Pretty Cool Prank

We can't help but share our favorite harmless prank. Add a couple of drops of food coloring (we like green) to your milk carton before your child goes to pour the milk. (Make sure to shake it up.) He'll get a surprise and a big kick out of the color!

Who Knew? Readers' Favorite

Sneak some calcium into your kids' food by adding powdered milk to their meals. It'll be inconspicuous to them in dishes such as mashed potatoes, meatballs, and peanut butter sandwiches (mixed in with the peanut butter).

The Right Bike

Before you get your kid that bike he's been begging for, make sure it's the proper size. When sitting on the seat with hands on the handlebar, your child should be able to place the balls of both feet on the ground. He should also be able to straddle the center bar standing up with an inch or so of clearance.

Toy Tamer

You could pay 50¢ a pop for links that secure your child's toys to his stroller. But for a less expensive substitute, try using shower curtain rings, which are available in 12-packs for less than $2.

Keep 'Em Guessing

We like to add a little more excitement and surprise to the holidays by labeling our kids' gifts with colorful stickers rather than gift tags. The stickers are color-coded for each recipient, and we don't reveal the code until gift-opening time on Christmas Day. It's a clever, fun, and inexpensive way to keep the kids guessing.

Add a Splash of Color

Make your kids' bath time colorful with this easy alternative to store-bought bath crystals: Simply put a few drops of food coloring into the bath water. Whatever color you choose, your children will still emerge from the bath squeaky-clean.

Placemat Fun

We love these unique placemats for your kids: Buy an inexpensive or secondhand picture book, then pull out the pages and laminate them using clear contact paper. They're waterproof, original, and cheaper than store-bought placemats.

Tone Down the TP Usage

If your potty-trained toddler enjoys pulling toilet paper off the roll, use this trick to keep his TP usage in line: Before putting the roll on the dispenser, squeeze the tube so that it flattens slightly. This will keep the roll from turning too easily, thus keeping the amount that comes off the roll manageable.

A Nutty Facial

If you're looking for a way to entertain your kids, put them to work with this fun chore. You can "wash" the faces of your daughter's dolls by smearing peanut butter on them, then wiping it off. The oils in the butter seep into the plastic, removing every last bit of grime.

Save Those Pennies

Teaching the kids about saving their money? An ice cream container makes a great piggy bank. Just clean it, cut a slot in the lid, and decorate the outside with wrapping paper, stickers, and ribbon.

Who Knew? Readers' Favorite

Almost all soft rubber balls, including tennis balls, can be brought back to life by spending a night in the oven with only the pilot light on. The heat causes the air inside the ball to expand. Just be sure to remove the balls before you turn the oven on!

DIY Finger Paints for Little Da Vincis

Keep your kids busy and encourage their creativity with homemade finger paints: Start by mixing two cups cold water with ¼ cup cornstarch, then boil until the liquid is as thick as, um, finger paints. Pour into small containers, swirl in some food coloring, and watch them create their masterpieces (just keep those colorful fingers away from walls!).

Dryer Lint Dough

Make a Play-Doh substitute for your kids with an unlikely ingredient: dryer lint! First save up 3 cups of dryer lint, then stick it into a pot with 2 cups water, 1 cup flour, and ½ teaspoon vegetable or canola oil. Cook, stirring constantly, over low heat until the mixture is smooth. Then pour onto a sheet of wax paper to cool.

Homemade Bubbles!

Summertime is bubble season for kids who want some outdoor fun. Here's an inexpensive homemade solution for blowing bubbles: Mix 1 tablespoon glycerin with 2 tablespoons powdered laundry detergent in 1 cup warm water. Any unpainted piece of metal wire can be turned into a bubble wand: Just shape one end of the wire into a circle. Blowing into the mixture with a straw will make smaller bubbles float into the air. For colored bubbles, add food coloring.

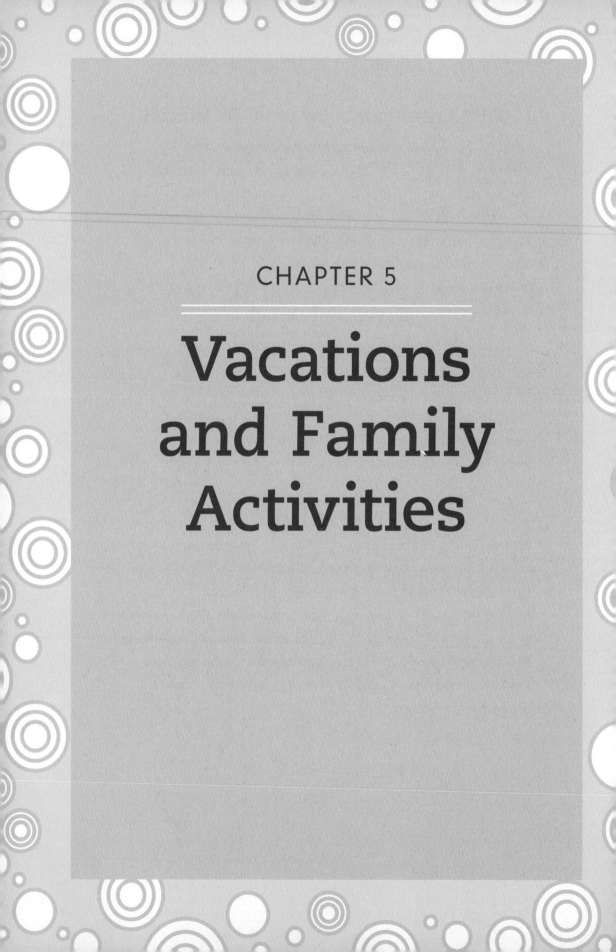

CHAPTER 5

Vacations and Family Activities

Flight days flexible? Try searching for trips that begin and end on a Tuesday or Wednesday, when we've found that flights throughout the US and Canada are cheaper.

Keep Checking Those Rates

Just because you've booked your flight doesn't mean you can't still save. Make sure to keep an eye on airfare prices, and rebook your flight if necessary. Even if your airline charges you $75 to cancel a ticket, you'll still save a bundle if a rival airline is offering tickets at $150 less than what you paid.

Go Direct

Planning a trip to a far-away locale? Before buying plane tickets, check out booking sites such as Expedia.com, Kayak.com, or Orbitz.com, which show the cheapest deals from every airline. Once you've found the best prices, check the airline websites directly. They'll offer either the price you've found online or an even lower one, and you'll save on the internet booking fees.

Get Past the Sponsors

When searching for travel deals online, make sure to scroll through a few pages of results before making your pick. Many sites have "sponsored results," which means that companies have paid to be featured at the top of search results.

Your Ticket to the Lowest Price

After you buy a plane ticket, visit Yapta.com. Enter your flight details and they'll email you if the price goes down. Even if you have to pay a fee to change your ticket, you'll find that fares often fluctuate by hundreds of dollars. This is an easy way to make sure you're getting the cheapest price.

The Five-Day Outlook for Travel

Farecast.com is one of our favorite sites for planning a trip. If your travel dates are flexible, it will tell you the cheapest days to travel. If you know exactly when you're coming or going, it will predict whether or not the price will go up or down. The coolest part is, it's not affiliated with a particular airline or travel site, so the advice is unbiased. If you want to lock in the price the site gives you, you can buy "insurance" for a small fee.

Last-Minute Deals in Travel

If you're looking for the best deals in travel, head over to AirfareWatchdog.com, which catalogs the cheapest fares as they are listed on travel and airline sites. This site requires a bit of work—you have to click through to other sites to find the rate yourself, but the "watch dog" will tell you which days of the week to search and in what date range. If you normally spend a lot of time trying different combinations of travel dates and nearby airports, this site will take a lot of the guesswork out of it for you.

If you've been to an airport lately, you've probably noticed that the ticket counters are staffed by fewer people than ever before. It's annoying on a regular travel day, but if there are lots of flight cancellations, this can mean a two-hour-plus wait in line. Save yourself a lot of time by skipping the line all together. Instead, call the customer service number for your airline and rebook your cancelled flight right over the phone.

Time To Get A Passport

In these bad economic times, it's hard to see a silver lining, but here's one for anyone who loves an exotic vacation: It's now cheaper than ever to travel to many fascinating destinations around the world like Reykjavik, Iceland; Montreal, Canada; and Sydney, Australia. Check out vacation packages on sites like Expedia.com and Orbitz.com or ask a travel agent for hot deals to faraway lands.

International Travel Tip

Before you travel internationally, pack a spare passport photo and write down your passport number and the date it was issued. If you lose your passport while abroad, you'll have all the materials you need to get a new one. Bring your photo and passport info to a nearby US Embassy: It'll take much less time to process your request if you come prepared.

Save in Europe

If you're aged 12–26, if you're a student of any age, or you're a teacher or faculty member, you qualify for the International Student ID Card , which gives you amazing savings in Europe. Available at ISECard.com, the card costs $25, but with it you get discounts on trains, rental cards, tourist attractions, and more. Best of all, they'll provide medical travel insurance up to $2,000.

Pile Up the Points

Traveling a lot this summer? Check out Points.com, a site that lets you keep track of your airline miles and other rewards points, all in one place. Better yet, you can swap points from one reward program to another!

Don't Pay for Location

Save money on car rental by not renting at the airport, which charges rental car companies concession fees. Instead, take a cab to a nearby location—even with the fare factored in, you'll be surprised how much you save.

—*Drey Luca, CA*

The Cheapest Rental Cars

When looking for great deals, Hotwire.com is a good place to turn. The downside to this site is that you don't know which airline you're flying or which hotel you're staying at until after you've booked. While we aren't always a fan of this format for flights or lodging, for cars, who cares what dealer it is, as long as it's at the airport?

Rent a Wreck

If you're renting a car for your vacation this year, try Rent-a-Wreck (RentAWreck.com), which offers older cars (that are far from being wrecks, by our standards!) at discounted prices. You can also try asking at local dealerships to see if they rent cars—many have begun to in an attempt to make extra cash!

An Alternative to Airport Parking

Find out the cheapest place to park at your nearby airport by visiting BestParking.com. You'll discover lots close to the airport that aren't run by the airport itself—and are often half the price.

Who Knew? Readers' Favorite

When digging for discounts on rental cars and hotels, always call the hotel or rental company directly. If the only phone number you have is a national, toll-free one, look up the local number for that particular location and speak to them directly instead. The closer you get to your travel date, the better—in fact, don't be afraid to call the day before to confirm your reservation and ask for a better rate.

Fun Website for Travelers

For ideas of inexpensive places to visit while on vacation, visit Localyte.com. Localyte is a free website that connects travelers with locals in the know. Post a question about your destination, and have it answered by a local expert!

Forgo The Foliage

The best summer vacation you'll ever take might not be in the summer. As soon as Labor Day goes by, the rates go down drastically on hotels and airfare to most vacation destinations. Some of the most-discounted areas are the Caribbean, Hawaii, California, and anywhere else there's a beach. In a warm climate, it will still be as hot as ever on the sand. But the price will be much less, and you'll get the added benefit of having a smaller crowd. Check out a travel site like Travelocity.com for good deals to your dream destinations.

Where to Find Cheap Cruises

If you're dying to get away on a cruise, check out CruiseDeals.com, which has packages to Alaska, the Bahamas, Hawaii, Mexico, and just about anywhere else you'd want to go on a boat. The company negotiates with some of the world's biggest lines to bring their customers the best rates on cruises. If you want to hit the water, this is the best place to start.

Timeshares

If you're staying somewhere for a week or longer, you may be able to save money on your accommodations by renting a timeshare. Timeshares are properties owned jointly by several different families, who split up their time at the property during vacation months. You'll often find people renting out their time, or landlords who rent out their properties on a week-to-week basis over the summer in tourist-filled areas. To find a cheap timeshare in your destination, search on Craig's List or Ebay. You can also try SellMyTimeshareNow.com and TimesharesOnly.com.

When you're on vacation, use your digital camera for more than just snapshots in front of the sights! Take photos of street signs and the fronts of stores to remember favorite shops you visited, and snap a photo of needed subway maps, too. That way, when you're looking for the subway you don't have to pull out a map and look like a tourist—just look at your photo!

Planning a Road Trip?

Find out exactly how much you need to budget for gas at FuelCostCalculator.com. Enter the make and model of your car and your origin and destination, and AAA will calculate how much it will cost you using the Environmental Protection Agency's fuel economy ratings and its own gasoline prices report. With rising gas prices and fluctuating airfare, this is a great site to visit if you're not sure taking the car will save you money.

Keep 'Em Fed

Going on a road trip? Make sure to pack plenty of food before you leave to cut down on meal expenses along the way. Periodically handing out food is also a great way to keep kids quiet(er)! Have several different types of snacks on hand so they don't get bored.

Make a Single-Night Stop Easy

Time for a family road trip? If you have an overnight stop on your journey, prepare for it by packing small, individual bags for each family member. That way, you won't have to dig around in the car for pajamas and toiletries for the one-night stay.

Going the Distance

Planning a road trip this summer? When it's time to fill up on gas, drive a little farther off the highway exit before choosing a station. The gas stations closest to the highway will often charge more per gallon than the ones located a bit off your course—you could save a few bucks by going the extra distance.

Save on Souvenirs

When you're on vacation, save money on souvenirs by staying away from gift shops and stores close to tourist areas. Instead, visit a local grocery store, where you'll usually find locally themed postcards, maps, key chains, magnets, t-shirts, and more, normally at discount prices.

Bring Some Easy Mac and Ramen When You Go

When booking a hotel for your summer vacation, make sure to choose one that offers a free breakfast or an in-room refrigerator and microwave. Eating a couple of meals at the hotel is one of the easiest ways to save while you're away.

—Rita Guerrero, Middlebury, VT

Packing with Pantyhose

Use a pair of nylons to store your socks and underwear. Keep the clean ones in one leg, then switch them to the other leg after you've worn them. It will make it super easy to find clean socks and undies in your suitcase.

Just in Case

When packing a suitcase for a trip, put at least one outfit in the suitcase of your spouse (or other travel buddy). If the airline loses your luggage, you'll have at least a few items of clothing to tide you over until it's found.

Who Knew? Readers' Favorite

Packing for vacation? Consider packing clothes in the same color family, and pants that can go with a lot of different shirts. You can more easily mix and match them, so you'll have to pack less. This trick will also come in handy when you spill something on yourself—if your blue shirt is soiled, you still have another in your suitcase.

A Hot Idea

A hair dryer can serve double-duty while you're traveling: It'll dry your hair and stand in for an iron. Wet the clothing you'd like to de-wrinkle and lay it on a table or other level surface. Smooth the wrinkles out with your hand while blowing warm air on the spot with the dryer.

Packing Presents?

When you have to pack tons of presents, it's usually more frugal to pay to ship the contents of your suitcase to your destination ahead of time. Most airlines charge between $15 and $30 for the first checked bag and much more for the second, while it only costs around $14 to mail up to 70 pounds via the post office.

Keep Your Necklaces Looking Nice

Don't waste any more time untangling necklace chains. Before packing them, cover each side with tape. If you didn't think ahead, use baby oil and a straight pin to work out the knots.

Another Neat Necklace Trick

Packing for a trip? Keep your necklaces safe and tangle-free by taping them to some bubble wrap. Then roll the wrap up and pack safely in your suitcase.

Shower Caps for Shoes

When you get plastic shower caps at hotels, save them for your suitcase. They make the perfect covers for dirty shoes!

Perfect for Accessories

Repurpose a plastic daily vitamin/pill container into a jewelry box that's perfect for trips. Rings, earrings, and even necklaces fit perfectly inside. You'll be accessorized for each day you're away!

When you're packing for a trip, keep some plastic wrap nearby. Before you pack shampoo, sunscreen, or other toiletries, take off the caps, place a layer of plastic wrap over the mouth of the container, and twist the cap back on. The plastic wrap will give you double the protection against suitcase spills.

A Sweet Solution!

If you use artificial sweetener for your coffee, you know what brand is your favorite! Make sure you always have some with you by using a business card holder to keep packets in your bag or purse.

Lighten the Load

Don't over-pack your vacation luggage—it could cause more pain than pleasure during your travels. To prevent a sore back, test the packing job before you leave: Pack your suitcase completely, and walk around the house with it for a few minutes. If it's too heavy, unload a bit or split your stuff into two lighter bags.

Keep Burglars Away

If you're concerned about your house being broken into while you're away, don't stop at automatic light switches. Ask your neighbor to park a car in your driveway, so robbers will think someone's at home.

Put Your Plants on Autopilot While You're Away

Place a large container of water near your plant (or if you have several plants, gather them into one spot to make it easy). Then place one end of a long piece of yarn into the water, and stick the other end into the plant's soil, near the roots. Lay the strand across the stalks of the plant. This will keep it moist until you return.

Plant Sitter

Now there's one less thing to worry about when you're on vacation. Water your plants yourself in absentia with this handy trick. Fill an ordinary plastic drink bottle with water and punch a little hole toward the bottom. Turn on its side and place on the soil near the plant stem to give a continual slow drip. Now go enjoy your trip and know you won't come home to a bunch of withering geraniums.

Save While You're Away

Many newspapers and magazines will allow you to suspend your home delivery or subscription. If you're going on a long vacation, make sure to call them up and stop service for the time you'll be away. You can also often do this for online movie rental and other services. You won't miss them while you're gone, and then you'll get an extra week or two when your subscription would normally be up.

Sometimes, vacation is all in your mind. If you can't afford to get away but you feel like you're ready to scream, consider taking a personal day off work, and convince your spouse or a friend to do it, too! Then enjoy an empty mall, a relaxing afternoon at the beach, or just a huge brunch (complete with mimosas). Whatever you do, get out of your house (which will just remind you of all your chores), and have fun! You'll be surprised how refreshed you feel after a day away.

Be A Day-Tripper

The most expensive part of any vacation is transportation and lodging, so consider taking several day trips during the summer rather than one week-long one. Commuter rail lines often offer discounts on train fare and tickets to theme parks and other attractions, or you may be overdue to take a drive to that nearby state park. For ideas of where to take day trips in your area, call your state's tourist board or type your state's name and "day trips" into a search engine.

For the Ski Buff

Like skiing? You'll love Liftopia.com. It offers discounts on lift tickets for more than 100 ski resorts across the United States and Canada. You can search by destination, or by categories like "good for beginners" and "nighttime skiing." You can also sign up for an email newsletter that will let you know about upcoming deals.

Smoother Skis

When you're getting ready to hit the slopes for the first time this year, take a few minutes to spray WD-40 on the bottom of your skis and snowboards before you scrape off the old wax. It will make your job much easier.

Keep Your Keys

If your vacation plans involve a boating excursion (or several), prevent drowned keys by sticking a few corks onto your key chain. Should the keys fall into the water, you'll find the corks bobbing along the surface.

Time to Go Camping!

Waking up to the sights, sounds, and smells of the forest can be one of the most peaceful things you'll ever experience—not to mention, the most inexpensive vacation you'll take in years. If you've never gone camping, it's time to start! If you don't have any equipment, ask friends if you can borrow theirs in exchange for lending them something of yours. You and your kids will enjoy working together while roughing it (and don't worry, "roughing it" can involve bathrooms and showers, electricity hook-ups, and even wireless internet). Best of all, with all that hard work each day, plus all the room in the world to run around in, your kids will get exhausted fast! To find campsites across the United States and Canada, visit ReserveAmerica.com, and for a great article for first-time campers, go to RoadAndTravel.com/adventuretravel/campingforfirsttimers.htm.

More Fun Activities Than You Ever Thought Possible

All you need to know when you're searching for fun things to do at Goby.com is what you're interested in and where you are (and, if you want, when you're going). Whether it's getting coffee, going to a playground, hitting up a museum, or more adventurous activities like sailing and horseback riding, Goby will tell you what's out there, and even give you a map to see where it is. The best thing about Goby is its straightforward, user-friendly design: no huge ads, no "sponsored results," no long loading times or signing up. For those of us who have spent a lot of time searching for things online, it's a welcome respite.

Cable: Not Always A Rip-Off

If you have cable, you may have movies and television shows available on-demand for free. Many cable systems offer a wide variety of old movies, as well as recent TV shows, that cable channels are trying to promote. Every system is different, but take a look and see if there is an option on your On-Demand menu that says "Free Movies," "Free Shows," or "Free On-Demand." You may also have to look through the shows and see which are listed as $0.

Going to the Movies

Even if you don't plan on getting snacks at the theater, it's hard to say "no" once you smell that popcorn popping! Always eat before you arrive; that way you'll be safe from snacking—and from spending. Find out which theaters in your area offer matinees, and also check to see if any membership programs you belong to offer free or discounted days. In some areas, Cablevision (also known as Optimum) offers free movies once a week for customers who sign up for cable, internet, and phone service.

Rent on the Cheap

What would the weekend be without a trip to the video store? With so many options for movie and video game rentals, the supply is up, so it's time to demand! Compare rates at your local video stores, and see if the store with the best perks—like being close to your home and letting you rent for the longest amount of time—will match the lowest price you can find. Since fewer and fewer people have VCRs these days, if you are still renting VHS cassettes, see if you can get a discount or a longer rental period when renting tapes instead of DVDs. Finally, keep an eye out for Redbox machines, which can be found in many drug and discount stores, where you can rent a DVD for one night for as low as $1.

Find Cheap Tickets More Easily

If you find Ticketmaster and other ticket sites as annoying as we do, you'll love ZebraTickets.com. Zebra Tickets collects ticket prices from around the web for sporting events, concerts, and plays, so you'll be sure to know which site is offering the best deal.

Free Summer Fun

For ideas on fun, free activities to do over the summer, try checking out your community center or park district. Most towns have tons of free summertime events, from sports clinics for kids to free concerts for adults. See if they have a website or pick up a calendar at your local branch.

Even if they normally have high admission prices, most museums offer opportunities for you to visit for free. If a museum gets money from the government, they're usually required to either offer free admission one day a week or charge admission as a "suggested donation"—that is, you only have to pay what you want. Other museums have late hours that are free to visitors once a week or month. If you like looking at art, also check out galleries, where you can find cool, local art displayed for free in the hopes that someone will buy it.

TV: Live and In-Person!

If you live near a big city, especially Los Angeles or New York, one of the most fun free activities you can do is attend a TV taping. Talk shows, sitcoms, and game shows are always looking for studio audience members, and it's not only a blast to see a show live, but also to get a peek at what happens behind the scenes. To get tickets to shows, visit TVTickets.com for shows in LA, or NYC.com for events and shows in New York (click on "TV show tapings" under "Top attractions."). NYTix.com offers an even wider range of New York tapings, but requires you pay $3 to take advantage of their "special relationships" with the shows. If a show you know and like is being taped in your area, try looking it or its network up online or seeing if there is a phone number at the end of the show to call for audience tickets.

Because a Good Game Is a Good Game

If you love going to see sports, but don't love the price tag of taking your whole family to a professional game, consider amateur sports instead. Colleges as well as intramural leagues have games every weekend for free or a few bucks. It's great to support local teams, and younger kids won't even know the difference in skill between a pro player and a Division Three league anyway.

Theme Park Savings

Nothing's more fun than taking the kids to an amusement park, especially when they've been begging you to do it for two summers now. Whether you're going to a local, Six Flags–type of park, or going all out for that Disney World vacation, here are some tips to keep your costs down.

+ A lot of organizations offer discount packages to local and national theme parks. Check with any organizations you belong to, such as the AARP, AAA, wholesale clubs like BJ's or Costco, or a branch of the military. Also look for promotions mailed out with your credit card bill.

+ Ask for a group discount. If you have at least 15 people in your party, you can usually get a good deal, depending on the time of year.

+ Visit AmusementPark.com, which has great deals on tickets to amusement parks around the country.

They also have savings on local tours, dinner cruises, museums, and tourist attractions.

✦ Keep an eye out for merchandise tie-ins. Many products—especially soda and chips—offer easy discounts such as bringing the wrapper or can to the park to get several dollars off.

✦ Check out the packages. Large theme parks such as Universal Studios and Disney World always offer package deals on—for example—a flight, hotel, and park tickets. These aren't usually significantly cheaper than buying tickets online through a site like Expedia.com or Orbitz.com, but they do often offer added incentives like free transportation or breakfasts.

✦ Call the park and ask them! Most parks (or their automated representative) will tell you about current deals being offered, and may offer promotions of their own. Also check the website of the individual park you're visiting.

✦ Before you get to the park, consider the real money-wasters: food and souvenirs. Bring lunches from home, and give each child a certain amount to spend at gift shops. For more indecisive kids afraid of hitting their limit, make sure to offer them the chance to go back for an item in a store if they don't find anything they like more (they usually will).

Keep It Cool on the Beach

Packing up your cooler for a day on the beach? Make sure it's at least 25 percent full of ice or cold packs. Otherwise, it won't be cold enough to keep your perishables cool.

A Shinier Straw Hat

Keep your straw beach hat looking like new with hair spray. Spray evenly over the entire hat, then rub your hand gently over it to push in any fraying ends. The hair spray will keep them all in place, and your hat will look shinier than ever before!

For Sand-Free Hands

Baby powder is the only known substance to immediately shake sand loose from human skin! Throw a cupful in a Ziploc bag and take it on your next ocean outing. When it's time to eat, dip your hands in the bag and rub off the sand. It works on other body parts as well.

Beachy Clean

Make homemade ice packs go further with this awesome trick. When you use up body wash or shampoo, add a bit of hand soap to the bottle and then fill with water. Keep in the freezer until you're headed to the park or the beach, then put in your cooler to keep everything cool. When it's time to leave, use the soapy water for quick cleanup!

Fog-Free Goggles

Goggles are necessary when swimming laps, but it's annoying when they fog over. Luckily, the solution is simple. Just coat the inside and outside of each lens with a layer of shaving cream. Leave on for a couple of minutes, then wipe away. The shaving cream leaves an imperceptible film that repels fog.

The Key to Keeping a Blanket in Place

Here's a great use for old keys: Use some thread or yarn to sew them to the corners of your beach and picnic blanket. It will help it stay put once you've laid it on the ground, even on the windiest days.

Who Knew? Readers' Favorite

When you're headed to the beach, make sure to keep your electronics in plastic freezer bags. Sand can easily get inside them, so the plastic makes the perfect see-through barrier, and you'll still be able to manipulate a touch-screen through the plastic.

Belly Up

As if you needed another excuse to sit at the bar, here's one more: many restaurants offer the same food at the bar as in the main restaurant, but for cheaper prices. You may have to order a few dishes to share since the portions may be smaller, but your savings will still be substantial. And since most restaurants also have table service in the bar area, you can still take the kids.

Daily Deals

Many chain restaurants have certain days each week on which they offer deals on particular entrees. Deals are especially easy to find for seniors and kids, but some restaurants offer buy-one-get-one-free options or discounts on appetizers for everyone. Know the "special days" at your local restaurants by visiting their websites or asking your waiter, and try to plan any dinners out so you're never paying full price for a meal.

A Big Week of Savings

Almost all big cities offer a "restaurant week" once or twice per year. During this week, you can dine at some of the nicest restaurants in town for the cost of eating at Applebee's! Most restaurants will offer a three-course fixed price, or "prix fixe," menu that allows you to choose from several different options for your lunch or dinner. This is an excellent opportunity to try that fancy restaurant you've read about or seen on TV, but could never afford. Just make sure you don't order off-menu! That cup of coffee could cost you half of what you just paid for your entire meal!

Winning Ways with Wine

The easiest way to make a dinner out an expensive one is to order a bottle of wine—but who can resist a little pinot with their pasta? Get rid of this extra expense by going to a BYOB (Bring Your Own Bottle) restaurant, which doesn't serve alcohol but will happily de-cork (or de-cap) yours and pour it into a glass. Restaurants that serve alcohol also often allow guests to bring their own anyway—call ahead and ask. Some will charge you a "corkage fee," but it's usually a smidgen of what you would pay ordering off the menu. If you'd only like one glass of wine, try asking if there's a "house wine" available. Many restaurants will pour you whatever is left in a bottle from behind the bar for as little as $3.

Who Knew? Readers' Favorite

If you often order take-out food, consider visiting your favorite restaurants at lunchtime. Most take-out joints offer lunch specials that are the same food as dinner for less money. They'll usually come in smaller sizes, but we've found that we usually don't need what the restaurant considers dinner-sized portions. Buy in the afternoon, stash in the fridge, and then reheat at dinner for savings!

Try Take-Out

How much do you spend each week eating out? To cut costs, find out if your favorite restaurants offer take-out, which is sometimes cheaper and will at least save you the tip. Pick it up on your way home from work and you'll have a restaurant-caliber meal without the temptation of impulse purchases like another drink or dessert. You'll just have to supply the silverware.

Get Your Coffee with Some Co-Eds

If you're a coffee fiend like we are, you know how costly those delicious coffee-shop lattes can be. If there's a college or university near your home, check out the campus coffee shop for your caffeine fix—they're less expensive and just as good as the local Starbucks.

Bistro Bargain

Want to try the that restaurant or cafe that just opened up down the street, but don't want to pay full price? Head over to Restaurant.com first, where you can find $25 gift cards to a wide array of restaurants for only $10 apiece. Many of the big chain restaurants aren't available, but if you like trying out local, family-owned restaurants, you have to check this website out!

CHAPTER 6

Holiday How-To

Bring Back the Mix Tape

You may not have made someone a mix tape since high school, but a collection of handpicked tunes can be a great, free Valentine's treat. Make a custom, romantic playlist to show your sweetie you care! If music isn't your thing, photocopy some of your favorite short stories or poems to present to your loved one as a "literary playlist."

DIY Easter Egg Dye

It's easy to make natural Easter egg dyes. Just add colorful ingredients to the water while you boil your eggs. Use grass for green, onionskins for yellow and deep orange, and beets for pink. If you plan to eat the eggs, be sure to use plants that haven't been treated with pesticides or other chemicals.

Better Than a Basket

The perfect holder for an Easter egg? The upside-down tops to soda and water bottles! For a little extra flair, glue a piece of Easter ribbon around the outside of them.

Halloween Pumpkin Preserver

A problem we used to have every Halloween was that our pumpkins got soft and mushy soon after they were carved. It turns out that this happens because air comes in contact with the inside flesh, allowing bacteria to grow. So to solve the problem of every jack-o'-lantern looking like an old man, we now spray the inside of the hollowed-out pumpkin with an antiseptic spray to slow down the bacterial growth and increase the time it takes for the pumpkin to deteriorate. Just make sure no one eats it!

Tart Trick for Jack-O'-Lanterns

To keep your jack-o'-lanterns fresh this Halloween, rub the insides with lemon juice before you put the lights inside. The lemon juice will prevent your pumpkin from rotting.

Make That Toothy Grin Last

Happy Halloween! Make this year's pumpkin last even longer by coating it with WD-40. It will stave off rot and keep critters from gnawing on it.

Save on Your Tree Skirt

Don't waste your money on an expensive tree skirt this Christmas. Instead, look for a small, round table cloth from a department store—they usually have a big selection and they're inexpensive, too. Cut a round opening in the center for the tree stand, and a straight line to one edge. Place the opening in the back of the tree and you're done.

Who Knew? Readers' Favorite

Making a popcorn garland for the holidays? Use dental floss! It's stronger than regular string and less likely to break when you wrap it around the tree.

A Personalized Calendar

For the holidays, consider giving a personalized calendar of your children's artwork as a gift. Pick up free calendars distributed by local companies, then paste drawings or paintings from the past year on top of each month's image. Your kids will feel proud of their work, and their grandparent, uncle, or godparent will love their new calendar.

A Twist on the Advent Calendar

Count down the days until Christmas with this fun family activity: Pull together all your holiday-themed books and wrap them as individual gifts. Let your children open one gift per night, and read the book together. Save "The Night Before Christmas" for the 24th. The pre-holiday festivities might keep your kids satiated enough to lay off the presents under the tree until Christmas!

An Exchange for a Change

If you have a large family, don't break the bank this holiday season by buying gifts for everyone. Plan a gift exchange instead: Have family members write their names on slips of paper, along with a few "wish list" items. Place the names into a bag and ask each person to draw one recipient. Everyone is sure to receive a good gift, and no one will go bankrupt!

Take Wrapping Presents in a New Direction

This holiday season, get creative (and thrifty) with your gift wrap. Got any travelers in the family? If you have old, unused maps sitting around the house, give them new life as wrapping paper. Mark any previous journeys on the map to add an extra-personal touch.

Festive Holiday Lights

Make your holiday lights even more festive by poking each bulb through a cupcake liner. The foil kind will make them even sparklier, while the paper kind will give off a soft light.

Long Live Christmas

We've been known to keep our Christmas tree up until well into January, and with this little trick, you can enjoy the holidays a little longer, too. Add a small amount of sugar or Pine-Sol to the water to extend the life of your tree.

Strand Storage

Once Christmas has come and gone, it's time to think about taking down the tree! When you're storing Christmas tree lights, wind each strand around a piece of cardboard cut to fit in a plastic bin, and they'll stay perfectly untangled. Think of the time you'll save next year!

Safe Storage for Holiday Decorations

When it's time to bring down the tree and lights, take great care with the delicate ornaments. Slip them into old socks or nylons; then for extra safety, place them in disposable plastic cups before storing. Old egg cartons are another ultra-safe (and eco-friendly) way to store bulbs and glass trinkets.

The Windup on Christmas Lights

When you take down your Christmas tree, always wrap the lights around the outside of a cardboard tube (try the tube from a roll of paper towels or wrapping paper) and secure with masking tape. They'll be easy to unwind next year, and you'll never have another nightmarish day of untangling all the lights while the kids wait to decorate the tree.

Zap the Sap

Pinecones are a family favorite during Christmastime, whether they're hanging on the tree, from a stocking, or simply radiating their delicious piney fragrance. But sometimes they're just too sticky to handle. To remove some of that sticky sap, place the pinecones in the oven at 300°F for 10 minutes.

Smells Like Christmas

Make your home smell wonderful during the holidays without buying manufactured home fragrances—customize your own spice potpourri instead! Select a few favorite spices from your kitchen, place them in an old nylon stocking, and tie the ends closed. Store the sachet near a cracked-open window, fan, or heating vent, and savor the spices of the season.

Ornament Storage Solution

If you ever get one of those plastic containers apples sometimes come in, make sure to save it for your Christmastime storage. They're the perfect holders for holiday ornaments, especially the classic glass orbs.

Festive Storage

Taking down the Christmas tree makes for a depressing afternoon. Make it a little less dreary this year by wrapping the ornaments. Dribs and drabs of holiday wrapping paper are a festive way to protect fragile angels and eggshell nativities for storage until next year. Plus, by skipping the newspaper route, you won't have to be reminded of last year's bad news at next year's tree-decorating party.

Ribbon Dispenser

Even if you don't have cats in the house, spools of ribbon can come undone (and tangled) up very easily. Keep your ribbon spools in a shoebox with holes cut in the sides for the end of each ribbon to go through.

Perfect Padding

Another great use for those self-multiplying plastic grocery bags—gift padding when you don't have bubble wrap or newspapers on hand. Bonus: they squeeze into all kinds of oddly shaped places.

Eco-Friendly Gifting

Say "no" to Styrofoam popcorn! Instead, save your old egg cartons for the holiday season—they'll come in handy when packing up gifts to mail. Cut them up and use the pieces as packing material. It's cheap and environmentally friendly.

Add Your Own Special Stamp

Mailing a gift and want to do something creative for that extra-special touch? Visit your local coin and stamp dealer to find unique, vintage postage sold at face value or less. Many dealers sell old yet valid stamps that aren't worth much to collectors, so you're likely to find a bargain on cool, old-fashioned postage.

CHAPTER 7

Pets

Feline-Friendly Food

Cats tend to get upset stomachs from super-cold food. Prevent tummy aches (and, more importantly, vomiting) by letting the food warm to room temperature before feeding.

Never Pay for a Milk-Bone Again

When getting a "treat" for being good, most dogs are just excited about a special snack, not that it's in the shape of a bone. The truth is, doggie treats have almost the exact same ingredients as dog food, and most dogs can't tell the difference. Instead of paying extra for dog treats, keep a separate container of dog food where you normally keep the treats, then give your dog a small handful when he's done something reward-worthy.

Remove Fur Stains

Our niece's white dog was always getting stains under her runny eyes until we tried applying our miracle liquid: vinegar. Rub a little vinegar into white fur to remove yellow or brown spots.

Sap Trap

Whether your dog is covered in sap or your cat's been hanging out under the car (or you have no idea what they've been up to!), use shampoo to remove that sticky substance from your pet's fur. Dab on a little and work it toward the edge. Pull out and rinse with water.

Quick Pick (Fur) Up

If you have pets, you probably also have pet hair all over your house. Help stop it before it starts with a dryer sheet. Just rub it over your pet and it will pick up any loose hairs thanks to static cling. It will also keep your pets smelling fresher!

Brew Up an Odor Buster

Here's a fantastic use for used tea bags. Let them dry, then cut them open. Mixed the used tea with your kitty litter to keep it smelling extra fresh.

Who Knew? Readers' Favorite

Crushed red pepper shaken onto tape and affixed to furniture is an effective "Keep Out" sign for cats. The noxious smell trumps the desire to scratch. (Just remember that you may have some explaining to do to your guests!)

Less Pricey Prescriptions

Pet medications are often insanely expensive. Luckily, we've discovered Omaha Vaccine, a website that offers great deals on meds that cost more elsewhere. Visit OmahaVaccine.com to search for your pets' medications, and get free shipping for orders over $49.

Kitty First Aid

If you accidentally cut your cat's claw too short, and it bleeds, fill a small bowl with cinnamon, and dip the paw in really quick. The cinnamon acts as a coagulant and the cat will clench its paw tighter and help stop the bleeding. Then go to the vet.

—Beth Peters, Waltham, MA

Make a Moat

Do ants keep sneaking into your pet's food? Secret tip: Ants can't swim! Place the bowl of dog or cat food into a shallow bowl filled with water.

Cooler Collar

No need to buy a fancy nighttime collar for your furry friends. Simply cover a regular collar with reflector tape and watch Rover roam all over, even in the dark.

Don't Be a Litterbug

If your cat leaves trails of litter around the house, set a sisal mat just outside her litter box, where she enters and exits the box. The fibers and grooves in the mat will catch any flyaway litter before it hits your floor.

Probiotics for Pets

Give cats and dogs yogurt to help their GI systems. Mix a few spoonfuls with their regular food once a day. Seek a veterinarian's attention if problems persist.

A Better Bath

If your dog hates taking baths, try placing a towel at the bottom of the tub before you fill it up. It will be much less slippery under your dog's paws, and that will help keep him calm.

Soothe Your Dog to Sleep

If it takes your dog a while to go to sleep, particularly on a cold winter night, use heat to ease her into slumber. Throw a large towel into the dryer for 5–10 minutes on high, then wrap around your dog's bedding. Dogs (especially older ones) will love the feeling of heat on their muscles and will settle down faster.

A Dandruff Deterrent

If your pet is suffering from dandruff, add some omega-3 fatty acids to his diet. Luckily, it's easy: Buy a can of sardines in oil, and chop up a few and add to his food. He'll love the taste, and his coat will love the nutrients. (Just be sure to check with your vet first.)

Who Knew? Readers' Favorite

In the hot summer months, you'd like to be able to give your dog a drink of water when you're out for a walk, but you haven't yet perfected how to train him to drink from a water fountain. Solve the problem by bringing a plastic shower cap with you. When you fill it with water, it will expand enough that you can hold it out as a bowl.

Keep Cats Away from Electrical Cords

If your cat likes chewing on electrical cords, we know you need a solution, and fast! Here it is: Unplug the electronics, then rub the cords with a wedge of lemon. Once they've dried, you can plug them back in. Cats hate the taste of lemon and will steer clear.

Help for Digging Dogs

If your dog likes to dig up plants in your yard (gee, thanks, Fido), sprinkle some cayenne pepper in his favorite spots. Dogs hate the smell, and will stay away.

Fat Cat?

Help your cat slim down by sprinkling a teaspoon of crushed wheat bran cereal on her food each day. It's low-fat, high-fiber content will keep her full. (Just make sure to check with your vet before changing your pet's diet.)

Decoration Dangers

Cat lovers, beware! When it's time to trim the tree, never use tinsel if you have a pet kitty. Cats love to play with tinsel and eat it, and it can be deadly if it gets stuck in their digestive system.

Laser-Sharp

A great way to keep your indoor cat mentally and physically fit is to keep a laser pointer next to your TV remote. Every time you watch TV you'll be reminded to shine a laser light for the cat to chase. This allows you to be a lot lazier than your cat, for once!

—Justin Ott, Weehawken, NJ

Vitamin Water

Vitamins and minerals are very important to your pet's health. Save the water from steamed or boiled vegetables or liquid from a slow cooker and mix it with your animal's food for additional nutrients—and a "human food" treat they'll love!

Quick Fix for Messy Paws

Forget about using soap and water on your dog's messy paws. It's faster and easier to simply wipe his paws with a baby wipe. It's a great way to remove dirt and mud—before he cuddles up with you on the couch.

Quieter Dog Days

It's great that your loyal canine is always by your side, but you could do without the accompanying jingle jangle of his ID and rabies tags. The same colorful vinyl caps that you use to easily identify keys will work to silence those ringing tags. Now the dogs can be like the kids—seen and not heard. (We can dream.)

CHAPTER 8

Your Green Thumb

Longer-Lasting Blooms

There are quite a few ways to prolong the life of fresh flowers. First, change the water and trim the stems every day. In addition, add a solution of 2 tablespoons white vinegar and 2 tablespoons sugar to a quart of water—or add ½ cup baking soda to a quart of water. When you get the flowers, submerge the stems in water, and trim an inch off the ends. This will ensure no air bubbles get caught in the stems, which will inhibit their ability to drink water. If you have roses, you can even crush the stems at the ends to encourage water absorption. If you have tulips, make a series of small holes down the length of their stems with a pin instead. And if you're displaying carnations, place them in carbonated lemonade (not the diet variety) rather than water. Change every four days.

Keep Your Overpriced Flowers Fresh

You've probably noticed that florists often keep flowers in refrigerated cases. That's because the lower temperature keeps them alive for longer. If you have a beautiful bouquet you'd like to keep around for as long as possible, place it in your refrigerator each night before you go to bed. Your flowers will age more slowly while you're not there to enjoy them. (Too bad we can't put ourselves in the fridge!)

Flat Soda for Flowers

The little bit of flat soda left in your can will revitalize and sustain fresh flowers. Pour it into the vase and let the sugar go to work keeping the flowers in bloom. Clear soda works best for a clear vase.

Vinegar for Vases

Don't put a beautiful bouquet of flowers in a cloudy vase! To make it shine like new, just pour a little white vinegar and uncooked rice inside, swish it around, and watch the clouds disappear.

Flower Arranging Done Easily

When arranging flowers, apply transparent tape in the shape of a grid across the mouth of the vase. Not only will it be easier to decide where to put each flower, but they'll stay more upright with the tape to lean against.

Who Knew? Readers' Favorite

Daffodils are one of our favorite flowers. Just remember not to mix them with other flowers when making an arrangement, as daffodils produce a toxin that kills other blooms!

A Fair Exchange

Do you have leftover vases from flowers that are long gone? Ask your local florist if she'd take them off your hands, and don't be surprised if you get a fresh bouquet of flowers in return!

Treat Your Flowers to a Cocktail

Add a drop or two of clear liquor like vodka or gin to a vase of flowers, and it will keep bacteria away from the flowers' stems, so they'll last longer!

A Beautiful Bud Vase

Finished with that glass bottle of salad dressing? Clean out the inside and peel off the label, and now you've got a brand-new vase! It'll be great for smaller bouquets, and no one will notice the difference—just tie some yarn or ribbon around the screw top and set your flowers in place.

Plants Love Starch

Your houseplants need nourishment, particularly in the dead of winter when the sunlight is limited, yet there's no need to buy expensive plant food. Just remember to save the water in which you boil potatoes or pasta, let it cool, and use it to water your plants. They love the starchy solution.

Humidity Helper

Wintertime is tough on houseplants—not only is there decreased sunlight, but there's the dry air from your furnace. If your plants are languishing, consider buying a furnace humidifier, or try a humidity tent: After watering, place a clear plastic bag over the plant, and tie the ends down around the pot with string.

Safe Transport for Your Plants

When transplanting, always use lightly moistened soil and peat moss to help retain moisture in the roots. If the soil is dry, it won't hold together well during the transplant, which might result in a messy move at best and a plant casualty at worst.

Who Knew? Readers' Favorite

If you are going to re-pot a plant, place a small coffee filter on the bottom of the new pot to keep the soil from leaking out the drainage holes. Not a coffee drinker? Try a paper towel or napkin instead.

The Right Pot for the Job

Small plants often don't do well in big pots, because the water seeps down to the bottom, below the roots. But if you only have a large pot, fill it three-quarters full with soil, then place a layer of plastic wrap on top and fill with more soil and your plant. The wrap will keep the water on the surface, but when your plant grows larger, its roots will poke through.

Soak It Up

Put a wet sponge in flowerpots before you fill them with soil. When you forget to water them, or are out of town for a day or two, the extra moisture will protect the plants from drying out.

The Garden News

Old newspapers make terrific weed screens when planting your garden. Just spread the paper on the dirt, hose it down, and cover with mulch or more dirt. Plant your garden right on top and the newspaper will keep weeds from invading your space.

Grow Your Seeds in the Daily Rag

What's black and white and warm all over? If you're a seed, the answer is newspaper. Seeds need warmth, but not light, to germinate, so if you place newspaper (black and white only) over a newly sown area, it will keep the seeds warm and block out the light.

Who Knew? Readers' Favorite

Eggshells are a great fertilizer for seedlings. Get a head start on your garden by first sowing them indoors in eggshell halves. Let them grow in an egg container, and when it's time to transplant them outdoors, just dig a hole for the shells.

Another Reason to Save Those Eggshells

Save eggshells for your garden plants. Just spread around the stems of your vegetables or flowers, and they'll help keep slugs and snails away.

Fruity Seed Starters

Save orange and grapefruit halves for use in your garden. They make great containers for starting seeds. Just fill them with soil and seeds, and plant them. After the seeds germinate, the holders will decompose, leaving nutrients in the ground.

Smarter Seed Planting

The next time you're planting seeds, save time and energy by marking one-inch measurements on the handles of your tools instead of using a ruler.

Garden To Go

Clear plastic take-out containers make great makeshift holders to jumpstart seed growing. Fill the container about halfway with soil, add the seeds, water, and close the lid. Seeds should sprout in no time when the container is left in the sun.

Soil-Free Seedlings

Grow seeds effortlessly! All you need is a wet sponge (squeezed out), a windowsill, seeds, and a misting bottle. Place the seeds in the holes of the sponge. They'll get a good start in life if you mist three times a week. Transfer to soil when your plants are an inch high.

Seed Spacing

Here's the perfect way to sow seeds while making sure they're perfectly spaced. Fill an old salt or spice shaker with the seeds and some sand, then sprinkle the mixture into the dirt when it's time to plant.

Spice Up Your Life

Here's a fun way to save money on your grocery bill while also coercing the kids into helping you around the house: grow a spice garden. Getting even a small variety of easy-to-grow herbs such as basil, mint, oregano, and thyme can save money and give you fresher ingredients to work with. (For a feline-friendly treat, try catnip, too!) Find the seeds at a home and garden center, or buy the plant starts at a nursery or farmer's market. Get the kids involved by putting the plants somewhere they can reach, and help them water them when necessary. Add the leaves—either fresh or dried—to elevate simple dishes to the next level. If your kids really get into it, you may even convince them to do a vegetable garden next year!

Who Knew? Readers' Favorite

If you have old seeds that may or may not be ripe for planting, test them out first: Pour a handful onto a moist napkin or paper towel, and cover with plastic wrap. Wait until the germination time has passed (check the wrapper for the correct time), and take a look at your seeds. If some are growing, the seeds are usable—just sow them heavily.

Storing Extra Seeds

If you have more seeds than you can use this spring, store them in a sealed container in your freezer. The cold will keep them fresh until next year.

Easy Plant Labels

Here's a cheap, easy idea for labeling plants—especially herbs, veggies, or anything you might consume. Use white or beige plastic knives, the kind you may have stashed from fast-food restaurants. Simply write the name of the plant on the knife with a permanent marker and stick into the ground. They're waterproof, and last forever.

Grow Your Own Garlic

Do you have a sprouting head of garlic? Put the whole bulb (sprout/pointy end up) in your garden and cover with an inch of soil. It will continue to send up shoots, and in a few months, a whole new bulb of garlic will have grown under the soil's surface. Best of all, garlic repels bugs in your garden!

Clear the Way for Lilacs

Lilacs hate grass. More specifically, they must compete with grass and any other vegetation for food and water. To help your lilacs flower beautifully, keep a 16- to 24-inch circle around the base free from grass. Lime and manure are great fertilizers for lilacs.

Give Pansies a Boost

If you've got pansies in your garden, take the time to pinch out the early buds. It encourages the flowers to grow, and you'll ultimately get more flowers this way.

Feed Your Fern

Banana skins and eggshells are excellent natural fertilizers for ferns, and the minerals they provide are not readily found in many synthetic fertilizers. Flat club soda is another great option for your garden: To perk up colors, give your plants an occasional sip or two.

Roses Look Better with a Little Fat On Them

Want to give your roses an extra dose of fuel? A small amount of fat drippings placed at the base of a rose bush will keep it healthier and make it bloom more frequently.

Gone Bananas

Rose bushes love potassium. Luckily, they're easy to come by in the form of banana peels. Bury the peels just under the soil near your rose's roots and it will feed your plant and help it resist disease.

Put Some Tea on Your Tea Roses

The tea that comforts you can also nurture your roses. Place tea bags or sprinkle loose tea in your rose garden, cover with mulch, and enjoy.

Watch That Hose!

When watering your garden with a hose, you don't want to drag the hose over your plants. Place a few short, heavy stakes in your garden to create an alleyway for the hose, which will restrain it from rolling around and distressing the delicate plants. If you don't have stakes, simply cut a wire hanger into six-inch pieces, bend them into arches, and use them to guide your hose.

Wooden Tools Need Love, Too

Care for wooden garden tools as you would your skin and your plants—moisturize! Over time, wood dries out and splinters. Apply a thin coat of linseed oil to wooden handles on rakes and shovels; it'll keep them safe and usable. A little goes a long way, so use the oil sparingly.

Don't Spread Disease

Use a solution of bleach and water to disinfect pruning sheers after you're done so you don't spread diseases among plants. Rinse with tepid water until the bleach is gone.

Shear Genius

Make sure your garden shears never rust by adding a little car wax. Just rub a little paste over the shears (including the hinge) to prevent them from getting stuck again.

Garden Caddy

Not sure what to do with that old golf club bag? Don't throw it away or stick it in the garage sale pile just yet. It's perfect for carting garden tools around your yard!

Tie Up Your Plants with Stuff You Don't Need

If you still have old, unused cassette tapes lying around, pull out the tape and use it to tie up your plants. Better yet, try old pantyhose: Just cut the nylons into narrow strips. This works even better than plastic ties because the pantyhose expands as the plant grows.

Turn Old Nylons Into Plant Holders

Got an unwearable pair of pantyhose? Don't trash 'em yet! Nylon stockings make excellent storage containers for plant bulbs. Air is able to circulate, which helps prevent mold. Store the bulbs in a cool, dry location.

For a Colorful, Sunny Garden

Be bold when planting flowers in sunny spots. Pastel-colored flowers can look washed out in bright sun, so consider red and orange blooms.

Get Rid of Garden Stains

To remove dirt, grass, and other garden stains from your hands, add ½ teaspoon sugar to the soap lather before you wash your hands. You'll be amazed how easily the stains come off!

Remedy for Super-Dirty Hands

Kids playing in the mud? Powdered laundry detergent makes an excellent hand cleaner for very dirty hands. It's specially formulated to get rid of grease and oil, and the powder will work as a mild abrasive.

Some Oat Action

Are your hands dirty from working in the garden? Keep some dry oatmeal handy, and add to your soaped-up hands. The oats' abrasive action will get your hands cleaner quicker. And don't forget—always scrape your fingernails along a bar of white soap before gardening, to keep dirt from getting under your nails!

Maintain Your Manicure

If you have a green thumb, but beautiful pink nails, try putting cotton balls into each finger of your gardening gloves to make your manicure last as long as possible. Rotate new ones in every few days or so (depending on how often you garden).

Weed Whacker

Bull and Russian thistle sound powerful, but they're no match for WD-40. When you need to get the prickly plants out of your way, give them a spray with this all-purpose formula. Our kids like to help with this chore, perhaps because spraying WD-40 in the garden feels somehow illicit!

Share the Wealth

You've heard of clothing and cookie swaps. How about plant swaps, where you share cuttings and roots with gardening friends? Make it an annual tradition and watch friendships grow along with your garden.

Who Knew? Readers' Favorite

In our family, we're never all ready to go at the same time. Since we love to garden, we keep a few pairs of garden gloves by the door so the early birds can pull out a few weeds while they're waiting. It prevents having to take the time to pull the weeds later—and keeps a certain someone from yelling at everyone else to hurry up!

After the Rain

Weeding is easier when the plants are wet. Save this dull task for post-rain or watering. When you give a yank, you'll be able to remove the whole weed down to the root.

Garden Cart

This gardening season, use your kids' winter sled as a handy cart for your garden. You won't have to buy a new one from a gardening or home supply store, and the sled's smooth bottom will allow it to slide easily over grass.

Soil Test

Good for you for remembering to water your garden! Just make sure you're not overdoing it. Here's a simple test. When you're finished with the hose, dig down half a foot or so and feel the soil. Moist is fine, but muddy means you should use a lighter hand.

Compile Your Compost

If you've been putting off having a compost pile because of the hassle of always having to tromp to the other side of the yard, simply keep scraps in your freezer until you're ready to compost. Banana peels, apple cores, eggshells, coffee grinds, etc. can all go right into a plastic container to wait until you're not feeling so lazy.

A Free Caffeine Fix for Your Compost Pile

Coffee grounds are a great fertilizer for plants that need a lot of nitrogen, like carrots and tomatoes. But even if you're not a coffee drinker, you can still get the grounds for free! Many Starbucks give away used grounds as part of their "Grounds for Your Garden" program. Just ask at your local Starbucks.

Stick a Toothpick in It

A leaky garden hose can easily be repaired with a toothpick stuck into the hole. (The hole itself should be easy to find—for obvious reasons.) Break off the part of the toothpick that hangs out and tape over the hole. Wood expands when wet so it will fit nicely after the first trial run.

Who Knew? Readers' Favorite

Got a hose that's full of holes? Turn it into a soaker hose for your garden by buying a cap for the end at a hardware store, repairing any large cracks with duct tape, and then using a fine nail to poke holes throughout its length.

Mulch with Grass Trimmings

Take extra care of your plants by laying grass trimmings around them. The grass provides nutrients and moisture, and also prevents nasty weeds.

All in a Row

Here's a tip if you have trouble planting your garden in neat rows. Run a hose in a straight line, then plant your new seedlings along the hose. Remove the hose and you'll have a perfect-looking flowerbed!

Drainage Booster

If you break a terra-cotta pot, don't toss it out—use it to help your garden drain more easily! Break it into tiny pieces, then mix with your soil to promote drainage. If they could, we're sure your plants would thank you!

Let Your Lawn Grow to Starve Weeds

Try to keep your lawn about three inches high. The higher the grass, the less direct sunlight for pesky weeds.

A Lazy Lawn

Did you know you can actually have a lazy lawn? If you feed your lawn too much, the roots won't need to reach down to find food. When it's hot, they'll dry out right away. The trick is to feed it once a year—in spring or fall. When the roots aren't pampered, they'll grow deeper and become stronger. Just like people.

A Greener Lawn

Don't worry about collecting clippings when you mow your lawn. It's a waste of landfill space, and you'll deprive your lawn of nutrients it can use through natural composting. Instead, take off the bag and leave the clippings in the grass.

A Great Grass Alternative

Patches of dirt in your yard where grass refuses to sprout? Try morning glory, wintercreeper, or lily-of-the-valley in hard-to-mow areas, or wherever grass has trouble growing. Forcing a picket-fence-green lawn is a waste of water and a missed chance to be a little more creative.

A Lawn to Inspire Envy

Make your lawn sparkle this summer with this nutritious homemade fertilizer: 1 cup baby shampoo, 1 can of beer, and enough ammonia to fill the rest of your hose-end sprayer. Shake it up, then follow the instructions on your sprayer for 2,000 square feet of lawn. Repeat once a month.

Who Knew? Readers' Favorite

The rain stopped just in time for your outdoor party, but not in enough time for the grass to dry before you want to mow it. To solve this problem, simply spray the blades of your lawnmower with vegetable oil, and the grass won't stick!

More Moss

We always thought moss looked quaint in between cracks in our sidewalk, so we learned how to grow our own. Pull up some common lawn moss and blend it with active-culture yogurt. Find a cool spot with lots of shade and paint it into nooks and crannies, stone walls, and flower pots.

CHAPTER 9

Shop 'Til You Drop

Haggling 101

Sure, you've always been able to haggle at car dealerships and mom-and-pop stores. But did you know that "big box" stores such as Home Depot and Best Buy are getting in on the act, too? With sales slipping, the staffs of chain stores are now being told that bargaining is OK. Here are some tips to make sure you get the most bang for your buck.

✦ To add extra ammo to your asking price, do a little preliminary research at competing stores or on the internet. If you can tell a salesperson that a nearby store is offering the same item for less, you'll be more likely to get it at that price.

✦ Be aware of "extras" that competing stores are offering. Even if you're not interested in an extended warranty or free engraving at the other place, you can use the incentive to your advantage when bargaining.

✦ Take a spouse or friend. One of the best methods for negotiating is the "good cop, bad cop" strategy. One of you acts really interested in the product, while the other continually points out the flaws and negative aspects. Because of the "good cop," the salesperson will remain hopeful that he can sell the product, but "bad cop" will make him work for it.

+ Find stores where there is no commission. A salesperson will be less likely to give you a discount if he will earn less from the transaction. But if it's only company money that will be lost, there's a higher chance he'll bow to your demands.

+ Buy accessories, too. Most stores have a higher mark-up on accessories for top-selling items. If you're buying a memory card and a carrying case for your new camera, you're more likely to get a discount on the camera itself.

Need Wood?

Looking for inexpensive, quality building supplies? Check out one of Habitat for Humanity's ReStores, which sell used and surplus materials for low prices. To find a location nearest you, visit Habitat.org/env/restores.

Reverse Wish List

To save money and space, keep a wish list for things you want now, but might not want in a few months. Whenever you get the urge to buy something, write it down, but don't buy it. Every few months, read through your list. Do you still want that leopard-print Snuggie, ultimate pet stroller, or personalized yoga mat? Chances are, you're willing to let most of them go. It's amazing how fast "I absolutely have to have this" turns into "That's so 2009."

—*Mara Berke*

You're shopping in your favorite store and notice that there are tons of markdowns. After you fill your arms with bargains, go home and mark the day on your calendar! Most stores receive shipments of new goods every 9–12 weeks and discount current merchandise to make room for the new stuff. Return to the store during that time frame to find more deals.

The Cure for Shopaholics

If you often find yourself making impulse buys, use this simple trick to cut back on spending: Once you've gathered everything you'd like to purchase, find a place to sit down for a couple of minutes and take a break. Make a phone call, play a game on your cell phone, or just sit back and relax. You'll find that clearing your mind will help you be more rational about what you really need and what you'll later regret buying.

The Best Discounts in Town

If you are an educator, a member of the military, or a government employee, always ask if there is a discount available to you! You'll often find travel and admission discounts offered to these groups. If you're over 60, of course, never ever buy anything without asking if there's a senior discount! Some discounts even start for those 50 and over. Even if you don't look your age, you might as well take advantage of the savings available to you!

The Best Places to Find Clothes Online

Shopping online is one the easiest and best ways to save money on clothing. Here are some of our favorite sites to find good, inexpensive clothes on the web.

✦ 15DollarStore.com is exactly what it sounds like—a store where all clothing is $15 or less. In addition to a large selection of women's clothing, the site also has belts, handbags, sunglasses, watches, jewelry, and some children's clothing.

✦ If you're trying to save money, it's probably a good idea to try to stay away from designer fashion labels. But if you just can't help yourself, Bluefly.com is the best place to go for a bargain. You'll find discounted prices on men's and women's designer clothing, including labels such as Kenneth Cole, Burberry, Armani, Marc Jacobs, Calvin Klein, and Prada. Just try to keep it to a couple outfits and a handbag!

✦ At Zappos.com, you'll find more shoes than you ever imagined possible, including men's, women's, and kids' sneakers; dress shoes; boots; and sandals. Not only do they have free shipping, but they also include a return shipping label with your order, so if you don't like the shoes once you try them on, you can easily return them for free.

- ✦ 6pm.com is where Zappos shoes go when they're on sale, so it's a great place to score some good deals on your favorite brands. You do have to pay for shipping, but the savings can be worth it because the selection and prices are usually quite good.

- ✦ If you love style, check out GoJane.com. Their focus is high-fashion clothing without the designer label or price tag.

Take It to the Tailor

Going to a tailor may seem like an expensive proposition, but it's often worth it if you unearth a good deal on a suit or other item that doesn't quite fit. Found some jeans for ten bucks that look great but are an inch too long? A jacket that's a steal, but a bit too baggy in the arms? For a low price, you can get these items custom-fitted at a tailor. And you'll still be saving a bundle from what the normal retail price would be.

The Seasonal Shopping Secret

For the best deals on clothes, always shop in the off-season. Buy spring and summer clothing in July and August, and fall and winter clothing in January and February. (You can often find the best sales right after the holiday season.) It's sometimes a bummer to buy something you're not going to be able to wear for six months, but when the time comes to switch seasons, you'll be happy you already have some new clothes to wear—all of which were purchased on sale!

Keep It Simple

When you're buying clothes, always go for classic looks rather than modern, trendy ones. A blue V-neck T-shirt will be fashionable year after year, while something with more exotic colors or patterns will go out of style quickly. By choosing the basics, you won't have to buy as many new articles of clothing each season.

Your Own Personal Shopper

At ShopItToMe.com, you enter your favorite brands of clothes and they do all the online searching for you. When items come up for sale on a department store's site, they'll send you an email, alerting you of the discount. The best part is, you can specify your size, so you won't have to waste your time wading through links only to find that the store is all out of extra-large!

Who Knew? Readers' Favorite

Here's an online shopping secret that can save you hundreds. When you're visiting a company's online store, make sure to hit up the "sale" section first. Many sites will also keep sale items in their original locations—without the prices marked down. Look in the sale section first to make sure you're getting the best price.

Thrifty? Try Shopping at Thrift Shops

Many people are intimidated by shopping at thrift shops. What's the best way to wade through all those clothes, organized in no particular order? How do you know you're getting something good? And what should you be wary of? First of all, it's more intuitive than you might think. If you're browsing through a thrift shop, and the clothes seem dingy or dirty, find a different shop. But for the most part, you'll find perfectly good clothes that are simply one or two seasons old. Make sure to check each item closely for rips or stains, and keep in mind that it may be worth it to buy something if you think you (or a tailor) can easily repair it. Many resale shops are organized by the color of the clothing, but most also use some kind of color-coded tag system (so that all items with a red tag are 50 percent off, for instance). Best of all, you can usually exchange your clothes for money or store credit. Make sure to ask if the store offers you more "money" for your item if you opt for credit rather than cash. And have fun looking for bargains! You never know what fantastic find you're going to get.

Take from the Rich

When going shopping at second-hand shops, try visiting wealthier neighborhoods for the best finds. Not only do they shop at these stores less often (leaving more goodies for you), they have nicer things to give away!

—*Lori McNaughton, Newport Beach, RI*

Begin in the (Bargain) Basement

How many times have you purchased an $80 sweater, only to find a nearly identical one later for much less? When you begin to look for clothes for the new season, always start at the least expensive store first. Since most clothing stores carry similar items each season, you'll make sure to get each piece for the best price. You should also try to buy most of your basics—solid-color T-shirts, socks, and so forth—at the cheaper stores. Save the expensive stores for the uniquely designed and patterned clothes, where you can see the difference in quality.

Befriend Those in the Know

If you have a favorite shop you find yourself spending a lot of time in, make sure to get friendly with the sales staff! Clothing stores often have unannounced sales, or they regularly begin sales on certain days of the week. If you're down with the people who work there, they'll often you tip you off. And if they really like you, they may let you put an item on layaway until it goes on sale a few days later.

The Mall Is a Money Pit

If you or your teen is looking for something to do, stay away from shopping malls! Although they're popular hangouts, they'll always lead you to spend money. Skip the stores and go to the park, a pool, or a matinee instead.

Don't Go into the Red on Black Friday

It's Black Friday—the craziest shopping day of the year. Before you head out to the mall, hit up FatWallet.com first. They keep track of each store's Black Friday deals, so you can keep an eye out for promised bargains and make a plan of attack for your day of shopping.

Your Site For Salon Savings

Addicted to fancy shampoo? Find all the same brands you buy at your salon for much less at SalonSavings.com. Shampoo and hair-care products are 10–80 percent off, and skincare products and fragrances are offered at much less as well. This site is also a great place to check if you have a favorite beauty product that has been discontinued.

Who Knew? Readers' Favorite

When trying to compare a pricey cosmetic with a less-expensive one, you only have to look at one thing: the active ingredients list. Products that have the same active ingredients are going to do almost the exact same thing, even if the percentages are a bit off. (The only thing you might have to worry about is which smells better.) You'll be surprised how many expensive brands—especially hair products like shampoo—have the exact same ingredients in them for vastly higher prices.

Never Pay Too Much for Cosmetics

When shopping for make-up and other cosmetics, avoid the department stores! Because of commissions for the salespeople and the cost to rent the space at the store, they're never a bargain. Instead, check out your local grocery store or discount store such as Walmart or Target—they almost always have similar brands for much less. If you can't find your favorites there, try a cosmetics discount outlet such as Ulta, or search for "discount cosmetics" online. If you still can't find your brand, consider switching to another brand you can find. Choose one a good friend uses, and ask her if she'd be willing to buy it from you if you don't like it. It shouldn't be too hard to find an affordable alternative.

Make-Up Must-Have

Most make-up is exactly the same, except for whether they call that shade of red you love "cherries jubilee" or "red crush." Make shopping for make-up easier by keeping an index card with your favorite colors on hand. Rub a bit of lipstick, blush, or eye shadow on the card, then mark down the brand and what the color is called. When it's time for more make-up, you can easily compare the colors of the sale brand with your card. Then write down what that color is called on your card. You'll soon have a list of all your favorite colors from each brand.

—*Arlene DeSantos*

Good Make-Up Doesn't Have to Be Expensive

For a great deal on cosmetics, head over to EyesLipsFace.com, where they have everything from lip gloss to nail polish for only a dollar apiece. They also have a great "Gifts" section, with cute box sets for unbelievable prices. For instance, you can find eye shadow, mascara, eyeliner, a brush, and an eyelash curler for only $5!

Who Knew? Readers' Favorite

Did you know that up to 30 percent of consumers never get around to returning items that they meant to take back to the store? If you're unsure about an item while you're in the dressing room, the best thing to do is to put it back on the rack. Once we began following this policy, we were shocked at how few never-worn garments ended up in our closets.

Use Your Phone to Check Prices

If you're lucky enough to own an iPhone, Android, or other smartphone, you're also lucky to have access to applications that make shopping easier. Once the applications are installed, you can use your phone's camera to take a snapshot of the barcode, or enter the UPC numbers underneath. Your phone will then give you a list of how much the item costs at locations near you and online. Search your phone's app store for Barcode Scanner on iPhone and Android, ScanLife on Blackberry, and ShopSavvy for

Windows phones. If you don't have a smartphone, you can still easily compare prices online. You don't get to use your phone as a scanner (which is half the fun), but you can enter the UPC code of any product to get prices from around the web by using Google's Product Search (Products.Google.com). Just type in the numbers found near the barcode and away you go!

Shopping for Electronics?

If you're in the market for a new TV, DVD player, portable music player, or other electronic device, the best time to buy is in the late spring and early summer. Prices will drop because new products are usually introduced in the late summer and early fall. New computers are also often released in February, so shop in January for savings.

Stream Free and Easy

Before you buy an expensive "streaming video" unit or get talked into buying a video game system "just so we can watch streaming Netflix on the TV," investigate your TV's hook-up options. Many TVs allow you to hook them right up to your laptop as a "second monitor." You may need to buy a couple of new cords, but they'll likely be much cheaper than new electronics.

Cheap Computing

Buying a new computer? Netbooks are smaller versions of laptops, and although they don't have nearly as many features as a full-size computer, they still work well for the basics (word processing, watching videos, searching the internet) and cost only about $200.

This may seem counterintuitive, but if you're buying a printer, try to buy one that uses as many different toner cartridges as possible. Not every household uses the same amount of every color, so you may be forced to throw away a tri-color cartridge that's out of, say, magenta, but still has plenty of yellow and cyan left. Printers with separate cartridges for each color solve that problem by ensuring that no toner is wasted. It's also a good idea, when printing, to specify a black-and-white printout in instances where color isn't really necessary.

Rah-Rah for Refurbs

If you're like most people, you probably shy away from buying refurbished electronics, but you shouldn't. We go out of our way to buy refurbs, which not only save cash, but also provide more or less the same level of reliability as brand-new items. Whether it's a cell phone, laptop, gaming console, or television, a refurbished item is arguably less likely to be defective than a new one, because these items are tested at the factory before they're resold. And in the rare instance where a refurb does fail, all of the other refurbs you've bought will have saved you enough money to replace it. Contrary to popular opinion, most refurbished units aren't simply broken items that have been repaired. They may have been returned to the maker for any number of other reasons. A customer may have returned a gift he didn't want, the packaging (but not the actual item) may have been damaged in shipping, the item might have a cosmetic blemish, or may have been missing a nonessential accessory. If you can live with those things, then refurbished items are definitely for you. Many of them even come with the original manufacturer's warranty intact.

A Game of Telephone

The most expensive place to buy a cell phone is at a cell phone store, even one run by your mobile provider. These stores count on foot traffic and impulse purchases, and usually price phones higher. When it's time to get a new phone, check out your phone company's online offerings, which will include several free or heavily discounted phones that the stores no longer carry.

Mobile Money

If you're buying a new cell phone, what should you do with the old one? Get cash, of course! Visit Cell4Cash.com and enter the brand and model of your old phone. The site will tell you if they're offering any money for it, and if they're not, they still allow you to send it in to be recycled. Plus, the shipping is free!

The Price You Pay

Looking to change your cell phone provider but aren't sure how much you're going to have to pay to get out of your contract? Head over to CellTradeUSA.com, which will tell you how much it will cost to cancel. The site also allows you to transfer your contract to another CellTrade user, if your cell company allows it.

Deals on Wheels

The internet can be a great resource for buying a car, particularly a new one. Instead of relying on a salesman's sketchy pitch, do your own online research on the pros and cons of each model. Go test-drive one to make sure you like it, but don't buy it right then. Instead, go home and hunt around for the best price among dealers in your region. Even if the dealership offering the best price is located far away, you may still come out ahead by having them deliver the car to you. We once paid $500 to have an out-of-state dealer ship a vehicle to us—and that was still $1,000 cheaper than buying the car locally.

—Jerri Thompson Barry

Buying Plants?

Always buy houseplants in the spring, when you'll find a better selection and prices that are 20–60 percent cheaper.

Who Knew? Readers' Favorite

If you're sending flowers for a special occasion, skip the national delivery services and websites. Instead, find a flower shop that is local to the recipient and call them directly. Most national services simply charge you a fee, then contact these very same stores themselves.

When to Buy Home Appliances

If you're looking for large appliances or household furnishings like a washing machine, dryer, dishwasher, refrigerator, or sofa, the best time to buy is in October. At this time of year, businesses are busy making room for their holiday inventory, so you'll find tons of sales on last year's merchandise. Go ahead, celebrate a little early!

Finding the Best Deals on Furniture

The best way to save on furniture is to browse your local store, then buy online. Seeing it in person will allow you to try it out and see its dimensions up-close, but buying online can give you a huge discount. If you see something you like, write down the manufacturer's name and, if available, the model number. Then do a search for the same piece and see what low prices you find.

Stop Squinting!

If you need new glasses and aren't sure how you're going to afford them, check out 39DollarGlasses.com. For around $45 (with shipping), you can get attractive (though bare-bones) glasses, including the lenses! Walmart also offers good deals on frames and lenses. If you've got to maintain your hipster image, try WarbyParker.com. They sell stylish $95 glasses including the prescription lenses with free shipping and returns. They'll even ship several frames to your house to try on and return. Plus, you can try out their glasses online "virtually" by uploading a picture of yourself. As a bonus, they donate a pair of glasses to someone in need for every pair that is sold.

Candle-Buying Benefits

If you like decorating your home with candles, buy them on clearance at after-holiday sales. There's nothing wrong with burning a pumpkin-scented candle in spring or a pine-scented one in August. If that feels weird, though, just stash the seasonal scents in the closet until next year's holidays come around.

Buy at Auction

Every month, hundreds of cars and other items are confiscated by the police. And hey, just because a criminal used it doesn't make that $100 laptop any less useful. Look in the classifieds section of your newspaper to find local auctions, or check out PropertyRoom.com or PoliceAuctions.com to find unbelievable deals on tools, electronics, bicycles, video games, and more, not to mention some truly bizarre items like a Freon tank, "assorted copper tubing," night vision goggles, and an adorable cement frog. And if you're OK with not telling the recipient where it came from, you should know that auctions are also one of the least expensive places to buy beautiful jewelry and gemstones.

Cheap Checks

When pawing through the coupon inserts in your Sunday paper, make sure to save the advertisements for checks. These companies aren't just for people who like cartoon characters next to "Pay to the order of." They're also for people who like to save! You'll always get them more cheaply than simply ordering them through your bank, and don't you give your bank enough money as it is?

Save, Then Spend

As Veruca Salt said in Willy Wonka and the Chocolate Factory, "I want it, and I want it now!" It's hard to break the habit of buying expensive items when we want them, then paying them off over the next several months. But saving up ahead of time has numerous benefits.

✦ First of all, you'll make sure you really want the item. If you have to save up for six months for a new TV, you'll have plenty of time to reconsider if the old 20-inch is good enough. And trust us, once you do finally have the money, it feels so much better to go home with a piece of merchandise that's bought and paid for, rather than one that has just put you further into the hole.

✦ When you open a new store credit card to pay for a big-ticket item, this credit card will pop up on your credit report as being opened and immediately maxed out. Obviously, this isn't good news for your credit score.

✦ Finally, not having to pay something off after the fact means no interest payments. And many mom-and-pop stores will give you a lower price if you pay all in cash.

Throw in the Towels

When you're shopping for towels in a superstore, skip housewares and go straight to the automotive section. You'll find packs of 12 white terrycloth towels, often for as little as $5. They're durable and can be used anywhere in the house.

Rent What You Rarely Use

Instead of buying something you'll only need rarely, how about renting it? Zilok.com puts you in touch with local businesses and individuals who are renting cars, vacation homes, tools, TVs, video game consoles, and more. Better yet, you can list your own items to rent! (Unfortunately, you can't rent out your kids.)

Built for the Battlefield—and the Playground

This school season, consider replacing your kids' flimsy backpacks with a sturdier (and cooler) alternative: military backpacks. These bags are built to last in the battlefields, so they'll certainly stand up to the wear and tear of the school year. You can find them in any Army/Navy Surplus store.

Don't Buy Hangers

In need of some new hangers? Try your local department store. When making a purchase, let the sales clerk know that you'd like to take the hangers, too. If you notice any empty hangers lying around the cash-out area, ask for those as well—it couldn't hurt!

Casino Coin Count

When you need to cash in loose change, avoid bank fees by taking your change to a nearby casino instead! Seem counterproductive? It's not. Bring your coins to the cashier, who will exchange them free of charge, then hustle out past the video poker machines to escape that urge to play!

Save Big

Save up the old-fashioned way by sticking money in a drawer on a regular basis. But instead of loose change in a piggy bank, stow a few dollar bills at the end of each day. Better yet, set up a "splurge fund" for your next big purchase or vacation—it'll give you incentive to be prudent with your cash.

Dump an Old Deal

That half-off Groupon deal for your boyfriend's favorite restaurant seemed like a good idea—until the two of you broke up. Luckily, all is not lost (at least in terms of your finances). Off-load your unwanted deals from sites like Groupon, Living Social, and Scoopst.com at CoupRecoup.com. And of course, if you're looking to get a great deal, this the place the visit first!

The Check Is in the Mail

Get free cash back just for shopping online at Ebates.com. Before you shop at your favorite sites (including HomeDepot.com, BN.com, Kohls.com, Target.com, and more), log in at Ebates.com. Then click through to your desired website. You get a certain percentage of cash back on each site, and a check will be mailed to you every three months. It's that easy!

Go Straight to Savings

If you're looking for deals online, your first stop should be PriceGrabber.com. It lets you see what's on sale in various categories, then takes you right to the site to get the bargain. Best of all, you can see the prices at different sites side-by-side, including sales tax and shipping!

Be a Membership Mooch

Just because you don't belong to a wholesale club like Costco, BJ's, or Sam's Club doesn't always mean you can't take advantage of their savings. Have a friend who is a member get you a gift card, and they'll let you shop there without a membership! (Make sure to check first.) Just show the gift card at the front desk.

Frugal Photo Printing

If you usually print out your digital photos using an online service, you know that there are a lot of them, and they often have promotions and sales. To help you figure out which one can give you the best deal right now, check out PrintRates.com. You indicate the number of prints and sizes you need, and it will tell you where to find the best deal.

Know the Code

Ever see that little box for "promo code" when you're buying something online? Always have something to put there with RetailMeNot.com, which has coupon codes for thousands of online retailers. Some stores offer more online codes than others, but you can usually find one that at least offers free shipping or a small discount.

Coupons for the Taking

Did you know that the websites of many malls now offer coupons? If you're headed to the mall, check their site for exclusive coupons and links to the coupons offered by the websites of the various stores inside.

Savings, Forwarded

Looking for coupons for big-ticket items for your home like washing machines, TVs, and more? Stop by your local post office and grab a packet for people who are moving and would like their mail forwarded. Even if you don't fill out the forwarding card, these packets often contain coupons from stores targeting those who have recently moved.

CHAPTER 10

Natural Remedies and First Aid

Longer Than Big Red

Bad breath? Eat some yogurt! The "good" bacteria in yogurt has been found to be effective in targeting the odor-causing bacteria in your mouth. Make sure you go for the plain kind, no sugar. Breath mints and sprays mask the odor but they don't help the underlying problem—eating yogurt does.

Great Breath Fast

You don't need expensive mouthwashes to get better breath. Simply gargle with a mixture of 1 cup water, ½ teaspoon baking soda, and ½ teaspoon salt. This combo will knock out any germs that are causing your bad breath.

Water, Water, Everywhere

How much water is enough water? Divide you body weight in half. The number you come up with is how many ounces of water you should be drinking daily. For example, if you weigh 150 pounds, you should consume 75 ounces of water each day.

Pepper Your Dishes

Why not use a sprinkling of cayenne pepper to help season your sauces? Derived from the plant Capsicum annuum, it has been reported to not only make you lose weight by elevating body temperature, but to improve circulation and to lower cholesterol. As it's a mild stimulant, it can also be added to hot water with lemon juice as an alternative to coffee.

Sage Advice

To cut down on how much you perspire, try drinking sage tea. Herbalists say it will take several weeks, but you'll see results!

Detox with Lemon

Lemon juice not only smells great, it tastes delicious, too. Mix it with hot water and try it as an alternative to hot tea and coffee. You may find it wakes you up just as well, and your body will thank you.

Kick Your Sweet Tooth's Habit

Here are two quick tricks to eliminate the craving for sweets (without hitting the fridge). One way is to place a small amount of salt on your tongue and let it slowly dissolve. The second: dissolve about a teaspoon of baking soda in a glass of warm water, then rinse your mouth out and spit (don't swallow). The salt or baking soda tends to stimulate the production of saliva, which eliminates your sweet craving.

Lutein for Healthy Eyes

Many people suffer from farsightedness, cataracts, glaucoma and other eye problems as they age. To keep your eyes healthy, increase your level of lutein—available in vegetables such as carrots, broccoli, spinach, Brussels sprouts and kale. Lutein can decrease the risk of cataracts and macular degeneration.

The All-Natural Prozac

The herbal supplement St. John's Wort can help ease feelings of depression and lift black moods. It is thought to increase the activity and prolong the action of the neurotransmitters serotonin and noradrenalin in a similar way to standard antidepressants, and will need to be taken for a few weeks before it starts working.

A Breath of Fresh Air

This is simple advice we've all heard before, but how often do we put it into practice? When you're feeling anxious or overwhelmed, take a deep breath. Take five, as a matter of fact. Start in your belly—envision blowing up a balloon there—and move to your chest, filling your lungs to their capacity. Exhale slowly. This is also a great method if you're having trouble falling asleep, since it signals to your nervous system that it's time to relax.

Furry Friends

Playing with or petting your pet is known to reduce blood pressure, improve your mood, and reduce stress. It been proven to work with all pets: dogs, cats, hamsters—everything but dust bunnies.

Relieve Stress in a Pinch

Many people hold stress in the area between their eyebrows, and in time, vertical stress lines will develop here. When you feel your brow knit together with concentration or stress, take a moment to pinch the muscle there, working from the center of the brow along the brow-line in each direction with a thumb and bent forefinger.

A Good, Stiff Drink

If you find you're often stiff after exercising, you probably just need more water. Dehydration is a major cause of post-exercise muscle soreness. Drinking water regularly while you work out should keep water levels high enough to combat pain.

Contrast Showers

You'll love the feeling of this simple routine that will help boost your immune and circulatory systems and even relieve stress. Toward the end of your shower, turn it up as hot as you can stand it and allow it to warm your body for three minutes. Then turn it down so the water is cool, and let it run over your body for 30–60 seconds. Repeat as many times as you like, ending on cold. When you get out of the shower, rub yourself vigorously with a towel to encourage circulation. Do not continue the contrasting temperatures, however, if you feel dizzy, nauseated, or excessively chilled.

Salt Sedation

Having trouble sleeping? We love this all-natural insomnia cure. At bedtime drink a glass of water, then let a pinch of salt dissolve on your tongue. (Just make sure the salt doesn't touch the roof of your mouth). Studies show the combination of salt and water can induce a deep sleep.

Rx, Vinegar

White vinegar stops nosebleeds. Just dampen a cotton ball and plug the nostril. The acetic acid in the vinegar cauterizes the wound. Who knew?

Cures for Canker Sores

Hydrogen peroxide may help reduce and relieve canker sores. Simply mix one part peroxide with one part water, then dab on any affected areas several times a day or swish around in your mouth for as long as possible. If you feel a canker sore coming on but it hasn't erupted yet, hold a slice of fresh garlic to the spot for ten minutes. It'll make your breath stink but it will also stop the sore from forming.

Get Rid of Cold Sores

If you have a cold sore, tea can help, thanks to the tannic acid in tea that helps relieve inflammation. Place a used tea bag on affected areas for 3 minutes. To make it feel even better, place the tea bag in the freezer for 10 minutes beforehand.

Homemade Heating Pad

Don't spend your money on an aromatherapy pillow! Instead, add uncooked, long-grain rice to a sock and tie it shut. Whenever you need a little heat after a long day, stick it in the microwave on high for 1–2 minutes and you'll have soothing warmth. To add a little scent to the pillow, add a few drops of your favorite essential oil to the rice.

Tiny Ice Packs

Get rid of the hundreds of condiment packets in your junk drawer and help ease the pain of smaller bruises, scrapes, and burns by keeping the packets in your freezer, then taping them to ouches with scotch or medical tape.

Soothe Bruises

If you have a bruise, soak a cotton ball in white vinegar, then apply it to the bruise for an hour. It will reduce the blueness of the bruise and speed up the healing process.

Toothpaste for Burns

Toothpaste is a great household helper, and it even comes in handy with burns. If you've sustained a minor burn, cover it with white, non-gel toothpaste to ease the pain and help it heal.

Slippery Solution

Soothe and help heal minor bruises and scrapes by using the inside of a banana peel to gently rub the injury. Treat as fast as possible to reduce bruising.

Try Honey, Honey

The ancient Egyptians relied on honey for cuts and burns long before antibiotics were around. Besides offering a soothing protective layer over minor wounds, the honey provides a natural antibiotic. Put a layer of pure honey on before a bandage.

Sanitize a Cut

You just got a nasty cut on your hand, but don't have anything to clean it out with before you put the bandage on. Luckily, there's something in your medicine cabinet that you may not have thought of—mouthwash. The alcohol-based formula for mouthwash was originally used as an antiseptic during surgeries, so it will definitely work for your cut, too.

Splinter Removal

Splinters used to be major events at our house until we discovered this trick: Vegetable oil softens the skin and helps the offending piece of wood slide back out. You can also put a drop of white glue over the offending piece of wood, let it dry, and then peel off the dried glue. The splinter will stick to the glue and come right out.

Keeping Finger Bandages Dry

You put a Band-Aid on your finger to cover up a scratch, but you still have to go through your day full of hand-washing, child-bathing, and dishes-doing. To keep the bandage dry while you work, cover it with a non-inflated balloon—any color will do!

PB&B

The blisters are gone but the Band-Aid tracks remain. Use peanut butter to get rid of the black marks and stop distracting everyone from your lovely pedicure!

Be Callous to Calluses

To remove hard calluses from your feet, try this old-fashioned but effective remedy: Grind a few aspirin tablets into a paste with equal parts lemon juice and water. Apply it to the calluses, then wrap your feet in a hot towel, cover in plastic bags, and stay off your feet for 30 minutes. When you unwrap your feet, the calluses will be soft and ready to be filed off with a nail file or pumice stone.

Another Cure for Calluses

Ugly callus got you down? Remove it easily and naturally with this simple fix: Take a piece of a lemon peel and tape it (yellow side up) over the callus using medical tape or packaging tape. Leave overnight, then remove and rub with an emery board or pumice stone in the morning. Repeat for a week and your callus will be gone!

No Need to Be Corny

To get rid of corns, soak a Band-Aid in apple cider vinegar, and apply it to the corn for a day or two. You can also try soaking your feet in a shallow pan of warm water with half a cup of vinegar. Either way, finish by rubbing the corn with a clean pumice stone or old nail file (just don't use it on your nails again).

Bee Careful

If you're stung by a bee, carefully grasp the stinger and pull it out as fast as you can. The less venom that enters your body, the smaller and less painful the resulting welt will be. Ice the area immediately to reduce the swelling. If it still hurts, try cutting an onion in half and applying the fleshy side to the sting. It should help ease the pain.

Help for Stings

Believe it or not, meat tenderizer works wonders on all sorts of stings—bee, wasp, even jellyfish. That's because it contains papain, which helps break down the proteins in venom. Make a paste with the tenderizer by adding a few drops of water at a time, then rub on the affected area.

Be Itch-Free

A great way to treat mosquito bites is with a dab of ammonia, which stops them from itching. In fact, ammonia is the main ingredient in many of the itch-relief products currently on the market. You can also try a dab of rubbing alcohol.

Getting Rid of Lice Naturally

Nothing strikes fear in the hearts of parents like the words "lice outbreak." The harsh chemicals that are used to fight lice are almost as bad as the lice themselves. Luckily, there is a cheap, more natural alternative, and it's as close as your refrigerator. Cover your child's head (or yours, if the little buggers have gotten you!) with a thick conditioner like Pantene Pro V. Put on a Disney movie to keep your kid busy, then get a wide-toothed metal comb.

Dip the comb into rubbing alcohol and comb through the hair, staying close to the scalp. Between each swipe, wipe the comb on a white paper towel to make sure you're getting the lice. Dip the comb in the alcohol again and keep going. Cover the hair with baking soda, and then repeat the process with the alcohol and the comb. Wash hair thoroughly when finished, and repeat this procedure each day for a week or until the lice are gone.

Poison Ivy?

To help relieve the itching of a rash caused by poison ivy, soak the affected area in a strong salt bath. Make sure the water is warm to fully get the itch out.

Diaper Rash Ointment

When your baby gets diaper rash, nix those pricey ointments and try a homemade remedy instead. Make a paste with about ¼ cup petroleum jelly and 1 tablespoon cornstarch, then spread it along your baby's irritated skin. Or try adding a cup of baking soda to your baby's bathwater.

Don't Horse Around with Aches and Pains

If you're suffering from aching muscles (either from illness or too much exercise), try this homemade cure. Mix 1 tablespoon horseradish with 1 cup olive oil. Let sit for 30 minutes, then apply it to aching areas.

Aid Arthritis with Oatmeal

Believe it or not, you can help relieve arthritis pain with oatmeal. Just mix 2 cups oatmeal with 1 cup water, warm the mixture in the microwave, and apply to the affected area.

Soothing Back Pain

If you have chronic back pain—especially associated with arthritis—or other sore muscles, try adding yellow mustard to a hot bath. Add a few tablespoons for mild pain, and up to a whole 8-ounce bottle if the pain is severe. The bathwater may look strange, but your aching back will thank you.

Help for an Stomach Ache

If your stomach is upset due to indigestion or a hang-over, try drinking a glass of club soda with a dash of bitters. It should help ease your pain.

Rub Away the Bloat

Feeling bloated? It could just be trapped gas. Encourage it to move by gently stroking from your right hip up towards your ribs, then across the bottom of your ribcage and down towards your left hip. Repeat several times.

Relieve Nausea Naturally

Nothing's worse than a bad bout of nausea. Try this simple trick to help relieve your discomfort: Drink a little ginger ale, then chew a handful of crushed ice, and finally sniff a piece of black-and-white newspaper. It may seem like an old wives' tale, but it works!

Root Out Morning Sickness

Ginger root, taken as a powder or in tea, works directly in the gastrointestinal tract by interfering with the feedback mechanisms that send sickness messages to the brain. Take some when you're feeling nauseated to help alleviate your symptoms.

Stop Motion Sickness in Its Tracks

If you get nauseated every time you ride in a car, boat, or train, take some lemon wedges with you. Suck on them as you ride to relieve nausea.

Sore Throat?

Aspirin does more than just relieve headaches! If you have a sore throat, dissolve two non-coated tablets in a glass of water and gargle. Just make sure to note that this only works with aspirin—don't try it with other pain relievers like ibuprofen.

Tasty Remedy

Relieve your sore throat with a time-tested home remedy. Slice one-third of a lemon off, then take the two-thirds-sized piece and place it on a shish kebab skewer or barbecue fork. Set your gas stove to high and roast the lemon over the open flame until the peel acquires a golden brown color. (This works on electric stoves too, although not quite as well.) Let the lemon cool off for a moment, then squeeze the juice into the smallest cup you have. Add one teaspoon of honey, mix well, and swallow.

Better than a Bloody Mary

In the peak of sore throat season, get a reprieve by gargling with this spicy mix: 1/3 cup tomato juice, ½ cup hot water, 5 drops pepper sauce. Gargle. It works even better if you gargle with lukewarm saltwater first. If you prefer sweet to salty, fill a shot glass with honey, then warm it in the microwave for about 10 seconds on high. Stir in ¼ teaspoon cinnamon, then drink.

Scallion Cure

Stuffy nose? Don't spend money on decongestant—head to your fridge instead. Cut the "root" end of two scallions and carefully insert the white ends into your nose (being cautious not to shove them too high!). You may look silly, but your nose will start to clear in a couple of minutes.

Onion Earmuffs

Oil found in raw onion is anti-microbial, which makes onions great cures for upper respiratory ailments. If you have a minor earache such as swimmer's ear, onion may help. Slice a fresh onion and heat it in the microwave on high for one minute. Wrap it in cheesecloth or another thin cloth so that it doesn't burn your skin, and then hold it against the ailing ear for 20–30 minutes. See a doctor if the pain gets worse or continues for longer than 24 hours.

Steam Away a Cold

Steam is a wonderful household remedy for colds, especially with some aromatherapy oils mixed in. Try pouring hot water into a bowl and breathing in as you lean over it. Stick your tongue out as you do it—this will open the throat and allow more steam through, which prevents membranes from drying out. Add aromatherapy oils to the water that are especially known to alleviate the symptoms of congestion, such as black pepper, eucalyptus, hyssop, pine, and sweet thyme.

Ancient Cold Relief

Ayurveda is a practice of natural medicine that's been used in India since around 1500 BC. Try this cold remedy that's been passed down through the ages: At the very first sign of a cold, mix 1 teaspoon water with 1 teaspoon raw honey and 1 teaspoon turmeric. Eat it every 30 minutes until symptoms disappear.

Watery Eyes?

If your eyes are itchy, try this quick fix to cut down on your misery: Rub a small amount of baby shampoo on your eyelids. It should reduce your symptoms dramatically.

Goodbye, Swimmer's Ear

If your children are prone to swimmer's ear, a bacterial infection of the ear canal, take this precaution when they've been in the pool: Dab a solution of one part vinegar and five parts warm water into each ear three times a day. The vinegar will ward off bacteria and keep your kids' ears pain-free.

Index

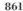

who knew?
online

Visit us on the web at WhoKnewTips.com!

* Money-saving tips
* Quick 'n' easy recipes
* Who Knew? products
* And much more!

Twitter.com/WhoKnewTips
Get a free daily tip and ask us your questions

YouTube.com/WhoKnewTips
Watch demos of your favorite tips

Facebook.com/WhoKnewTips
Daily tips, giveaways, and more fun!

Learn The Secrets To Couponing

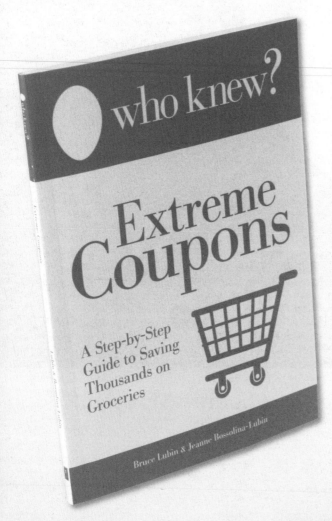